The Start of Something BIG:

Your Ultimate Guide to Writing a Dynamic Business Plan

3rd Edition

By

Kimberly L. Johnson

Copyright

Copyright © 2017 Bolingbrook, Illinois
Universal. Innovative. Intelligent, Inc.
Third edition, 2017
Second edition, 2005
First edition 1997
Printed in the United States of America

Library of Congress Cataloguing-in-Publication (CIP) Data

Name: Johnson, Kimberly, Writer/Editor.
Title: The start of something big: your ultimate guide to writing a dynamic
business plan / K. L. Johnson
Description: Bolingbrook: Universal. Innovative. Intelligent, Inc., [2016] |
    Includes glossary and index.
Identifiers: | LCCN 94027946 (print) | ISBN 1-884933-01-7 (lib. bdg.) | ISBN 1-
    884933-07-6 (2nd edition) | ISBN 1-884933-10-6 (3rd print and digital editions)
Subjects: | Business enterprises — Planning. | Corporate planning. | Business
    writing.
Classification: LCC HD30.28.J653 1996 (print) | DDC 658.4'012 — dc20
LC record available at https:// https://lccn.loc.gov/94027946

Printed in the United States of America

3 4 5 6 7 8 9 10 / 1 2

The Publisher nor the Author take any credit for the success or failure of any business using this Guide for the purpose of starting a business, growing an existing business, acquiring capital or otherwise. This publication is written solely for the purpose of providing information. The Author nor the Publisher is engaged in rendering professional advice. Send all inquiries to Universal. Innovative. Intelligent, Inc. (U3I), Post Office Box 1711, Bolingbrook, Illinois 60440 or via email at info@universal3i.com. Visit our web site www.universal3i.com.

Dedication

The 2017 print and digital editions of
"The Start of Something BIG:
Your Ultimate Guide to Writing a Dynamic Business Plan"
is dedicated to the loving memory
of our beloved mother and grandmother,
Mary Louise Richardson and Nellie Carr.

Acknowledgements

A great many thanks to those who unreservedly supported all my efforts in the preparation of the third edition of *"The Start of Something BIG: Your Ultimate Guide to Writing a Dynamic Business Plan."*

Dr. Ollie Anderson who so patiently listened and provided valuable input in the development and promotion of this edition. I thank her for the ecclesiastical inspiration she bestowed upon me. Ms. Ruth Smith for the design and creativeness she brought to every event we attended.

Zachary Beasley III for his unrelenting determination to make all website technological and structural features and functions perform properly. Jocelyn Poe for all her wonderful and amazing branding, graphics and design concepts.

I am eternally grateful to my family members who've showered me with the unyielding love and support needed to make all my dreams a reality. To my Triumph Community Church family for being there and reminding me to look to the Almighty for strength, and to *". . . seek first his kingdom and his righteousness, and all these things will be given to you as well."* (NIV Matthew 6:33).

And as always, my sons, Marcus, Daniel and James who have continuously believed with reckless abandon in my every endeavor.

I thank and love you all so much!

TABLE OF CONTENTS

PART I - PROLOGUE

Foreword XV

Preface XVII

Where to Begin XVIII

Chapters in this Guide XVIII

Assisting You Every Step of the Way XXIII

PART II - THE START-UP PHASE

CHAPTER 1 - THE START OF SOMETHING BIG

From Concept to Reality.. 3

Your Product or Service 4

Proof of Concept (POC) 6

Research and Development 7

Legal and Regulatory Issues 8

Barriers to Entry or Exit 11

Operational Risk Management 12

Value Proposition 13

Your Mission Statement... 14

Entrepreneurial Traits 16

Assessing Your Readiness for Entrepreneurship... 17

Taking the Entrepreneurial Leap 19

Assessing Your Personal Strengths and Weaknesses.. 21

Assessing Your Skills and Abilities 22

    Exhibit 1 – Assessment of Personal Strengths and Weaknesses............................... 26

Personal Finances 27

Setting Personal Financial Goals and Addressing Concerns 27

TABLE OF CONTENTS

Exhibit 2 – Setting Personal Financial Goals and Addressing Concerns *28*

Assessing Your Current Personal Financial Status **29**

Exhibit 3 – Current Personal Financial Status *30*

Getting Your Personal Finances in Order **31**

Your Personal Credit History **31**

Preparing Your Monthly Budget **34**

Exhibit 4 – Monthly Budget *35*

Start-up Costs **36**

Assessing Your Start-up Costs **37**

Exhibit 5 – Assessment of Start-up Costs *38*

Organizing the Development of Your Business **39**

Your Business Model **40**

North American Industrial Classification System (NAICS) **41**

Researching Your Market and Industry **42**

Conducting Research Online **43**

Exhibit 6 – Google Advanced Search *44*

Conducting Research Offline **45**

Legal Structure **46**

Exhibit 7 – Legal Forms of Business *47*

Naming Your Company **53**

Your Company Logo **54**

Filing Your Fictitious Business Name **55**

Business Bank Account **56**

Federal Employer Identification Number (FEIN) **57**

Exhibit 8 – SS4 – Application for Employer Identification Number *58*

Selecting and Registering Your Domain Name **60**

E-mail (Electronic mail) **61**

Internet Service Providers (ISPs) **62**

TABLE OF CONTENTS

Social Media 63

Building Your Brand 63

Developing Your Website 65

Technology for Your Business 66

Selecting Your Business Location 67

City and County Ordinances 70

Business Licenses or Registrations 70

Financial Accounting System 71

Filing Income Taxes 72

Dun & Bradstreet (DUNS) 73

Quality Certifications 73

Professional Licenses 74

Hiring Employees and Contractors 75

Outside Professional Services 77

Small, Disadvantaged, Minority, Woman, Veteran-Owned & Service-Disabled Veteran Business
Enterprise Certification 78

System for Award Management (SAM) Registration 78

Insurance 79

Bonding 82

Intellectual Property 84

Contracts, Agreements and Execution 86

Licensing Agreements 87

U.S. Federal, State and Local Government 89

Exhibit 9 – Federal, State and Local Government Agencies 91

Educating Your Customer 102

Preparing Your "Elevator Pitch" 102

Using Metrics to Measure Business Success 103

What Gets Measured and How 104

TABLE OF CONTENTS

Business Execution Excellence 105

Operational Efficiency 106

Business Valuation 107

Moving Ahead 110

Capacity Constraints 110

Start-up Checklist 111

Next Step: Writing Your Business Plan 111

    Exhibit 10 – Business Start-up Checklist *112*

PART III - THE BUSINESS PLANNING PROCESS

CHAPTER 2 - UNDERSTANDING BUSINESS PLANNING

What is a Business Plan? 115

Purpose of Writing a Business Plan 116

Why is Business Planning Important: The Journey 117

Writing Your Business Plan 118

Why Some Entrepreneurs Don't Write a Business Plan 119

What Your Business Plan Will Tell You 119

CHAPTER 3 - THE ANATOMY OF A BUSINESS PLAN

Developing Your Business Plan 121

Using this Guide 122

Navigating Through the Process 122

Getting Started 122

The Finished Document 124

Update Your Business Plan Regularly 125

The Sample Plan 125

The Cover Page 126

TABLE OF CONTENTS

Components of the Cover Page 126

    Exhibit 11 – Cover Page 128

The Cover Letter of Introduction 129

Components of the Cover Letter of Introduction 129

    Exhibit 12 – Cover Letter of Introduction 131

The Table of Contents 132

Components of the Table of Contents 132

    Exhibit 13 – Table of Contents 133

The Authorizations Page 134

Components of the Authorizations Page 134

    Exhibit 14 – Authorizations Page 135

The Executive Summary 136

Components of the Executive Summary 136

    Exhibit 15 – Executive Summary 138

The Operating Plan 140

Components of the Operating Plan 141

    Exhibit 16 – The Operating Plan 143

    Exhibit 17 – Fixed Asset Inventory List 146

    Exhibit 18 – Key Operating Metrics 147

The Marketing Plan 148

Components of the Marketing Plan 154

    Exhibit 19 – The Marketing Plan 156

    Exhibit 20 – Product & Service Pricing Models 159

    Exhibit 21 – Breakeven Analysis 160

    Exhibit 22 – Press Release 161

    Exhibit 23 – Customer Acquisition Model 162

    Exhibit 24 – Fact Sheet 163

    Exhibit 25 – Market Position & Annual Industry Sales 164

    Exhibit 26 – Key Marketing Metrics 165

    Exhibit 27 – Service Contract 166

    Exhibit 28 – Limited Warranty 167

TABLE OF CONTENTS

Exhibit 29 – Money Back or Replacement Guarantee.. 168

The Management Plan 169

Components of the Management Plan... 170

Exhibit 30 – The Management Plan... 171

Exhibit 31 – Organizational Chart.. 174

Exhibit 32 – Staffing Plan Chart 176

Exhibit 33 – Résumé/Curriculum Vitae 178

Exhibit 34 – Key Management Metrics 179

The Financial Plan 180

Purpose of Financial Planning 180

How Financial Planning Begins... 181

Establishing a Financial Accounting System 181

General Accounting/Financial Information 182

Pro Forma Statements 182

Components of the Financial Plan... 183

Exhibit 35 – Balance Sheet... 185

Exhibit 36 – Income Statement.. 186

Exhibit 37 – Cash Flow Analysis 187

Exhibit 38 – Operating Budget... 188

Exhibit 39 – Estimated Projections & Forecasts Statement 189

Exhibit 40 – Key Financial Metrics (Terms, Ratios & Formulas) 190

The Strategic Plan 193

What are Goals and Objectives? 196

Project Plan... 197

How Strategic Planning Begins 198

Setting Goals & Objectives.. 199

Identifying Key Results Areas (KRAs)... 199

Problem Solving to Reach Goals 200

Strengths, Weaknesses, Opportunities or Threats (SWOTs) 201

TABLE OF CONTENTS

Components of the Strategic Plan 201

    Exhibit 41 – Strategic Plan 203

    Exhibit 42 – Goals & Objectives 209

    Exhibit 43 – Key Results Areas (KRAs) 210

    Exhibit 44 – Strengths, Weaknesses, Opportunities & Threats (SWOTs) 211

    Exhibit 45 – Strategic Implementation Plan 212

    Exhibit 46 – Status Report 213

    Exhibit 47 – Key Strategic (Long Range) Plan Metrics 214

The Succession Plan 215

Business Continuation 215

Transfer of the Business 216

Preparing the Succession Plan 217

Components of the Succession Plan 217

    Exhibit 48 – Succession Plan 218

    Exhibit 49 – Key Succession Plan Metrics 222

The Appendix 223

    Exhibit 50 – Appendix 224

The Glossary of Terms 225

    Exhibit 51 – Glossary of Terms 225

PART IV - THE BUSINESS ASSISTANCE CENTER

CHAPTER 4 - ACCESS TO MARKETS

Accessing Your Market 229

Which Markets Do You Choose 230

Research Resources 230

Qualifying as a Supplier 231

Understanding Your Competitive Advantage 232

Common Mistakes Business Owners Make 232

Choosing the Best Market 233

Contracting Rules and Regulations 233

TABLE OF CONTENTS

Federal Contracting Opportunities..234

Registering for Government Contracting Opportunities.......................................235

General Services Administration (GSA) Schedules..235

Technical Assistance 236

State, Local and Quasi-Government Agencies..236

The Private Sector...237

Not-for-profit Organizations 238

Associations and Foundations 238

International Markets 240

Is Your Company Export Ready? 240

Risks of Doing Business Abroad...241

Technical Assistance 241

E-business – Marketing on the Internet 243

Reverse Auctions 244

Building Customer Relationships..245

Customer Relationship Management..246

Supplier Development Initiatives..247

Supplier Development 247

Supplier Diversity...248

Strategic Alliances..248

Mentor-Protégé Programs 249

Preparing Bids & Proposals 251

Offer and Acceptance of Bids/Proposals 255

Contract Performance...256

CHAPTER 5 - EMAIL, SOCIAL MEDIA, EMAIL MARKETING & USING YOUR WEBSITE

Email and Social Media: The Science...257

TABLE OF CONTENTS

Email: The First Social Media 257

Unwanted and Unsolicited Email Messages 258

Creating Effective Email Messages 259

What is Social Media? 262

Social Media Platforms 263

Social Media Planning 265

Email Marketing 268

Marketing Using Your Website 269

Creating Your Blog 270

RSS (Really Simple Syndication) Feed 274

Search Engine Optimization (SEO) 275

How SEO Works 275

Affiliate Marketing 276

Social Media Metrics 278

Social Media Marketing ROI (Return on Investment) 279

CHAPTER 6 - ACCESS TO CAPITAL

Understanding Financing Needs 281

Types of Financing 282

Selecting the Best Source of Capital 282

Sources of Capital 283

Government Financing 284

Equity Capital 290

Franchises 291

Going Public 292

Angel Networks 292

Other Sources of Financing 292

TABLE OF CONTENTS

Meeting with Potential Lenders 293

Crowdfunding 296

When to Seek Financing 298

Obtaining Financing 298

Preparing Your Loan Proposal 299

Collateral for Your Loan 301

Negotiating the Loan 301

Loan Repayment 302

Rejected Loan Proposals 303

Credit and Creditworthiness 304

Credit Reporting Agencies 304

UCC (Uniform Commercial Code) Filing 306

    Exhibit 52 – UCC Financing Statement *307*

CHAPTER 7 - BUSINESS TECHNOLOGY

The Evolution of Technology 309

Technology Impact on Business 309

Benefits of Technology 311

Technology Planning 312

Types of Technologies 313

Implementing Technology in Your Business 315

Cloud Computing 315

Technical Service & Support 318

CHAPTER 8 - SMALL, DISADVANTAGED, MINORITY, WOMEN, VETERAN-OWNED, SERVICE-DISABLED VETERAN BUSINESS ENTERPRISE DEVELOPMENT

History of Small Business 319

Small Business Size Standards 320

TABLE OF CONTENTS

Minority, Disadvantaged Business Enterprise Development 321

Women Business Enterprise Development 322

Veteran-Owned and Service-Disabled Veteran Business Enterprise Development........................... 323

Current State of Small Business Development 324

Section 8(a) Business Development Program 325

Business Certification.. 325

CHAPTER 9 - BUSINESS RESOURCES

Your Resource Center 329

PART V - EPILOGUE

SELECTED READING

Suggested Publications 359

GLOSSARY OF TERMS

Business Terms 365

APPENDIX

List of Exhibits.. 399

INDEX

Index... 401

ABOUT THE AUTHOR

KIMBERLY LOUISE JOHNSON... 409

PART I

PROLOGUE

PROLOGUE

Foreword

More than 12 years have passed since the 2nd Edition of *"The Start of Something BIG: Your Ultimate Guide to Writing a Dynamic Business Plan"* was published (19 years for the 1st Edition). Since then, so much has changed in world and in business. One example is the gentrification that has emerged in every major U.S. city. More significantly, we've become a much more global, educated, and technologically-astute world. Additionally, we've spent billions of dollars each year shopping online, and to top it off, there's an "app" for EVERYTHING!

We can't discuss change without making mention of the 2008 election which brought into office the first African American President of the United States, Barack Obama. With this Administration came the Affordable Care Act (ACA), more popularly known as "Obamacare," which provided healthcare coverage for millions of Americans. And after eight productive years of the Obama Administration, the 2016 election took America and the world by surprise when Donald Trump became the 45th president, a businessman with no previous government experience.

The 2009 crowdfunding phenomenon arose as a major funding source for entrepreneurs bringing more products to market faster and easier than ever before. Financial technology had taken over and forced more stringent lending practices making it more difficult for traditional banks to loan money and earn stockholders the desired return on investment thus making crowdfunding a viable funding option.

In 2005, U.S. cell phone sales revenue was $3.8 billion; in 2016, revenues reached over $422 billion. Social media exploded onto the scene and dramatically changed how the world communicates and does business. Also in 2005, 7% of adults used social media; in 2016, that number skyrocketed to 65%. We've also become a more laid-back world. CEOs are called by their first names and blue jeans are appropriate office attire. Cubicles have been removed and enter the open-office concept.

Since the 911 attacks in 2001, we've become a closer nation. Even with today's controversial issues such as the "repeal and replace" proposal for the ACA, ongoing civil and human rights debates on both sides of the political aisle, the major disagreements on immigration reform, the overhaul of the Voting Rights Act of 1965, the institution of same-sex marriage, the legalization of medical marijuana, more lenient gun control laws, the opposing views on global warming, and environmental protection issues, we remain a united front.

PROLOGUE

On a less serious note, in 1999 came the release of the first "urban" dictionary defining terms like *"foodie"* (someone who enjoys food), *"awesome sauce"* (more awesome than awesome), *"baller"* (someone who is good at what she/he does), *"e-quaintance"* (an electronic acquaintance), and my personal favorite, *"fleek"* (smooth or nice). Also, the Merriam-Webster's dictionary has been updated adding hundreds of new words used daily in the English vernacular. Terms such as online, offline, social media, ping, and wikis have become so commonplace it's hard to remember their absence.

For all these reasons and more, it was necessary to update, *"The Start of Something BIG: . . ."* Brand new to this digital edition are hundreds more websites in **CHAPTER 9, BUSINESS RESOURCES** beginning on page 329 that quickly direct you to agencies, organizations, corporations, and information needed to conduct essential research to get your business operational and your business plan completed. A 22-page social media section provides the most popular and current technologies needed to develop and implement social media campaigns. Additionally, there are more helpful offline resources.

Metrics at the end of each section will help with identifying, evaluating and measuring all major and minor activities in your business to determine whether success in each area has been achieved. With metrics, goals can be better set, trends can be tracked, feedback can be evaluated, and appropriate changes can be made.

With this world moving and changing at warp speed, *"The Start of Something BIG: . . ."* print and digital editions were developed to keep pace with the growing changes in business, industry, and entrepreneurial education. In preparing this Guide, our goals were to provide information geared to the concerns unique to small businesses and present them in a utilitarian fashion. Any individual with basic business skills, knowledge and experience in their industry, and a strong willingness to go the distance can use this Guide effectively.

I extend a very warm and sincere "thank you" to all who were so gracious in supporting previous editions, my conference appearances and other speaking engagements. For this I am truly grateful. This year we advocate continued striving for greatness through entrepreneurship. We're pleased to be a part of your impending business success and hope our goals are accomplished. Best wishes, again, to you all in your entrepreneurial endeavor!

Kimberly L. Johnson

Preface

If you ask successful entrepreneurs how they got started in business, you might be surprised to find out that a large number of them came about it by happenstance. Some simply had circumstances (e.g., layoffs, inability to work away from home, military duty/deployment, spousal relocation, etc.) that made opening a business their best option. Others were awarded a contract because of an extraordinary skill, ability or knowledge they possessed. And then there are those who just wanted a second career. That now begs the question, are they really *"in business"*, or are they just *"doing business*?" Believe it or not, there is a difference.

Regardless of how their venture came about, for many it was done without a clear understanding of the implications or ramifications of being in business. For example, because an individual has outstanding culinary skills doesn't mean they can run a restaurant. More than expertise in the products or services one provides is necessary to be successful in business. Some level of expertise in marketing, accounting, finance, management, as well as the related industry, is crucial. In addition, a solid, workable plan is imperative to take an idea or opportunity from start-up all the way to growth and sustainability.

Entrepreneur

"One who organizes and assumes the risks of a business or enterprise"

Entrepreneurial firms have always played an integral role in our economy via experimentation and innovation in ways that lead to new technologies and increased productivity. Whether it's a new approach to an old idea or a new idea entirely, America depends greatly on entrepreneurship to keep its economy healthy and thriving.

Research confirms that small business is the most significant contributor to the U.S. economy and society. It's a fact that small business is the largest job creator in the country, employing more than half the workforce in the private sector. Small business creates more than two out of three new jobs and generates 50% of the nation's gross domestic product (GDP).

Economy

"Structure of economic life in a country, area or period"

Where to Begin

To proceed with the critical planning and to address issues typically encountered by entrepreneurs, *"The Start of Something BIG: Your Ultimate Guide to Writing a Dynamic Business Plan"* is here to help. This business plan Guide presents a step-by-step systematic approach to organizing and developing your business. It takes you from conception to implementation if you're just starting out in business. And, for those who are already in business, provides the tools and information needed for growth, expansion and sustainability.

As you move forward in making your entrepreneurial dream a reality, research should be the one constant in your journey. An incalculable number of books, magazines, newsletters, and courses on the Internet, at the library, in bookstores, with government agencies and business development centers are available to assist you in devising a plan and bringing your business idea to fruition.

"The Start of Something BIG: . . ." is another one of those resources. The information contained is easy to understand and does not require an MBA degree. However, recognize that the ability to comprehend basic business concepts is prerequisite for starting and maintaining a business of any kind.

To better assist you in locating or following up on the resources throughout this Guide, company names, government agencies, trade organizations, management and technical assistance centers, and their complete website addresses are included. Forms and examples are also included to help you format documents needed in organizing your business and preparing your business plan.

Chapters in this Guide

CHAPTER 1, THE START OF SOMETHING BIG beginning on page 3 will assist you in assessing your readiness for entrepreneurship and thinking through all the necessary and logical steps to develop your business. **Exhibit 10 – Business Start-up Checklist** on page 112 are the steps for the start-up phase, listing forms and sample documents. This section will help you understand, identify, develop and/or prepare:

1. your business idea;

2. your product or service;

3. barriers to entry and exit;

4.   proof of concept;

5.   legal and regulatory issues;

6.   traits of an entrepreneur;

7.   entrepreneurship readiness;

8.   personal strengths, weaknesses, skills and abilities;

9.   setting financial goals and addressing concerns;

10. assessing start-up costs;

11. personal and business finances;

12. how to structure your business;

13. management and operational efficiency;

14. researching your market; and

15. contracting opportunities.

CHAPTER 2, UNDERSTANDING BUSINESS PLANNING beginning on page 115 will provide insight on what business planning entails. In it you will learn:

1.   what a business plan is;

2.   the purpose of business planning;

3.   why business planning is important; and

4.   what the completed document will tell you.

CHAPTER 3, THE ANATOMY OF A BUSINESS PLAN beginning on page 121 breaks down each component of the business plan. The definition, purpose of each component, and sample documents are included in the form of an actual business plan. It explains:

1.   how to best use this Guide to develop your business plan;

2.   how to use the finished document (internally and externally); and

3.   updating your business plan regularly.

CHAPTER 4, ACCESS TO MARKETS beginning on page 229 describes access to entry in the public and private sectors, not-for-profit organizations and international markets. It will assist you in:

1.   determining which products/services best meet current market needs;

2.   identifying and researching the market(s) best suited for your products/services;

3.   capitalizing on your competitive advantage;

4.   utilizing the most effective and profitable channels of distribution (e.g., the Internet, retail outlets reverse auctions, importing/exporting);

5.   qualifying as a supplier, supplier development initiatives, proposal preparation; and

6.   managing customer relationships.

CHAPTER 5, EMAIL, SOCIAL MEDIA, EMAIL MARKETING & USING YOUR WEBSITE beginning on page 257 provides information on using email and social media in your business. You will learn:

1. the history of email and social media;

2. creating effective email messages;

3. social media platforms;

4. social media planning;

5. email marketing;

6. developing your website and using it as a marketing tool;

7. creating a blog; and

8. social media return on investment.

CHAPTER 6, ACCESS TO CAPITAL beginning on page 281 provides information you will need to locate debt or equity capital, and organizations to contact and secure it. You will learn:

1. how to determine your financing needs;

2. how to locate the best funding sources available to meet those needs;

3. about your credit and creditworthiness; and

4. what loan preparation and packaging entails.

CHAPTER 7, BUSINESS TECHNOLOGY beginning on page 309 provides information to assist you in understanding the technology needs for your business. You will learn:

1. the evolution of technology;

2. technologies that impact business;

3. technology planning;

4. the benefits of integrating the proper technology in your business; and

5. the various business solutions available today.

CHAPTER 8, SMALL (SBE), DISADVANTAGED (DBE), MINORITY (MBE), WOMEN (WBE), VETERAN-OWNED (VOBE) & SERVICE-DISABLED VETERAN (DVBE) BUSINESS ENTERPRISE DEVELOPMENT beginning on page 319 discusses the history of small, disadvantaged, minority, women, veteran-owned and service-disabled veteran business ownership. In it you will learn:

1.   the history of small business;

2.   what constitutes a small, disadvantaged, minority, woman, veteran or service-disabled veteran business enterprise;

3.   the various programs available for small, disadvantaged, minority, women, veteran and service-disabled veterans; and

4.   the certification process.

CHAPTER 9, BUSINESS RESOURCES beginning on page 329 lists hundreds of public and private agencies and organizations across the country that can provide you with assistance in the areas of business start-up, technical assistance, financing your business, current industry information, research, certification, business technology, building business relationships, legal issues, and more.

A **SELECTED READING** section beginning on page 359 includes book titles that may be useful in researching your industry and brushing up on a variety of business concepts, issues, principles and practices. Titles are categorized and represent a very small number of books that may supplement the information and knowledge your currently have.

The **GLOSSARY OF TERMS** beginning on page 365 defines terms throughout this Guide that may be unique, confusing or unclear. You should include a glossary in your business plan to define all terms that are specific to your business and its industry.

The **APPENDIX** beginning on page 399 developed for *"The Start of Something BIG: . . ."* contains a list of all exhibits throughout this Guide. You should include an appendix in your business plan that contains necessary supplemental information that can strengthen it (e.g., licensing agreements, financing agreements, contract information, consultant agreements, property or equipment leases, etc.).

And finally, the **INDEX** beginning on page 401 lists major topics throughout this Guide to assist you in quickly locating specific information.

Assisting You Every Step of the Way

The 400+ pages of this Guide contain vital information on nearly every aspect of business start-up, planning and management. It would be difficult (actually impossible) to describe each topic contained within in too much greater detail. Fortunately, there are volumes upon volumes of information available online, in libraries and via many other means that cater to entrepreneurial education. *"The Start of Something BIG: . . ."* provides a high level, introductory explanation and examples to help you along in the process.

While *"The Start of Something BIG:. . ."* delivers a significant amount of information on the most critical areas of business, it should also be used as a resource that will direct you in locating and identifying more in-depth information online and offline about business and your industry. It's imperative that you take the time to look further into every topic relevant to your business and its industry.

Now that we've discussed the "what" of entrepreneurship, **CHAPTER 1, THE START OF SOMETHING BIG** beginning on page 3 will take you step by step through the "how." Review each chapter and its contents carefully and give each item ample attention. Always remember that research is never ending, and that the only constant in business is *change*. Business success hinges on being able to consistently meet the ever changing course of your business and the needs of your customer.

"I have learned

that success is to be measured

not so much by the position

that one has reached in life

as by the obstacles

which he has overcome

while trying to succeed."

--Booker T. Washington
Up From Slavery, 1901

PART II

THE START-UP PHASE

CHAPTER 1

THE START
OF SOMETHING
BIG

From Concept to Reality

Going into business has crossed the minds of most people at one time or another in their lives. With a dream of being one's own boss, images of working their own hours, making all final decisions and earning lots of money fueled their desires. Next with the vision of operating a successful enterprise, they entertained thoughts of great money-making prospects. They evaluated the type of work they were performing for their current employer, their hobbies or just something of interest.

Vision

"Unusual wisdom in foreseeing what is going to happen"

Many moved forward to pursue their dream, acting on their ambitions of achieving business success. Even with the proper planning, execution, follow through and follow up, unfortunately for some, that success never materialized. Studies have shown that over 60% of all businesses started in the U.S. each year fail within the first two years. The number one reason for failure is poor planning to include poor management and undercapitalization.

Capitalization

"Total investment of the owner(s) in a business enterprise"

One important consideration when starting your business is believing you are starting your business for the right reason. Having a goal of "making a lot of money" is the grandfather of all wrong reasons to go into business. Certainly no

3

one starts a business looking to fail, but when you don't go about it for the right reasons, it will be difficult to do the proper planning to make the business a success. Wanting to "make a difference", "solve a problem", or "make the world better" are all good reasons to start a business.

A common mistake most budding entrepreneurs make is believing that business success can be achieved simply with a great idea, desire and passion. While this in some respects is very true, a great idea, desire and passion alone are necessary, but not sufficient. Even the best idea with the most extreme amount of desire and passion can make for a bad business.

In order to be successful in business there must be a clear definition and understanding of the business and its mission. When bringing products or services to market, basic business and industry knowledge are prerequisite. In addition, a product or service that the world needs and/or makes life better, and a workable business model that aligns with the business purpose are all required for business success.

Your Product or Service

Deciding what products, services or products and services your company will offer should be one of the must joyous events in the start-up phase. Maybe you want to sell an innovative product for which you have an idea or have created. Or you want to turn a hobby into a business. Maybe you want to provide a service for which you have skills and experience. Or you may want to operate a franchise. Either way, you need to be specific about the business you are about to embark upon.

Innovation

"Introduction of a new idea or method"

It's so easy to get caught up in trying to be all things to all people, but this kind of a start can quickly turn into disorder and chaos. The smartest way to begin is by making a list of all the products and/or services you would like to offer. Then pare down the list to what you believe you can successfully do. The fewer, the better. This doesn't mean other products and services won't come in to play at a later date. You just need to take baby steps because there's so much work to be done. And the larger your product/service line is, the more work there will be, and the easier it will be for things to spiral out of control.

When selecting products/services to offer in your business, choose those:

- that solve a problem that many people will pay for;
- that have relevance and credibility in the marketplace;
- where you can dominate the market;
- for which you have interest and experience;
- in a market or industry not already saturated;
- where the market is emerging and not declining;
- that doesn't require a large staff to perform;
- that production can be financed as needed; and
- that can be extended to create new products/services in the future.

Starting off with a small number of products/services directed towards a unique and select customer base can be most beneficial. In servicing any niche market, you will need to be laser focused on the specialty of your product/service and how it meets the specific needs of customers.

Niche

"A market where products or services are sold to only a particular kind or group of people"

The medical community is a great example of companies that cater to a large number of niche markets. An example of a niche product in pharmaceuticals would be:

> - *A new vaccine that cures chicken pox*
> - *For children between the ages of 5 and 10*
> - *Children not yet contracted or exposed to chicken pox*
> - *Children attending public or private school*

In this example, the cure for chicken pox excludes children under the age of 5 and over the age of 10. Children who have already contracted the virus, as well as children not attending public or private school, possibly home schooled.

One major advantage of offering products/services to a specific group is that it is more cost effective to promote. For example, if your product/service is geared to the likes of only those of a certain demographic (e.g., young females, ages 10 to 15, attending private school), then your marketing dollars can be specifically directed towards them. This then excludes all adults both male and female, all females ages 9 and under and 16 and older, all young males, and all females attending public school or home schooled.

Give yourself plenty of thought time for making product/service offering decisions before settling on any. It's important that you do much contemplation before making a large investment of time, money and energy at this point. Allow yourself the flexibility to make crucial changes very early on. In addition, decide on a product/service line that can be augmented for future business growth.

This allowance of time is particularly important in a product-oriented business where costs for design, development, patents, prototypes, equipment, machinery, production, alpha and/or beta testing, inventory, etc. can be considerably high. But even after an investment of this type is made, a good entrepreneur knows when to give up on an idea because it simply does not work. It could be due to the wrong timing of its launch, the wrong market, poor execution, poor management, inadequate suppliers, materials, shortages, or a multitude of other reasons.

Proof of Concept (POC)

The phrase, "there's nothing new under the sun" comes from the Book of Ecclesiastes 1:9, for which many believe there is *some* truth. However, ideas that can be considered *new* are introduced to the world every day. But *how* are these ideas introduced to the world? The easy answer is "proof of concept."

Proof of concept OR proof of principle

"Demonstration that a concept or theory is feasible and has the potential for real-world application"

Proof of concept (also referred to as proof of principle) is verification that an idea, product, theory or method has the potential to be realized. Simply stated, something created has been thought out, tested, has applicability in the world, and could feasibly be produced and sold, even if it has not been fully developed. This concept is widely used in both business and industry.

An example of proof of concept in business would be the actual development of a prototype for a product that may have the potential to meet the needs of a customer base. The idea comes to mind, a design is created, and finally a sample is made which provides something that can be seen, tested and used. Developing a prototype is the best way to test a product without a large investment.

In the television and film industry, proof of concept would be a pilot television program that could become a series. A popular example is the 1982 pilot of the television sitcom, "Cheers" which ultimately became a series running 11 seasons. A slightly different term, "proof of mechanism," is used in the medical field and describes testing drugs on bacteria, enzymes or organisms before performing clinical trials with human subjects.

The importance of proving a concept when introducing a new idea, product, theory, etc., is that investors, partners, potential customers, even employees get a real sense of what is being created before excess money, time, resources and energy are invested. Proof of concept is the instrument that brings a creation to life and allows stakeholders to actually see and touch what has been created. There have been many instances where there was no interest or real-world application for a creation and thus the projects never enter the marketplace.

Research and Development

Research and development (also referred to as R&D) is more commonly known in the science, medical and technology communities. The concept of R&D is used in business and industry by where companies, organizations or institutions of higher learning (colleges and universities) continuously improve their products or processes to keep pace with fast-changing technologies and to surpass the competition.

Some large high-tech, biotech, computer and pharmaceutical companies, as well as the military, have R&D units within their organizations. These specialized units research and develop specific scientific or technological products for the future. However, depending on how intense the research is, some companies outsource this function to government agencies or universities.

Research and development (R&D)

"The creation of new technology or information aimed to improve the effectiveness of products or make the production of products more efficient"

Small businesses don't generally have a need, funding or the resources to conduct R&D. Projects of this caliber can be capital intensive and require very specialized knowledge and expertise. However, small businesses in the high-tech space benefit tremendously from R&D to grow their businesses, and attract investors.

Legal and Regulatory Issues

It's unfortunate, but true, that entrepreneurs don't immediately think about the legal issues that could affect their businesses in the start-up phase. Relying on family members or friends whose businesses or professions have little or nothing to do with practicing law is where most entrepreneurs obtain legal advice. It's normally not until there's a problem that expert legal counsel is sought. And sometimes it's a little too late.

As a small business owner, being a legal "expert" is not a requirement, however, there are business matters where the advice of a qualified attorney is indispensable. Some of these issues include:

- deciding on the best legal structure for the company;
- understanding the barriers to entry in a market or industry;
- understanding risks of starting the desired type of business;
- knowledge and adherence to federal, state and local laws and regulations that govern that type of business;
- protecting the business from lawsuits;
- adhering to the laws and regulations for hiring employees;
- applicable environmental issues;
- truth in advertising and promotion;
- contracts and negotiations;
- protecting intellectual property or licensing to and from others;
- length of time records are to be kept;
- taking on investors; and
- understanding the barriers to exit.

As part of your business start-up and in preparing your business plan, all of the issues above and more need attention and consideration. Any questions you have should be directed to attorneys who specialize in each of those areas. Don't risk trying to figure out a legal problem just to save money. It's true that attorneys can be expensive, but the cost is much greater if you have to hire one to mitigate or repair any damages that have arisen.

Discrimination, harassment, dissatisfied customers, product or service breaches, disgruntled employees, intellectual property infringement, tax litigation, and contract disputes are just a few issues encountered in business where legal help is necessary. Litigating any one of these issues and others can quickly put you out of business. Below are the benefits of hiring an experienced and qualified attorney in the start-up phase because they can:

- review contracts and interpret the language that a novice can miss or misunderstand;

- understand personal liability as it pertains to insurance claims and other legal matters, such as determining the best legal structure for your business;

- understand risks associated with taking on investors or borrowing money;

- protect you against and/or represent you in the event there's litigation;

- provide assistance in employment laws and help ensure they are adhered to;

- carefully and clearly explain any area of law in terms you can understand; and

- give you security in knowing that you have a legal advocate and representation to serve your business, and when necessary, personal needs.

Thoroughly vetting and not just merely hiring an attorney is very important. It's unfortunate that there are attorneys that don't have their client's best interest at heart, only their own. If you happen to hire an attorney that is less than ethical, you have the right (and obligation) to report them to the bar association in the state where your business is located.

9

THE START-UP PHASE

Unethical legal practices are frowned upon in the law, and alleged violators will be investigated, can be prosecuted, and even lose their license. Conversely, you as the business owner also have an obligation to your customers to provide your products/services with the highest, most honest and ethical standards. If you find yourself embroiled in a legal dispute with customers, vendors, etc., and litigation is pursued, make sure you understand the doctrine of "clean hands." You cannot expect the "long arm of the law" to rule in your favor if you have unsavory business practices, in other words, unclean hands.

Clean (Unclean) Hands Doctrine

"A rule in the law that a petitioner (defendant) for a court order must be free from unfair or unethical conduct with regard to their own matters in the case"

A good way to have legal assistance when needed is to join an organization such as Legal Shield (formerly Prepaid Legal), Rocket Lawyer, or Nolo Law for low-cost legal assistance. For a monthly fee, you are provided with legal services in all areas of law with just a phone call. Under "**LEGAL**" in **CHAPTER 9, BUSINESS RESOURCES**, beginning on page 340 are legal sources and their websites for your convenience.

Regulatory (regulations) issues have a dramatic impact on how you are legally required to operate your business. The purpose of regulations is to ensure all relevant parties comply with applicable statutes passed in the jurisdiction where they conduct business. Depending on the nature of your business, you may be required to abide strictly by federal regulations. Highly regulated industries include financial services, healthcare, producers of chemicals, and energy/utility companies, which are not typically small or start-up.

Regulatory

"A rule or order having the force of law issued by an executive authority of government"

Regardless of the nature of your business, some regulations affect all businesses. These include posting signs on employee rights in a visible location, and the new rules on overtime pay. Another example, in 2016, new credit card security measures were put in place. This measure was in response to the credit and debit card fraud problems that have plagued society. Merchants are now required to install EMV (Europay, MasterCard and Visa) terminals and implement processes for the new chip-enabled cards.

Consequences for not abiding by regulations could be financially catastrophic. The cost of litigation alone could bankrupt a company, especially a small business. Not to mention the fines, penalties or liquidated damages that can be assessed to violators. Here again where a qualified legal expert can be invaluable.

Barriers to Entry or Exit

The ease of entering an industry (or market) varies greatly depending on the players already in that space. Some examples of industries that are difficult to enter include fashion, entertainment, professional athletics, television broadcasting, medical and some technological. Some obstacles that exist for a newcomer trying to make a mark in these industries and others include:

- high start-up costs;

- high capital and equipment investment;

- heavy governmental regulations;

- inability to obtain necessary licenses;

- gender domination (male or female);

- customer loyalty to the competition;

- higher cost of goods (economies of size);

- lack of access to necessary talents or agents; and

- unequal access to distribution channels or markets.

Barriers to entry OR exit

"The existence of obstacles that prevent a company from entering or exiting a market"

In terms of exiting a market, some major barriers include the inability to sell or dispose of specialized equipment or machinery that cannot be used elsewhere, or specialized skills that don't transfer to other industries. This situation unfortunately can leave the business to continue with low profits (or no profits) because the cost of exiting is too high.

In your overall strategic planning, always be cognizant and consider how, when necessary after entering a market, you will exit that market. As difficult as either can be, if you believe you have the talent, expertise and resources, nothing should stop you from realizing your dream. Just understand that there are issues that might make your journey a little more vexing. Make sure your plan clearly outlines what happens to all the assets of the business, who will be responsible for their disposition, the assignment of a fair and equitable valuable, and the timeframes for disposition.

Operational Risk Management

Processes and procedures are put in place to ensure an operation functions as effectively and efficiently as possible. However, there are instances when these processes and procedures fail. For this reason, an operational risk management plan is necessary to keep business operations moving while problems can be diagnosed, solutions can be deployed, and when necessary, new processes and procedures can be developed and put in place.

Operational risk

"The risk of loss that can result from inadequate or failed internal processes, people, systems or external events"

Internal problems such as flaws in production or employee fraud are considered the most common risk factors in business. As are external events such as natural disasters or loss of a company's physical assets. Whether internal or external, high risk or low risk, these are issues that can severely disrupt business operations and cause big losses. To stay ahead of these potential threats, an operational risk management plan is important. In developing an operational risk management plan, you must:

- identify any potential areas at risk of exposure in your business;
- assess the magnitude (high or low impact) of that exposure;
- develop a set a procedures to mitigate any damages resulting from that exposure;
- appropriate capital to pay for potential losses;
- devise a system to monitor potential and subsequent threats;
- review and monitor new systems on a regular basis to ensure their effectiveness.

The financial industry, for example, has a tremendous amount of risk exposure as compared to other industries. Credit, liquidity, compliance, data breaches or losses, failed processes, illegal transactions, and human factors all play a part. In the event of a failure, your risk management plan will guide you in assessing the situation, deploying the appropriate resources to mitigate damages, communicating the situation at all levels, monitoring and reviewing results, and implementing new processes and procedures.

Value Proposition

Your value proposition is a statement that tells your customer why they should do business with you and not your competitor. This statement should be clear and in language that is easy for anyone to understand. Elements of a value proposition include:

- why your product(s)/service(s) is/are superior to that of your competition;
- what your product(s)/service(s) do;
- how well your product(s)/service(s) do what they do;
- how well it will benefit them;
- how well you can deliver; and
- what sets your company apart from the competition.

Value proposition

"A business statement summarizing the reasons why a company's products or services offers more value than other companies"

One example of a great value proposition is the social media platform, Pinterest. Their value proposition is, *"Pinterest: the world's catalog of ideas."* Another is the credit card reader company, Square, *"Square works for every business."* Both companies describe in only a few words who they are and what they do.

Another value proposition can be as simple as an act that can set you apart from the competition such as free shipping, a money-back guarantee, volume discounts, customization or a bonus (e.g., double number of products ordered or a different product). All those extras add value to the products/services you provide and could easily entice a prospective customer to do business with you.

13

THE START-UP PHASE

Your Mission Statement

Establishing the mission for your company is an important early step. The mission statement gives customers an idea of your company's or organization's direction. It is a short statement created to inform employees, customers, partners, the media, etc. of your company's core beliefs, competencies and goals.

Mission statement

"A brief statement describing why an organization exists, its products/services, customers served, and its goals and philosophies"

An example of a mission statement for our imaginary staffing agency, *CareerTemps* would be:

> *"CareerTemps Temporary Staffing Agency" is committed to providing small, medium and large businesses with incomparable temporary assistance, employing the most qualified and well-trained clerical and technical personnel available in the local marketplace.*

With a clear mission and vision for the company, the next step in determining whether to start a business begins with answering critical questions to include the following:

1. Is this a bona fide business, a hobby or simply an idea?

2. What products/services does the world need?

3. Are the products/services in a new or existing category?

4. Why does the world need these products/services?

5. What problems will the products/services solve?

6. Do products/services serve a public good?

7. Is the associated industry or industry sector in a start-up, growth or decline mode?

8. What are the barriers to entering this market?

14

9. What are most efficient and profitable ways to bring these products/services to market?

10. How much will it cost to produce each product or perform each service?

11. How much will customers be charged; what will the market bear?

12. Who is purchasing comparable products/services today?

13. Where are comparable products/services being sold today?

14. Where are products being manufactured/produced or services being performed?

15. What are customers currently paying for these products/services?

16. Why will customers buy these products/services from me?

17. What are the core competencies of the company?

18. What is the company's clear differentiation (competitive advantage) from the competition?

19. Is there anything proprietary about the products/services provided?

20. What will it cost to start the company?

21. What will the legal structure of the company be?

22. Where will the company be located?

23. What are the plans to grow the company?

24. What will be the manpower needs for the company?

25. What is the exit strategy or barriers to exit?

Trait

"A distinguishing quality"

Entrepreneurial Traits

Clearly entrepreneurship is not for everyone. But how do you know whether it's for you? Some people seem to have a penchant for entrepreneurship. They are truly born to be business owners. And then there are others who like the idea of owning and controlling their own business, but unfortunately find out that they are not cut out for it. Regardless of how you earn your living, there are character traits for every person in every occupation. As for the entrepreneur, major character traits include, but not limited, to:

1. **Strong leadership qualities**
   A self-starter who is agile and takes charge to get the job done, but understands to importance of delegating, listening and accepting the advice of others, even subordinates. Works tirelessly to solve problem and adapts well to change.

2. **Excellent communications skills**
   Speaks and writes with clarity at any level and conveys messages in language that is easy to understand, particularly when there is a crisis. A great storyteller.

3. **A decision maker**
   Not afraid or hesitant about making decisions impacting any area of business and takes steps to remedy issues to keep business on track.

4. **Consistently builds skills**
   Always willing to grow and learn new skills as well as teach. Stays abreast of changes in their business and the associated industry. Reads voraciously about business and industry.

5. **Self-motivated and able to motivate others**
   Very passionate about their ideas and driven to produce. Strong sense of ethics, honesty and the ability to inspire others. Provides the opportunity for others to learn and grow.

6. **Innovator and risk taker**
   A true visionary who always seeks to develop new ideas and improve processes. Never afraid to take chances, ask questions or make mistakes. Will admit to any error made and move forward to correct. Not humiliated by what can be construed as failure, but understands when it' necessary to go in another direction.

7. **Makes a difference**
    Willing to make sacrifices. Takes actions designed to benefit others. Listens to the needs and desires of others, and helps fulfill them.

8. **Works well with professionals**
    Has a well-established network of professionals who are willing to provide consultation and referrals. Also makes time to assist and support colleagues when called upon.

9. **Strong ego and desire to be wealthy**
    Relishes a sense of accomplishment and enjoys the financial rewards that accompany it.

10. **A strong willingness to go the distance**
    Not easily discouraged or distracted when adversity arises. Always looking to solve any problem, meet any challenge and continuously seek out new opportunities.

If you're a person who exhibits most of these or similar characteristics, entrepreneurship may be for you. To take it a step further, the next section will help you assess your readiness.

Readiness

"Prepared mentally or physically for some experience or action"

Assessing Your Readiness for Entrepreneurship

Readiness to start a business is comparable to starting a family. How do you really know whether you are ready? To ascertain whether you are ready to start a business, ask yourself the following questions and answer as candidly and in as much detail as possible.

1. Why do I want to start a business? OR Why am I in business?

2. At what do I excel?

3. What do I consider to be a worthwhile or enjoyable use of my time?

4. Are my strengths greater as a leader or a follower?

17

5. Am I a team player? Am I able to work well with others, be it employees, contractors or other businesses or organizations?

6. Am I physically, mentally, financially, and emotionally capable of starting and operating a business?

7. Do I have the temperament to respectfully accept advice, counsel even criticism from those whom I work or interact?

8. Do I have the social and financial support of family, friends and other professionals to accomplish my goals?

9. Do I possess the necessary skills and abilities to start and control the day-to-day operations of a business?

10. Do I have up-to-date working knowledge of technology necessary for efficient operation in order to keep pace in the business world?

11. Do I have the ability to exercise sound professional judgment in people and ideas?

12. Is my past education and experience in the industry sufficient?

13. What sacrifices and risks am I willing to take to be successful?

14. What financial level of success am I seeking to achieve?

15. Have I made proper provisions for income and insurance (health and life) while waiting to achieve business success?

16. How will I balance family and business?

17. Will I be able to devote the necessary time, resources and capital to be successful in business?

18. Why do I believe I can make this type of business work?

19. Why do I believe this type of business is sustainable?

20. Do I have the ability to work to grow the business as it is today, while working to innovate, improve or change it for tomorrow?

The previous questions are intended to assist you in addressing the most fundamental issues generally encountered in the start-up phase. Your responses should give you an indication as to whether you're ready to start your business or continue in business. But once completed, it is strongly advised to revisit this section periodically throughout the life of your business.

Taking the Entrepreneurial Leap

If your business has not yet begun operating and most of your answers are negative, then you will need to carefully re-evaluate whether you should go into business at the present time or stay in business. Any uncertainty can lead to business failure as well as putting relationships and finances in serious jeopardy.

Evaluate

"Determine significance by careful appraise and study"

If on the other hand your answers are affirmative, then you may be ready to enter the world of entrepreneurship. In this case, you're ready to move ahead. In preparation for that day, you should do the following:

1. Make regular visits to your local library, office of the Small Business Administration, small, women and minority business development center (SBDC or MBDC), or procurement and technical assistance center (PTAC). Utilize the many helpful technical assistance services they provide. You will find contact information in **CHAPTER 9, BUSINESS RESOURCES** under "**TECHNICAL ASSISTANCE**" beginning on page 354.

2. Set aside at least an hour a day to conduct research using the Internet. There is virtually nothing in the world you can't find by surfing the web. There are free (and some paid) webinars you can attend virtually on a host of business topics. They are generally about an hour and you will be able to ask questions of the presenters on most of them.

3. Continue to seek business opportunities to find the ideal business for you. A franchise might be a great venture to pursue. If this is so, check the International Franchise Association (IFA) online at www.franchise.org/.

4. Find full- or part-time employment in a similar business or volunteer in an organization to gain first-hand working knowledge of the business and industry.

5. Stay abreast of current trends in the industry by reading local and national trade association publications. It's the best way to keep up with what's going on around the globe.

6. Attend general business and other industry-related seminars and workshops. Local chapters of SCORE (Service Corps of Retired Executives at www.score.org) centers hold business development workshops on a variety of business topics, and they are usually free of charge. Attending workshops and seminars provides interaction with others giving you the networking experience you'll need to build and grow your business.

7. Enroll in business classes at your local community college to brush up on business skills you may be lacking or just need refreshing. If time doesn't permit you to get away and take classes, there are online classes (some are free) at www.Lynda.com. Check with your local library for access from the library or from home.

8. Ask questions of professionals and consultants. This includes people you work with or even family and friends.

9. Read EVERYTHING you pass by. That means every book, newspaper, magazine, brochure, sales piece, sign, billboard, etc. Do so even if it doesn't appear at first glance to have any relevance to the type of business you're interested in starting.

10. Research all legal and regulatory information about your prospective business and its associated industry through your local, state and federal government agencies. Their websites should have a listing by department that will be helpful. Remember that ignorance of the law (or regulations) is no excuse for not abiding by it.

Skill

"A learned power of doing something competently"

Assessing Your Personal Strengths and Weaknesses

Regardless of your reasons for going into business, assessing your skills and abilities (and those of your potential employees) will be helpful to you in determining the role you and your employees, partners or contractors will play in the company. Performing this analysis will enable you to optimize performance in areas you rely on as strengths and improve in areas where there are weaknesses.

In the real world, few business people have or know it all. Some people excel at numbers while others excel at written and/or oral communications. And others excel at technology. It's a fact that in order to be successful in business, you, your employees, a contractor or outside consultant must possess certain required skills and abilities in every area of business. They include having:

1. a strong grasp of business basics;

2. strong ethical standards;

3. focus and a clear direction on where the business should go;

4. goal setting capabilities and follow through;

5. the ability to mitigate challenges effectively;

6. ability to develop new and innovative ideas for continuous growth;

7. good negotiation skills;

8. sound management and leadership skills;

9. experience in the industry;

10. technical expertise;

11. mechanical expertise (where necessary);

12. computer and analytical skills;

13. planning and reasoning abilities;

14. the ability to determine when necessary skills are lacking;

21

15. excellent social skills; and

16. excellent oral and written communications skills.

Some entrepreneurs are more technical than managerial so understanding limitations is critical. Always remember, good products and services are a dime a dozen, but good people, proper execution of plans, and sound management skills are not. Most entrepreneurs cannot hire the expertise they need initially, so keep in mind contracting or bartering services is an excellent way to get the professional services needed for the business.

Ability

"Natural talent or acquired proficiency"

Assessing Your Skills and Abilities

Regardless of how well you know what you know or how well you do what you do, there's always room for skill building to make sure you are always at the top of your game. This includes taking online courses, attending webinars, attending seminars, brushing up on new technologies, and reading about what's going on with your competition.

In assessing your *technical* and *technological skills*, evaluate your knowledge and expertise with computers, technical writing, product design, processes, troubleshooting, data analysis, reporting, and developing presentations. Assessing your m*echanical skills* includes the understanding and expertise in the selection of, purchase of, building or repairing of products, equipment or machinery to be used in your business.

Troubleshooting

"Solving serious problems for a company by tracing and correcting faults"

Social skills are communications skills that are learned and developed over time. This includes the ability to listen as well as speak. While human beings are very social by nature, some aspects of communications are difficult. Not everyone is a great orator or literary genius, but speaking to groups and written correspondence are business imperatives.

If communications isn't your strong suit, identify someone (internally or externally) whose it is. However, you should consider developing your public speaking and presentation skills by joining a speaker training organization such as Toastmaster's International, TED, or possibly taking a course at your local community college. In **CHAPTER 9, BUSINESS RESOURCES** under "**SPEAKING ORGANIZATIONS**" beginning on page 353 are organizations that can help.

Management is practically a science in and of itself. It entails managing time, people and processes, decision making and organization. Leading and/or directing others, even negotiating a consultant or other business contract is a daunting task for many. Not to mention delegating. If managing people and projects is difficult for you, hire someone who can be effective. As a rule of thumb, never hire anyone you would feel reluctant or uncomfortable firing, especially friends, a spouse or other relatives, in particular.

Management

"The process of dealing with or controlling people or things"

The *decision-making* aspects of management can easily make or break a company. The ability to make sound decisions on any issue affecting your business it critical. Steps to sound decision making include, but are not limited, to:

1. clearly defining the issue with as much specificity as possible;

2. gathering relevant information;

3. using information attained, determining the pros and cons of its use and seeking the advice of experts where necessary;

4. determining the best possible outcomes for the company; and

5. devising a written plan to remedy the issues to include new or revised methods, or processes and procedures to prevent these issues from recurring in the future.

Being organized and making *effective use of your time* is the cornerstone of good management. Prioritizing tasks from the most important to the least important, getting rid of any distractions that can inhibit the ability to get a job completed, establishing timeframes for start to finish on each job, and keeping a positive attitude and outlook will help you stay motivated and on task.

THE START-UP PHASE

Starting each day with a clear direction on what needs and should be accomplished is key. Once the work day has ended and before going to bed each night you should do each of the following:

1. Clear your work area so that you return to it uncluttered.

2. Review your calendar to remind yourself about any meetings or events to occur, where they will be held and their times. If the meetings or events are offsite, make sure you know exactly where you need to be and how long it will take you to get there.

3. Make a written list of the next day's tasks (by priority, large and small) and assign the most appropriate time of day to complete.

4. Identify and locate individuals, information, tools, documents, etc. needed to complete each task, or for each meeting or event.

Education and *training* are essential in business, even though not all successful business owners are MBAs or have a college degree of any kind in any field. If you don't possess a degree, certification or license, you can and should, hire, consult or partner with someone who does. If possible, work on securing the applicable credentials so you won't have any dependency on someone else's. At no time do you want to be found practicing in any licensed profession illegally.

Credentials

"Qualification, achievement, title to credit, personal quality, or some aspect of one's background that indicates they are an authority or have official power"

Experience in the industry is very important and a lack thereof could make for a very bumpy ride. Changes in every industry occur frequently. In the technology space, changes seem to occur every second. Make learning your industry and keeping abreast of the changes a priority by either working in a similar business, hiring, consulting or partnering with an expert.

Industry

"An economic activity concerned with the processing of raw materials and the manufacture of goods in factories"

Good *physical health* is vital to the perseverance and endurance needed to go the distance. In business there are few 40-hour workweeks (usually 60 to 80, but not recommended), and for some, no vacations or sick days off are par for the course (also not recommended). Make it a practice to see your doctor regularly to ensure that you are in the best physical condition. A good diet and exercise should be a part of your daily regimen because being in business takes a lot of time and energy. In addition, make sure to get plenty of sleep each night. Some of the most successful people in business get at least six hours sleep each night. Also, wake up to your favorite music, have a healthy breakfast, and at some point in the day, get some sunshine. Oh yes, and BE HAPPY!

As for *mental health*, meditation and just taking a break and/or lunch away from your desk and computer can contribute significantly to your ability to put in a full and productive day's work. Even a power nap (a 30-minute nap during the day) can help you refuel and finish the day on top and avoid burnout. But as often as it makes sense, take time off. Even if not for a full week at a time, being away from it all helps thwart burnout and helps you recharge. While away be sure you make time to meditate in peace and quiet to think and relax without any interruptions.

A healthy mind and body, as well as a neat appearance are much more attractive than this world's current standard of beauty. Unfortunately we live in a society where "good looks" are prevalent. Today we seem to have an obsession with beauty as evidenced by the hundreds of thousands of "selfies" posted each day on Facebook and Instagram. While beauty can be both a strength and a weakness, unless you are in an industry where *that* standard matters, it doesn't matter anywhere else.

Exhibit 1 - Assessment of Personal Strengths and Weaknesses on page 26 will aid you in evaluating your personal and professional strengths and weaknesses. A true assessment will signify areas where you will need to focus your expertise and where to contract out or hire others. Take personal inventory of where you are in each of the areas of skill. Be honest with yourself in assessing your strengths as well as your weaknesses.

In the following table, there are just a few examples of skills needed to be successful in business. However, it is important that you come up with others that apply specifically to you and your business. You may even want to conduct the same assessment with each person in your business. This information will be very valuable in helping you determine what skill areas your company is lacking or not as proficient as need be. But on a positive note, it will show you where you and/or individuals in your company perform best.

Exhibit 1 – Assessment of Personal Strengths and Weaknesses

AREAS OF SKILL	MY STRENGTHS	MY WEAKNESSES
Technical/Mechanical • Computers • Technical writing • Analytical/statistical • Financial/mathematics • Reporting • Presentations • Building/constructing • Processes • Troubleshooting	High proficiency with PC and Mac platforms. High proficiency with SAP. Excellent in developing processes and procedures. Will always complete any task that has been started.	At times, have to move deadlines to make sure product is perfect.
Social • Personality • Oral/written communications • Social media • Speaking/listening • Telephone • Person to person • Marketing/public relations	Strong written and oral communications skills. Proficient with Facebook, and Instagram. Experienced public speaker in large and small groups. Humble with own point of view and good listener.	Don't always take the opportunity to discuss business when meeting people, which could mean missed opportunity. Sometimes thinks ahead of conversations.
Management • Leadership agility • Legal/negotiating • Organizational • Administrative • Teaching/training • Decision making • Delegating/time manager	Able to deal with multiple issues and make decisions 10 years senior management experience with staff sizes of 5 to 10. Training expert in marketing and entrepreneurship.	Sometimes procrastinates. Don't delegate as much as could, but not a micromanager.
Education/Training • Degree(s) • Certification(s) • Licensing	Master's Degree in Communications Bachelor's Degree in Business	Needs more education in product licensing. Need more training in social media
Experience • Number of years • Area of expertise	35 years management in corporate and public agency	N/A
Health • Physical/appearance • Mental • Emotional	Excellent, physical, mental and have emotional support of family.	Would like to lose 25 pounds Get more than 5 hours per night sleep

Personal Finances

Much of what we do or accomplish in life is predicated on our personal financial position. Those who keep their credit clean, save money and invest well, obviously fare best. However, there are millions of Americans who are in serious financial trouble today. They have too much unsecured debt, no savings, late bill payments, and no formal plan for getting their situation under control.

Without question these factors negatively impact one's personal financial status. For those seeking to become entrepreneurs, this situation must be resolved, or it'll eventually impact their businesses. If the aforementioned mirrors your current situation and you have a fear of any kind in dealing with it, this is the time to confront and conquer. A poor personal financial position can be immobilizing to you in your entrepreneurial journey.

Business success doesn't come over night. In fact, it's often said that overnight success takes about 10 years. So it's important to implement a plan that will ensure financial security for you and your family prior to the start of your new venture. The following section will help you examine, understand and systematically master the art of managing your personal finances.

Financial status

"An individual's existing financial position"

Setting Personal Financial Goals and Addressing Concerns

Begin by identifying your personal financial goals and any concerns you may have that could inhibit your reaching them. Let's take a hypothetical situation. Assume you're currently employed full time. You're devising your transition plan to move (voluntarily or involuntarily) from employee to entrepreneur.

Completing **Exhibit 2 – Setting Personal Financial Goals and Concerns** on page 28 will guide you in this process. Just remember that after you've set your goals, be sure to follow through, keep accurate records, and it's always a good idea to seek professional assistance.

Goal

"The end toward which effort is directed"

THE START-UP PHASE

Exhibit 2 – Setting Personal Financial Goals and Addressing Concerns

ITEM	GOALS	CONCERNS	DATE
1	Pay off $14,000.00 in unsecured debts in 18 months.	Too much unsecured debt and inability to save money to invest in business venture: Credit cards: $6,000.00 Personal loan: $8,000.00	Begin 2/XX End 8/XX
2	Save 10% of monthly salary	Cut back on recreational expenditures (e.g., health club, eating out, etc.)	2/XX to indefinite
3	Create and manage a monthly budget	Currently have no written plan to measure monthly spending	2/XX to indefinite
4	Keep better financial records	Receipts are disorganized and not in a centralized location or lost	2/XX to indefinite
5	Use cash more often	Credit and debit cards enable overspending	2/XX to indefinite
6	Get rid of all credit cards except one	Have too many credit cards that are to the limit	2/XX
7	File delinquent tax returns	Past 2 years of federal and state tax returns have not been filed	2/XX
8	Change life insurance coverage from whole life to term	Whole life is much more expensive and doesn't have the value	2/XX
9	Change auto insurance plan to exclude comprehensive	Paying too much for auto insurance because both cars are paid for and are over 5 years old	2/XX
10	Begin apply at least $200 more money per month to mortgage for early pay-off	Need to save money on the interest being paid to mortgage company	2/XX

Assessing Your Current Personal Financial Status

Follow up your financial goals with taking stock of your assets and liabilities to determine your personal net worth. Completing **Exhibit 3 - Current Personal Financial Status** on page 30 will give you a true picture of your financial status. Understanding and having a handle on your personal finances (including tax filings) is a prelude to handling the finances of your business.

If you have unfiled or unpaid federal taxes and need help settling a tax debt, contact the Internal Revenue Service (IRS) at www.irs.gov as soon as possible. For unfiled and/or unpaid state taxes, contact your state department of revenue. Private tax firms are also available to assist for a fee, but seek assistance through the IRS or local department of revenue first. Their services are free of charge.

Personal net worth

"What you own minus *what you owe"* (Assets – Liabilities)

Assets

- **Current Assets** - Monies or resources that can be converted into cash in 6 months or less

- **Securities** - Publicly-traded stocks, bonds, mutual funds, futures, contracts, warrants and options

- **Real Estate** - Includes first and second homes, condominiums, rental properties, etc.

- **Long-term Assets** *(Investments)* - Instruments with a true value that's known after several years or even decades

- **Personal Property** - Personal items valued at whatever one believes it is worth in its present condition

Liabilities

- **Current liabilities** - Debts that are due and payable in six months or less

- **Real Estate** - First and second mortgages on primary residences or mortgages on rental properties

Exhibit 3 – Current Personal Financial Status

At January 31, 20XX

ASSETS		LIABILITIES	
Current Assets		**Current Liabilities**	
Asset	**Current Value**	**Liability**	**Balance due**
Checking accounts	$ 6,000.00	Automobile	$ 2,300.00
Savings accounts	$ 2,500.00	Home improvement	$ 1,500.00
Treasury securities	$ 5,000.00	Education	$ 20,000.00
Money market mutual funds	$ 2,500.00	Utilities	$ 250.00
U.S. savings bonds	$ -	Medical	$ 310.00
Treasury bills	$ -	Dental	$ 150.00
Other	$ -	Unpaid taxes	$ 5,000.00
Securities		**List other debts**	
Corporate bonds	$ -	Leases	$ -
Government bonds	$ -	Credit card	$ 1,500.00
Preferred stock	$ 5,000.00	Credit card	$ 500.00
Common stock	$ -	Credit card	$ 250.00
Mutual funds	$ -	Personal loan	$ 5,000.00
Futures contracts	$ -		
Warrants	$ -		
Options	$ -		
Real Estate			
Residence	$ 200,000.00		
Condominiums	$ -		
Rental properties	$ -		
Other properties	$ -		
Long-term Assets (Investments)			
Pension	$ 15,000.00		
IRAs	$ -		
Keogh	$ -		
Annuities	$ -	**Real Estate**	
Cash value of life insurance	$ 50,000.00	Residence	$ 350,000.00
		Condominiums	$ -
Personal Property		Rental properties	$ -
Automobiles	$ 10,000.00	Other properties	$ -
Household furnishings	$ 10,000.00	Other	$ -
Art, collectibles	$ -	**TOTAL LIABILITIES**	$ 386,760.00
Clothing, jewelry	$ 15,000.00		
TOTAL ASSETS	**$ 321,000.00**	**NET WORTH**	**$ (65,760.00)**

Getting Your Personal Finances in Order

If as shown in **Exhibit 3 – Current Personal Financial Status** for example, your home is valued at $200,000 (asset), but the balance on your mortgage is $350,000 (liability), this snapshot shows you a $150,000 deficit, meaning you owe more on your home than it's worth. Also, examine the cash on hand in the example ($8,000 asset) versus the current debt ($36,760 liability). Again, if this is your situation, having more current debt (liabilities) than you have cash (assets), you will need to devise a plan to pay off this debt.

Bottom line, this example shows a negative personal net worth of $(65,760). This information is critical because it not only tells you whether you have enough cash or credit to start your business, but it also gives you the information every banker requires prior to loaning you money when needed. Having a negative personal net worth won't preclude you from being successful in business, but be advised that it makes it more difficult to maintain a positive cash flow or secure the necessary credit for your business.

Now that you have a clear picture and understanding of your personal net worth, it's time to work through whatever issues you may have with your finances and credit. Understand that personal net worth changes constantly with the increase or decrease of assets and liabilities.

Your Personal Credit History

Your personal credit history plays a critical role in obtaining the credit you may need for your business. Most people have no idea what has been reported on their credit profile until they apply for credit of some kind or apply for a job. Note that credit is also used when determining one's rates on common items such as car insurance premiums, cell phone contracts and apartment/housing rental.

To review your credit profile you must order a copy via mail or online. You can receive your credit report annually at no charge from the three major credit bureaus. Credit reporting companies such as FreeCreditReport.com can also provide you with your credit report online. However, a credit card is required for some, which may be charged $1 and you may be signed up for unwanted credit monitoring services. Just remember to cancel the service within the allotted timeframe (usually 7 days) or you will be charged a monthly fee, around $21 or more per month. You can find credit and credit reporting agencies in **CHAPTER 9, BUSINESS RESOURCES** under "**CREDIT & REPORTING**" on page 334.

THE START-UP PHASE

It's important to get a copy from all three credit bureaus because not every creditor reports to all three. It is not uncommon to see and item reported on only one of the three credit bureaus as opposed to all three. You can contact them online at:

1. **Experian**
   www.experian.com

2. **Trans Union**
   www.transunion.com

3. **Equifax**
   www.equifax.com

Once you have obtained a copy of your credit report, review it thoroughly. It's not unusual to have inaccuracies reported, and inaccurate information can be removed. As a consumer you have a right to dispute any item that you believe to be incorrect. All three credit bureaus have an online dispute process where you can file a dispute. Positive and negative information remain on your credit report for varying amounts of time as shown in the table below:

REPORTED ITEM	DESCRIPTION	DURATION
Payment activity	Open and active accounts	Indefinitely/ongoing
Open and active accounts	Open and active accounts	Indefinitely/ongoing
Identifying information	Name, aliases, current and past addresses	Indefinite/ongoing
Credit inquiries	Hard inquiries resulting from an application for credit. Only those over the previous 2 years impact FICO Score.	24 months
Chapter 13 Bankruptcy	Allows you to pay back some or all of your debts with lenders.	7 years
Civil Judgments	Paid and unpaid rulings, generally lawsuits.	7 years
Collections	Any credit account from the date of the first delinquency.	7 years
Paid tax liens	Unpaid tax liens from the filing date.	7 years
Late payments	From original delinquency date even if payment is made and the account is current or closed, and payment is never received.	7 years

REPORTED ITEM	DESCRIPTION	DURATION
Chapter 7 Bankruptcy	No repayment of any debt, and can be petitioned or discharged. If dismissed, however, will remain on your credit report for 7 years from filing date.	10 years
Unpaid tax liens	Liens remain from filing date.	10 years
Paid closed accounts	Non-delinquent or derogatory credit cards, mortgages, school loans, car payments, utilities.	10 years

The credit scoring system used by most lenders most often is called FICO®, which stands for the Fair Isaac Corporation, the inventor of credit scoring. These scores are calculated using the credit data in your profile, and considers both positive and negative information. Basic FICO® scores range from as low as 300 to as high as 850. The credit score breakdown is as follows:

- 35% - Payment history – on time and late payments

- 30% - Amount of money owed

- 15% - Length of credit history

- 10% - New credit accounts

- 10% - Credit mix – types of credit (e.g., mortgage, credit cards, etc.)

You can learn more about your FICO® score, credit and credit reporting online at http://www.myfico.com/. Be careful not to pay so-called "credit repair" companies that promise to remove negative credit from your report. You can easily do this yourself. Just note that if the reported item is accurate, it cannot be removed until the required reporting period has expired.

For more information on fair credit reporting, the Federal Trade Commission (FTC) "pursues vigorous and effective law enforcement; advances consumers' interests by sharing its expertise with federal and state legislatures and U.S. and international government agencies; develops policy and research tools through hearings, workshops, and conferences; and creates practical and plain-language educational programs for consumers and businesses in a global marketplace with constantly changing technologies." You can visit their website at https://www.ftc.gov/about-ftc.

Preparing Your Monthly Budget

If you don't already do so, your next step in getting your finances in order is to prepare a monthly budget. If you are starting your business because you've been laid off your job or your income has been reduced for any reason, preparing a budget will still be extremely helpful to you. You may ask, "*how do I budget with little or no income?*" This is not an easy question to answer, but know that budgeting is even more important in that instance.

A budget serves as a spending plan that will assist you in balancing your income with your expenses. Preparing a budget each month allows you to determine how much money you have, how much money you will need to cover your monthly expenses, and whether you have enough to cover those expenses. It will also aid you in working your way out of debt.

What's great about establishing and maintaining a budget each month is that it forces you to take a look at your spending. You'd be surprised to see how much money you spend carelessly each month, while bills continue to pile up and ultimately spiral out of control. Keeping track of all expenditures can put you on the path to becoming debt free, allowing you to pay off debts and save for your business and future.

Most of us have experienced financial challenges at some point in time in our lives for a number of reasons. This includes unemployment, underemployment, unexpected illness, death of a spouse or partner, divorce, retirement, etc. Overcoming these difficulties is not easy, but possible. Being honest and identifying each source of your challenge is the best way to eradicate problems. It may take time, but you can do it.

Creating a budget and understanding finances can be a painful task which takes time and a lot of commitment to make it work. Dave Ramsey's Financial Peace University (FPU) is a biblically-based money handling plan that uses video teaching, class discussions and interactive small group activities combined with practical steps to get you from where you are to where you've dreamed you could be. This plan shows you how to get rid of debt, manage your money, spend, save and give wisely, and much more! For more information, or to locate a class near you, visit the FPU website at http://www.daveramsey.com/fpu/.

If you have been diligent in handling your monthly finances, you probably already use a budget. But if you've never put one together, **Exhibit 4 – Monthly Budget** on page 35 is an example of typical household budget that is an easy and simple way to proceed.

Exhibit 4 – Monthly Budget

HOUSEHOLD BUDGET
For the month of January 20XX

	BUDGETED	ACTUAL	DIFFERENCE (+/-)
INCOME (Take home)			
Salary 1	$ 3,500.00	$ 3,500.00	$ -
Salary 2	$ 2,500.00	$ 2,500.00	$ -
Other income	$ 500.00	$ 500.00	$ -
TOTAL INCOME	$ 6,500.00	$ 6,500.00	$ -
			$ -
EXPENSES			$ -
Mortgage/rent	$ 1,500.00	$ 1,500.00	$ -
Utilities			$ -
Gas	$ 75.00	$ 66.00	$ 9.00
Electric	$ 125.00	$ 90.00	$ 35.00
Water	$ 60.00	$ 70.00	$ (10.00)
Cable	$ 105.00	$ 105.00	$ -
Trash	$ 35.00	$ 35.00	$ -
Phone	$ 120.00	$ 120.00	$ -
Food	$ 300.00	$ 400.00	$ (100.00)
Installment payments			$ -
Car payment	$ 400.00	$ 400.00	$ -
Credit card	$ 50.00	$ 50.00	$ -
Credit card	$ 60.00	$ 40.00	$ 20.00
Personal loan	$ 125.00	$ 125.00	$ -
Student loan	$ 250.00	$ 250.00	$ -
Clothing	$ 200.00	$ 100.00	$ 100.00
Transportation	$ 75.00	$ -	$ 75.00
Gas	$ 160.00	$ 155.00	$ 5.00
Repairs	$ 100.00	$ -	$ 100.00
Other	$ 65.00	$ -	$ 65.00
Insurance	$ 125.00	$ 125.00	$ -
Auto	$ 245.00	$ 245.00	$ -
Mortgage/rent	$ 80.00	$ 80.00	$ -
Life	$ 200.00	$ 200.00	$ -
Other expenses	$ 100.00	$ -	$ 100.00
Donations/tithes	$ 200.00	$ 250.00	$ (50.00)
TOTAL EXPENSES	$ 4,755.00	$ 4,406.00	$ 349.00
			$ -
TOTAL INCOME LESS EXPENSES	$ 1,745.00	$ 2,094.00	$ (349.00)

ANALYSIS: For the month of January total income budgeted and actual was $6,500.00. Total expenses budgeted was $4,755.00 and total actual was $4,406.00. There was a total of $349.00 difference in the budgeted amount and the actual expenses.

Start-up Costs

Obtaining bank financing is difficult (and these days nearly impossible) when you're starting out in business. So it's no surprise that most businesses are initially financed with personal funds (usually from savings, retirement accounts, family, friends, credit cards, insurance proceeds, pension, loans, settlements, real estate, etc.). Even if you have good credit, a bank loan for your business requires the financials that your new business does not have which makes financing your business with personal funds all the more necessary.

Regardless of whether you're able to secure outside financing or you finance your business yourself, there are non-recurring and recurring start-up costs of some kind. To ascertain how much will be needed to start your business, it's necessary to perform an analysis. Determining what your start-up costs will be is predicated on the type of business you are starting.

If you are in a service-oriented business, generally start-up costs are fairly low. That's because these types of business don't require much in terms of expensive heavy or major equipment or even commercial office space. Basic office equipment such as up-to-date computers and software, office supplies, and probably small equipment or appliances are all that's necessary to run the business. And the business can conceivably be run from a home office.

On the other hand, if you are running a product-oriented business, there's much more to consider, and costs can be significantly higher. You may need commercial space to stock inventory and store materials and supplies as well as equipment that needs space, significant electrical power and ventilation to function properly. In addition, if products are manufactured elsewhere (in another city or state or abroad), they may need to be trucked in. Therefore, access for trucks to deliver products, materials, or supplies is crucial.

Non-recurring costs are generally one-time expenses. These include deposits on office space, leasehold improvements (if applicable), certain licenses and permits, office furniture, computers and peripherals and other office equipment. Remember these items will need to be upgraded or renewed from time to time, or in the case of business expansion, you may need to purchase additional units.

Non-recurring OR recurring

"Not to occur OR to occur again after an interval"

Recurring costs are your regular monthly or quarterly expenses. These are expenses that you will have throughout the life of your company. They include your monthly rent/lease on your office space (or a portion of it if your business is home based for tax purposes), lease payments on equipment, payroll, taxes, insurance and transportation. These payments are somewhat fixed meaning they don't vary much or at all from month to month.

Other recurring costs such as utilities, inventory, raw materials and supplies may vary from month to month. For example, during slow periods, less in terms of inventory, raw materials and supplies is needed. Some bi-annual or as-needed expenses include professional services, marketing and promotion, memberships and subscriptions, printing, licenses and other fees. These, too, are expenses that may be variable, but occur periodically as opposed to just one time.

Assessing Your Start-up Costs

Exhibit 5 - Assessment of Start-up Costs on page 38 is a list of typical start-up expenditures that, when completed, will show you how much money you will need to start your business and a total of what your monthly expenditures could be. It includes the non-recurring costs and recurring costs that can be used for either product- or service-oriented businesses.

Begin by identifying the line items applicable to your business. For example, under the non-recurring costs column, if you are operating from a home office, rent/lease deposits, tenant improvements, and other deposits would not apply. And under the recurring costs column, monthly rent/lease, parking, cleaning and maintenance would also not apply. If your business is service oriented, then line items under the recurring costs column such as inventory, raw materials may not apply. However, if you have a product-oriented business, most all line items, non-recurring costs and recurring costs, may apply.

This analysis is best performed on an electronic spreadsheet (e.g., Microsoft Excel) where costs can be calculated easily and accurately. Line items can be added or deleted based on the specific costs associated with your type of business. When completed, you will have the most accurate picture of what costs should be considered, how often these costs will occur, and how much will be needed to cover them. As a rule of thumb, at least six months of expenses should be available when starting your business. This cushion will enable monthly expenses to be paid on time and serve as a means to monitor cash flow, especially when the reality exists of being paid by some customers is 60 to 90 days later.

Exhibit 5 – Assessment of Start-up Costs

January 20XX

NON-RECURRING COSTS			RECURRING COSTS		
Set-up Costs			**Commercial or Home Office Space**		
Line item	Cost		Line item	Cost	
Licensing/permits	$	75.00	Rent/lease, parking	$	2,500.00
Corporate/business filing	$	250.00	Cleaning/maintenance	$	75.00
Legal fees	$	500.00			
Corporate documents	$	65.00	**Utilities**		
			Gas	$	250.00
Office Space			Electric	$	100.00
Rent/lease deposit	$	5,000.00	Water	$	75.00
Tenant improvements	$	-	Cable	$	250.00
Other deposits	$	-			
			Telecommunications		
Computer			Telephone	$	300.00
Hardware	$	8,000.00	Cellular/paging	$	300.00
Software	$	750.00	Internet access	$	150.00
Printer	$	500.00			
Peripherals	$	600.00	**Insurance**		
Supplies	$	800.00	Business	$	80.00
Other digital devices			Bonding	$	-
Equipment			**Lease/rental**		
Fax machine	$	250.00			
Copier	$	450.00	Equipment	$	-
Other	$	-	Automobile	$	350.00
Telecommunications systems	$	2,500.00	Other	$	-
Furniture/Fixtures			**Production Costs**		
Desks	$	6,000.00	Inventory	$	1,000.00
Chairs	$	4,000.00	Raw materials	$	1,500.00
Shelving	$	600.00	Supplies	$	500.00
Cabinets	$	150.00			
Tables	$	100.00	**Professional Services**		
Other	$	-	Accounting	$	200.00
			Legal	$	150.00
Professional Services			Marketing/promotion	$	400.00
Accounting	$	200.00	Printing	$	600.00
Consulting	$	250.00	Consulting	$	200.00
Graphic design	$	400.00			
Printing	$	525.00	**Taxes**		
Social media management	$	250.00	Federal	$	2,000.00
Website design	$	1,000.00	State	$	800.00
			Local	$	-
			Other	$	-
			Other		
Other			Licenses/fees	$	25.00
Office supplies	$	500.00	Memberships/subscriptions	$	25.00
Signage	$	-	Equipment supplies	$	150.00
			TOTAL RECURRING COSTS	$	11,980.00
TOTAL NON-RECURRING COSTS	$	33,715.00	**TOTAL START-UP COSTS** (Non- + recurring) costs	$	45,695.00

38

The assessment in **Exhibit 5** shows typical start-up line items and estimated costs for a company that will be operated in commercial space. As you can see, total non-recurring costs are $33,715. This is presumably the initial amount of money needed to secure all needed licenses, equipment, supplies, furniture, etc. for the company. Total recurring costs of $11,980 is an estimate of monthly expenses. This means that a total start-up cost of $45,695 (the sum of non-recurring and recurring costs) is what could be needed to start the business.

When identifying line items and costs for your business, it's important to determine which items are essential and which are optional. There is the "nice to haves" and then there is the "need to haves." Just remember, the "nice to haves" can come later, so there is no need to splurge right from the beginning.

Again, as a rule of thumb, you should have at least six months of expenses covered before signing any leases or purchasing any furniture or equipment to fill commercial space. Note that these start-up estimates do not include employee salaries, benefits and related taxes.

Organizing the Development of Your Business

Now that you've made an honest assessment of your personal strengths and weaknesses, an analysis of your personal financial position, and your start-up costs, you're ready to take the leap. Begin with fully developing your business idea. In starting your specific type of business, take an "outside-in" view to determine "what the world needs." This means that instead of simply selling a great idea, you're actually solving a problem, fulfilling a need or providing entertainment. It's now time to develop your mission, what your company is about and what it stands for.

Mission

"What the business wants to do for its owners, customers, and employees"

Make sure you have chosen a product and/or service with which you have skill, knowledge or interest. Going into business to sell an unfamiliar product/service can severely increase your chance of failure. You may want to conduct a survey among family, friends and business associates. They can give you a feel for whether you're on the right track, and can offer suggestions that could very well strengthen your business.

39

THE START-UP PHASE

Now it's time to take a "formal approach" to organizing the development of your business. This means responding to each of the items listed and defined on the following pages such as legal structure, naming your business, licensing, technology, accounting systems, etc. Instituting this approach at the onset offers the protections you will need in your business, and will save you time, energy, money and agony as you continue on.

In building your business, consider what it takes to be a world-class operation. While you may be just starting out or growing your existing business, always look to the best in class as an example. This includes Fortune 500 companies as well as businesses that are local or regional, and depending on the nature of your business, national or international. Part of your research should include studying related companies individually and the industry as a whole.

Organize

"To arrange or form into a coherent unit or functioning whole"

Your Business Model

Defining and developing your business model will help you in the preparation of your business plan. It describes the value of how your company converts its products and services into revenue. For example, if your company provides products/services such as food services or hair styling, that business model is considered "on demand." Amazon.com is one such business; order today and receive in a day or two. Other familiar types of businesses include direct sales, consulting, online subscription-based, contract manufacturing, distribution, retail, franchise (or turnkey) or multi-level marketing. Examples of a textual (conceptual) and a graphical (illustrative) business models can be found on page 140.

Business model

"A conceptual, textual and/or graphical representation of an organization including its core products, services and customers"

The business model is important in that it lays the groundwork on which the business is built taking into account all aspects of the business to include:

- problems the products or services solve;
- how products and services are provided;

- economics of providing products and services;
- markets for products and services;
- how revenue will be generated;
- competitors in the marketplace;
- how market share will be garnered;
- competitive strategy; and
- environment in which the business functions (e.g., technologic, economic, political, legal, social or cultural)

North American Industrial Classification System (NAICS)

NAICS (pronounced "Nakes"), formerly known as SIC (Standard Industrial Classification), is a unique, all-new system for classifying business establishments by type of activity in which they are engaged. This system functions as part of the U.S. Department of Commerce, Bureau of the Census (www.census.gov/eos/www/naics/).

The purpose of NAICS is to facilitate the collection, tabulation, presentation and analysis of data relating to establishments and for promoting uniformity and comparability in the presentation of statistical data collected by various agencies of the federal and state governments, trade associations, and private research organizations. This is also important when filing your taxes so that your industry accounts for all the monies made under specific classifications. This information is reported, made public and lets us know how much money an industry is earning as a whole or if that industry is in a decline.

Classification

"Systematic arrangement in groups or categories according to established criteria"

NAICS reflects the structure of today's economy in the U.S., Canada and Mexico, including the emergence and growth of the service sector and new and advanced technologies. This six-digit system, in contrast to the four-digit system of the SIC code, recognizes important industries below the level at which comparable data will be shown for all three countries. Below are the main categories for the publishing industry:

Division 51 - Information
511110   Newspaper Publishers
511120   Periodical Publishers
511130   Book Publishers

41

Researching Your Market and Industry

Research is the key to determining the market potential of your product/service. It begins at the inception of your company and continues throughout its life. This very crucial practice involves discovery and interpretation of new or existing facts and statistics, accepted theories or laws and their practical application. The key to proper research is to determine the NAICS code(s) for your business, and to use it to monitor and measure your business as it compares to your competition and its industry or industry sector.

Regular visits to your local library, chamber of commerce, business development centers, related trade association or government agency will be very helpful to you in researching your market. These entities carry and subscribe to a multitude of invaluable resource materials, books, white papers, magazines, periodicals and newsletters that have the most current and historical industry information. Because changes occur in business and industry much faster than we can keep pace, it's critical that you stay abreast of changes by way of either or all sources.

Research

"Search or investigate exhaustively"

You don't have to spend a lot of money on market research because you are your best market researcher. Visiting similar businesses in person can give you an idea of how your type of business is doing in your specific area or region. In addition, utilizing the Internet is an excellent method for researching your market and industry electronically locally, nationally and internationally.

Demographic, analytical and financial information on virtually every industry can be found online. It only costs time. However, there are paid solutions such as ESRI Business Information Solutions (www.esri.com) and LexisNexis Group (www.lexisnexis.com) that can be of tremendous help in obtaining demographic data and data analytics, respectively.

When conducting research for your business and industry, make sure to:

- Stay as organized as possible. Keep copious notes including where the information was obtained.

- Not take everything you read at face value. Consider the source from which the information is derived.

- Double-check each source. Bias is almost inevitable depending on the source.

- Use the information you find to locate other information.

- Exercise common sense in your research. When things don't make sense, chances are the information is incorrect or invalid.

- Whenever possible, interview the source. This is not always an option, but when it is, take full advantage.

Conducting Research Online

In the current information economy, we are bombarded with hordes of resources we can use to conduct research on virtually any subject known to man. With quick access to information via technology, we get information faster and in more depth than ever before. Desktop, laptop and tablet computers, mobile devices, and now watches can download information and communicate instantly and in real time.

Information economy

"An economy in which knowledge is the primary raw material and source of value"

When conducting research online, simply typing a word or phrase in the search bar of a search engine can yield literally hundreds of thousands, even millions of results to your search. The problem is the vast majority of the results are most likely not relevant to your search. Using an advance search function on a search engine (e.g., Google [Chrome] or Bing [Internet Explorer]) can drastically narrow your search results and save a lot of time.

Remember to make sure the topic of your search is clear and specific. Long phrases and multiple words will produce far too many results to be useful. In **Exhibit 6 – Google Advanced Search** on page 44, Google has created an exercise for conducting an Advanced Search for a "tri-colour rat terrier." Using your own search criteria, you can get the information that specifically meets your research needs.

Exhibit 6 – Google Advanced Search

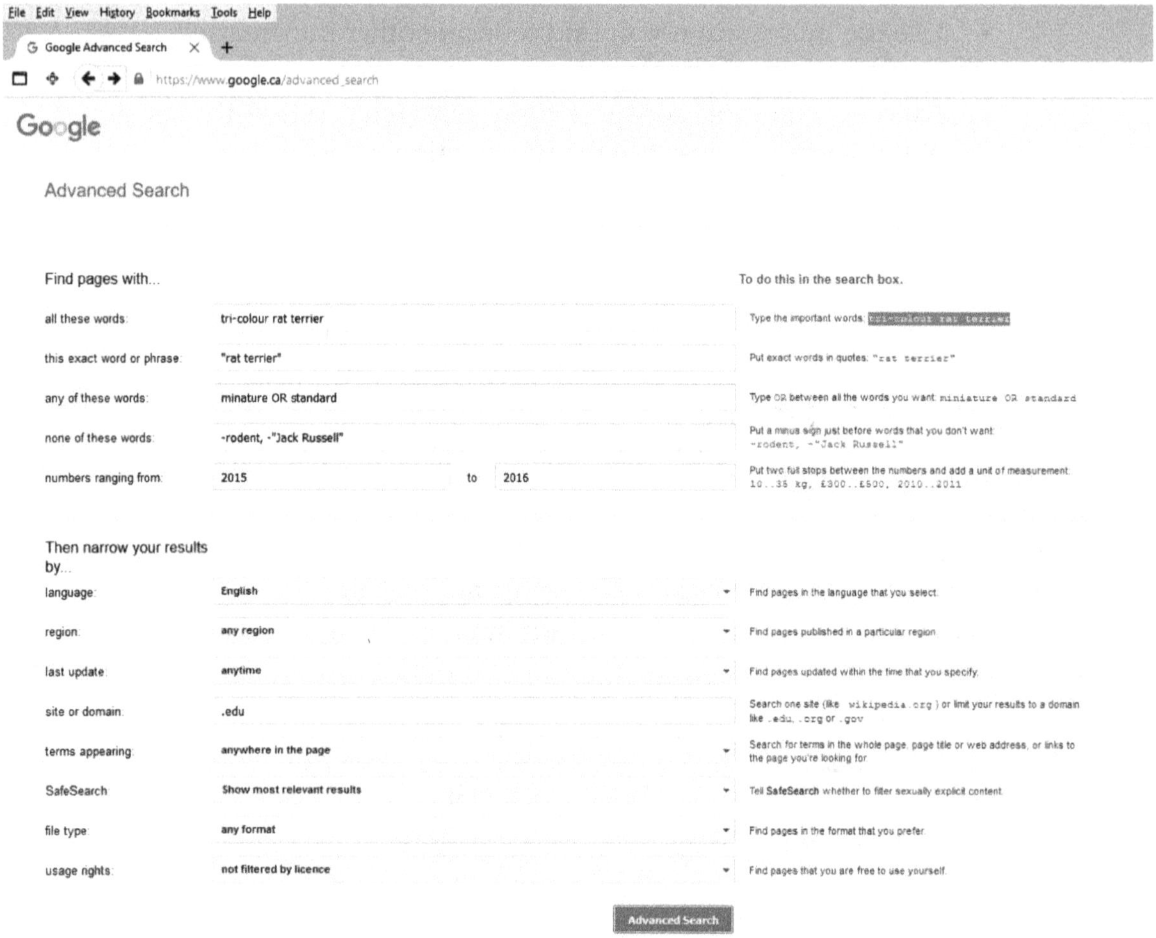

Completion of this exercise yielded only 19 search results. However, when conducting a normal search, "All", the search yielded 217 thousand results. As you can see, conducting an Advanced Search not only yielded significantly fewer results, but the results were very specific based on search criteria.

Another popular online research tool is Wikipedia. Wikipedia defines itself as a *"multi-lingual, web-based, free-content encyclopedia project supported by the Wikimedia Foundation based in San Francisco, California."* This organization raises money, distributes grants, develops and deploys software, controls the servers, and does outreach to support Wikimedia projects.

Wikipedia is a portmanteau (blend of words) of the Hawaiian word "wiki" meaning quick and encyclopedia. Its articles provide links designed to guide users to related pages with additional information. Wikipedia is written collaboratively by largely anonymous volunteers who contribute information without pay. Anyone with Internet access can write and make changes to articles except in limited cases where editing is restricted to prevent disruption or vandalism.

The following are additional online resources that could prove very helpful in researching current and historical industry, customer, legal, demographic and geographic information on private corporations, not-for-profit corporations, and international companies.

- **Encyclopedia of Associations**
  http://find.galegroup.com/

- **American Society of Association Executives (ASAE)**
  https://www.asaecenter.org/en/about-us

- **Securities & Exchange Commission EDGAR (Electronic Data Gathering and Retrieval)**
  https://www.sec.gov/about/whatwedo.shtml

- **GuideStar**
  http://www.guidestar.org/

Conducting Research Offline

Offline research is simply research by means other than electronic (e.g., personal computers, mobile devices, or tablets). This method, though can be equally as thorough, is more time consuming and requires some foot work, possibly some travel. Regardless of the preferred research method, there are advantages and disadvantages. For this reason, it will be important to do some of both. Some offline research methods include:

- visiting local public or college libraries and their bookstores;

- visiting local retail bookstores, even resale shops;

- subscribing to magazines or periodicals;

- joining relevant trade associations;

- conducting interviews of experts in the field and industry;

- conducting surveys with relevant individuals;

- attending local workshops, tradeshows or conferences;

- participating in networking events or forums; and

- viewing television or listening to radio programming.

Offline research requires locating and making personal contact with desired and relevant sources. With this research method, you can literally reach out and touch potential customers or experts in your field or business. It does, however, take a lot of time, but depending on the type of business you are in, it is imperative. And more importantly, offline research can lead and guide you to other sources.

Legal Structure

When determining the best legal structure for your business, taxes, liability, goals and objectives, contribution of owners, and management and control are major factors to be taken into consideration. The most common forms of business are sole proprietorship, corporation, general partnership, franchise, joint venture and not-for-profit. But regardless of which business formation you choose, there are advantages and disadvantages to them all.

Legal structure

"Formal business status established by law"

Carefully review all forms of business to determine which legal structure will work best for you. **Exhibit 7 – Legal Forms of Business** beginning on page 47 provides each type of legal structure and some advantages and disadvantages of forming each of them. However, if you are unsure about which legal structure would work best for your company, it is strongly advised that you consult with an attorney or CPA.

Exhibit 7 – Legal Forms of Business

The following are the most common legal forms (legal structures) of business (there are others). Depending on the nature of the business, there is a legal structure that is most appropriate. For example, sole proprietorships are for single owners, LLCs and LLPs are best suited for professional services firms such as medical/dental practices, law firms, engineering firms, etc. Corporations are for businesses that have shareholders. And not-for-profits are for entities that serve social good. As a business grows or changes, the legal structure can, and in some cases, should also change.

SOLE PROPRIETORSHIP

This is the most common and simplest form of business and is presumed to be operated under one owner or a husband and wife. Some advantages and disadvantages of forming a sole proprietorship include:

Advantages
- Easy and inexpensive to form
- Owner's ability to make all management decisions
- Losses without limits can be deducted on individual federal income tax return
- Minimal government control

Disadvantages
- Not a legal entity
- Owner has unlimited financial liability
- Creditors can attach owner's personal assets and those of the business
- Business ceases to exist upon the death or termination of the owner(s)

To form a sole proprietorship if the owner(s) name is not being used, a fictitious business statement must be filed in the county clerk or county recorder's office. Once contacted, further instructions will be given on the recordation of the business.

CORPORATION

A corporation is the second most common form of business. It is formed as either a for-profit or a not-for-profit entity. Owners (referred to as shareholders in a for-profit entity) elect a board of directors who are responsible for the management of the business. The board of directors appoints officers to manage the day-to-day operations.

With a corporation, the ownership and management are separate. Shareholders don't necessarily manage, and managers, directors or officers aren't necessarily shareholders. Some advantages and disadvantages of forming a corporation include:

Advantages
- Is a legal entity
- Shareholders have limited liability for the corporation's debts

THE START-UP PHASE

- Can survive after the death or withdrawal of its owners, partners or shareholders

Disadvantages
- More expensive to start than a general partnership or sole proprietorship
- Subject to both state and federal taxes

To form a corporation of any kind, an application must be filed and approved with the Secretary of State's office in your state. Prior to the filing, it would be wise to consult with an attorney to review the application, articles of incorporation and by-laws.

CLOSE OR CLOSELY-HELD CORPORATION

Close and closely-held corporations have few shareholders whose shares aren't available to the general public. While they're subject to the same rules under state corporate law, they're given a greater degree of latitude. Some advantages and disadvantages of forming a close or closely-held corporation include:

Advantages
- Precise form and content of the articles of incorporation are open ended, therefore, there are no set guidelines as to how the business is managed or financed
- Controlling shareholders are the only managers of the business
- Not necessary to elect a board of directors
- Can operate as though it were a partnership

Disadvantages
- Number of shareholders cannot exceed 35
- Cannot operate without the cooperation of all shareholders

SUBCHAPTER S CORPORATION

Also known as an "S" Corporation, the Subchapter S Corporation is treated like a partnership for federal purposes. Some advantages and disadvantages of forming a Subchapter S Corporation include:

Advantages
- A legal entity, therefore, shareholders' liability is limited to their contributions
- Has the ability to raise large sums of capital
- Shareholders report income on their individual income tax returns
- Remains unaffected upon death or termination of any shareholder

Disadvantages
- Expensive to form
- Ownership difficult to transfer because of restrictions on who and how many shareholders there may be

THE START OF SOMETHING BIG

GENERAL PARTNERSHIP

This is a business formation in which two or more competent persons combine their skills, property, other assets or labor to conduct business. While general partnerships aren't considered legal entities, the Uniform Partnership Act provides for some degree of legal uniformity. Some advantages and disadvantages of forming a general partnership include:

Advantages
- Business can be conducted by agreement or by default
- Management decisions are shared equally
- Partners can agree to add a purchaser of interest as a partner
- All profits are divided among the partners
- Income is reported on individual federal income tax returns

Disadvantages
- Not a legal entity
- All partners are personally liable for all obligations of the business
- Any partner can be held liable for more than their share
- Unless otherwise stated in an agreement, the business ceases to exist upon death or termination of any partner
- Business ceases to exist upon bankruptcy of any partner regardless of the agreement

To form a partnership of any kind, it is imperative that and attorney is consulted to assist in drawing up all the agreements to protect the interest of all partners. Second, there must be a fictitious business name statement in the county clerk or county recorder's office of the primary place of business.

LIMITED LIABILITY PARTNERSHIP (LLP)

This is a business formation formed with one or more general partners AND one or more limited partners. This formation is most appropriate for businesses seeking large capital contributions. The general partners manage the day-to-day operations of the partnership; the limited partners contribute capital, have limited liability for the obligations, but have no right to manage the day-to-day operations. However, if they do manage, they'll lose their right to limited liability.

Some advantages and disadvantages of forming a limited liability partnership include:

Advantages
- Liability of limited partners is limited to capital contributions
- Have the ability to attract large amounts of capital
- Losses from the business are deducted from individual federal income tax returns without limits
- Can be created by default, however, a partnership agreement is necessary
- Can continue after the death or withdrawal of a limited partner
- General partner can also be a limited partner at the same time

Disadvantages
- General partners have unlimited liability
- General partners are liable for criminal acts of other partners if they know about them or are a part of them
- Estate of any limited partner is liable for all liabilities of the limited partner
- Dissolved upon the death or withdrawal of a general partner unless there is an agreement that states otherwise

PROFESSIONAL OR PERSONAL SERVICES PARTNERSHIP

This business formation (sometimes called a limited liability partnership [LLP]), is preferred by professionals such as accountants and attorneys who elect not to incorporate.

Some advantages and disadvantages of forming a professional or personal services partnership include:

Advantages
- All partners make management decisions equally unless otherwise agreed
- Profits and losses are deducted on individual federal income tax return
- Ownership interest is not freely transferred

Disadvantages
- Must comply with limited partnership statutes
- Requires filing with Secretary of State
- Must carry professional liability insurance
- Ceases to exist upon death or termination of any partner unless otherwise stated in the partnership agreement

FRANCHISE

A franchise is one of the fastest growing forms of business today. It's an agreement in which a franchisee has the right to sell goods and services under a marketing plan prescribed by a franchisor. The Franchise Investment Law was enacted to alleviate the many problems created in establishing a franchise.

Some advantages and disadvantages of owning a franchise include:

Advantages
- Receives assistance from franchisor in setting up the business and training employees
- Benefits from national marketing and advertising
- Must be registered with the commissioner of corporations in most states

Disadvantages
- Franchise territories limited as to where to operate, thus limiting the ability to meet demands of areas with increased population

To establish a franchise, contact the franchisor directly via their website or the International Franchise Association at www.franchise.org/ or the American Association of Franchisees & Dealers at www.aafd.org/.

JOINT VENTURE

A joint venture (also known as a "JV") is a specialized type of business formation used particularly in the construction industry. Partnership law generally applies to joint ventures. In a joint venture, two or more companies combine resources and expertise to construct a major project.

Some advantages and disadvantages of forming a joint venture include:

Advantages
- Enhances the ability of each enterprise to perform on a project where the magnitude is such that neither entity can perform utilizing its own existing resources
- Limited to a single project; remains in effect until its purpose is accomplished or until it has been determined that it's impossible to accomplish
- Not taxable entities, therefore, co-venturers are liable for income taxes only in separate and individual capacities
- Profits and losses from the project are shared equally

Disadvantages
- Co-venturer holding or acquiring title to property for the joint venture is only a trustee even if it was paid for with their own funds
- Negligence of one joint venturer acting on behalf of the joint venture is imputed to the other joint venturer
- Contract or agreement to form a joint venture need not be expressed in a formal instrument
- Death or termination of a co-venturer terminates the joint venture

To form a joint venture, all venturers must participate in drafting a joint venture agreement. This agreement is considered a legal document and should be reviewed by an attorney before submitting it as final.

LIMITED LIABILITY COMPANY (LLC)

More commonly known as an LLC, the limited liability company may soon take the place of the S Corporation and the limited partnership. It operates much like a partnership, but offers the benefits of limited liability like a corporation.

Some advantages and disadvantages of forming a limited liability company include:

Advantages
- Owners are generally not liable for debts of the LLC

THE START-UP PHASE

- Unless treated like a corporation, owners report income on their individual federal income tax returns
- Can engage in any type of business, including professional, with only a few exceptions

Disadvantages
- Not all states have adopted the LLC, so protection would not be available in those states
- Must have at least two owners, except for in a few states

NOT-FOR-PROFIT (NFP)

A not-for-profit (or sometimes called a non-profit) is an organization that does not pass its income to its members but instead uses the income to further a goal that benefits the community. Contrary to popular belief, the not-for-profit can be profitable, and many of them are, but they may not use the profits to benefit private parties.

The most common types of not-for-profits are:

- 501(c)3 – corporation or association organized and operated exclusively for religious, charitable, scientific or educational purposes, public safety testing, prevention of cruelty to children and animals, and to foster amateur sports.

- 501(c)4 – lobbying, social welfare or local association of employees whose earnings are earmarked for charitable, educational or recreational purposes.

- 501(c)6 – business leagues, chambers of commerce, and professional football leagues.

  Some advantages and disadvantages of forming a not-for-profit include:

Advantages
- Exempted from taxes depending on the organization type and the state in which it's located
- Contributions made by taxpayers are deductible on taxpayer's income tax return
- Eligible for private and government grants
- Lower costs for postage and electronic and print media advertisements
- Can raise money by issuing tax-exempt bonds

Disadvantages
- Limitations on how much control a contributor can have
- Can only perform functions listed in tax laws
- Most are prohibited from contributing to political campaigns
- Financial records are open for public scrutiny

To form a not-for-profit corporation, contact the Secretary of State's office in writing or online to obtain the necessary information. For more information on the many types of not-for-profit organizations contact the Internal Revenue Service (IRS) online at https://www.irs.gov/Charities-&-Non-Profits.

Naming Your Company

Choosing a name for your company is one of the single-most important steps in starting your business. With over one million businesses starting in the U.S. each year, it's becoming increasingly more difficult to find a name that's unique and doesn't violate trademark laws. Be sure to select a name that gives a good impression of your company and name recognition in the marketplace.

Business name

"A word or phrase that constitutes a distinctive designation"

Whether you hire a graphic designer or image consultant, conduct a formal and informal survey, or name your company after yourself, select a name that:

1.   is short, simple, distinctive and easy to remember;

2.   doesn't imply the business is something that it's not;

3.   doesn't have connotations in English or other languages that can be construed as negative or insulting;

4.   has an acronym that's not negative or insulting;

5.   you can secure the ".com" or other extension (e.g., ".net", or ".org" for not-for-profits; ".edu" is for educational institutions and ".gov" is government agencies);

6.   will stand the test of time and isn't dated in a short period;

7.   can expand to national or global proportions;

8.   includes the nature of your business or its products or services in it;

9.   will help build your company brand; and

10.   has the potential for mass public appeal.

Choose several names and conduct an online search to ensure those names are available for your use. You can quickly and easily conduct your search using the following sources:

1. **Patent & Trademark Office (USPTO)**
   www.uspto.gov

2. **Dun & Bradstreet**
   www.dnb.com/us/

3. **Secretary of State**
   (Check online for the office in your state)

4. **County Recorder**
   (Check online for the office in your county)

Your Company Logo

As with the naming of your company, your company logo is a representation of you. If you are not an experienced or skilled graphic designer or artist, hiring one is strongly advised. A freelance graphic designer is a very important contributor to your business and image. The experienced designer understands the messaging you will need to put a "face" (in text or graphics) to your company.

When hiring a graphic designer make sure to:

1. ask other business associates for references;

2. hire one that is experienced;

3. be clear about what you are looking for and the message you want to convey, but since they are the professional, it's wise to remain open to their suggestions;

4. ask to see a portfolio of their work;

5. check out their website. An experienced designer should have one;

6. get rates for initial concept and revisions;

7. proofread the work very carefully when completed; and

8. clarify that you want 100% ownership of the work.

The creation of your logo should be a collaborative effort between you and your graphic designer. But the final decision must be yours. If you are not completely and fully satisfied with the job, let it be known. This is *your* company and *you* should have the utmost satisfaction in how it's being presented. A great place to find a graphic designer at a very low cost is Fiverr (www.fiverr.com). It is a creative and professional services marketplace where you can choose from hundreds of providers in the areas of graphic design, digital marketing, and other online services.

Filing Your Fictitious Business Name

A fictitious business name (also known as "assumed name" or "DBA" [doing business as]) is a business name used instead of the business owner's name. The filing is intended give the legal protections needed against illegal use of your company name. To file an assumed name or DBA with your local county clerk or county recorder's office, you must:

1. Complete a certificate of ownership or business application (application name varies by county or state).

2. Have the application signed and notarized.

3. Pay the filing fee (a nominal fee of usually $10.00, however, could be more in some counties).

4. Upon receipt of Legal Notice announcing your DBA filing, an ad must be published in an adjudicated or publication of record.

5. Identify and contact the chosen publication of record to publish your business name.

6. Obtain a Certification of Publication and file it with the original clipping at the county clerk or county recorder's office. The process should take about five weeks and cost about $50, however, costs varies depending on the publication

---

Fictitious business name

"A business name that is conventionally or hypothetically assumed or accepted"

For demonstration purposes, we will use imaginary *"CareerTemps Temporary Staffing Agency"* as an example of a fictitious business name. Even though its legal structure is a sole proprietorship, the name speaks specifically to the type of business it does as opposed to the name of the business owner. In this case, a fictitious business name filing must be made in the county clerk or county recorder's office in the county where the business is located.

If you've named your company after yourself, the business name would be considered non-fictitious. An example would be, "Sally P. Wilson *CareerTemps Temporary Staffing Agency*." As a sole proprietorship or general partnership in some counties, it's not necessary to file a fictitious business name. However, it may be wise to do so in the event someone else wants to use the name you've selected.

Business Bank Account

Regardless of the size of your business, all business transactions from the sale of your products/services, as well as expenses paid should be kept separate from your personal finances. This practice is not only fundamentally sound, but it also alleviates confusion in recordkeeping, budgeting and filing income taxes. Commingling of business and personal finances is never a good idea.

Transactions

"A business deal, act or process"

After receipt of your FEIN (you can use your social security number if you're a sole proprietorship with no employees), and your fictitious business name filing, open a separate bank account for your business. Be sure to select a banking institution that specializes in dealing with small businesses. These banking professionals are familiar with the needs unique to small business, offering products and services specifically geared to them.

Any monies (e.g., cash, checks, money orders, electronic payments) earned from the sale of your products or services should be deposited into your business bank account. When accepting cash, it's not unusual for a business owner to collect monies and spend it without properly recording it. The downside to not depositing these funds is that they won't appear on your bank statement and could possibly be missed when filing your income taxes. Consequently, when you're ready to borrow money, it'll be difficult to prove to a lender how or if your business has been profitable.

In addition, use your business bank account to pay all the bills and expenses of your company. In doing so, you will be able to easily track all disbursements made. This will help you in making sound business decisions, monitoring and managing cash flow, and preparing financial statements.

Disbursement

"Funds that are paid out"

Federal Employer Identification Number (FEIN)

A federal employer identification number (FEIN) is a nine-digit number (e.g., 12-3456789) assigned to sole proprietors with employees, corporations, partnerships, estates, trusts and other entities for tax filing purposes. It's used in connection with your business activities only in the same manner your social security number is used for personal filings. You must apply for an FEIN if you:

1. start a new business;

2. have hired or will hire employees, including household employees;

3. open a bank account;

4. change legal structure of your company;

5. purchase an existing business that doesn't already have one;

6. create a trust or pension plan as plan administrator;

7. are a state or local agency;

8. are a single-member LLC; and

9. are an S or C corporation.

To apply for an FEIN and to obtain other tax-related forms, visit the Internal Revenue Service (IRS) website and download a copy of Form SS-4 at https://www.irs.gov/pub/irs-pdf/fss4.pdf as shown in **Exhibit 8 – SS-4 Application for Employer Identification Number** on page 58. Instructions on how to complete the form and where to file via telephone, fax or mail are included.

Exhibit 8 – SS4 – Application for Employer Identification Number

Form **SS-4**
(Rev. January 2010)
Department of the Treasury
Internal Revenue Service

Application for Employer Identification Number
(For use by employers, corporations, partnerships, trusts, estates, churches, government agencies, Indian tribal entities, certain individuals, and others.)
▶ See separate instructions for each line. ▶ Keep a copy for your records.

OMB No. 1545-0003

EIN

Type or print clearly.		
1 Legal name of entity (or individual) for whom the EIN is being requested		
2 Trade name of business (if different from name on line 1)	**3** Executor, administrator, trustee, "care of" name	
4a Mailing address (room, apt., suite no. and street, or P.O. box)	**5a** Street address (if different) (Do not enter a P.O. box.)	
4b City, state, and ZIP code (if foreign, see instructions)	**5b** City, state, and ZIP code (if foreign, see instructions)	
6 County and state where principal business is located		
7a Name of responsible party	**7b** SSN, ITIN, or EIN	

8a Is this application for a limited liability company (LLC) (or a foreign equivalent)? . . . . ☐ Yes ☐ No
8b If 8a is "Yes," enter the number of LLC members . . . . ▶

8c If 8a is "Yes," was the LLC organized in the United States? . . . . ☐ Yes ☐ No

9a Type of entity (check only one box). Caution. If 8a is "Yes," see the instructions for the correct box to check.

☐ Sole proprietor (SSN) _____
☐ Partnership
☐ Corporation (enter form number to be filed) ▶_____
☐ Personal service corporation
☐ Church or church-controlled organization
☐ Other nonprofit organization (specify) ▶_____
☐ Other (specify) ▶

☐ Estate (SSN of decedent) _____
☐ Plan administrator (TIN) _____
☐ Trust (TIN of grantor) _____
☐ National Guard ☐ State/local government
☐ Farmers' cooperative ☐ Federal government/military
☐ REMIC ☐ Indian tribal governments/enterprises
Group Exemption Number (GEN) if any ▶

9b If a corporation, name the state or foreign country (if applicable) where incorporated | State | Foreign country

10 **Reason for applying** (check only one box)
☐ Started new business (specify type) ▶ _____
☐ Hired employees (Check the box and see line 13.)
☐ Compliance with IRS withholding regulations
☐ Other (specify) ▶

☐ Banking purpose (specify purpose) ▶_____
☐ Changed type of organization (specify new type) ▶_____
☐ Purchased going business
☐ Created a trust (specify type) ▶_____
☐ Created a pension plan (specify type) ▶_____

11 Date business started or acquired (month, day, year). See instructions. | **12** Closing month of accounting year

13 Highest number of employees expected in the next 12 months (enter -0- if none). If no employees expected, skip line 14.

Agricultural	Household	Other

14 If you expect your employment tax liability to be $1,000 or less in a full calendar year **and** want to file Form 944 annually instead of Forms 941 quarterly, check here. (Your employment tax liability generally will be $1,000 or less if you expect to pay $4,000 or less in total wages.) If you do not check this box, you must file Form 941 for every quarter. ☐

15 First date wages or annuities were paid (month, day, year). Note. If applicant is a withholding agent, enter date income will first be paid to nonresident alien (month, day, year) . . . . ▶

16 Check **one** box that best describes the principal activity of your business.
☐ Construction ☐ Rental & leasing ☐ Transportation & warehousing
☐ Real estate ☐ Manufacturing ☐ Finance & insurance
☐ Health care & social assistance ☐ Wholesale-agent/broker
☐ Accommodation & food service ☐ Wholesale-other ☐ Retail
☐ Other (specify)

17 Indicate principal line of merchandise sold, specific construction work done, products produced, or services provided.

18 Has the applicant entity shown on line 1 ever applied for and received an EIN? ☐ Yes ☐ No
If "Yes," write previous EIN here ▶

Third Party Designee	Complete this section **only** if you want to authorize the named individual to receive the entity's EIN and answer questions about the completion of this form.	
	Designee's name	Designee's telephone number (include area code) ( )
	Address and ZIP code	Designee's fax number (include area code) ( )

Under penalties of perjury, I declare that I have examined this application, and to the best of my knowledge and belief, it is true, correct, and complete.

Name and title (type or print clearly) ▶ | Applicant's telephone number (include area code) ( )

Signature ▶ Date ▶ | Applicant's fax number (include area code) ( )

For Privacy Act and Paperwork Reduction Act Notice, see separate instructions. Cat. No. 16055N Form **SS-4** (Rev. 1-2010)

Do I Need an EIN?

File Form SS-4 if the applicant entity does not already have an EIN but is required to show an EIN on any return, statement, or other document.[1] See also the separate instructions for each line on Form SS-4.

IF the applicant...	AND...	THEN...
Started a new business	Does not currently have (nor expect to have) employees	Complete lines 1, 2, 4a–8a, 8b–c (if applicable), 9a, 9b (if applicable), and 10–14 and 16–18.
Hired (or will hire) employees, including household employees	Does not already have an EIN	Complete lines 1, 2, 4a–6, 7a–b (if applicable), 8a, 8b–c (if applicable), 9a, 9b (if applicable), 10–18.
Opened a bank account	Needs an EIN for banking purposes only	Complete lines 1–5b, 7a–b (if applicable), 8a, 8b–c (if applicable), 9a, 9b (if applicable), 10, and 18.
Changed type of organization	Either the legal character of the organization or its ownership changed (for example, you incorporate a sole proprietorship or form a partnership)[2]	Complete lines 1–18 (as applicable).
Purchased a going business[3]	Does not already have an EIN	Complete lines 1–18 (as applicable).
Created a trust	The trust is other than a grantor trust or an IRA trust[4]	Complete lines 1–18 (as applicable).
Created a pension plan as a plan administrator[5]	Needs an EIN for reporting purposes	Complete lines 1, 3, 4a–5b, 9a, 10, and 18.
Is a foreign person needing an EIN to comply with IRS withholding regulations	Needs an EIN to complete a Form W-8 (other than Form W-8ECI), avoid withholding on portfolio assets, or claim tax treaty benefits[6]	Complete lines 1–5b, 7a–b (SSN or ITIN optional), 8a, 8b–c (if applicable), 9a, 9b (if applicable), 10, and 18.
Is administering an estate	Needs an EIN to report estate income on Form 1041	Complete lines 1–6, 9a, 10–12, 13–17 (if applicable), and 18.
Is a withholding agent for taxes on non-wage income paid to an alien (i.e., individual, corporation, or partnership, etc.)	Is an agent, broker, fiduciary, manager, tenant, or spouse who is required to file Form 1042, Annual Withholding Tax Return for U.S. Source Income of Foreign Persons	Complete lines 1, 2, 3 (if applicable), 4a–5b, 7a–b (if applicable), 8a, 8b–c (if applicable), 9a, 9b (if applicable), 10, and 18.
Is a state or local agency	Serves as a tax reporting agent for public assistance recipients under Rev. Proc. 80-4, 1980-1 C.B. 581[7]	Complete lines 1, 2, 4a–5b, 9a, 10, and 18.
Is a single-member LLC	Needs an EIN to file Form 8832, Classification Election, for filing employment tax returns and excise tax returns, or for state reporting purposes[8]	Complete lines 1–18 (as applicable).
Is an S corporation	Needs an EIN to file Form 2553, Election by a Small Business Corporation[9]	Complete lines 1–18 (as applicable).

[1] For example, a sole proprietorship or self-employed farmer who establishes a qualified retirement plan, or is required to file excise, employment, alcohol, tobacco, or firearms returns, must have an EIN. A partnership, corporation, REMIC (real estate mortgage investment conduit), nonprofit organization (church, club, etc.), or farmers' cooperative must use an EIN for any tax-related purpose even if the entity does not have employees.

[2] However, do not apply for a new EIN if the existing entity only (a) changed its business name, (b) elected on Form 8832 to change the way it is taxed (or is covered by the default rules), or (c) terminated its partnership status because at least 50% of the total interests in partnership capital and profits were sold or exchanged within a 12-month period. The EIN of the terminated partnership should continue to be used. See Regulations section 301.6109-1(d)(2)(iii).

[3] Do not use the EIN of the prior business unless you became the "owner" of a corporation by acquiring its stock.

[4] However, grantor trusts that do not file using Optional Method 1 and IRA trusts that are required to file Form 990-T, Exempt Organization Business Income Tax Return, must have an EIN. For more information on grantor trusts, see the Instructions for Form 1041.

[5] A plan administrator is the person or group of persons specified as the administrator by the instrument under which the plan is operated.

[6] Entities applying to be a Qualified Intermediary (QI) need a QI-EIN even if they already have an EIN. See Rev. Proc. 2000-12.

[7] See also Household employer on page 4 of the instructions. Note. State or local agencies may need an EIN for other reasons, for example, hired employees.

[8] See Disregarded entities on page 4 of the instructions for details on completing Form SS-4 for an LLC.

[9] An existing corporation that is electing or revoking S corporation status should use its previously-assigned EIN.

Selecting and Registering Your Domain Name

Once you have selected your company name, you must research whether the domain name is available. Selecting your domain name is the first step in establishing your company's presence online. This includes establishing your website address and email addresses. Your domain name should be as close as possible to your company name if not exactly. This is one of the ways in which you will build your company brand. Give your domain name the same consideration as your company name.

Domain name

"A name that identifies your website"

There are many companies you can use to research and register your domain name. The registrations are paid by the year and the fees range in price from around $35 per year. However, many companies offer specials of $1.00 for the first year. A few domain name registration companies are:

1. **Register**
   www.Register.com/

2. **Internic**
   www.InterNIC.net/

3. **Check Domain**
   www.checkdomain.com/

The purpose of registering your domain name is to prevent anyone else from using it without your permission, even before you start your business, establish email, or develop your website. But be very careful of "cyber squatters" who purchase domain names with no intention of ever using them, only to resell them at a premium. You may also want to register your domain name with the U.S. Patent & Trademark Office (USPTO) along with your company name and logo.

A web address or URL (Uniform Resource Locator) is the standard way developed to specify the location of particular resource in your website. Using our imaginary *"CareerTemps"*, an appropriate web address could be "www.careertemps.com."

E-mail (Electronic mail)

Email is as critical in business communications as the telephone connecting millions around the world. Some of the most significant advantages of using e-mail as a communications tool in business are its ability to:

1.   provide real-time communications internally and externally;

2.   allow for clear and direct communication;

3.   enable cohesion in any organization;

4.   quickly and easily access any individual regardless of where they are in the world; and

5.   serve as a legal record that can withstand a court challenge.

When instituting e-mail in your business, establishing a specific format for e-mail addresses is very important. You should use some form of the *name of the addressee @ the company name .com* (or other extension such as ".org", ".edu", ".net", etc.). This type of address gives your company a professional image and makes it appear larger than it may well be. Again, using our fictitious staffing agency, "*CareerTemps*", an example of a typical company e-mail address could be "swilson@careertemps.com or sally.wilson@careertemps.com."

There are basic codes of conduct for using e-mail commonly known as "netiquette" or network etiquette. Just as written correspondence should be well thought out, organized and free of grammatical and typographical errors, so should your business e-mail. Make it a company policy that all e-mail be proofread carefully before distributing. The tone of your e-mail is also a critical factor. For instance an e-mail typed using ALL CAPITAL letters may give the impression of anger or impatience.

When sending e-mail, always bear in mind that anything written can be:

1.   easily repeated or misrouted;

2.   unintentionally misconstrued from what is actually meant; and

3.   while an effective marketing tool, spam (officially known as Unsolicited Commercial Email [UCE]), is illegal.

Also, the overuse of colors, fonts and backgrounds can give your organization a very unprofessional appearance. This kind of personalization is fine for personal use, but be careful when constructing e-mail for business purposes.

Internet Service Providers (ISPs)

Internet Service Providers (ISPs) are organizations that provide the connection that enables you to surf the web and exchange e-mail. Today, the most popular connections are made via local cable companies using broadband technology.

There are literally thousands of ISPs in the world offering similar services at varying prices. A few large ISPs include Comcast, Time Warner Cable, Verizon, and AT&T. Others are small businesses that may only provide services to small, local populations. If you are a traveler, then a large online services provider would be best for you.

Before settling on an ISP, check out their website or simply ask other Internet users to give you some insight into the ones they use. Review the short list of the most well-known service providers in **CHAPTER 9, BUSINESS RESOURCES** under "**INTERNET SERVICE PROVIDERS**" beginning on page 340. But whichever ISP you choose, evaluate their services based on your needs in terms of:

1. footprint or service territory;

2. technical support;

3. security features;

4. response time you can expect on any inquiry;

5. number of additional e-mail addresses you can receive;

6. freebies (e.g., auctions, chat rooms, bulletin boards, etc.); and

7. services that you can use today and in the future.

Also, note that changes and consolidations occur rapidly in the technology industry so do your homework to see whether the ISP you've selected will be around tomorrow.

Social Media

Social media has proven to be one of the best (to many users, the best) marketing tools you can use in your company. With it, you can reach millions worldwide in real time. This engagement has earned millions of dollars to many businesses large and small in a very short period of time. The key, however, to a successful social media campaign is one that connects with the appropriate audience and builds a brand.

CHAPTER 5, EMAIL, SOCIAL MEDIA, EMAIL MARKETING & USING YOUR WEBSITE beginning on page 257 will guide you in:

1. determining the best social media platforms for your business;

2. developing your social media plan;

3. email marketing; and

4. social media return on investment.

Building Your Brand

When you hear, *"I'm lovin' it,"* naturally you think of McDonald's. Without reservation, images of the "golden arches" come to mind. How about, *"It's mmm, mmm good."* Of course, it's Campbell's Soup. And, *"We'll pick you up."* We all know this is Enterprise Rent-A-Car. These are a few of America's (and the world's) greatest brands.

Becoming a great brand is more than just a logo or a slogan. It involves the engagement of customers and consumers at many levels to build and maintain loyalty. Television and radio ads, social media, blogs, and conversations are all platforms used to build brands. Branding is sometimes used synonymously with marketing, but they are in fact, different even though they work hand in hand. With marketing, a mix of activities and processes (tactics) that involve creating campaigns and identifying a target market are employed to influence consumer behavior and garner market share.

Brand(ing)

"A marketing strategy involving the creation of a differentiated name and image to establish presence in consumers' minds"

Branding refers more to "who I am" as opposed to "what I'm trying to sell" as is with marketing. Branding is the experience customers enjoy when they engage with the messages you send, and then share these messages with others. If you ask anyone to describe you, what would he or she say? Would they say you are attractive or not, smart or not, kind or not? Whatever answer they give is generally based on the messages they've received from you. That perception is your personal brand. It works the same for your company. What people see or hear, and their experiences with your company or product/service dictate their engagement.

So what makes a good brand? The following are characteristics of a good brand:

1. **Having a purpose**
   You must have a good sense about who you are and have laser focus on what you do, how you do it and for whom you do it. Demonstrating a clear sense of who you are gives customers confidence in your products/services.

2. **Leading as a united front**
   As the leader of your company, it's critical that there's a coordinated effort among all parties. You must be able to get everyone in harmony with company mission, vision and processes.

3. **Having a unique quality**
   Being innovative and distinctive and setting yourself and your company apart from competitors.

4. **Having a memorable design**
   Create a logo and slogan that's catchy and easy to remember. For example, today when someone mentions "Apple" the mind tends to go towards the iPhone or Mac computer more often than a gala or a red delicious.

5. **Understanding its target market**
   Knowing who to communicate to, where they are and what messages to send.

6. **Being passionate about what you do**
   The ability to strive for greatness drives innovation that keeps your brand thriving in the eyes of the consumer. It will make them continue to buy and share their experiences with family, friends, business associates, etc.

7. **Having a consistent message and level of quality**
   Customers want to buy from companies that consistently deliver quality, respond quickly to their needs, and seek to make life better for them.

8. **Willingness to make needed changes**
   Not all ideas work. Understanding when they don't, and making the necessary changes is a must. Just admit something went wrong and move on. Customers greatly appreciate honesty.

9. **Standing out above the competition**
   Continuously delivering coherent brand messages that show customers you are always on an upward trajectory.

10. **Keeping in touch**
    Developing a presence on a variety of social media platforms allows for real-time conversations with customers.

There are many more ways to build your brand. But if you always think in terms of keeping the conversations going, delivering quality products and services, continuous process improvements and making a difference, you can build a respected and powerhouse brand.

Developing Your Website

The use of a website today should be a major marketing and communications tool in your business. Today, over 77% of the world uses ecommerce to make purchases. While it's possible to be successful in business without a website, having one helps you to build market awareness, build your brand, and gain market share. Website builders such as Wix, iPage, Yahoo, and GoDaddy make building a website possible. But for those who are technologically challenged, freelance website designers can quickly and easily build a website for you that could make you more competitive.

In developing your website, be sure:

1. that it loads quickly and is simple to use;

2. it has your company logo on all pages to help build your brand;

3. that the content is well written, useful and interesting;

4.   the navigational tools make locating information easy and fast;

5.   it has contact information available via an e-mail link;

6.   to update your site regularly; remove all outdated and non-relevant material;

7.   to use your website for marketing;

8.   to create your blog and provide useful content regularly;

9.   that allows access to all social media accounts; and

10.   to establish affiliate marketing relationships.

Technology for Your Business

The proper technology for your business is as critical to business as is the products or services your business provides. It simplifies and streamlines processes that once were conducted manually making your business function more efficiently. In addition, connects your company with customers, vendors and suppliers instantaneously. Technology encompasses computers and peripherals, telecommunications systems and other digital devices.

Technology

"A technical method of achieving a practical purpose"

Today, if a company is to compete, it must incorporate state-of-the-art technology throughout its operations. Understand that all technology is not created equal. What works for one business won't necessarily work for another, even if they are in the same industry. To determine what technology will work best for your company, it's imperative that you understand your business and its processes. **CHAPTER 7, BUSINESS TECHNOLOGY** beginning on page 309 will help you understand the importance and types of technology available for your business. Selecting the wrong technology for your business can be very costly and inefficient.

Selecting Your Business Location

When selecting the location for your business, your operations and customers should be the determining factor. This will affect whether you move into commercial office or retail space (bricks and mortar) or operate from home. An office away from home can be great and may be necessary depending on the nature of your business. But whatever decision you make regarding your business location, your decision must be customer and operations driven.

Bricks and mortar

"An office or store where business is conducted face to face that is owned or rented"

There are over 500,000 homebased businesses operating in the U.S. Consulting, bookkeeping, data/word processing, medical billing, and the like, generally operate from a home office. Businesses whose success is predicated on heavy foot traffic (e.g., retail outlets, medical/dental practice, beauty/barber salon, repair shop, etc.), the use and storage of major equipment, large inventory, materials and supplies (e.g., manufacturing, storage, etc.), or have employees (permanent or temporary), generally operate in commercial space.

Today, technological advances in office and communications equipment allow businesses to operate globally from home. State-of-the-art equipment have become very affordable and has made it virtually impossible for customers to know that a business is home based. But once you've outgrown the spare bedroom, basement or garage, commercial space is the next step.

Whether your business is located in commercial space or in your home, be sure to occupy space that enables you to function professionally and efficiently. There are presumed advantages and disadvantages to both which include:

BUSINESS LOCATION	ADVANTAGES	DISADVANTAGES

Homebased	• Flexible work hours
	
	• Saving of commute time
	
	• Cost savings
	  o Fuel
	  o Parking, tolls
	  o Vehicle wear
	  o Dry cleaning
	  o Meals
		• Need for discipline
		
		• Isolation from public contact
		
		• Personal distractions from family
		
		• Tendency to do more family-oriented work
		
		• Tendency to work endlessly

BUSINESS LOCATION	ADVANTAGES	DISADVANTAGES
	• No day care expense (if applicable) • Isolation from public contact • Potential fewer distractions from workers • Balance of work and home	• Difficulty in separating home from work • Clients, customers, meet in the home instead of meeting space

Commercial space	• Disciplined work habits
	
	• Getting away from home for a period of time
	
	• Public interaction
	
	• More structure in schedule
	
	• Greater focus on business activities
		• Associated costs
		  o Leased space
		  o Utilities
		  o Telecommunications
		  o Meals
		
		• Being away from home
		
		• Shared office space
		
		• Associated costs
		  o Fuel
		  o Parking, tolls
		  o Vehicle wear
		  o Dry cleaning
		
		• Day care costs (if applicable)
		
		• Co-worker distractions
		
		• Convenient for meeting with clients, customers, etc.

When making your business location decision whether homebased or in commercial office space, consider the following:

1. **What is the nature of your business?**
   Are you a retailer, manufacturer or service business? Depending on the nature of your business and zoning requirements, you may legally be able to operate from your home or you may have to secure commercial space, especially if you have employees.

2. **Do you depend on moderate or heavy customer or client visits?**
   If your business deals directly with the public and high traffic volume is critical to its success, or if you're a manufacturer of any kind, then commercial space would definitely be the appropriate choice.

On the other hand, if you're a consultant of any kind, an alternative to working from home would be an executive suite or incubator arrangement which provides personal space for your business as well as an office environment where clients can visit instead of coming to your home office. These locations are professional and can meet commercial office space needs without a high cost of operation.

3. **How much space are you going to need?**
   Measure the workforce, production, shipping and distribution space needs of your company. If either exceeds the amount of space you have available in your home and your budget permits, the obvious choice would be commercial space.

4. **How much money do you have budgeted for commercial space?**
   Commercial space can be very expensive. If your business doesn't require it, you may want to hold off on signing that lease until it's necessary for you to do so. This money can be used to grow your business until you're ready.

5. **Are large pieces of equipment, machinery or office furniture needed in the operation of your business?**
   Large pieces of equipment, machinery and furniture can require extra space, ventilation and a greater amount of electrical power. If this is the case, then commercial space is the better option.

6. **Do you have inventory and how much?**
   If you have inventory, you will need adequate storage and space to efficiently roll out your products or services. Again, commercial space could be the better option.

7. **What are the zoning laws for your area?**
   If your desire is to work from home, be sure to check out local ordinances and regulations to make sure that it's legal to operate your type of business from home. Parking, excess noise, odors or fumes and vehicle traffic can be a nuisance to your neighbors. If reported, your business can be shut down.

If heavy public traffic is necessary for business success, check with your local department of transportation or association of governments to obtain detailed traffic studies available to assist you in determining the best location for your business.

City and County Ordinances

City and county ordinances are municipal regulations put in place to promote and protect the public health, safety, morals, comfort and general welfare of its citizens. In addition, they serve to protect and preserve the qualities of a city as it grows, reshapes and revitalizes itself through community redevelopment.

Incorporated municipalities are allowed to enact laws provided that those laws do not supersede state or federal law. These laws are created and/or modified as a result of the wants, needs and desires of the community at large and can only be changed by the voters via referendum. If you live in an unincorporated area, you may still want to check with your local township to make sure you are operating within the limits of all laws.

Ordinances

"Laws set forth by governmental authorities"

Your city charter is the document that addresses the local form of government and specifies the manner in which governmental powers are distributed. The local government is generally the city council or the city commission. To obtain a copy of the ordinances in your city or county visit your county clerk's office, city attorney's office, public library or surf the Internet.

Business Licenses or Registrations

Many incorporated cities require businesses to obtain a business license (otherwise known as a local tax registration or certification) regardless of the size or whether it is home based. The fees are generally low and are assessed annually. If your business is operated in a rural or unincorporated area you may or may not be required to obtain a business license or certification. To ensure that you aren't operating illegally if your business is located in either of these areas, contact your county clerk's office.

License

"Permission granted by competent authority to engage in a business or occupation or in an activity otherwise unlawful"

Registering your business allows the local government to collect taxes from the sale of your products and services. Different cities use different tax structures depending on the nature of each business. For example, one city may assess a flat fee for vending machine operators while another city may charge a percentage of gross receipts. If your business sells a tangible product of any kind, you may also be required to obtain a seller's permit.

There's a distinct difference between local, state and federal registrations. Local registrations tend to focus on whether your business poses any risk or threat to public safety (e.g., environmental, noise, traffic, etc.). State regulations focus on the type of work you plan to do and your qualifications to perform (e.g., cosmetology, auto repair, waste management, etc.). At the federal level, the focus is primarily trades and services that are regulated by the federal government (e.g., financial services, interstate trucking, manufacturing of food, alcohol, tobacco products, etc.) to name a few.

Financial Accounting System

Accurate financial, accounting, sales and other management records are vital to the profitability, success and long range planning of your business. Improper recording and use of inaccurate financial information can be very costly. Additionally, if inaccurate information is used in any decision making, significant losses in revenue, time and resources are likely to result.

Accounting

"A system of recording, summarizing, analyzing and verifying business and financial transactions and reporting the results"

You don't have to be a Certified Public Accountant (better known as a CPA) to be successful in business or understand the finances of your company. However, you must incorporate a good financial accounting system. Today there are several software programs on the market that can efficiently record and report sales transactions of your business. Quickbooks by Intuit is one of the most popular small business accounting systems.

While software programs are designed to easily, quickly and efficiently handle the financial reporting of your business, the software alone is not the answer. You will still need a clear understanding of what numbers need to be calculated and what they mean.

71

In **CHAPTER 3, THE FINANCIAL PLAN** beginning on page 180, you will find samples of the most used financial statements and key financial terms to give you an understanding of what financial accounting entails. Also, **Exhibit 40 – Key Financial Metrics (Terms, Ratios & Formulas)** beginning on page 190 lists and describes financial terms important to your business.

Filing Income Taxes

Federal and state income taxes are a fact of life for all working Americans. And not filing on time, or even worse, not filing at all can have serious consequences. As with assessing your readiness, finances and start-up costs for entrepreneurship prior to embarking on your venture are vitally important, so is taking stock of your tax situation.

Taxes

"A charge imposed by authority upon persons or property for public purposes"

If your personal taxes (or payroll taxes for employees) go unpaid and no effort is made to remedy this indebtedness, your state department of revenue or the IRS (Internal Revenue Service) could take such actions as levying bank accounts, wages, other income, or seizing other assets. In addition, a lien could be filed having a detrimental effect on your credit standing and could negatively impact your chance of obtaining financing of any kind.

The IRS always encourages taxpayers to pay taxes owed in full. In situations where this is not possible, a taxpayer could qualify for an extension to pay depending on the circumstances. In this event, the IRS can request a Collection Information Statement (CIS) to compare individual or business monthly income with expenses and assist in establishing a payment plan.

There's a considerable amount of invaluable resources developed by the IRS for small businesses or self-employed persons. This information is free, and to place an order for publications regarding taxes for Small Business/Self-Employed visit the IRS website at https://www.irs.gov/Businesses/. You can also pick up publications at your local IRS office. If you need personal assistance, you can make an appointment with a tax specialist at your local IRS office to discuss any tax issues you may have.

Dun & Bradstreet (DUNS)

Just as individuals have a credit rating, so does your business. In today's global economy, the DUNS (Data Universal Numbering System) number has become the standard for keeping track of the world's businesses. Established in 1841 as a credit-reporting agency, it continues today as one of the leading providers of business-to-business credit, marketing, purchasing, receivables management and decision-support services worldwide.

Credit rating

"An estimate or evaluation of an individual's or business' standing or level of responsibility"

The DUNS number is a nine-digit identification sequence that provides unique identifiers of single business entities, while linking millions of corporate family structures. Used by the world's most influential standards-setting organizations, it's recognized, recommended and required by the government and global, industry and trade associations. There's no charge to obtain a DUNS number for your company. You can quickly and easily apply online at https://fedgov.dnb.com/webform/pages/CCRSearch.jsp to receive your DUNS number within one business day. For more information, visit the Dun & Bradstreet website at www.dnb.com/us/.

Quality Certifications

Quality certifications serve as formal recognition that individuals have demonstrated their proficiency and expert knowledge of a specific subject. Quality organizations exist for its members to share relevant knowledge and develop international standards for their industry. The world's most recognized quality organizations include:

1. **ISO (International Organization for Standardization)**
   http://www.iso.org
   Quality certification for the manufacture of a product, information technology and information technology management

2. **ASQ (American Society for Quality)**
   http://asq.org/cert
   Quality certification for Six Sigma and professional engineers, inspectors, technicians, etc.

3. **TL 9000 QuEST Forum**
   http://www.questforum.org/
   Quality certification for the telecommunications industry

4. **NAHQ (National Association for Healthcare Quality)**
   http://www.nahq.org
   Quality certification for the healthcare industry

Professional Licenses

Professional licenses are issued through the Secretary of State office in each state. This office within the state department is legislatively charged to administer and enforce specific laws relating to the licensing and regulation of certain occupations and professions. Licensure requires each applicant meet minimum standards (e.g., age, education, training certification, etc.) for their respective occupation or profession.

Professional

"Acting or exhibiting specialized knowledge usually after long and intensive academics or training"

There are 60 or more categories of licensure, and the majority of these categories include several individual license classifications. Check the Secretary of State's office in your state for a list that may include, but not limited to, common occupations and professions that require a license:

Accountant	Design or Interior Decorator	Nail Technician
Acupuncture	Detection of Deception	Naprapath
Advance Practice Nurse	Examiner	Nurse
Alarm Contractor	Detective	Nursing Home
Architect	Dietician	Nutritionist
Armed and Unarmed Security	Electrologist	Occupational Therapist
Force	Engineer	Optometrist
Associate Marriage & Family	Environmental Health	Orthodontist
Therapy	Practices	Pharmacist
Audiologist	Esthetician	Physical Therapist
Chiropractor	Euthanasia Agency	Physician's Assistant
Collection Agency	Firearms	Physician
Construction Contractors	Funeral Director	Podiatrist
Controlled Substance Drug	Geologist	Prosthetist
Distributor	Land Surveyor	Psychologist
Cosmetologist or Barber	Locksmith	Respiratory Care
Clinical Counselor	Mail Order Ophthalmic	Shorthand Reporter
Dental Hygienist	Provider	Social Worker
Dentist	Massage Therapist	Veterinarian

Hiring Employees and Contractors

When starting out in business, it's expected that you will be chief, cook and bottle washer. This is because hiring employees at the start-up of your business is not likely. But since no one can be an expert in every aspect of business, utilizing the services of others is necessary, and making hiring decisions is a process that should be carefully executed.

When making hiring decisions, be sure to select individuals who believe in the company, its mission and vision. Also, consider each employee's fitness for duty. There are many reasons an employee may be unfit for a position which could include not being fully qualified for the specific position, past criminal history, health challenges, even substance abuse.

Fitness for duty

"An employee's physical and mental capability of safely and competently performing the essential functions of their position"

Before hiring employees, you will need to understand and consider matters such as:

1. Why do you need to hire?

2. What services do you need?

3. What is the timeframe for hiring?

4. How many employees do you need to hire?

5. What areas of expertise are required?

6. What level of education does each individual need?

7. How many years of experience does each individual need to have?

8. What will the specific responsibilities of each employee be?

9. What level employee will you need for each position (e.g., executive, management, administrative, line, other)?

10. Will they be full-, part-time, intern, contractor, contract employee, freelance, other?

11. How many hours will they work per week?

12. How much do you have budgeted for their compensation?

13. Will they be paid hourly, salary or commission?

14. To whom will they report or manage?

15. What fringe benefits will you offer (e.g. medical/dental/vision insurance, group life insurance, equity in the company, education assistance, company cell phone, childcare assistance, cafeteria plans, parking, company car, employee discount, employee stock options, paid time off, etc.)?

16. Will they be provided orientation and/or training?

Fringe benefits

"Benefits provided by an employer to an employee, contractor or partner (some tax-exempt) when certain conditions are met"

Regardless of your hiring needs and the type(s) of employees you need to hire, be sure to educate yourself on employment and labor laws from both federal and state labor departments. Most important laws include:

- Americans with Disabilities Act (ADA)
- Equal Pay Act (EPA)
- Fair Labor Standards Act (FLSA)
- Family and Medical Leave Act (FMLA)
- Occupational Safety & Health Act (OSHA)
- State "At Will" and "Contract Employee" laws

There is so much to know about hiring employees at any level. You may want to consider hiring a payroll and tax company such as ADP (www.ADP.com), Paychex (www.paychex.com) or others. These companies are experts in providing automated payroll, electronic tax filing, timekeeping, and other human resources assistance including the preparation of an employee handbook.

Outside Professional Services

Outside professional services should be utilized early in the business development and planning process. Waiting until your business is in trouble before contacting an accountant, attorney or insurance agent can be the most costly mistake you could make. It's important that each professional perform services solely in their field of expertise. In other words, don't use your attorney to handle accounting functions or your insurance agent to act as your attorney.

Expertise

"Expert skill in a particular field"

Identifying individuals to provide legal, accounting, insurance and other professional services, such as a banker or other consultants in your field of business and industry, should be done with much scrutiny. Choose each professional with the intention of developing a long-term relationship. So "letting your fingers do the walking" through the yellow pages or using "Craigslist" to identify a professional service provider of any kind may not be the best way to go.

Begin your search by asking close friends, family members, colleagues or business associates for referrals. They could quite possibly know of someone they would be happy to refer. When vetting professional services providers and consultants, make sure that each professional is:

1. willing to teach you about their profession as it relates to your business as opposed to simply doing the work and sending you a bill;

2. not threatened by your asking any questions at any time and has no issue with your disagreeing with what they have presented;

3. a person that will work with you like a partner who's genuinely concerned about the success of your business;

4. a person you believe to be trustworthy and competent;

5. skilled and experienced with issues unique to small business; and

6. understands and is up to date on trends, laws, regulations that affect your business and industry.

And last, but certainly not least, make it a practice throughout the life of your business to get **ANY AND ALL** agreements (e.g., contracts, letters of intent, etc.) in writing, signed and dated by all parties. Whether you're establishing a partner, consulting or supplier relationship, agreements will keep all aspects of the relationship clear and help clarify roles, responsibilities and costs of each party involved. If there's a dispute of any kind, your executed agreement is legally enforceable. Also, any changes to a written agreement **MUST** be made in writing. The legal community only recognizes written amendments to written agreements.

Small, Disadvantaged, Minority, Woman, Veteran-Owned & Service-Disabled Veteran Business Enterprise Certification

If your business is owned and controlled 51% or more by one or more minorities, women, veterans or service disabled veterans, you may be eligible to participate in certain public and private initiatives that offer contracting opportunities. The first step in determining eligibility is to contact a government agency or a third party certifier and obtain documentation to apply for certification. **CHAPTER 8, SMALL, DISADVANTAGED, MINORITY, WOMEN, VETERAN-OWNED & SERVICE-DISABLED VETERAN BUSINESS ENTERPRISE DEVELOPMENT** beginning on page 319 will provide details of the certifications available and the certification process.

System for Award Management (SAM) Registration

Doing business with the federal government can be very lucrative if you are fortunate and qualified to land a contract. But there are steps to take before any consideration can be given to your company. The System for Award Management (SAM, formally known as Central Contractor Registration [CCR]) is the official U.S. government system that consolidated the capabilities of CCR/Federal Agency Registration, Online Representations and Certifications Application (ORCA) and Excluded Parties List System (EPLS).

SAM was created to streamline the process for collecting, validating, storing and disseminating data in support of agency missions. Current and potential government vendors are required to register in order to be awarded contracts by the DoD, NASA, DOT and Treasury departments. Vendors must complete a one-time registration and provide basic information relevant to procurement and financial transactions. Registration must be updated or renewed annually or bi-annually to maintain an active status.

SAM validates the vendor's information and electronically shares the secure and encrypted data with the federal agencies' finance offices to facilitate paperless payments through electronic funds transfer (EFT). Additionally, SAM shares the data with several government procurement and electronic business systems. However, registration does not guarantee business with the government.

Before conducting the online registration at https://www.sam.gov, you must have the following information available:

1.   federal employer identification number (FEIN);

2.   a DUNS number (Dun & Bradstreet);

3.   legal company name;

4.   physical street and mailing addresses;

5.   financial information;

6.   banking information

7.   point of contact; and

8.   EDI capabilities, if available.

Before you begin the SAM registration, be sure to first secure a DUNS number because it is REQUIRED. If you don't already have one, contact Dun & Bradstreet to obtain one (see Dun & Bradstreet on page 52). You will be unable to register without it.

Insurance

Insurance needs will vary depending on the size and nature of your business. It's imperative that you are able secure at least $1 million in liability insurance if you plan to do business with any government agency or large corporation.

Insurance

"Coverage by contract whereby one party agrees to guarantee another against a specified loss"

There are hundreds of types of insurance. The following is a list and brief description of some of the types of insurance that may be important for your type of business:

1. **Liability Insurance** – Covers legal responsibility for the harm it may cause to others (i.e., things that you or your employees fail to do in your business that may cause bodily injury or property damage due to defective products, faulty installations and errors in services).

2. **Business Umbrella Insurance** – Adds another level of protection when liability coverage is not sufficient and ensures your business is protected when serious situations arise.

3. **Health and Dental Insurance** – Covers the cost of the covered individuals' medical and surgical expenses for overall health and dentistry.

4. **Disability Insurance** – Replaces income lost during a short-term (e.g., pregnancy, accident, etc.) or permanent (e.g., long-term illness or condition) disability.

5. **Property Insurance** – Provides coverage for a building and its contents.

6. **Business Interruption Insurance** – Covers loss of income resulting from a fire or other catastrophe that disrupts the operation of the business.

7. **Directors and Officers Liability Insurance** – Offers reimbursement for losses or advancement of defense costs in the event an insured suffers a loss as a result of a legal action brought for alleged wrongful acts while in the capacity as a director or officer.

8. **Workers Compensation Insurance** – Provides payments to injured workers for time lost from work and for medical and rehabilitation services without regard to who was at fault in the accident. It also provides death benefits to surviving spouses and dependents.

9. **Key Person Insurance** – Provides a death benefit to the company when a key employee dies. Policy is owned by the company that pays the premiums and that company is the beneficiary.

10. **Professional Liability Insurance** – Protects professionals deemed to have extensive technical knowledge or training in their particular area of expertise. If they fail to use the degree of skill expected of them, they can be held responsible in a court of law for any harm they cause to another person or business.

11. **Errors & Omissions Insurance** – Coverage for professional liability limited to acts of negligence.

12. **Commercial Auto Insurance** – Usually the same coverage for personal auto insurance (e.g., liability, collision, comprehensive, personal injury) only it carries the name of the company.

13. **Employment Practices Liability Insurance (EPLI)** – Covers the business against claims by workers when their legal rights as employees have been violated. It includes claims of:

    a. Sexual harassment
    b. Discrimination
    c. Wrongful termination
    d. Breach of employment contract
    e. Negligent evaluation
    f. Failure to employ or promote
    g. Wrongful discipline
    h. Deprivation of career opportunity
    i. Wrongful infliction of emotional distress
    j. Mismanagement of employee benefit plans

14. **Identify Theft Insurance** – Protects individuals whose personal information has been unlawfully used to impersonate them, steal from bank accounts, establish phony insurance policies, open credit card accounts or obtain bank loans.

15. **Kidnap and Ransom Insurance** – Covers some of the expenses of dealing with kidnappers and their demands to include hostage negotiation fees, lost wages and ransom amount.

Consult with your insurance agent to determine what types insurance is required for your type of business. The Insurance Information Institute (III) publishes a host of helpful pamphlets and books that provide accurate and timely information on insurance subjects. For more detailed information, visit their website at www.iii.org.

Bonding

Surety bonds or bonding is defined as *"an agreement under which one party (the surety agent) guarantees to another (the owner of the project or business concern) that a third party (the contractor performing the work) will perform on a contract in accordance with contract documents."* There are two types of surety bonds: contract surety bonds and commercial surety bonds.

Bonding

"An insurance agreement pledging surety for financial loss or caused to another by an act or default"

Contract surety bonds provide financial security and construction assurance on building and construction projects by assuring the project owner that the contractor will perform the work and pay certain subcontractors, laborers and material suppliers. Some contract surety bonds include:

1. **Bid Bond** – Provides financial assurance that the bid has been submitted in good faith and the contractor intends to enter into the contract at the price bid and provide the required performance and payment bonds.

2. **Performance Bond** – Protects the owner from financial loss should the contractor fail to perform the contract in accordance with its terms and conditions.

3. **Payment Bond** – Guarantees the contractor will pay certain subcontractors, laborers and material suppliers associated with the project.

4. **Maintenance Bond** – Normally guarantees against defective workmanship or materials for a specified period.

5. **Subdivision Bond** – Guarantees to a city, county or state that the principal will finance and construct certain improvements such as streets, sidewalks, curbs, gutters, sewer and drainage.

Commercial surety bonds guarantee performance by the principal of the obligation or undertaking described in the bond and usually required by government agencies for the purpose of protecting a portion of the general public that interacts with the principal licensee. Some commercial surety bonds include:

1. **License and Permit Bond** – Required by state law or local regulations in order to obtain a license or permit to engage in a particular business (e.g., contractors, motor vehicle dealers, securities dealers, employment agencies, health spas, warehouses, liquor and sales tax).

2. **Judicial and Probate Bond** – Also referred to as fiduciary bonds, secures the performance on fiduciaries' duties and compliance with court orders, (e.g., administrators, executors, guardians, trustees of wills, liquidators, receivers, etc.).

3. **Judicial Proceedings Court Bond** – Provides for injunction, appeal, indemnity to sheriff, mechanics lien, attachment, replevin and admiralty.

4. **Public Official Bond** – Guarantees the performance of duty by a public official (e.g., treasurers, tax collectors, sheriffs, judges, court clerks, notaries).

5. **Federal Bond** (non-contract) – Required by the federal government (e.g., Medicare and Medicaid providers, customs, immigration, excise and alcoholic beverages).

6. **Miscellaneous Bond** – Provides for lost securities, leases, guarantee payment of utility bills, guarantee employer contributions for union fringe benefits and workers compensation for self-insurers.

The U.S. Department of Transportation (USDOT) and the U.S. Small Business Administration (SBA) have surety bond guarantee programs to assist. To obtain more information on surety/insurance seminars, classes, continuing education courses, federal and state legislation, visit the National Association of Surety Bond Producers' (NASBP) website at www.nasbp.org.

Intellectual Property

A company's intellectual property (IP) is as valuable to the company as its fixed assets, management expertise and the products/services it provides. Types of intellectual property include patents, trademarks, copyrights and trade secrets. Companies use their intellectual property to demonstrate their influence and product positioning (or service) in the marketplace.

The federal government offers protections for owners of intellectual property. The unlawful use of (e.g., use, reproduction, distribution, etc.) is a breach of the owner's rights. Using any protected work without the owner's consent is a violation and punishable by fines and/or imprisonment.

A patent excludes others from making, using or selling an invention in the U.S., its territories and possessions for 17 years. Items covered by a patent include:

1. **Novelty** – not previously known to or used by others in the U.S. or patented or described in a printed publication anywhere;

2. **Unobvious** – not known to a person having ordinary skill in the relevant art; and

3. **Utility** – has a useful purpose, actually works and is not frivolous or immoral.

A trademark is a work, design or a combination of them used by a manufacturer or merchant to identify his goods and distinguish them from others. They include:

1. brand names identifying goods (e.g., Pepsi-Cola);

2. service marks identifying services (e.g., Hyatt Hotels);

3. certification marks identifying goods or services meeting certain qualifications (e.g., UL for appliances meeting safety standards of Underwriter's Laboratory, Inc.); and

4. collective marks identifying services or members of a collective organization (e.g., AFL-CIO for union locals).

For more information on patents and trademarks, visit the U.S. Patent & Trademark Office website at www.uspto.gov.

A copyright promotes literary and artistic creativity by protecting, (for life plus 50 years), what the U.S. Constitution broadly calls writings of authors. The creator is given the exclusive rights to reproduce the work, to distribute the reproductions, to display and perform it publicly, to prepare derivative works based on it and to authorize others to do any of these things. Copyrightable works include:

1.   literary, musical and dramatic works;

2.   pantomimes and choreographic works;

3.   pictorial, graphic and sculptural works (including the non-utilitarian design features of useful articles);

4.   motion pictures and other audiovisual works;

5.   sound recordings;

6.   computer programs; and

7.   compilations of works and derivative works.

For more information on copyrights, visit the U.S. Copyright Office website at www.copyright.gov.

Trade secrets include formulas, patterns, programs, methods, techniques or process. In order for the standard of trade secret to be used, it must be used in business and serve as an economic advantage over competitors who don't know or use it.

Examples of trade secrets are the *"11 herbs and spices"* used in the Kentucky Fried Chicken recipe. Or the formula for Coca-Cola. These secrets may be communicated to certain employees during the course of employment and must be held in strict confidence. Unlike patents or copyrights, there are no time limitations on the protection of trade secrets and they have no registration.

Any information developed by a company that is not generally known, and cannot be patented or copyrighted under federal law, will be protected under state law as long as it is kept secret. For more information on trade secrets and protection, contact the U.S. Patent and Trademark Office online at http://www.uspto.gov/patents-getting-started/international-protection/trade-secret-policy.

Contracts, Agreements and Execution

There was once a time when a handshake was considered a bona fide agreement between two or more parties. As long ago as the existence of Babylon, the handshake symbolized "coming in peace" or "good faith." Out-stretched hands were proof that all parties could be trusted and that neither party was holding a weapon of any kind. And as a precaution, there would be an up and down motion ("shake") to release any weapons that might be hidden in a sleeve.

In later times, the handshake symbolized that "a man's word was his bond." Instead of writing a formal contract, parties would agree, shake hands, and that meant the deal was done. Today, we know that a contract not in writing or mutually-agreed upon could be problematic. Courts are full of more cases than they can quickly resolve because of contract disputes. Without having a clear offer and acceptance in writing, signed and dated by all parties, there's a potential for litigation. Verbal (or oral) contracts are valid as well as long as there is a "meeting of the minds." But when a dispute arises, it could be difficult for a judge or mediator to determine which of the litigants is at fault based on what is being said.

Contract (agreement)

"An offer and acceptance of a promise for performance by another party"

In order for any contract (or agreement, preferable in writing) to be valid, there must be:

1. **Offer** – a promise of one party (offeror) for exchange of a service, product, act, etc., received by another party (offeree) for money or something of value

2. **Acceptance** – the offer must be accepted by the offeree

3. **Consideration** – the mutual benefit to both the offeror and offeree in the offer and acceptance

4. **Mutuality** – the understanding that both parties in the contract are bound to it or neither is

5. **Competency** and **capacity** – that both parties are legally competent and have the capacity (e.g., not a minor, incapacitated or intoxicated) and can legally enter into a contract and be held liable

6. **Written** instrument – can be in the form of a letter, website, email, fax, behavior, and is signed and dated

All these elements constitute a legally-defensible contract. However, contracts can be nullified or terminated under certain circumstances with or without a counteroffer. Only the parties to the contract may terminate it. Reasons for ending a contract include, but not limited, to:

1. **Impossibility of performance** – one of the parties is unable to or it's impossible for them to perform

2. **Breach of contract** – when one of the parties intentionally does not meet its contract obligation

3. **Prior agreement** – if there's a prior agreement in place that makes either party unable to perform

4. **Rescission of a contract** – when one of the parties has misrepresented themselves, acted illegally or made a mistake

5. **Completion** – once all obligations in the contract have been met and the contract ends

While a handshake or verbal agreement can constitute a contract, a smart business person will always get everything in writing. Business relationships, family relationships and friendships can turn into warfare for virtually any reason or no reason, so make sure you have a contract that meets the criteria of a legally-enforceable document in the event litigation is necessary. If you are in need of legal assistance or representation, under "**LEGAL**" in **CHAPTER 9, BUSINESS RESOURCES**, beginning on page 340 are legal sources and their websites for your convenience.

Licensing Agreements

Licensing is the extension of a brand for marketing purposes to another entity. If your product/service lends itself to applying for a trademark or patented technology owned by another company, then a license is what you need. Popular examples of licensing include professional sports teams (e.g., NFL, NBA, NHL, etc.), fictional characters (e.g., Hello Kitty, Disney, etc.), and in the fashion industry (e.g., Nike, Chanel, Yves St. Laurent).

Licensing

"Leasing of a single or combination of legally-protected trademarks, patents, designs, slogans, characters, etc. owned by another entity"

Depending on the entity for which licensing is sought, the cost of securing an agreement can be expensive. For example, at this writing, a license for the National Football League is a $100,000 to meet the royalty guarantee required by the NFL. Licensees must pay the entire royalty guarantee each year. This means that annual sales from licensed products should exceed the $100,000 guarantee to make a profit from those sales.

Royalties

"Monies paid to one party from another for the right to use an asset"

A company's brand is their public image. Company officials are always concerned with how their brand is used. Therefore, permission must be granted before using a company brand for any reason. In addition, they want to know that their brand is not associated with any political opinions, negative propaganda, or in contrary to the company's mission or vision.

So, if licensing is the path you want to explore, here are the steps to take to secure a license:

1. Visit the website or contact the company or organization by phone in which you would like to secure a license. Locate the department in charge of reviewing requests.

2. Download and print all information that explains the organization's policy on licensing their brand.

3. Complete all forms (e.g., permission request form, etc.) and include any supplemental information requested in the form of attachments.

4. Documentation should explain in explicit detail:

   a. The format in which the brand will be used

   b. The medium in which the brand will be used (e.g., video, print, online)

     c. For print, send a printed page or screenshot sample of the layout.

     d. For video, upload the video or send a screenshot of the video layout.

5. Make sure all contact information is clear and correct.

6. If the option is available, prepare a letter making the request and include space at the bottom for approval or declination of the request.

If a license is granted, it may come with an agreement that can be complicated (one more instance where having legal expertise on hand is important). Licensing agreements generally contain the same basic information. A few of them include the:

1. Scope of the agreement

2. Financial structure (e.g., fees, guaranteed minimum sales, royalties, etc.)

3. Ownership of the licensed products

4. Restrictions for use (e.g., territories, quality of products, disposal of unsold products, etc.)

5. Beginning and termination dates and renewals

Because of the serious legal nature of licensing and agreements, it's always best to consult with an attorney to ensure that all agreed-upon aspects of the contract is understood by all parties. Unlawful use of a license could result in a cease and desist order as well as financial penalties.

U.S. Federal, State and Local Government

The role of the federal government is founded in the Preamble of the Constitution of the United States. While states are permitted to enact their own laws and prosecute crimes, they are considered "subdivisions" of the federal government. Under the Tenth Amendment, all powers not granted to the federal government are reserved for the states and the people.

The federal government is composed of three branches:

1. **Executive Branch** - The Office of the President who also serves as the Commander-in-Chief, and the Vice President who stands ready to resume the presidency when necessary. Responsible for implementing and enforcing laws written by Congress, and appoints the heads of all federal agencies.

2. **Legislative Branch** – Responsible for initiating revenue bills, impeaching federal officials and election of the President in the event there is an Electoral College tie. Consists of the 435 elected members to House of Representatives.

3. **Judicial Branch** – The only Branch were members are appointed by the President and confirmed by the Senate and not elected by the people. Congress has significant discretion to determine the shape and structure of the federal judiciary, including the number of Supreme Court Justices that will serve.

It's important to understand that all levels of government play a significant role in how we do business. Ignorance of any law in any jurisdiction is no excuse for breaking the law. You may need to consult with one or more agencies when filing the appropriate documents and obtaining other necessary information about operating you type of business. Visit each applicable agency's website to see if any documents can be filed online prior to taking a trip to their office.

Doing business with federal, state and local government agencies can be quite lucrative. Chances are your products/services appropriately suited for the military, schools and universities, city or county offices, as well as quasi-government agencies (e.g., water districts, utility companies, etc.). Contact each agency to find out what their purchasing procedures are. It may take patience and perseverance, but it can well worthwhile.

Exhibit 9 – Federal, State and Local Government Agencies beginning on page 91 lists and describes federal, state and local government departments and agencies. It is intended to help you locate, understand and navigate through the many levels of government to find important information such as policies, procedures, laws, and regulations that may affect your business.

Exhibit 9 – Federal, State and Local Government Agencies

U.S. FEDERAL GOVERNMENT

Provides defense, war prosecution, peace, foreign relations, foreign commerce and interstate commerce. Protects the constitution rights of its citizens. Establishes federal courts, copyright protection, coining of U.S. currency, postal services, national set of universal weights and measures, and taxation needed to raise the needed to perform essential functions.

Department of Agriculture (DOA)
www.usda.gov
Provides leadership on food, agriculture, natural resources, rural development, nutrition, and related issues based on public policy, the best available science, and effective management.
- Farm and Foreign Agricultural Services
- Rural Development
- Food, Nutrition and Consumer Services
- Food Safety
- Natural Resources and Environment
- Marketing and Regulatory Programs
- Research, Education and Economics

Department of Air Force
www.af.mil
Provides compelling air, space, and cyber capabilities for use by the combatant commanders. Excels as stewards of all Air Force resources in service to the American people, while providing precise and reliable Global Vigilance, Reach and Power for the nation.

Department of Army
www.army.mil
Conducts both operational and institutional missions. The operational Army consists of numbered armies, corps, divisions, brigades, and battalions that conduct full spectrum operations around the world. Institutional organizations provide the infrastructure necessary to raise, train, equip, deploy, and ensure the readiness of all Army forces.

Department of Commerce (DOC)
www.commerce.gov
Works with businesses, universities, communities, and the nation's workers to promote job creation, economic growth, sustainable development, and improved standards of living for Americans.
- Bureau of Industry and Security
- Economic Development Administration (EDA)
- Economics and Statistics Administration (ESA)
- International Trade Administration (ITA)
- Minority Business Development Agency (MBDA)
- National Institute of Standards and Technology (NIST)
- Patent and Trademark Office (PTO)

- National Oceanic and Atmospheric Administration (NOAA)
- National Telecommunications and Information Administration

Department of Defense (DOD)

www.defense.gov

Manages an inventory of installations and facilities to keep Americans safe. The Department's physical plant is huge by any standard, consisting of more than several hundred thousand individual buildings and structures located at more than 5,000 different locations or sites. When all sites are added together, the Department of Defense utilizes over 30 million acres of land.

- Defense Logistics Agency (DLA)
- Department of the Air Force
- Department of the Army
- Department of the Navy
- U.S. Marine Corps (USMC)
- Joint Chiefs of Staff
- National Guard Bureau
- Defense Advanced Research Projects Agency
- Defense Commissary Agency
- Defense Contract Management Agency
- Defense Finance and Accounting Service
- Defense Information Systems Agency
- Defense Intelligence Agency
- Defense Security Cooperation Agency
- Defense Security Service
- Defense Technical Information Center
- Defense Threat Reduction Agency
- Missile Defense Agency
- National Security Agency
- National Reconnaissance Office
- National Geospatial-Intelligence Agency
- Naval Criminal Investigative Service
- Pentagon Force Protection Agency
- United States Pentagon Police
- American Forces Information Service
- Defense Prisoner of War/Missing Personnel Office
- Department of Defense Education Activity
- Department of Defense Dependents Schools
- Defense Human Resources Activity
- Washington Headquarters Services
- United States Military Academy at West Point

Department of Education

www.ed.gov

Establishes policies on federal financial aid for education, and distributing as well as monitoring those funds. Collects data on America's schools and disseminating research. Focuses national attention on key educational issues. Prohibits discrimination and ensuring equal access to education.

- Office of Communication and Outreach (OCO)
- Office of the General Counsel (OGC)
- Office of Inspector General
- Office of Legislative and Congressional Affairs (OLCA)

- Office for Civil Rights (OCR)
- Office of Educational Technology (OET)
- Institute of Education Sciences (IES)
- Office of Innovation and Improvement (OII)
- Office of the Chief Financial Officer
- Office of Management
- Office of the Chief Information Officer
- Office of Planning, Evaluation and Policy Development
- Office of the Under Secretary (OUS)
- Office of the Deputy Secretary (ODS)
- Office of English Language Acquisition, Language Enhancement and Academic Achievement for Limited English Proficient Students (OELA)
- Office of Special Education and Rehabilitative Services (OSERS)
- Office of Innovation and Improvement

Department of Energy (DOE)

www.energy.gov

To ensure America's security and prosperity by addressing its energy, environmental and nuclear challenges through transformative science and technology solutions.

- Energy Information Administration
- Federal Energy Regulatory Commission
- National Laboratories & Technology Centers
- National Nuclear Security Administration
- Power Marketing Administration

Department of Health and Human Services (HHS)

www.hhs.gov

Enhances and protects the health and well-being of all Americans by providing for effective health and human services and fostering advances in medicine, public health, and social services.

- Administration on Aging
- Administration for Children and Families
- Agency for Healthcare Research and Quality
- Centers for Disease Control and Prevention
- Centers for Medicare and Medicaid Services
- Food and Drug Administration
- Health Resources and Services Administration
- Patient Affordable Healthcare Act Program
- Indian Health Service
- National Institutes of Health
- Public Health Service
- Substance Abuse and Mental Health Services Administration

Department of Homeland Security (DHS)

www.dhs.gov

Secures the nation from the many threats through the dedication of more than 240,000 employees in jobs that range from aviation and border security to emergency response, from cybersecurity analyst to chemical facility inspector with a goal of keeping America safe.

- Federal Emergency Management Agency (FEMA)
- Federal Law Enforcement Training Center
- Transportation Security Administration (TSA)
- United States Citizenship and Immigration Services

THE START-UP PHASE

- United States Coast Guard (USCG)
- United States Customs and Border Protection (US CBP)
- United States Immigration and Customer Enforcement
- United States Secret Service

Department of Housing and Urban Development (HUD)
www.hud.gov
Sponsors housing counseling agencies throughout the country that can provide advice on buying a home, renting, defaults, foreclosures, and credit issues.
- Federal Housing Administration (FHA)
- Federal Housing Finance Agency

Department of the Interior (DOI)
www.doi.gov
Responsible for the construction of the national capital's water system, the colonization of freed slaves in Haiti, exploration of western wilderness, oversight of the District of Columbia jail, regulation of territorial governments, management of hospitals and universities, management of public parks, and the basic responsibilities for Indians, public lands, patents, and pensions. In one way or another all of these had to do with the internal development of the nation or the welfare of its people.
- Bureau of Indian Affairs (BIA)
- Bureau of Land Management
- Bureau of Ocean Energy Management
- Bureau of Reclamation
- Bureau of Safety and Environmental Enforcement
- Federal Consulting Group
- Fish and Wildlife Service
- National Park Service
- Office of Insular Affairs
- Office of Surface Mining
- United States Geological Survey

Department of Justice (DOJ)
www.justice.gov
Enforces the law and defends the interests of the United States according to the law; ensures public safety against threats foreign and domestic; provides federal leadership in preventing and controlling crime; to seek just punishment for those guilty of unlawful behavior; ensures fair and impartial administration of justice for all Americans.
- Antitrust Division
- Asset Forfeiture Program
- Bureau of Alcohol, tobacco, Firearms and Explosives (AFT)
- Civil Division
- Civil Rights Division
- Community Oriented Policing Services
- Community Relations Service
- Criminal Division
- Drug Enforcement Administration (DEA)
- Environment and Natural Resources Division
- Executive Office for Immigration Review
- Executive Office for Organized Crime Drug Enforcement Task Force
- Executive Office for United States Attorneys

- Executive Office for United States Trustees
- Federal Bureau of Investigation (FBI)
- Federal Bureau of Prisons (FBP)
- Foreign Claims Settlement Commission
- INTERPOL
- Justice Management Division
- National Crime Information Center
- National Drug Intelligence Center
- National Institute of Corrections
- National Security Division
- Office of the Attorney General
- Office of Dispute Resolution
- Office of the Federal Detention Trustee
- Office of Information Policy
- Office of Intergovernmental and Public Liaison
- Office of Intelligence and Analysis
- Office of Justice Programs
- Office of Legal Counsel
- Office of Legal Policy
- Office of Legislative Affairs
- Office of the Pardon Attorney
- Office of Privacy and Civil Liberties
- Office of Professional Responsibility
- Office of Public Affairs
- Office of Sex Offender Sentencing, Monitoring, Apprehending, Registering and Tracking
- Office of the Solicitor General
- Office of Special Counsel
- Office of Tribal Justice
- Office on Violence Against Women
- Professional Responsibility Advisory Office
- Tax Division
- United States Attorneys
- United States Marshals
- United States Parole Commission
- United States Trustee Program

Department of Labor (DOL)
www.dol.gov
To foster, promote, and develop the welfare of the wage earners, job seekers, and retirees of the United States; improve working conditions; advance opportunities for profitable employment; and assure work-related benefits and rights.
- Bureau of International Labor Affairs
- Bureau of Labor Statistics (BLS)
- Center for Faith-Based and Neighborhood Partnerships
- Employee Benefit Security Administration
- Employment and Training Administration (ETA)
- Job Corp
- Mine Safety and Health Administration
- Occupational Safety and Health Administration (OSHA)
- Veterans' Employment and Training Service (VETS)
- Wage and Hour Division
- Women's Bureau

Department of Navy

www.navy.mil

To maintain, train and equip combat-ready Naval forces capable of winning wars, deterring aggression and maintaining freedom of the seas.

- United States Navy
- Marine Corps

United States Department of State

www.state.gov

The United States federal executive department responsible for the international relations of the U.S, equivalent to the foreign ministry of other countries.

- National Council for the Traditional Arts
- United States Foreign Service

Department of Transportation (DOT)

www.transportation.gov

Serves the United States by ensuring a fast, safe, efficient, accessible and convenient transportation system that meets vital national interests and enhances the quality of life of the American people, today and into the future.

- Bureau of Transportation Statistics
- Federal Aviation Administration (FAA)
- Federal Highway Administration (FHWA)
- Federal Motor Carrier Safety Administration
- Federal Railroad Administration
- Federal Transit Administration (FTA)
- Maritime Administration
- National Highway Traffic Safety Administration (NHTSA)
- Office of Intelligence, Security and Emergency Response
- Pipeline and Hazardous Materials Safety Administration
- Research and Innovative Technology Administration
- St. Lawrence Seaway System
- Surface Transportation Board

Department of the Treasury

www.treasury.gov

Responsible for promoting economic prosperity and ensuring the financial security of the United States. Responsible for a wide range of activities such as advising the President on economic and financial issues, encouraging sustainable economic growth, and fostering improved governance in financial institutions.

- Alcohol and Tobacco Tax and Trade Bureau
- Bureau of Engraving and Printing
- Bureau of Fiscal Service
- Community Development Financial Institutions Fund
- Financial Crimes Enforcement Network
- Internal Revenue Service
- Office of the Comptroller of the Currency
- Office of Financial Stability
- United States Mint

Department of Veterans Affairs
www.va.gov
Serves America's veterans and their families with dignity and compassion, and to be their principal advocate in ensuring that they receive medical care, benefits, social support, and lasting memorials promoting the health, welfare, and dignity of all veterans in recognition of their service to this nation.

- National Cemetery Administration
- Veterans Benefits Administration
- Veterans Health Administration
- Board of Veterans' Appeals
- Center for Faith-Based and Community Initiatives
- Center for Minority Veterans
- Center for Veterans Enterprise
- Center for Women Veterans
- Office of Advisory Committee Management
- Office of Employment Discrimination Complaint Adjudication
- Office of Survivors Assistance
- Office of Small and Disadvantaged Business Utilization (OSDBU)
- Veterans Service Organizations Liaisons

INDEPENDENT AGENCIES AND GOVERNMENT-OWNED CORPORATIONS

The following section lists each of the independent agencies and government-owned corporations of the U.S. federal government:

- Elections
    - Election Assistance Commission
    - Federal Election Commission
- Administrative Agencies
    - Administrative Conference of the United States
    - National Archives and Records Administration
- Civil Service Agencies
    - Merit Systems Protection Board
    - Office of Government Ethics
    - Office of Personnel Management
    - Office of Special Counsel
- Commerce Regulatory Agencies
    - Federal Trade Commission (FTC)
    - Consumer Product Safety Commission (CPSC)
    - Federal Communications Commission (FCC)
    - Federal Housing Finance Agency (FHFA)
    - U.S. Trade and Development Agency
    - U.S. International Trade Commission
- Education Agencies
    - Corporation for Public Broadcasting
    - Helen Keller National Center
    - Institute of Museum and Library Services
    - International Broadcasting Bureau
    - National Constitution Center
    - National Endowment for the Arts (NEA)

- o National Endowment for the Humanities
- Energy and Science Agencies
    - o National Aeronautics and Space Administration (NASA)
    - o National Science Foundation (NSF)
    - o U.S. Antarctic Program
    - o U.S. Arctic Program
    - o Nuclear Regulatory Commission
    - o Office of the Federal Coordinator, Alaska Natural Gas Transportation Projects
    - o Tennessee Valley Authority
- Foreign Investment Agencies
    - o African Development Foundation
    - o Export-Import Bank of the United States (Ex-Im)
    - o Inter-American Foundation
    - o Overseas Private Investment Corporation (OPIC)
    - o United States Agency for International Development
- Interior Agencies
    - o Advisory Council on Historic Preservation
    - o Environmental Protection Agency (EPA)
- Labor Agencies
    - o Federal Labor Relations Authority
    - o Federal Mediation and Conciliation Service
    - o Federal Mine Safety and Health Review Commission
    - o National Labor Relations Board (NLRB)
    - o National Mediation Board
    - o Occupational Safety and Health Review Commission
    - o Office of Compliance
- Monetary and Financial Agencies
    - o Commodity Futures Trading Commission
    - o Farm Credit Administration
    - o Federal Reserve System
    - o Federal Deposit Insurance Corporation (FDIC)
    - o National Credit Union Administration
    - o Securities and Exchange Commission (SEC)
    - o Securities Investor Protection Corporation
    - o Small Business Administration (SBA)
- Postal Agencies
    - o Military Postal Service Agency
    - o Postal Regulatory Commission
    - o United States Postal Services (USPS)
- Retirement Agencies
    - o Armed Forces Retirement Home
    - o Federal Retirement Thrift Investment Board
    - o Pension Benefit Guaranty Corporation
    - o Railroad Retirement Board
    - o Social Security Administration (SSA)
- Federal Property and Seal of Government Agencies
    - o Court Services and Offender Supervision Agency
    - o General Services Administration (GSA)
    - o National Capital Planning Commission
- Transportation Agencies
    - o Amtrak (National Railroad Passenger Corporation)
    - o Federal Maritime Commission
    - o National Transportation Safety Board (NTSB)
- Volunteerism Agencies
    - o Corporation for National and Community Service

- o Peace Corps
- Defense and Security Agencies
  - o Central Intelligence Agency (CIA)
  - o Defense Nuclear Facilities Safety Board
  - o Office of the National Counterintelligence Executive
  - o Office of the Director of National Intelligence
  - o Selective Service System
- Civil Rights
  - o Commission on Civil Rights
  - o Equal Employment Opportunity Commission (EEOC)
  - o National Council on Disability
- Proposed Government-owned Corporation
  - o Strategic Economic and Energy Development
  - o Digital Opportunity Investment Trust
- Inspectors General
- Quasi-Official Agencies
  - o Legal Services Corporation
  - o Smithsonian Institution
  - o John F. Kennedy Center for the Performing Arts
  - o State Justice Institute
  - o United States Institute of Peace
  - o National Trust for Historic Preservation
  - o Brand USA
  - o Graduate School USA
- Private Regulatory Corporations
  - o Public Company Accounting Oversight Board
  - o Internet Corporation for Assigned Names and Numbers
  - o Municipal Securities Rulemaking Board
  - o National Futures Association
- Government Entities Created by Acts, But Not An Independent or Other Entities
  - o American Institute in Taiwan
  - o COMSAT
  - o Cotton Incorporated
  - o Dairy Management, Inc.
  - o In-Q-Tel
  - o Protestant Episcopal Cathedral Foundation
  - o Financial Industry Regulatory Authority
  - o National Consumer Cooperative Bank
  - o National Corporation for Housing Partnerships
  - o National Endowment for Democracy
  - o National Fish and Wildlife Foundation
  - o National Technical Institute for the Deaf
  - o Neighborhood Reinvestment Corporation
  - o Pennsylvania Avenue Development Corporation
  - o The Financial Corporation
  - o Sister Cities International
  - o United States Olympic Committee

THE START-UP PHASE

STATE GOVERNMENT

The 10th Amendment of the U.S. Constitution granted all states the power to control everyday dealings in their states. State governments are responsible for the administration of policies decided by voters, law makers and the state constitution. These dealings include:

- Education
- Transportation
- Motor vehicle registration, drivers licensing
- Professional licensing
- Birth and death certificates
- Unemployment compensation

COUNTY GOVERNMENT

County governments are governed by an elected Board of Supervisors, even though their roles and responsibilities are established by their state. However, "home rule" or "charter" counties have more flexibility in their dealings with the counties served. County government focuses on public records, elections, infrastructure and transportation, economic development, law enforcement, public health and safety, and the implementation of federal, state and local programs.

The National Association of Counties (NACo) is an organization comprised of America's over 3,000 county governments. The organization brings county officials together to advocate collectively on national policy, exchange ideas, and enrich the public's understanding of county government, among many other activities. For more information on NACo visit their website at www.naco.org.

Primary departments within county government include:

- Animal Control
- Auditor
- Board of Review
- Cable TV Franchise
- Coroner
- County Board
- County Clerk
- Court Services
- Development
- Emergency Management
- Environmental Health
- Finance
- Forest Preserve
- Health Department

- Jail
- Jury Commission
- Juvenile Justice
- Law Library
- Liquor Commission
- Merit Commission
- Personnel
- Public Defender
- Purchasing Recorder Regional School Office
- Sheriff
- States Attorney
- Supervisor of Assessments
- Transportation
- Treasurer

LOCAL GOVERNMENT

Local governments serve as the public administrators of towns, cities, counties and districts. They work with county and municipal governmental structures to run city utilities, local law enforcement, libraries, fire departments, public swimming pools, parks, and other amenities needed for everyday living. Some departments of local government include:

- Administration
- Ambulance
- Animal Control
- Assessor
- Building & Zoning
- Cemeteries
- Chamber of Commerce
- City Clerk
- City Hall
- Civic Activities
- Community Development
- Community Resource
- Customer Service, Information & Complaints
- Economic Development
- Electrical
- Emergency Management
- Engineering
- Finance
- Fire Department
- Garbage & Recycling
- Inspections & Permits
- Highway Commission
- Housing Authority
- Libraries
- Maintenance
- Motor Vehicle
- Neighborhood Redevelopment
- Parks & Recreation
- Parking Violations
- Permits & Inspections
- Personnel/Human Resources
- Planning
- Police
- Public Arts Commission
- Public Property
- Public Schools
- Public Works
- Purchasing
- Preservation Commission
- Senior Citizens
- Street Maintenance
- Voter Registration
- Wastewater Treatment
- Water & Sewage
- Youth Activities

Educating Your Customer

The use of some products/services is not easily understandable, particularly if they are niche, new or unusual. This means that educating prospective customers is necessary. Materials that educate customers can also be used for marketing and can help increase sales by turning prospects into customers for life. This education process can also provide prospective customers with information in other areas of your field that can be helpful and useful.

For example, if your company is a provider of cookware, you may want to email or snail mail prospects recipes that work well using that cookware, utensils that work best with the cookware, the best types of cleaners for the cookware, or other uses and users of the cookware. Educational materials should:

- Provide prospects with a clear description of your products/ services and your company.

- Let prospects know how the use of your products/services benefits them and other products you have they could be interested in.

- Provide them with other related information that could help them in other areas of your field.

- Provide a way for customers to reach you by phone and online.

Creating YouTube video demonstrations, Facebook, Instagram and Pinterest posts, as well as blogs, are excellent ways to educate your customers while simultaneously marketing your products and services.

Preparing Your "Elevator Pitch"

It can be difficult to introduce yourself to a stranger in just a few words. Even though you know your business, sometimes your business description can evade you. Unless you have prepared an "elevator pitch" you could find yourself verbally stumbling to find the right words to tell someone who you are and what you do in a few words.

Elevator pitch

"An approximately 60-second overview of your business, products or services used in face-to-face business networking"

Your elevator pitch is intended to serve as an ice breaker about you and your business when meeting people for the first time. After your greeting, your elevator pitch should include your:

- **Full name** - Titles such as Mr., Mrs., or Ms. are not necessary. However, the title Dr. is fine if you are a bona fide doctor in any area of medicine or a Ph.D. Regardless of the person's educational background, common courtesy in addressing them should always be exercised.

- **Company name and your title** - Your listener needs to know specifically who is addressing them.

- **What your company does** - Should be consistent with your mission statement.

- **Major customer(s)** - This should be your target or largest audience.

- **Your unique selling proposition** – Describe what makes your business unique or the best compared to its competition.

- **Follow-up conversation** – Give and get a business card or contact information to continue the conversation.

Before attending any networking event or if you are going to be around people you are not acquainted and who you could potentially do business with, you should prepare an elevator pitch. Put your elevator pitch in writing and practice until you are comfortable and confident with how you introduce yourself and your business to acquaintances. When people see and hear that you are comfortable and knowledgeable about your business, they are more willing to continue the conversation and possibly do business with you.

Using Metrics to Measure Business Success

There's an old adage, "what gets measured, gets done." In every aspect of business, be it marketing, management, finance or long range planning, metrics play an important role in helping determine what strategies work, and more important, which ones don't work. Expressing business activities in words is important, however, expressing business activities in numbers is critical.

Metrics provide the statistical information you need as a business owner to explain what has happened over a specific period of time, determine what the issues are, and make projections for the future. Regardless of the industry in which your business is associated, you need metrics to ascertain how well your business is doing, where problems lie, how to resolve them, and what the next outcomes should be.

Metrics

"A measuring system that quantifies an art, process, science, trend, dynamic or characteristic"

What Gets Measured and How

Understanding metrics can be challenging. You must know specifically *what* areas need to be measured and *how* these areas are to be measured. Depending on the nature of your business, measuring activities differ in importance. Determining what to measure is the first step. Keep in mind your goals and objectives for measuring business success are a good way to start. Ask yourself:

1. What are the key results areas where overall company goals and objectives need to be measured? One example would be increasing online presence by opening social media accounts.

2. Will meeting goals and objectives in these areas mean success? If the company employs social media, how much business can it expect to gain from its use?

3. How is success measured? It could be defined in terms of dollars, percentage increase/decrease, or number.

For our imaginary *CareerTemps* Temporary Staffing Agency, some examples of metrics could include measuring, but not limited, to:

- Number of applicants in the database currently placed

- Number of available applicants in the databased ready for placement

- Number of available positions for placement

- Percentage applicants placed

- Number of requests for temporary staffing in the service area
- Number of available applicants for placement
- Number of available applicants with technology experience
- Number of applicants via the CTSA website and social media
- Duration each applicant remains in a position
- Number of applicants from job fairs

Each area of your business plan will require you to identify metrics for success in those areas. Some metric suggestions are presented, but you will need to add others based on your business type, goals and objectives.

Business Execution Excellence

Throughout the business start-up and business planning processes, defining and executing established strategies and using best skills and abilities to meet desired goals is the formula for business success. Developing strategies and a well thought-out business plan are of no use if you don't properly or effectively execute the details of them to meet your goals.

Execution excellence

"Occurs when people, processes and products/services are in total alignment to meet overall company goals and achieve business success"

Business execution excellence requires that all human resources and business resources are in lock step. This alignment ensures that each area of the company understands their specific roles and work within the prescribed framework to meet established goals. And when this alignment is absent, procedures to ameliorate any issues must be put in place. Company leaders must regularly create and communicate the overall company goals to all employees and consultants.

For effective execution excellence, your company must have:

- a strategic plan that defines overall quantifiable and attainable company goals;

- employees or consultants with the right skills sets in the right positions doing the right work to ensure the best use of human resources;

- senior or executive staff that creates effective communications across all levels of the company that are clearly understood, motivating and engaging;

- processes in place that ensure that manufacture/production of products/services is streamlined, cost effective and operates efficiently; and

- an efficient cash management system that properly collects and records all transactions, strictly adheres to budgets, monitors all spending, and conducts monthly financial reporting, including bank reconciliation.

Operational Efficiency

There's a saying, "if it ain't broke, don't fix it." This statement assumes that an operation is currently working efficiently, in no need of reparation, there are no threats and no lost opportunities. To maintain that efficiency, an operation must be broken (figuratively speaking) so that a plan can be devised to fix it BEFORE it is actually broken.

This is operational efficiency. It not only encompasses cost cutting measures, but it is also about how well company resources are utilized in delivering value and quality products/services to its customers in an effort to reach its overall goals and objectives. Simply put, it means using the right actions and resources in the right ways at the right time to produce the best outcomes without sacrificing value and quality. And when issues arise, there's a plan for rectification and remediation to maintain that value and quality.

Operational efficiency

"Capability of an enterprise to deliver cost effective products/services to its customers and ensuring value, high quality and support"

To ensure operational efficiency exists in an organization, some factors to consider include:

- overall planning and setting goals and objectives;
- use of technology, equipment, machinery, space, labor and skills;
- efficient use of inputs (materials) for maximum outputs (products/services) with minimal waste;
- meeting production schedules, efficient use of time;
- safety standards adherence;
- production maximization using best practices and scalability;
- proper and competitive price points, fluctuations; and
- how the industry is performing nationally, globally.

For both service- and product-oriented businesses, there are three levels of operations: 1) strategic; 2) tactical; and 3) operational. Each level requires specific tasks be accomplished in order for operational efficiency to prevail. But, since service-oriented businesses don't have the same types of production issues, planning must have a greater focus on customer service.

At the strategic level, all planning and decision making occurs. This includes all areas that affect finances, marketing and management. The tactical level involves the planning and organizing for the use of materials, time and other resources for product/service output. And finally, the operational level involves the actual manufacture/production of products/services.

The use of industry best practices is the best path to operational efficiency. This is where being part of an industry group can be extremely beneficial. Those working in your industry have already identified approaches to the production/manufacture of products/services (both similar and dissimilar) to yours, and understand which activities or methods work best. In **CHAPTER 9, BUSINESS RESOURCES** under "**PROFESSIONAL ASSOCIATIONS**" beginning on page 346 and "**RESEARCH ORGANIZATIONS**" beginning on page 350, you will find information on locating your business industry.

Business Valuation

Placing a value on any business can be difficult. The basis of and for valuation and the value itself changes in every stage of the business' life. Matters used to impute valuation are different in the start-up, growth, and mature phases of every business. In the start-up phase for example, valuation could be based on the number of buyers for products/services, the reputation of the owners or the strength of the industry. Whereas valuing a mature business would include financials and assets.

Business valuation

"Process and procedures used to estimate the economic value of an owner's interest in a business and the price a business can be sold for"

Before a business' valuation can be determined, reasons and circumstances surrounding the valuation must be specified using standards of value (e.g., fair market, investment and intrinsic values). This is the hypothetical condition under which the business is valued. Or the premises of value (e.g., going concern, assemblage of assets, orderly disposition, liquidation). This value relates to assumptions such as the business' inevitable continuance, or that the business is based on the proceeds from sale of assets minus any debt.

Some of the most common reasons for valuing a business include:

- Attracting investors
- Borrowing money
- Employee stock option incentive plans
- Mitigate shareholder disputes
- Marital dissolution
- Estate planning
- Buyout/buy-in agreements
- Succession planning

Since there is generally little or nothing in sales in the start-up phase, the value is anyone's best guess. There are several factors used in determining the fair value of a business. But understand that valuations can vary based on the methods used. The easiest approaches to business valuation include:

1. **Asset approach** – (Assets - liabilities = value)
   This assumes placing a value on business assets, both tangible (e.g., equipment, machinery, inventory, etc.) and intangible (e.g., intellectual property, accounts receivables, and other non-physical objects). Other assets can be difficult to value because there may not be a book value for these items (e.g., office equipment, furniture, some inventory).

2. **Market approach** – (Value compared to similar businesses)
   Compares the business to similar businesses sold. Much like "comps" used in the real estate industry to determine the amount a house is being appraised for in the same area.

3. **Income approach** – (Financial information)
   This approach uses the company's financial information and formulas to consider future economic expectations and the rate of risk or return.

For the small, start-up business seeking equity financing, there is a simple method for imputing its value. Let's assume you're seeking a $50,000 equity investment with earnings of $75,000. For the $50,000 the investor receives a 25% equity stake in the company. This means there's an imputed $200,000 value for the company. The calculation is as follows:

- The $50,000 investment represents 25% of the company

- Meaning 25% is ¼ of the entire company (4 x 25 = 100)

- 100% of the company is $200,000

- The 25% is multiplied by the $50,000 investment for total valuation of $200,000

Another easy valuation method is the revenue multiple. This is calculated by determining the value of the company divided by its profit. One example would be to:

- Begin with earnings. A multiplier suggests the number of times earnings must be met to get the value of the business.

- If earnings are $75,000, then there is a multiplier of 2.6666

Using the multiplier method in the example above, the company must have 2.6666 times earnings ($75,000) to have a value of $200,000. Other valuation methods could include of multiplier of 5 times cash flow or 1.5 times revenue.

Understanding business valuation encompasses much more than the non-financial or non-attorney person can comprehend. So many factors have to be taken into account. Weighted average, cost of capital, discount or capitalization rates, or capital asset pricing model are just a few of the many terms used in business valuation that must be understood. This is why it's always important to consult with an attorney and/or CPA. They will know the best approach to take based on the business situation and the reasons for needing a valuation.

Moving Ahead

Being in business is one of the most challenging, yet exciting undertakings you will ever experience. At a minimum it'll require long, hard hours, total commitment, and most importantly, perseverance. But the rewards are tremendous. Just remember that research of your product/service, industry and competition, as well as self-evaluation doesn't end with a completed business plan. Research and self-evaluation should continue throughout the life of your business for you to achieve and maintain a desired level of success.

Perseverance

"Continuance of something to an exceptional degree beyond a desired point"

The steps and information provided in this Guide are clearly designed to assist you in introducing your company and its products and services to the world (at least your locale or region). Hopefully now with the help of *"The Start of Something BIG. . ."* launching your new venture is a little less intimidating and perplexing. Always look at being in business as a continuous learning experience. It's impossible to know everything about everything so it's important to keep an open mind. Even people with no business experience can teach you something about your own business. Therefore, egos must be checked at the door or take up residency elsewhere.

Capacity Constraints

Your dream of business success can become a reality. But you will need to start conducting business at a pace you can comfortably handle. Understanding capacity constraints will keep you from taking on more than your business can handle at any given time. This could even mean passing on what appears to be a great business opportunity. Too much too soon could easily mean failure for you. Easily costs can be higher than anticipated and profits lower than expected. Setting small or short deadlines for yourself that are attainable and not overly ambitions can keep you on track.

Capacity constraints

"The level at which production comes to a bottleneck due to overscheduling"

Start-up Checklist

Exhibit 10 - Business Start-up Checklist on page 112 can help ensure that each item in this section has been addressed. Here's where the foundation for your business is laid. Not everything in this book will apply to your business. However, in preparing this Guide, most all elements of business and business start-up were taken into consideration. It is important to know and understand your business and its industry. In knowing this, you will be able to determine which issues should be addressed and which ones simply don't apply.

Next Step: Writing Your Business Plan

The preceding pages were intended to lay the groundwork for structuring and organizing your business. We've identified the major steps necessary for starting a business and being successful. While they are many in number, they are not intended to be exhaustive or overwhelming. Once all steps (and there will be others depending on the nature of your business) have been addressed, your business will begin to take shape. You should now have an understanding of:

- How to go from an idea to a business.
- Structuring and organizing your business.
- What products/services you will provide.
- Legal aspects of starting and operating a business.
- How to manage the business.
- Your personal and business finances.
- Measuring business success.

Remember, first and foremost, organization is critical. The entire business start-up and business planning process will necessitate the collection and use of a multitude of information and materials. Keep order and organization a top priority. Take notes and create a filing system that will enable you to locate any information when it is needed.

CHAPTER 2, UNDERSTANDING BUSINESS PLANNING beginning on page 115 will define business planning and the process. **CHAPTER 3, THE ANATOMY OF A BUSINESS PLAN** beginning on page 121 will provide step-by-step instruction as well as a sample plan for you to follow. Read and re-read each section or research collected as necessary because it is difficult to absorb everything all at once.

Let the planning begin!

Exhibit 10 – Business Start-up Checklist

INITIAL RESEARCH
_____ Begin researching a "need" for your product/service
_____ Determine the type of business you want to start, its mission, vision

CONDUCT ASSESSMENTS
_____ Readiness for entrepreneurship
_____ Personal strengths and weaknesses
_____ Current personal financial status
_____ Set financial goals and address concerns
_____ Start-up costs

STRUCTURING THE BUSINESS
_____ Determine sources of funding to cover start-up costs
_____ North American Industrial Classification System (NAICS) Code
_____ Legal structure (sole proprietor, partnership, corporation)
_____ Naming your company
_____ Fictitious business name filing in county where business is located
_____ Domain name registration
_____ Internet service provider
_____ Electronic mail (e-mail)
_____ Identify website hosting company
_____ Open social media accounts
_____ Develop website
_____ Select business location
_____ Research computer and telecommunications technology
_____ Review city and county ordinances
_____ Apply for FEIN (federal employer identification number) IRS form number SS-4
_____ Open business bank account
_____ Research accounting systems and/or companies
_____ Secure Dun & Bradstreet (DUNS) number
_____ File for business license/registration in county where business is located
_____ Secure quality certifications, if applicable
_____ Professional license(s) in state where business is located
_____ Identify outside professional services
_____ Apply for small/disadvantaged/minority/women/service disabled veteran certification
_____ Register with System for Award Management (SAM, formerly CCR)
_____ Secure necessary insurance and bonding
_____ Apply for any patent, trademark or copyright
_____ Write business plan

PART III

THE BUSINESS PLANNING PROCESS

CHAPTER 2

UNDERSTANDING BUSINESS PLANNING

What is a Business Plan?

When properly prepared and well thought out, a business plan is essentially a management and operating tool. It is often referred to as a "roadmap" to starting and operating a business of any kind. It will clearly define professional and personal goals and objectives regardless of whether you are:

- starting a business;
- borrowing money;
- expanding an existing business;
- purchasing a business or franchise; or
- transferring, selling or closing a business.

Plan

"An orderly arrangement of parts of an overall design or objective"

When completed your business plan should clearly address:

- products and services offered;
- company goals and objectives;
- financial goals and position;
- management team;
- your customer;
- contingency plan;
- measurements for business success; and
- what the future holds for the company.

THE BUSINESS PLANNING PROCESS

Purpose of Writing a Business Plan

The purpose of writing a business plan is two-fold: the first is for internal use by your company to plan, grow, monitor and measure business success. The second is a modified version for external use when seeking funding from an outside source. For either purpose, your business plan will:

1. provide you with a roadmap for working through all the steps necessary to manage and build a successful enterprise;

2. serve as a means for specifying the exact business you are in, the products and services you are providing, and who your customers are and how you will reach them;

3. serve as the "bible" for your business especially when responding to bids and proposals;

4. provide lenders and investors with a detailed plan of your business for the purpose of securing financing; and

5. assist you in setting and attaining goals, maintaining control, monitoring and measuring progress, and planning for the future.

Purpose

"Something set up as an object or end to be attained"

Each stage of development of your business must be carefully planned and realistic goals must be set. Business failure inevitably results when:

1. strategies for operating the business are incorrectly defined;

2. details of implementing business strategies are lacking or unclear;

3. goals and objectives aren't stated in quantifiable terms;

4. no plans exist for mitigating issues or conflicts that arise;

5. commitment of owners and key persons is insufficient;

6. owners and employees don't share a common view or philosophy of the company's purpose, mission or future; or

7. management and employees don't have the requisite expertise or skills to perform at assigned levels of the company, which subsequently takes the operation out of sync.

Why is Business Planning Important: The Journey

To illustrate the importance of writing a business plan, let's look at what it would take to travel by car from coast to coast as an analogy. A prudent person would obviously never embark upon such a long and potentially tedious journey without first devising a plan and determining:

1. **Purpose – Why does the business exist?**
   a. Why does the journey need to happen at all
   b. What is the destination
   c. What is the best route
   d. What happens upon arrival to destination

2. **Timeframe – When will the business start, be sold, close?**
   a. When will the journey begin
   b. How long will it take
   c. When will the journey end

3. **Offering – What will the business offer?**
   a. What are the products/services
   b. What problem(s) does/do products/services solve
   c. How are products/services manufactured or produced
   d. How are products/services promoted and sold

4. **Customer – Who will the business serve?**
   a. Who are the customers
   b. Where are they
   c. Why do they need products/services
   d. How are they currently being served

5. **Tools – What tools, equipment or supplies are needed?**
   a. What is the proper vehicle for taking the journey
   b. What tools, equipment and supplies are needed
   c. How are tools, equipment and supplies utilized

6. **Staff – How is the business staffed and managed?**
   a. Who will be on the journey

THE BUSINESS PLANNING PROCESS

    b. What is their role

    c. What are their qualifications

7. **Finances – How is the business funded?**
    a. How much will the journey cost
    b. Where will the money come from
    c. Is there a budget
    d. What will money be spent on and when

8. **Strategy – What is the plan for the journey?**
    a. Where to stop along the way
    b. When to reroute or make other changes
    c. What to do in an emergency
    d. Plans for safe return or moving forward

9. **Measurements – How do you know the journey was successful?**
    a. What metrics are being measured
    b. What constitutes success

This is exactly what your business plan is intended to do. It will force you to think through every aspect of your business and guide you step by step in accomplishing your goals. The lack of or an inadequate plan can cost you a lot of money, time and energy. Consequently you will quickly find yourself lost and off course.

Writing Your Business Plan

There are many business and management consultants who are very experienced in business plan writing, and for a fee (usually a pretty hefty one) will write your business plan for you. However, understand that while hiring a consultant may sound quite attractive, it may not be as beneficial to the management and success of your business as you might think. This is by means to say that the assistance of outside professionals (e.g., accountants, attorneys, marketers, etc.) is not needed. But you should, at all cost, take charge of writing your business plan.

Researching your market and preparing your business plan yourself can send you well on your way to becoming an expert in your business and its industry. You will not only learn more than you could've ever imagined, but you will also know where pitfalls lie and how to confidently, competently handle and control them.

Why Some Entrepreneurs Don't Write a Business Plan

Some entrepreneurs go into business and ironically are very successful for many years without ever having written a business plan. Others who take that same route are not so fortunate. There are numerous reasons entrepreneurs neglect to write a business plan to include, but not limited, to:

1. not taking the time because they are so immersed in the day-to-day operations of their businesses;

2. lack of expertise or confidence in writing business plans;

3. not wanting to put their ideas in writing for fear someone may take and replicate them;

4. not understanding that the business plan is a valuable tool; and

5. simply putting it off and not making their planning a company priority (e.g., borrowing money or seeking investors).

What Your Business Plan Will Tell You

As the owner, you should know more about your business than anyone else on the planet. Whether you hire a consultant or write it yourself, your completed business plan will tell you specifically and in great detail:

1. what products/services you will offer and at what price;

2. what problems do your products/services solve or what purpose do they serve;

3. how will products/services be manufactured/produced;

4. who your customers are and how you will market to them;

5. what your customers' needs are and how they're currently being met;

6. how your products/services can better meet customer needs;

7. what your manpower needs will be;

8.   what your initial investment should be;

9.   how much money you will need invested or borrowed, how it will be repaid and what will be the return on investment;

10.   whether the company has met sales and performance expectations as planned;

11.   how the business will be scaled;

12.   what new products/services will be introduced and when;

13.   as products/services expand, who will be the new customers;

14.   how will new products/services be priced;

15.   where your business is headed and how it'll get there;

16.   what to do in the event the business needs to be transferred, sold or closed;

17.   what to do in the event of a catastrophe or emergency;

18.   whether this type of business is sustainable;

19.   what metrics will be used to measure success; and

20.   what is considered success.

Remember to take your time and consider all aspects of your business and the related items in this business plan Guide. As stated before, not all issues and items included here will apply to your business, but make sure you give ample consideration to make sure no issue is overlooked.

Now that you understand what a business plan is and does, you're ready to begin the business planning process. **CHAPTER 3, THE ANATOMY OF A BUSINESS PLAN** beginning on page 121 gives you all the components of a business plan and provides sample documents that will help you move ahead. Don't be discouraged about the amount of time it takes to complete any section. Just take your time and research, leaving no stone unturned throughout the process.

THE ANATOMY
OF A
BUSINESS PLAN

Developing Your Business Plan

Now it's time to develop and assemble your business plan. There are many different formats for writing a business plan that can be found in books at the library, bookstore and online. *"The Start of Something BIG: . . ."* is one. In this section, we will cover the various components, including sample documents. But regardless of the format used, your business plan should include, in some form, the following:

- Cover letter (for external use)
- Cover page
- Executive Summary
- Operating Plan
- Marketing Plan
- Management Plan
- Financial Plan
- Strategic (Long Range) Plan
- Succession Plan
- Appendix
- Glossary of Terms

In preparing your business plan, take as much time as necessary to complete. Business planning is a process, so note that it's not unusual to take six months to a year or more to write. The length shouldn't be of primary concern. However, keep in mind that a business plan that appears too short may give the impression that essential information may have been omitted. On the other hand, one that's too long may give the reader the impression that you may be unclear about your business or industry.

THE BUSINESS PLANNING PROCESS

Using this Guide

Responses to questions or statements throughout this Guide should be thorough. Disregard those that are clearly irrelevant to your business or industry. But be as clear and concise as possible. Don't assume your reader (internal or external) knows your business as well as you. Even if that is the case, she/he is primarily interested in seeing how much YOU know. Industry terms that are unique to your business should be included in the Glossary.

Provide statistical data whenever possible. When obtained from a credible source, statistics lend strong support to the narrative portions of your business plan. However, be sure not to overload your business plan with facts and figures that could mean little or nothing to the reader. Some sources of information could include well-known local or national publications, business and trade associations, state and local governmental agencies, chambers of commerce, business development centers, the U.S. Small Business Administration, U.S. Census Bureau, U.S. Department of Commerce, U.S. Department of Defense, trade organizations, and others.

A lender or investor could request some or many of the documents included herein. Other documents such as professional licenses, lease/rental agreements, inventory lists, suppliers lists, franchise agreements, licensing agreements, articles of incorporation, by-laws, quality certifications, current client lists, current or past executed contracts, letters of intent, purchase orders, etc., could also be requested.

Navigating Through the Process

As you begin, you should find yourself moving from section to section. This is because when ideas are put in writing they oftentimes paint a new and completely different picture than what was initially envisioned. So you will need to revise each section until the entire business plan is in sync.

Getting Started

In developing your business plan, we suggest that you start the process using the following easy steps:

STEP 1 Label separate folders as follows:

- Introduction (includes the Executive Summary and Table of Contents)
- Operating Plan
- Marketing Plan
- Management Plan
- Financial Plan
- Strategic (Long Range) Plan
- Succession Plan
- Appendix
- Glossary

STEP 2   Gather all information you have collected about your business and its industry. This includes white papers, reports, magazine or newspaper articles, brochures, samples, etc. Place each document in the applicable folder.

STEP 3   Begin the business planning process.

1. **<u>Operating Plan</u>** – Begin the business planning process with the Operating Plan. This section is needed to provide details of the business you're in, your products/services, and how they are manufactured/produced.

2. **<u>Marketing Plan</u>** – This section should follow the Operating Plan. It'll help you determine how you will promote and sell your products/services, and the marketing and your promotion activities, including social media campaigns.

3. **<u>Management Plan</u>** – Next you will need to determine what your manpower needs will be to perform. Detail how you will staff your operation.

4. **<u>Financial Plan</u>** – You should now have a clear picture of what your business looks like. The next step is to put costs (or projected costs) on all business operations and activities you've identified.

5. **<u>Strategic (Long Range) Plan</u>** – No business will survive without planning for the future in the beginning.

Determine where you think your business will be in the next year, three years and five years.

6. **Succession Plan** – While we don't like to think about the business ceasing to exist, this section will assist in devising and implementing a plan for transferring, selling or liquidating the business if or when it becomes necessary.

7. **Executive Summary** – This portion of the Introduction briefly summarizes every aspect of the business and all information contained within the body of the completed business plan and is prepared last.

8. **Appendix** – This section includes any type of documentation that supports your business plan (e.g., agreements, licenses, corporate documents, studies, articles, etc.).

9. **Introduction** – This includes the cover page, cover letter, executive summary and table of contents. While these documents are placed in the front of the business plan, they are always prepared last.

10. **Glossary** – Include all terms that are unique to your business or industry. Don't assume the terms throughout your business plan are familiar to individuals in your company, bankers or investors. Even if they are familiar, adding a glossary can ensure that all parties understand how each term is used specifically in your business.

11. **Table of Contents** – List and number each section of the business plan. It makes it easy for persons reviewing it to quickly locate their area of interest.

The Finished Document

Once completed, make sure your business plan is free of typographical errors, is constructed in a neat and legible format and all pages are numbered. Also, appearance is as important as content. Hiring a professional word processor is highly recommended. Assign or hire one or more individuals to proofread. Once completed, each copy should be laser printed or copied with the best equipment available then bound before use and distribution.

Even if your business plan was not written for the purpose of borrowing money, you should share it with your banker. This type of interaction will help you establish and build that all-important banker-customer relationship early on. The role of a banker is to assist their clients in assessing their financial needs and meeting their financial goals. They also keep up with market and industry trends, both locally and globally. Further, your banker can provide valuable input and assist you in preparing for the day you will need to borrow.

Update Your Business Plan Regularly

As an internal document, it cannot be overemphasized that business planning is an ongoing process. Updating your business plan regularly is an absolute must if you intend to stay in business and be profitable. One of the biggest mistakes entrepreneurs make in preparing a business plan is neglecting to update or revise it on a regular basis.

Because changes in your business and its industry occur frequently, it's important that your business plan reflects these changes as they affect your business. This includes trends, laws, financial status, technology, management techniques, customer needs, and most important, product/service. In making the update of your business plan a priority, set aside time each month or each quarter and force yourself to make revisions. This practice can easily become a habit and help keep your business organized and your business plan current and relevant.

The Sample Plan

The following section is formatted as an actual business plan. It is only one of many formats that can be effectively used as a template or sample. Understand, the nature of your business will dictate the information that your business plan will contain and how long your business plan will be.

To illustrate each step of the business planning process, we will use the imaginary *CareerTemps* Staffing Agency (CTSA) throughout this Guide. CTSA is described as a start-up (in business less than 1 year), small (under 500 employees) and woman-owned business. It provides temporary staffing to small, medium and large businesses in the metropolitan area of Anycity, Illinois. CTSA currently employs 10 full-time employees and has a database of 250 available employees, 200 of which have been placed. Future plans include expanding operations throughout the Midwest.

The Cover Page

The cover page is a single page used to graphically identify your company. It is the first impression of your company that your reader sees as an introduction to your business and your brand. It should have a neat, clean and professional appearance and let your reader know what the document is and where it's from.

Upon completion of your business plan, the cover page should be printed in color if your logo has any color. It should also be printed on a heavier stock of paper (#80 or heavier card stock) with a mylar cover to protect its contents. The back cover of your business plan should be the same weight of card stock as the front. The back cover need not have any printing, and does not necessarily have to have the mylar back.

Components of the Cover Page

It should include:

1. **Company name** – Spell out your company name completely even if it's more popularly known by its acronym. But it is proper that you include the acronym on the cover page and in your business plan. You never want the name of your company to be confused or unclear to your reader regardless of which format of your company name you choose to use.

2. **Company logo** – Your logo gives your company brand identity. Using your company logo on all company information and documentation keeps your brand in the forefront of all who see or take interest in your business.

3. **Street address or post office box** – Provide the address you want used in sending and receiving your business communications. Make sure your reader understands the best address to send information to you.

4. **Telephone and fax numbers** – Contact phone and fax numbers for the individuals sending and receiving communications regarding your business and your business plan. Make sure your reader understands the best numbers to communicate and send information you.

5. **Website address** – Gives your reader the impression that your company is technologically savvy and offers them the opportunity to look further into your company. Make sure your website is live and the information it contains is current and accurate. Your reader must always be able to locate any information you present to them (that is not private or confidential) on your website.

6. **"Business Plan"** – The two words specifically identify the document as your business plan and alleviates confusion as to what the document is. Letting your reader know that it is a "business plan" signifies that the document is important business information and not just any type of document, and that this information should be safeguarded at all times.

7. **Date prepared** – Give the month and year (use of the day is also appropriate) to show when the document was completed and that it is the latest version. Revisions should occur regularly, so you want your reader to know and you want to be sure, they are receiving the latest edition.

8. **Preparer's name and title** – Give the name and title of the person responding to any questions or comments. Only include the names and titles of the individual(s) who are authorized and can effectively respond to any questions within the business plan.

9. **Protection clause** – This clause alerts readers that the document is proprietary and warns against illegal distribution of your work. This doesn't guarantee that your work will not be given to anyone other than the person you submitted it to, but it will at least let them know you do not want your work distributed.

The use of company letterhead can also be used as your cover page. Just make sure it contains all the elements above. Generally, letterhead has company name, logo, sometimes a motto, phone, fax, address, email and website information in its header and footer. This too is acceptable. However to some, it may not look like a cover.

Exhibit 11 – Cover Page on page 128 is an example of a business plan front cover page. It shows each of the elements listed above. While there is not actually a graphic logo, it does have the company name "*CareerTemps*" large and italicized as its logo.

Exhibit 11 – Cover Page

CareerTemps

Temporary Staffing Agency

111 West Main Street
Anycity, Illinois 69471
Phone: 321-987-7890   Fax: 321-987-7895

Web address: www.xcareersx.com

BUSINESS PLAN
January 20XX

Prepared by

Sally P. Wilson
President & Chief Executive Officer

This business plan is the property of *CareerTemps* Temporary Staffing Agency. It contains confidential and proprietary information, and is not to be reproduced at all or in part. Also, may not be discussed with anyone not authorized by *CareerTemps*, and must be returned upon request.

The Cover Letter of Introduction

The following is a sample cover letter of introduction. It is used when distributing externally to introduce your company and state the purpose and objective of the business plan, especially when seeking financing. Here's where you give the WHO, WHAT, WHEN, WHERE, WHY, HOW and ACTION to be taken regarding your purpose for submitting it. Remember, it's a representation of your company and should give the best first impression.

Components of the Cover Letter of Introduction

The cover letter should be one page in length, always prepared on company letterhead and include the following:

1. **Date** – Use the actual date the letter is to be sent even if it was written prior.

2. **Inside address** – The "WHO." It's imperative that your cover letter be addressed to a specific person. Their name and title should be correct and complete. The worse thing to happen is that your proprietary information be delivered improperly or received by the intended person long after it had been sent.

3. **Full company name** – Spell out the full name of the company unless it's more popularly known by its acronym (e.g., IBM, 3M, etc.). Make sure the company name, street address, suite or room number (if applicable) and the city are complete. It's proper to use the two-letter state abbreviation (e.g., IL for Illinois). And for the fastest delivery, always include the zip code (+4 if known).

4. **Salutation** – Unisex names such as Courtney, Sydney, Terry, or Corey are very common, so be sure that conventional titles (e.g., Mr., Mrs., Ms., Dr., Rev., etc.) are correct. If you're unsure whether the individual is male, female, married or single, it's proper to call the company and simply ask to avoid embarrassment or looking as though you haven't done your homework.

5. **Subject: or RE:** - This is the subject or reference that lets your reader know immediately what the document is. In five words or less, state the purpose.

6.   **Paragraph 1** – In three to five sentences, state your financing objective; the WHAT and WHY about your wants or needs. Be very specific, clear and concise.

7.   **Paragraph 2** – In five sentences or less, explain the WHEN, WHERE and HOW. Tell your reader (probably a lender, investor or lessor) when you need it, where you're going to need it, and how you plan to use it.

8.   **Paragraph 3** – Finally, ACTION. Let your reader know that you will be in contact with them for further discussion or to arrange a date to speak or meet. A good rule of thumb is to give them a week from the day you believe they received the information (approximately 8 to 10 days from the date of mailing).

Be sure to leave the best telephone number or e-mail address for them to reach you or another person if they have questions or comments. Always remember to thank them in advance for their time and consideration.

9.   **Complimentary close** – The most commonly used are "Sincerely,", "With regards," or "Best regards,".

10. **Author and title** – Spell out the author's name completely as they would like to be known and their full title. Exclude the conventional titles, as they are not necessary in the close.

11. **Typist's initials** – If the letter was typed by someone other than the author, their initials should follow the author's initials (capital letters) followed by a colon and the typist's initials in lower case letters.

12. **Enclosure(s)** – You can also use "Attachment(s)" to denote there is/are document(s) accompanying the letter.

Exhibit 12 – Cover Letter of Introduction on page 131 is an example of a cover letter. It contains each of the elements listed above. Make sure your letter is free of typographical errors and reads clearly and distinctly.

Exhibit 12 – Cover Letter of Introduction

CareerTemps
Temporary Staffing Agency

January 2, 20XX

Ms. Ann Jones, Assistant Vice President
1st National Bank of Anycity
Commercial Lending Department
987 Broadway, Suite 1200
Anycity, Illinois 69480

Dear Ms. Jones:

RE: Business Loan Request

    CareerTemps Temporary Staffing Agency (CTSA) is seeking financing in the amount of $75,000.00 (seventy-five thousand dollars). The funds will be used as working capital for a contract recently awarded to CTSA by the Illinois Department of Employment & Training. Enclosed is our business plan detailing our business and use of funds for the project.

    The Notice to Proceed has been issued with a start date of March 1, 20XX and terminating December 31, 20XX. As the employer of record, CTSA will place five (5) clerical persons in the Records Management Department to perform data entry functions using the agency mainframe computer system.

    I will contact your office in the next 10 days to schedule an appointment to meet with you to discuss further. If you should have any questions, please feel free to contact me by phone at 321-987-7890 or via e-mail at swilson@careertemps.com. Thank you in advance for your consideration.

Sincerely,

Sally P. Wilson
President & CEO

SPW:abc
Enclosure

111 West Main Street • Anycity, Illinois 69471
Phone: 321-987-7890 • Fax: 321-987-7895 • www.xcareersx.com

The Table of Contents

The Table of Contents serves to direct the reader to the section of your business plan in which she/he is most interested. It should not be more than two pages in length. However, one page is sufficient. Because many readers depend on a table of contents, make sure all pages are numbered correctly and are exact in the Table of Contents.

Components of the Table of Contents

Make sure all major headings of the business plan are included. It would be appropriate to include subheadings if desired, especially if they're documents listed in the **APPENDIX**. Third level headings are not necessary.

Each document in the Appendix should be listed in order as they appear in the business plan. Be sure the title of each document and page number is listed in the Table of Contents as they are on the document itself. **Exhibit 13 – Table of Contents** on page 133 is an example which includes main and subheadings.

Exhibit 13 – Table of Contents

TABLE OF CONTENTS

Page

Executive Summary.. XX

Operating Plan... XX

Marketing Plan... XX

Management Plan.. XX
- Organizational Chart... XX
- Staffing Plan XX
- Résumé XX

Financial Plan
- Balance Sheet XX
- Income Statement XX
- Cash Flow Analysis XX
- Operating Budget XX
- Estimated Projections & Forecasts Statement.................................... XX

Strategic Plan XX

Succession Plan XX

Appendix... XX
- Document 1 XX
- Document 2 XX
- Document 3 XX
- Document 4 XX
- Document 5 XX
- Document 6 XX

Glossary of Terms XX

The Authorizations Page

Following the Table of Contents is the Authorizations page. It typically accompanies an individually-prepared strategic plan or proposal (solicited or unsolicited). The purpose of the Authorizations page is to demonstrate that the contents and implementation thereof have been approved, and is being supported by the appropriate board of directors, advisory board, executives or other applicable parties.

Components of the Authorizations Page

It should include:

1. **Title of the document** – AUTHORIZATIONS, BUSINESS PLAN AUTHORIZATIONS, etc., or some variation of.

2. **Statement of use** – A brief statement for advising the reader the purpose of the document.

3. **Signature, printed name, title and date lines** – From one to five or required number of persons giving approval for the document.

4. **Notary** – Provide space in the event a notary is required from the individual, organization or institution receiving the document.

Exhibit 14 – Authorizations on page 135 is an example. Depending on the number of authorizations required, the number of signatories will be fewer or greater. Be sure to include notarizations for proposals submitted if required. Notary language can be modified based on signatories and authorities.

Exhibit 14 – Authorizations Page

AUTHORIZATIONS

The following are authorized signatories approving the contents and the implementation of this *(business or strategic)* plan as presented herein:

(1)_____   _____   _____
Signature   Title   Date

_____
Printed name

(2)_____   _____   _____
Signature   Title   Date

_____
Printed name

(3)_____   _____   _____
Signature   Title   Date

_____
Printed name

* * * * * *

NOTARY

I, _____,_____ certify that the names on this instrument have been declared to the undersigned officer as authorized to execute this document.

_____   _____
Signature and title   Date

State of _____   **SUBSCRIBED AND SWORN TO BEFORE ME**

City of _____   This ____ day of _____

Signature of Notary Public _____

Address _____

City _____

State _____

My Commission expires _____

THE BUSINESS PLANNING PROCESS

The Executive Summary

The Executive Summary (sometimes titled the Introduction, Business Description, Statement Purpose, etc.) is used to summarize the details of your business plan. In addition to your mission and vision statements, you may want to include your company's value statement (describes a company's intrinsic value, importance or desirability) and guiding principles (describes what the company views as its rule or code of conduct).

While the Executive Summary is located at the beginning of the business plan, it's always prepared last. This is because its purpose is to summarize all the details contained within the body of your business plan. It should be two to four pages in length, and give the reader a concise synopsis of your business.

If you are seeking outside financing, the Executive Summary should pique the interest of the reader enough to read further, and ultimately finance or invest.

Components of the Executive Summary

Each question should be answered briefly from the information contained in the body of the business plan. In-depth descriptions are not necessary here as they are covered in detail in the body of your business plan. Each section should be one to two paragraphs in length as described below:

1.   **The Business** – Describe the nature of your business and its core competencies. Simply ask yourself, *"What business am I in?"* Briefly describe and/or illustrate your business model. See examples on page 140.

2.   **Mission Statement** – The purpose of a mission statement is to describe your business, commitment, customer and philosophy as it is today.

3.   **Vision Statement** – The purpose of the vision statement is to describe your business, commitment, customer and philosophy as they are projected to be in the future. An example of a vision statement would be:

     "CareerTemps Temporary Staffing Agency" will reach revenues of $2 million by the year 20XX becoming the largest provider of temporary staffing assistance to small, medium and large businesses throughout the Midwest."

4. **Business Objective** – Based on the mission and vision of your company, your objective should state what you would achieve. Your mission and vision statements, as well as core values, should support your objective and only be changed when major changes in your business or industry occur. Describe the company's brand image; how will the company prefers to be most popularly known as or for.

5. **Operating Plan** – Briefly describe each product and service. Discuss how each product/service will be manufactured/produced. Discuss the licensing and certification requirements necessary to operate this type of business.

6. **Marketing Plan** – Discuss your marketing strategy:

    a. *Product* (or service) – Description and unique features
    b. *Price* – What is the selling price of each product/service
    c. *Promotion* – Advertising and other communication methods for bringing your product to market.
    d. *Place* – Demographic and geographic data about your customer and customer needs
    e. *Position* – Market position in the industry
    f. *Process* – How products/services are produced and delivered
    g. *Profit* - How profitable the company is

7. **Management Plan** – This section describes the owners, key persons and employees in your company. Briefly discuss their roles, responsibilities and capabilities.

8. **Financial Plan** – Discuss the initial investment in the company. If seeking financing or investing, describe the type of financing, amount, purpose and use of the funds.

9. **Strategic (Long Range) Plan** – Discuss your view about where the company is and its future. Describe the growth strategies to be employed for expansion or diversification of products or services.

10. **Succession Plan** – Describe how the business will be transferred, sold or liquidated in the event it becomes necessary to do so.

Exhibit 15 – Executive Summary

EXECUTIVE SUMMARY

The Business

What is the name of the business? What is the nature of the business? What are the company's core competencies? How long has the business been in existence? What industry is the business associated? Where is it located? What are the hours of operation?

What is the legal structure (e.g., sole proprietorship, partnership, corporation, etc.)? Is it a new, existing, purchased, or franchise business? If the business was purchased, why was it sold? What are the terms and conditions of the sale? What is the value of the business? How, if applicable, is value calculated?

Describe the business model using text or illustrations. Does the company own any intellectual property? Who owns the intellectual property (e.g., copyrights, patents, trademarks) and what is their ownership interest in each?

Mission Statement

What is the company's mission statement?

Vision Statement

What is the company's vision statement?

Value Statement

What is the company's value statement?

Objective

Discuss the purpose of writing the business plan and what it is intended to accomplish (e.g., starting a business, expanding an existing business, forming a joint venture, borrowing money, etc.).

Operating Plan

What product(s)/service(s) are being offered? What is their purpose/function? Describe the technology and its use in the operations of the business? What role, if any, does the government play in this industry? What, if any, are the licensing/certification requirements for providing each product/service? What risk factors are involved with operating this type of business? What, if any, are the insurance and bonding requirements?

Describe how product(s)/service(s) will be provided. How will operations continue in the event of natural disaster, material or supply shortage? Describe how and what products or services will be offered when or if the market experiences a dramatic decline in demand. What will sustain this business?

Marketing Plan

In what categories are products/services associated? What is the market need? Define your customer (e.g., primary, secondary, tertiary markets). Where are these markets located (e.g., locally, statewide, nationally or internationally)?

Describe current contracting relationships. Describe potential contracting opportunities. Who are the top competitors? Where are they located? Who is their customer?

What advertising or marketing mediums are currently being used? What are the future plans for advertising and marketing? What social media platforms will be used?

Management Plan

Who are the owners and key persons in the company? What role do they play? What contributions have they made to the company (e.g., cash, capital equipment, fixed assets, expertise, etc.)? What are their percentages of ownership? What is the policy for the buyout or selling shares of any owner? How many full- and part-time employees are there? Is there a Board of any kind (e.g., advisory, directors)? What outside professional services will be used? Briefly describe how employees and outside professionals will be compensated.

Financial Plan

How much money was initially invested in the company? How much is needed to accomplish established goals? What is the current value of the business? What method of valuation was used to determine that value?

If applicable, how much money will be borrowed? What type of financing is being sought (debt or equity)? For equity financing, what will be the return to investors? How will the financing contribute to the profitability of the company? What type of collateral will be used to secure the financing? For what will funds be used? What are the plans for repayment?

What were previous years' sales? How were there sales derived? How much revenue was generated from each product/service? What percentage of revenue derived from each product/service?

Strategic Plan

What are the plans for growth and/or expansion? Describe future opportunities in the business and industry. Will new products or services be added, productivity levels increased or both? How soon? Are there plans for franchising in the future? How soon? How will these changes affect manpower and staffing needs?

Succession Plan

Describe how the business will continue in the event of death, disability, divorce, retirement or buyout of the owner(s) or key persons. What insurance and/or buyout provisions have been made for the owner(s) or key person(s)? What are the plans for assigning someone to act as executer? Will it be an owner, other employee or outside entity?

The Operating Plan

The Operating Plan is used to list and describe, in detail, each product/service of your business, their purpose, how and where they will be manufactured/produced, processes and procedures, the facilities used, their distribution, and how all functions of the operation are tracked and reported. This section could include your business model (textual or graphical). Two examples of business models for our fictitious firm *CareerTemps* are shown below:

TEXTUAL/CONCEPTUAL BUSINESS MODEL	GRAPHICAL/ILLUSTRATIVE BUSINESS MODEL
1. CTSA takes a percentage of the hourly wage for employees placed in a position. 2. CTSA charges a finder's fee (flat rate or percentage of employee's annual salary) for employees referred to a company and subsequently hired permanently.	CTSA → Temporary candidate (% hourly wage) → Permanent candidate (% annual salary); Employer

This is tactual portion of the business plan that provides the specifics on the execution of the manufacture/production of all products/services and can identify both operational efficiencies and inefficiencies. The Operating Plan should contain as many pages as necessary to give a clear idea of your company's core competencies. Some or most of the following documents may be included as part of the Operating Plan or in the Appendix:

- location of facilities and the floor plan (overhead view of plant or office where manufacturing or production takes place) of the operations

- technology, equipment or machinery used in the manufacture or production of each product/service

- inventory control systems

- distribution channels

- list of raw materials suppliers, subcontractors and the services they provide

- staffing plan of those who produce products/services

- forms, graphs, charts, flowcharts, specifications, diagrams, schematics, prototype sketches (product design and manufacturing processes and quality certifications)

- brochures, pamphlets, line cards (marketing, promotions and sales materials)

- intellectual property agreements (e.g., approval for use of patents, trademarks and copyrights)

- trade secrets (internal use only)

Intellectual Property

The creations, inventions, literary and artistic works, symbols, images, designs, trade secrets, etc., are the intellectual property (IP) used in business and industry. Your intellectual property is considered an asset of your company and has tremendous value. These assets can be used to secure loans and attract investors once value has been determined. Your Operating Plan should describe any intellectual property in your business. Include the owners of any patent(s), trademark(s), or copyrights.

As part of your **"internal use only"** Operating Plan, you may want to include any trade secrets. A trade secret is defined as a formula, process, compilation of information, or device used in a business that is not published or divulged, and that thereby gives a company a competitive advantage. There are no governmental protections for trade secrets, so be sure that this information is kept tightly under wraps so you won't be in danger of losing one of your most important company assets.

Components of the Operating Plan

Information contained within the Operating Plan includes:

1. **Products/Services** – Describe in detail each product/service in your company and their unique features. How many SKUs (stockkeeping units) are associated with each category of products?

2. **Intellectual property** – Describe any patents, trademarks, copyrights or trade secrets owned by the company. What individual(s) own the intellectual property and what is their percentage ownership?

3. **Business Location** – Provide a physical description where each product/service is manufactured or produced. Whether you operate from a home base or in commercial space, describe the costs and advantages of doing business at that location.

4. **Staffing & Administrative Functions** – Describe the staffing and administrative functions required to facilitate manufacture or production of your products/services. Discuss operating policies and procedures.

5. **Manufacturing & Production** – Discuss each manufacturing or production process. Describe any safety (including UL), governmental and/or environmental issues associated with the manufacture or any product. Describe the type(s) of capital equipment, machinery or fixed assets used. Compile a list as shown in **Exhibit 17 – Fixed Asset Inventory List** on page 146. Describe process controls in manufacturing, inventory, production and quality control. Discuss any alpha or beta testing done.

6. **Management Information Systems (MIS)** – Describe the type(s) of information within the company gathered and what systems and methods are used.

7. **Information Management Systems (IMS)** – Describe how the information is collected, used, analyzed, stored and retrieved.

8. **Product Packaging & Distribution** – Describe, where applicable, how products are packaged and how products and services are delivered.

9. **Expansion & Improvement** – Discuss future plans for expanding and/or improving current product/service line. Discuss product/service process improvement plan.

10. **Operations Metrics** - List and describe the key and specific metrics used to measure and assess the success of each area of operations.

Exhibit 16 – The Operating Plan

OPERATING PLAN

Product(s)/Services(s)

List and describe in detail each product/service? How many SKUs are there? How were products/services ideas conceived? Discuss the purpose of each. Discuss their unique features. How does each product/service compare in quality, feature, design, etc. to the competition? What are the strengths and weaknesses of each product/service? What are the benefits of each product/service? Is there a prototype for each product? If so, what is the current status? What are the plans for expanding the product/service line? What is the industry standard for the manufacture/production of each product/service?

Intellectual Property

Describe the intellectual property for each product/service. This includes all patents, trademarks, copyrights and trade secrets. Who owns them and what is their ownership breakdown? Is there any prior art for products? What is proprietary about the product?

Business Location

Describe the plant or facilities (land and building) and the location in which manufacturing or production takes place. What is the square footage? Can it be expanded when necessary? Why was this location chosen? Are there similar businesses located in this area? If so, describe each. Is this location rented, leased or owned? Are there any lease or purchase options? Is it accessible to foot and/or freeway traffic? Is this location accessible to public transportation (e.g., bus, rail, airport)? Is there ample parking and accommodations for the disabled? Will this location accommodate delivery of equipment and supplies? What is the cost of operating from this location? Are there tax incentives (e.g., HUB zone, rural areas, etc.)?

Staffing & Administrative Functions

What staffing and administrative functions are required for the operation of the business (e.g., management, technical and clerical support)? Is there an administrative manual detailing operations, contract management, bidding, ordering materials and supplies, managing inventory, scheduling, testing, equipment use, personnel, etc.? Describe risk management policies. What is your exposure (e.g., disaster, loss, damage, liability) to equipment, facilities, damaged goods or injuries? What insurance coverage or bonding do you carry?

Manufacturing & Production

For both product- and service-oriented businesses: Who are the principal and alternate suppliers? What do they supply? Where are they located? How are supplies and materials ordered? Discuss uncontrollable factors that can affect manufacturing/production (e.g., economic, legal, social, technological, environmental). Discuss the critical path, if applicable, for project or production completion.

THE BUSINESS PLANNING PROCESS

Discuss process and quality control procedures. Describe the equipment and/or machinery needed. How are equipment and/or machinery serviced or maintained? Compile fixed asset inventory list. Describe, in detail, environmental risk factors associated with operating this type of business. Discuss safety plan. What Occupational Safety & Health Administration (OSHA) regulations govern the manufacturing/production of this type of product/service? How is operational efficiency maintained? Describe, if any, trade secrets your company may have.

For product-oriented businesses: Describe how product(s) will be engineered, manufactured and/or produced. If applicable, have UL (Underwriters Laboratories) Standards being applied to products? Describe production lead times. Are there any capacity constraints in the manufacture of products? Describe each phase of development. What technology is involved? Discuss reliability testing and maintainability. To what quality standards does your company adhere? What quality certifications does your company hold (e.g., ISO, TL)? How, if at all, is Six Sigma applied to your operations? If applicable, for software-related companies, discuss any alpha or beta testing.

What are the peak and slow production seasons? What, if any, are alternate production methods? Discuss production monitoring systems and inventory controls. Discuss any make or buy decision processes.

Discuss handling, storage or obsolescence. What is the shelf life of the finished product? Describe inventory control systems. What is the total number of stockkeeping units (SKUs)? What are the product categories? What inventory pricing method will be used (e.g., first in, first out [FIFO], last in, first out [LIFO], weighted average)?

For service-oriented businesses: Describe in detail each service and the process by which they are performed.

Management Information Systems (MIS)

How are computers used in the day-to-day operations of your business? What platform(s) (e.g., Windows, Apple, mainframe)? What software programs do you use and what version(s)? Describe the use of each software program (e.g., wordprocessing, databases, customer relationship management [CRM], spreadsheets, computer-aided drafting [CAD], presentations, etc.). Describe the methods used for collecting data.

How is system reliability tested and by whom? How are the systems maintained and by whom? What mechanisms are in place to change any process or procedure when necessary? Is there a standard operating plan in place detailing these procedures? Describe, in detail, manual systems(s) used to manage information.

Information Management Systems (IMS)

Describe, in detail, the reported information generated from each program. What is the purpose of each report? What is the reported information expected to tell you about your current operation? How does the reported information influence decision making? What impact is this influence expected to have on current operations? How is reliability of the reported information determined with regard to its accuracy and use? What are the retention times for documentation?

144

Describe, in detail, each of the following processes and the responsible person in each of the following areas. What systems will be used handle each process?

1. Data collection
2. Data input
3. Data classification
4. Data calculation
5. Data analysis
6. Data summary
7. Data storage
8. Data retrieval

Describe, in detail, data security systems in place. Describe who will be authorized to access or share information at each process area and at what level. Describe how reported information is communicated to appropriate persons. How will it be determined how much information or access will any person be granted?

Product Packaging & Distribution

Describe how products will be packaged. Describe product packaging processes. Will packaging be performed in-house or outsourced? Describe the fulfillment process.

Describe delivery and shipping processes (e.g., free on board [FOB], first/second/third/fourth class mail, UPS, express mail, courier, etc.). What are the channels of distribution? What, if any, are the distribution constraints? Discuss turnaround time (e.g., hours, days, weeks).

Expansion & Improvement

Discuss improvement and/or expansion of present products/services. Discuss future uses of current products/services. What is the plan, if any, for product/service diversification? Describe possible new products/services.

How will the operating plan change with product/service expansion and/or improvement (e.g., staffing, equipment, resources, space, etc.)? How will expansion and/or improvement increase the profitability of the company? How much bandwidth will be needed for each area of product expansion?

Operating Metrics

What metrics will be used to measure and assess operations? List and describe each metric used. Why were those metrics used? What does each metric intended to tell you about your operations efforts? How is each metric constructed? What is the output of each metric (e.g., content, dollars, numbers, percentage, rating, etc.)?

What are the success factors? What rationale will be used to determine what success looks like in each metric? How will metrics that are not reaching the level of expectation be handled? How will it be determined that other measurements should be used? At what point will these determinations be made?

Exhibit 17 – Fixed Asset Inventory List

CareerTemps **Temporary Staffing Agency**
20XX Fixed Asset Inventory List

Description	Manufacturer	Model number	Qty.	Date purchased or leased	Total purchase price
Computers	Dell	TC1100	4	01/01/20XX	$2849.00
Printers	Epson	WP-44550	4	01/01/20XX	$1,289.00
Plotter	Canon	Y363-PL	2	01/01/20XX	$600.00
Heat press	Steampro	TR-9863	2	01/01/20XX	$1,010.00
Overhead projector	Optoma	HW-386	1	01/01/20XX	$750.00
Flat-screen TVs	Toshiba	468375AB	3	01/01/20XX	$1,150.00
Storage cabinet	At Work	ST-38681	3	01/01/20XX	$719.00
Refrigerator	Amana	AM-57367	1	01/01/20XX	$450.00
File cabinets	Spectrum	CA-35714	6	01/01/20XX	$1,435.00
Conference table	Square	CO-1687	1	01/01/20XX	$2,500.00
Conference chairs	Morgan	PH-6295	10	01/01/20XX	$1,250.00
Work tables	Finish	PY-06847	2	01/01/20XX	$210.00
Executive desk	Huntington	EX-4825	1	01/01/20XX	$1,500.00
Executive chair	Morgan	PH-5726	1	01/01/20XX	$250.00
Credenza desk	Contemporary	DK-352	4	01/01/20XX	$3,200.00
Desk chair	Stonehenge	CH-330	4	01/01/20XX	$375.00
Waiting room sofa	Burhill	OP-4622	1	01/01/20XX	$425.00
Receptionist area	Marquee	YI-3425	1	01/01/20XX	$1,100.00
Executive office sofa	Thornhurst	GQ-2688	1	01/01/20XX	$550.00
Lunchroom table	Café Fav	BR-59175	2	01/01/20XX	$250.00
Chairs	Vista	GN-2426	4	01/01/20XX	$445.00

Exhibit 18 – Key Operating Metrics

CareerTemps Temporary Staffing Agency
20XX Key Operating Plan Metrics

METRIC	KEY INDICATOR	CONSTRUCTION	INPUT/OUTPUT
Manufacturing/production release of finished products/services	Whether products or services are completed on time	Scheduled order date to scheduled production date to scheduled delivery date	Amount of time taken from order to finish a product or complete a service
Quality improvements	Number of rejects, revisions, returns	Number of times a product/service is rejected, revised, returned / total number approved	Percentage of times required to improve products/services to those approved and accepted
Throughput	Amount of production from each resource (e.g., machine, unit, line, person etc.) over a period of time	Quantity produced by each resource / the total number of resources	Percentage of products/services produced
Delivery times	Whether deliveries are made according to schedule	Scheduled delivery date from the scheduled start date	Number of days deliveries made on time or late
Customer fill rate	Frequency by which customer orders filled to specification and delivered on time	Number of orders filled to specification on time / total number of orders	Percentage of times orders are filled to specification and delivered on time
Incident (accident) count	Lost operation time	Number of incidents per month / number of days of productivity	Percentage of productive days versus unproductive days
Time to resolution	Number of times the same issue is reported	Number of days from time issue is reported to time issue is resolved	Amount of time taken to resolve an issue from time reported
Escalations	Number of times an issue is escalated	Number of levels an issue escalates to before resolution	Level at which an issue has reached at resolution

The Marketing Plan

The Marketing Plan is used to define your marketing strategy. Its purpose is to detail the objectives and tactics necessary to achieve your overall marketing goals. It should also describe, in detail, the market need, the target market, your company's value proposition, the market potential for each product/service, and how and where they be promoted and sold.

A well-prepared marketing plan includes strategies for each of what has been known as the 5 Ps of marketing. Today some marketing experts identify 7 Ps of marketing. They are the metrics by which marketing activities can be measured. They include:

1. **Product** (or service) – what you are selling

2. **Price** – the price of the product/service

3. **Promotion** – how you will promote your product/service

4. **Place** – where and to who you will promote and sell your product/service

5. **Position** – where you are compared to your competition

6. **Process** – how products and services are delivered to customers

7. **Profit** – how profitable your company is

Product/service

Your **PRODUCT/SERVICE** should be determined by taking an "outside-in" approach to business by identifying a need. Simply ask yourself, *"What does the world need?"* Generally speaking, people buy products/services for one or more of the following reasons:

1. to solve a problem;

2. to fulfill a need;

3. to derive pleasure; or

4. for entertainment.

In defining your product/service, present a clear and relevant need and value proposition. Discuss what makes your products or services unique as compared to the competition. Be specific about the products/services you want to provide. Describe the worth and importance of your products/services to potential customers and how you will create a desire for them to purchase from you as opposed to your competitors. You must demonstrate that your product/service will provide the specific solutions each customer seeks.

Pricing

PRICING objectives and policies must be established and guided by your company objectives. Your objectives and policies should explain:

1.   how flexible prices will be;

2.   how does pricing compare to the competition;

3.   price points to be set over the product life cycle;

4.   how transportation (shipping) and delivery costs will be handled;

5.   to whom and when discounts, service charges and allowances be made;

6.   refund and exchange policies; and

7.   giveaways and other promotions.

The simplest pricing method is often based on cost plus a desired mark-up. This is a pricing model that most accountants prefer. The mark-up is expressed as a percentage of the selling price added to the cost. Sometimes mark-ups are a determined standard set by middlemen in a channel by industry.

Whatever pricing method you use, carefully consider what the market will bear. Be sure not to underprice your product/service because that is definitely the formula for going out of business. A good profit margin is somewhere between 40% and 50%. It's not necessary to compete on price if you're offering more value for the going rate. **Use Exhibit 20 – Product & Service Pricing Models** on page 159 to determine what price you should charge your customer.

Once you've established prices for each product/service, you will need to perform a breakeven analysis. This analysis will provide you with sales objectives expressed in dollars or units of production at which your business will break even. This is the point at which your business is neither making a profit nor losing money. The breakeven point can be calculated for a one-product/service company or a multi-product/service company. This critical information gives you

149

a definite target you can plan to reach. **Exhibit 21 – Breakeven Analysis** on page 160 will help you determine at what point your business will be profitable.

Promotion

Once you've identified your target market, you will need to develop a **PROMOTION** strategy to build your brand and company image. This is accomplished via advertising, social media, electronic media, print media or public relations, or networking activities designed to inform, persuade and remind customers about your company and to buy your products/services. In developing promotion strategies and campaigns, determine:

- what needs to be said;

- by whom will it be said;

- to whom it needs to be said ;

- why it needs to be said;

- how it needs to be said; and

- when it needs to be said.

Today, social media is the most popular and cost effective form of promotion. Costs are free or minimal, and regardless of the platform used (e.g., Facebook, Twitter, Instagram, LinkedIn, Pinterest, et al.) millions can be reached instantaneously, worldwide. And for those not embracing social media, email is used as widely by nearly every person in the world. It is understood that social media is not for everyone, but not employing a social media campaign in your business could easily mean lost revenue.

Electronic media consists of paid television and radio advertisements. This is the most expensive form of mass selling. Print media, on the other hand, consists of paid advertisements via newspapers, magazines, external paid newsletters or billboards and is considered less expensive than electronic media. Publicity or public relations are a free form of promotion. It can take the form in either electronically or in print, in-house newsletters, press releases, attending networking events or speaking engagements.

Exhibit 22 – Press Release on page 158 and **Exhibit 24 – Fact Sheet** on page 161 are examples of promotion pieces that will be helpful in spreading the word about your business.

Customer Acquisition

There is always a cost or costs to acquiring new customers. Whether you are using social media, which is for the most part free of charge, there is a cost for the time spent identifying a target market and posting your product/service information. As your business becomes better known and sales increase, you should inevitably acquire more customers. The formula for customer acquisition is:

Cost of sales and marketing expenses at a given time
The number of customers acquired at that time

You will always want to make sure you are prepared when the time comes to acquire more customers. Nothing is worse than having a successful marketing campaign, and being unable to provide the products/services promoted. And understanding what it costs to acquire those customers will let you know whether earning that customer was worth the resources expended. **Exhibit 23 – Customer Acquisition Model** on page 162 will help you determine whether expenditures in any medium were worth the cost for acquiring the customers they attracted.

Always remember that no single promotion strategy works for everyone. Regardless of the medium you use, it need not be expensive. Promotions are ineffective when they don't reflect the product/service for the intended audience. But whatever your campaign strategy entails, all efforts should be well understood by everyone in the company as well as customers.

Place (Target Market)

The **PLACE** should describe where and to whom your products or services will be sold. Whether local (within your city or surrounding areas), regionally (in the Northern, Southern, Eastern or Western regions of the U.S.), nationally (the continental U.S., Alaska, Hawaii and Canada), or internationally (other parts of the world), knowing where your customers live, work or play is important for creating an effective strategy to reach them.

Identifying your target market and knowing its size is critical in developing your advertising and promotion activities. Your customer could be the end user (consumer), government, wholesaler, retailer, manufacturer or distributor. Describe the customer using demographic information (e.g., age, ethnicity, sex, religion, income level, occupation, marital status, education level, lifestyle, sexual orientation, etc.). Or using psychographic information (e.g., personalities, values opinions, attitudes, interests, culture, etc.). When you know whom you're selling to, you can then figure out what and how best to sell to them.

151

Position

Market **POSITION** is described as market share. In order to be successful in business, you must gain market share in your product/service category. Determine the size of the market and how much of the market your company has or intends capture as it compares to your competition. An effective positioning strategy includes knowing your market, proper pricing, and directing promotional activities towards it. The competition could be globally, nationally, regionally or locally. **Exhibit 25 – Market Position & Annual Industry Sales** on page 164 will help you determine your potential market share.

Process

The **PROCESS** by which your products or services are manufactured or produced is directly related to how much you can sell them. Operational efficiency has a direct positive impact on your bottom line. If the costs of producing your products or services are too high, this will affect pricing and in turn, affect sales. The unnecessary waste of time and materials can make your products or services too expensive for you to compete in the market.

Profit

PROFIT is what doing business is all about. It's the way in which business success is measured. Even if sales goals are made or surpassed each year, inefficiencies can cause a company to lose money and ultimately be put out of business. Profitability leads to growth and business continuation. It also makes a company attractive to investors.

Measure and Review

Measuring and reviewing all advertising and promotion activities is a must in tracking and reporting on how well each activity is working. With each advertising and promotion medium, setting goals and monitoring each activity daily, weekly, and at a minimum, monthly will let you know how effective your campaigns are and whether you need to continue, change or discontinue any campaign.

Licensing Agreements

Before you include any trademarked or patented information of other companies in your business plan, make sure you have valid licensing agreements in place. Using the trademark or patent of any brand in your business in any way will result in lawsuits. Include any licensing agreements in the Appendix of your business plan. This also includes any licenses issued to others for the use of your products or brand. Here again you need to make sure you consult with a legal expert that specializes in licensing and licensing agreements.

Service Contracts

Service contracts for repair, maintenance or replacement of a product (or its parts) can serve as a value-add to any sell. For no cost or minimal cost to customers, service contracts can give the assurance that your company will make concessions in the event something goes wrong after a purchase. The Federal Trade Commission (FTC) insists that service contracts be specific in what they cover and what they do not cover, a time frame in which its terms can executed, how and where claims are to be made, and contact information for further assistance. **Exhibit 27 – Service Contract** on page 166 is an example of what a service contract should entail.

Limited Warranty

A limited warranty is a promise that clearly describes what a seller promises about its products. Warranties are not meant to be "the law", however, FTC guidelines insist that warranties are not deceptive or unfair. **Exhibit 28 – Limited Warranty** on page 167 is an example of the information that meets FTC guidelines.

Money Back or Replacement Guarantee

A guarantee is a written assurance that a product/service provided will meet certain specifications. It's typically a pledge that what is stated about the product/service is true and what the remedies will be if the product proves to be defective or faulty, or a service is performed inadequately. **Exhibit 29 – Money Back or Replacement Guarantee** on page 168 is an example.

Marketing Metrics

There was a time when marketing was considered an art. Campaigns were created with virtually no way to determine how effective marketing efforts were. Now with the use of metrics, all marketing efforts can be monitored and measured. But determining what to measure is key. We now use marketing metrics to serve as key performance indicators that let us know which marketing efforts are working, which ones are not and why.

There are literally hundreds of online and offline metrics that can be used for measuring marketing activities. You would practically have to be a financial scholar to understand them all. This is where your financial experts can be invaluable. But just to give you an idea of some of the most significant metrics are, they include, but are not limited to:

Online

1. Website visits

2. Downloads

3. Engagement

4. Subscribers

5. Conversion rates

6. Customer retention

7. Click-throughs

8. Unique landing pages

9. Discount codes

10. Coupons redeemed

11. Abandoned carts

Offline

1. Industry growth/decline statistics

2. New and existing distribution channels

3. Customer acquisition costs

4. Cost of promotion

5. Cost of returns

6. Changing demographics

Exhibit 26 – Key Marketing Metrics on page 165 is a chart that will help you identify, list and describe each marketing metric.

Components of the Marketing Plan

Information contained within the Marketing Plan includes:

1. **Industry Outlook** – Describe the need for your product/service. Discuss the potential future of the industry. Describe the anticipated sales and growth trends for your business as it relates to what's happening in the industry.

2.   **Marketing Objective** – Discuss the value proposition. Describe how the products and services you provide will give you a competitive advantage. Include quantitative (numerical) and qualitative (descriptive) data to support each objective.

3.   **Sales Objective** – Describe how your products/services will be sold and each sales channel. Determine what sales goals your company intends to meet the time frame, and what the sales terms of your products or services will be. Describe any licensing agreements to sell others' products/services.

4.   **Product/Service Pricing** – Describe how products/services are priced for customers (e.g., wholesalers, retailers, end users).

5.   **Advertising & Promotion** – Describe the advertising mediums for your business. Devise a method to measure advertising and promotion response. Describe your company's brand image and strategies to build it. Describe premiums, giveaways or bonuses with each sale.

6.   **Competition** – It's important that you know who and where your competitors are. Describe how they are currently meeting customer needs and at what price.

7.   **Customer Service** – Describe customer relationship management tools used. Describe how customer service issues will be handled and by whom. Describe the methods to be used in measuring customer feedback and satisfaction.

8.   **Measure and Review** – Discuss the process of measuring the effects of your advertising and promotion campaigns.

9.   **Service Contracts** – Discuss service contracts, if any, for products/services and the conditions under which they will be honored.

10. **Warranties or Guarantees** – Describe the terms and conditions, if any, for which warranties or guarantees are offered to customers.

11. **Marketing Metrics** – List and describe the key and specific metric used to measure and assess the success of each marketing campaign or activity.

Exhibit 19 – The Marketing Plan

MARKETING PLAN

Industry Outlook

Provide history and background of the industry (i.e., when and where did industry begin). Include historical data, news releases, clippings etc. How has the industry changed or grown in the past three years? Describe the environment the company functions within (e.g., technology, economic, political, legal, social, cultural). What factors contributed to those changes (e.g., economics, technology, market conditions, government, competition, etc.)? Discuss current trends. How large is the market currently? Is the market in a growth or decline mode? What, if any, are the barriers to entry?

Marketing Objectives

What product/service categories are products/services associated? What are the needs that exist? Discuss your value proposition in fulfilling those needs. Describe current and potential customers (e.g., the end user, government, wholesaler, retailer, manufacturer, distributor). What are your customer demographics (e.g., age, marital status, ethnicity, religion, sex, income level, education level, occupation, lifestyle, etc.)? What are customer psychographics (e.g., personalities, values opinions, attitudes, interests, culture, etc.)?

What methods will be used to research this market (e.g., Internet, libraries, government agencies, trade associations, etc.)? How has products/services been proven in the market? What methods will be used to test this market (e.g., surveys, focus groups, introductory specials, giveaways, etc.)? Discuss the budget for each marketing activity. This includes cost of selling, advertising and promotions.

Sales Objectives

How are products/services sold (e.g., online, retail outlets, direct sales, mail order, sales force, distributors, brokers, EDI, shopping television, strategic alliances, franchising, etc.)? How is sales volume for each product/service broken down (e.g., by region, store, product, salesperson, monthly, quarterly, etc.)?

What are projected sales for the first year? Second year? Third year? Are any of these products/services seasonal? Discuss peak and slow sales periods. Discuss pricing policies for each product/service. Prepare pricing model. Discuss mark-up, gross margins, discounts. What are the actual costs for products/services? Include labor and materials. How does pricing compare to that of the competition? How often are prices increased or decreased? What is the breakeven point?

Are there any licensing agreements in place to sell brand-name products/services of other companies? List each company where licensing has been attained. What are the products/services to carry the license? What is the scope of the agreement? Describe the financial arrangement, length of the agreement, renewal options, restrictions of use, etc.

What is the product/service demand (i.e., how often is each product/service purchased)? What is the size of the market? Where are customers located geographically (locally, regionally, nationally, internationally)? How are their needs currently being met? Why would customers buy this product/service from you? As products/services expand, who will be your future customers? How large is the retail footprint for stocking products in retail space?

Discuss sales terms; is credit offered to customers, checks and credit cards accepted, orders by fax, cash only, deposits, purchase orders, COD, etc.? Discuss back-end sales plans. Discuss collection policies.

Advertising & Promotion

Will advertising and promotion be handled in-house or through an outside agency? How is brand awareness built? What advertising medium will be used (e.g., social media, online ads, email marketing, television, direct mail, radio, magazines, newspaper, classified ads, yellow pages, special events, co-op advertising, coupons, transit, outdoor, etc.)? How much does it cost to acquire each customer? Describe method of measuring advertising response.

What are the social media strategies? Which platforms will be used and how often? Describe the use of each social media platform.

What types of public relations activities will be used (e.g., networking, community events, telemarketing, trade shows, newsletters, press releases, speaking engagements, seminars, personal letters, etc.)? What results are expected? Describe method of measuring public relations response. How much will be budgeted for advertising and promotion?

Competition

Who are your top five competitors? Where are they located? What is their size? What are the annual sales in the industry for these products/services? What percent of the market does each competitor have? What dollar amount does this percentage make up? What advantages and disadvantages do your products/services have over the competition?

Customer Service

How will customer concerns and complaints be handled (e.g., online, by phone, in writing, in person, etc.)? Will a customer service center be established? Who will handle concerns and complaints? Will they be handled during normal business hours only, 24 hours per day, 7 days per week, holidays? Will a toll free number be available or will collect calls be accepted?

What method will be used to evaluate customer service performance (e.g., online surveys, phone surveys, results of customer satisfaction tools, management staff, etc.)? How will customer satisfaction be measured (e.g., analyzing surveys, comment cards, follow-up phone calls, etc.)? Describe customer relationship management tools.

Measures & Review

What documents or systems will be used to measure the effectiveness of the marketing plan (e.g., customer accounts, sales records, warranty claims, ad response, returns, complaints, interviews, business reply cards, etc.)? Who is responsible? How will feedback be handled? How frequently will changes be made?

Service Contracts

Will you offer service contracts on products you provide? What will the contract cover? What is the time frame in which the service contract will be honored? Under what circumstance will service contracts be used, for what products, and at what cost, if any?

Warranties & Guarantees

Will a written warranty or guarantee be offered with products/services? Specifically what parts, repairs or modifications will be covered? Will the warranty cover consequential damage (i.e., damage the product caused)? What conditions will the warranty have (e.g., limitations on personal use as opposed to business use, shipping charges and instructions, repairs to be made by approved dealers, etc.)? What is the warranty time limit? Will there be a labor charge with the warranty? Will there be refunds, exchanges or both under the warranty or guarantee? If so, for how much of the purchase price?

Marketing Metrics

What metrics will be used to measure and assess performance online and offline? List and describe each metric used. Why were those metrics used? What does each metric intended to tell you about your marketing efforts? How is each metric constructed? What is the output of each metric (e.g., content, dollars, numbers, percentage, rating, etc.)?

What are the success factors? What rationale will be used to determine what success looks like in each metric? How will metrics that are not reaching the level of expectation be handled? How will it be determined that other measurements should be used? At what point will these determinations be made?

Exhibit 20 – Product & Service Pricing Models

PRODUCT PRICING MODEL		SERVICE PRICING MODEL	
[1]Cost of goods sold	$4,500.00	[1]Material costs	$5.00
[2]Operating expenses	$13,050.00	[2]Operating expense	$2,000.00
[3]Labor	$14,000.00	[3]Labor (2 hrs. $18.00/hr.)	$36.00
[4]Mark-up percentage 40%	$12,620.00	[4]Mark-up percentage 40%	$816.40
[5]Taxes at 0.75%	$3,312.75	[5]Taxes at 0.75%	$214.31
[6]Selling price	$47,482.75	[6]Total charge	$3,071.71
Unit product price (selling price/number of units)	$31.66 ea.	Unit service price (total charge = price for each service of this type)	

TO CALCULATE PRICING

ASSUMPTION:

A product-oriented business purchasing total of 1500 widgets at $3.00 per unit. After operating expenses, labor, mark-up and taxes, the total price for 1500 widgets is $47,482.75 at a cost of $31.66 each.

CALCULATION:

1. Use the total cost of producing a specified number of units at a specified time (COGS).

2. Add operating expenses (from income statement) for that same time period.

3. Add labor (from income statement for that same time period).

4. Multiply total by desired mark-up percentage.

5. Add applicable sales tax.

6. Result: projected selling price.

ASSUMPTION:

A service-oriented business (calculated operating costs significantly lower than a product-oriented service) providing service to one customer at an hourly rate of $18.00 for a total cost for the service of $3,071.71.

CALCULATION:

1. Use the total cost of materials used in providing each service.

2. Add operating expenses (from income and expense statement) for that project.

3. Add labor.

4. Multiply total by desired mark-up percentage.

5. Add applicable sales tax.

6. Result: projected charge

Exhibit 21 – Breakeven Analysis

Product/Service	Revenue	Fixed Costs	Variable Costs	Breakeven Point
1. Technical support	$15,000.00	$2,000.00	$75.00	7.8 units
2. Clerical support	$25,000.00	$2,000.00	$35.00	12.7 units
3. Sales person	$15,000.00	$2,000.00	$45.00	7.7 units
4. Customer service	$18,000.00	$2,000.00	$22.00	9.1 units
5. Janitorial	$12,000.00	$2,000.00	$20.00	6.1 units

TO CALCULATE BREAKEVEN POINT

Formula: Total fixed costs / Selling price per unit – variable unit cost

Example

1. Product/Service A	$100.00	$24,000.00	$70.00	**800 units**

Using the "Product/Service A" example above, we must figure out how much in product/service must be sold before the costs (fixed and variable) are exactly equal to the revenue (income or sales). The equation looks like this:

$$\$100X = \$24,000 + \$70X$$

To solve using a simple algebraic equation, we must determine the value of "X" (quantity) by subtracting the variable cost ($70) from the revenue ($100). The equation now looks like this:

$$\$30X = \$24,000$$

Finally, we divide the fixed costs ($24,000) by the revenue minus the variable cost ($30) to get the value of "X." The equation now looks like this:

$$X = 800$$

ANALYSIS:
Our computation shows us that in order to 'break even" we must sell 800 units (products or services) priced at $100 each. We can check for accuracy by substituting "800" (the value of "X") in each equation. The next step is to determine:

1. the feasibility of pricing each product/service at this rate;

2. how does this pricing compare to that of competitors; and

3. can this number of sales be met considering current market conditions.

THE ANATOMY OF A BUSINESS PLAN

Exhibit 22 – Press Release

Press Release

CareerTemps
Temporary Staffing Agency

FOR IMMEDIATE RELEASE (Otherwise state time and date)

SUBJECT: Expansion of CareerTemps Temporary Staffing Agency
In Anycity, Illinois

CONTACT: Sally P. Wilson, President & CEO, 321-987-7890

ANYCITY, IL – This is a sample news or press release. It's typed on 8-1/2 by 11 paper with company masthead (or on letterhead). All releases must be typed double spaced, with wide margins. Information contained in a news release should be concise and factual (who, what, where, when, why, how). A fact sheet (see Exhibit 17 on page 89) may be submitted to give the reader supplemental or detailed information.

If the release is only one page in length, 5 pound (# # # # #) signs should appear bottom center of the page. If the release is more than one page in length, the word "more" should be placed bottom center of the first page(s) and # # # # # signs should be placed bottom center of the last page. Under no circumstances should a release be typed on both sides of the page.

# # # # #

Exhibit 23 – Customer Acquisition Model

CareerTemps **Temporary Staffing Agency**
From January 3, 20XX to January 31, 20XX

Advertising & Promotion Medium (1)	Date of Placement/ Event (2)	Cost of Placement (3)	Number of New Customers (4)	Total Sales by Medium (5)	% of Total sales (6)
Anycity Trib ½-page ad	01/03/XX	$350.00	0	$0.00	0.00%
Facebook posts	01/03/XX	$0.00	100	$6,000.00	4.19%
Twitter posts	01/03/XX	$0.00	75	$0.00	0.00%
Website	01/03/XX	$0.00	250	$35,000.00	24.46%
Website blog posts	01/03/XX	$0.00	100	$4,500.00	3.14%
Orland Voice ½-page ad	01/03/XX	$75.00	85	$2,500.00	1.75%
Daily Bugle ½-page ad	01/10/XX	$500.00	45	$2,500.00	1.75%
Job & Business Fair	01/15/XX	$85.00	55	$40,000.00	27.95%
Women's Trade Show	01/22/XX	$200.00	115	$42,000.00	29.35%
Total Trade Show	01/28/XX	$60.00	105	$1,500.00	1.05%
1500 direct mailers	01/28/XX	$875.00	200	$500.00	0.35%
		TOTAL EXPENSE		$143,100.00	

TO MEASURE CUSTOMER ACQUISITION COSTS

1. List each promotion medium or event (e.g., social media, print advertising, direct mail, job fair, trade show, television, radio, etc.)

2. Include the date for each placement or the event.

3. Include the cost of the placement.

4. Include the number of new customers derived from each medium.

5. Calculate the dollar amount of total sales derived from each medium.

6. Divide the cost of the ad placement or event by the total sales.

The total sales derived from all ad placements and events are $143,100.00. You can now see the percentage sales from each ad placement and events make up the total sales for the month of January 20XX.

Exhibit 24 – Fact Sheet

CareerTemps
Temporary Staffing Agency

FACT SHEET

SUBJECT: Expansion of CareerTemps Temporary Staffing Agency
In Anycity, Illinois

A fact sheet is used to provide pertinent detailed information not contained within the news release. It should be printed on 8.5 x 11 paper with company masthead (or letterhead) and should not exceed two pages. Double spacing nor wide margins are necessary, particularly if the fact sheet exceeds one page.

Each fact sheet should contain pertinent details as follows:

BACKGROUND: Describe how the event came about the key persons involved.

HISTORY: Past programs or activities similar in nature.

COMMENTARY: Articles or reports written by other individuals.

STATISTICS: Number of participants, associated dollars, comparison figures.

When possible, provide photographs. They are an indispensable supplement to any news release. This is simply because visuals give what oftentimes cannot be conveyed in words.

Exhibit 25 – Market Position & Annual Industry Sales

Employment Placement Agencies
NAICS Code 561311
(In the Midwest region)

	Competitor Name Location	Location	Sales by Competitor	% Market Share
1.	ABC Staffing	Broadview, Illinois	$3,560,000.00	0.14%
2.	Anycity Employment Agency	Anycity, Illinois	$3,490,000.00	0.14%
3.	Yearlong Staffing	Chebanse, Illinois	$2,445,000.00	0.10%
4.	LMN Staffing & Employment	Iola, Illinois	$2,398,000.00	0.10%
5.	Jobs, Inc.	New Athens, Illinois	$2,365,000.00	0.09%
6.	CareerTemps Staffing Agency	Anycity, Illinois	$199,250.00	0.08%
7.	Remaining competitors	Regional agencies	$2,286,942,000.00	99.0%
		TOTAL REGION	**$2,500,000,000.00**	**100.0%**

TO CALCULATE MARKET POSITION

1. Identify the NAICS code for the temporary employment industry.

2. Locate the annual industry sales for the industry as a whole and the area in which you are doing business. In the example above, annual sales for this industry in a specified area total $2,500,000,000.00.

3. Locate the annual revenue for the top competitors in the area(s) in which you will compete (locally, statewide, regionally, nationally, or globally). For this purpose we'll use the top 6. The number 7 place will be the total remaining competitors.

4. Divide Sales per Competitor by TOTAL REGION to get the market share for each competitor.

ANALYSIS:
The example above shows that ABC temps has a 0.14% market share of the $$2.5 billion the temporary staffing industry made in the selected area in the past year. Knowing the market share of the top competitors will give you an idea of what you will need to capture to compete and the market potential.

Exhibit 26 – Key Marketing Metrics

CareerTemps Temporary Staffing Agency
20XX Key Marketing Plan Metrics

METRIC	KEY INDICATOR	CONSTRUCTION	INPUT/OUTPUT
Customer acquisition cost	Cost to acquiring customers through various means	Amount spent / number of customers added	Dollar amount to acquire the number of customers added
Unique online visitors	Number of new visitors to the website	Number of individuals visiting the website	Number of individuals visiting the website
Page views	Total number of individual pages visitors click on	Pages clicked on	Cumulative number of pages
Bounce rate	Visitors who leave the website before taking any action	Number of times visitors leave the website	Cumulative number of individuals leaving the website
Total conversions	Number of visitors that take some action	Number of visitors / number of visitors who take some action	Amount of sales or the number of actions taken
Conversion rate	Percentage of visitors visiting the site and take some action	Number of visitors / the number of times they take specific actions	Percentage of visitors that take specific actions
Customer retention rate	Number of customers that return and make purchases	Number of customers / the amount of spend or action taken	Calculates the value of customers
Revenue market share	Measure of competitiveness	Sales revenue / total market sales revenue	Percentage of market by a specific entity
Market penetration	Measures popularity of a product or brand	Number of customers purchasing a product / total population	Percentage of the relevant market captured
Unit margin	Difference between selling price and cost	Selling price - cost per unit	Amount remaining after costs are covered

Exhibit 27 – Service Contract

CareerTemps
Temporary Staffing Agency

Service Contract

Customer Information

_____
Name

_____
Address

_____
City, state, zip code

Seller Information

Your company name
Address
City, state, zip code
Phone
Fax number

Description of Purchase(s)

Product _____
Model_____
Serial number _____
Date of purchase _____

Covered Services

Describe in detail each repair and/or maintenance provided for under this contract and not provided for in the warranty. Under what conditions will the service contract cover any product? It may only cover certain parts or specific repairs. Describe specifically each repair and/or maintenance NOT provided for under this contract.

Coverage Terms

What is the time period covered? What is the deductible amount per claim, if any? What is the total cost of the service agreement?

Claims Procedure

Describe in detail the process for making a claim for repair and/or maintenance. Describe, if any, authorizations needed to begin work. Describe process for shipping products for repair, maintenance or replacement if necessary.

Customer Responsibilities

Describe what the customer is required to do. This includes advising customers that they must retain receipts, service contract information, original packaging, serial numbers, etc.

Service Locations

List name, address and phone number for each service location.

For More Information

Provide customer with contact information in the event they need additional issues or have concerns, preferably a toll free number.

Exhibit 28 – Limited Warranty

Limited Warranty

CareerTemps
Temporary Staffing Agency

Customer Information

_____
Name

_____
Address

_____
City, state, zip code

Seller Information

Your company name
Address
City, state, zip code
Website address
Phone number
Fax number

Description of Purchase(s)
Product _____
Model_____
Serial number _____
Date of purchase _____

Warranty Period
What is the time period covered by the warranty?

Products Covered
Specifically what products are covered by the warranty? Under what conditions are they covered? Is the warranty for parts and labor separate?

Products Not Covered
Specifically what products or parts are NOT covered by the warranty?

Your Rights
Do you exclude any obligation for incidental or consequential damages related to the failure of products to function properly under the conditions set forth?

To Obtain Service
List name, address and phone number for each service location.

For More Information
Provide customer with contact information in the event they need additional issues or have concerns, preferably a toll free number.

Exhibit 29 – Money Back or Replacement Guarantee

CareerTemps
Temporary Staffing Agency

Money Back or Replacement Guarantee

Seller Information

Your company name _____   Fax number _____
Address _____   Phone number_____
City, state, zip code _____   Web address _____
E-mail _____

Description of Purchase(s)
Product _____
Model_____
Serial number _____
Date of purchase _____

Guarantee Period
What is the time period covered by the guarantee?

Statement of Guarantee
All our products are carefully manufactured, tested and inspected. We unconditionally guarantee such products against defects in material or workmanship from the date of purchase as follows:

(List and describe products by name and number and include period of time from date of purchase they are guaranteed.)

Products Not Covered
Specifically what products or parts are NOT covered by the guarantee?

Sellers Rights
What, if any, exclusions or obligation for incidental or consequential damages related to the failure of products to function properly?

Remedies
If any item proves defective due to faulty material or workmanship, we will (state what you will do, replace, repair, refund, or other).

To Obtain Service
List name, address and phone number for each service location.

For More Information
Provide customer with contact information in the event they need additional issues or have concerns, preferably a toll free number.

The Management Plan

The Management Plan is a representation of the company's principals, employees, temporary staff, outside professionals, contractors, subcontractors, freelancers, and their backgrounds, responsibilities and capabilities. It is the detailed structure of all the company's human resources, compensation and benefits. As part of your business plan, include résumés, curriculum vitae, or employment/contract agreements for key personnel here or in the Appendix.

If you are just starting out in business, you will need to give serious consideration as to whether it's necessary to hire employees. It may be more cost effective to simply use outside professionals. For permanent hires, however, make sure you are aware of and adhere to federal, state and local employment laws and regulations. That includes avoiding asking questions that cannot be asked legally in the interviewing process or after hiring. But either way, you need to be sure that roles, responsibilities and compensation are clearly defined and disseminated in writing.

Developing hiring and contracting procedures prior to making any hiring or contracting decisions will prove extremely useful. Details can be described in the form of a policies and procedures manual or guide. This type of document will enable your company to follow an orderly and consistent process for recruitment, hiring, contracting and compensation. Details for each hire/contractor in the policies and procedures manual should include, but not be limited, to:

1. The full recruitment process for hiring/contracting.

2. Employer and employee rights and responsibilities as legislated by federal, state and local government agencies.

3. The organizational structure and following the chain of command.

4. Identifying specific roles and responsibilities of each hire/contractor.

5. Compensation and benefits for each hire/contractor.

6. Orientation at the start of the hire/contract and exit interviews at termination of hire/contract

7. Any necessary initial, ongoing or periodic training and/or development for each hire/contractor.

Components of the Management Plan

Information contained within the Management Plan includes:

1. **Personnel** – Describe, in detail, recruitment for hiring/contracting practices. Describe orientation for hires and/or contractors. List and describe each employee and contractor roles and responsibilities. Discuss their qualifications and expertise in the areas they will be performing. Assess their fitness for hire. **Exhibit 33 – Résumé/Curriculum Vitae** on page 178 is an example.

2. **Compensation & Benefits** – Describe how each employee will be compensated. Discuss fringe benefits.

3. **Outside Professional Services** – List and describe the professional services (e.g., outside contractors or subcontractors) for your business. Discuss their role and qualifications. It's important that you select professionals who are skilled in your industry.

4. **Advisory Board/Board of Directors** – An advisory board or board or directors can be very helpful in guiding the direction of your company. Select individuals whose expertise and influence can be leveraged to move your business in the right direction.

5. **Organization Chart** – The organization chart is a graphic depiction of your company. It should show each position and the chain of command. **Exhibit 31 – Organizational Chart** on page 174 is an example.

6. **Staffing Plan Chart** – The organization plan is used to show how your company is staffed by category in a one-year period. **Exhibit 32 – Staffing Plan Chart** on page 176 is an example.

7. **Consultant/Contractor/Subcontractor Agreements** – Consultant, contractor or subcontractor agreements (even freelance) are used to specifically detail the areas of responsibilities, payment terms and duration of assignment for each consultant.

8. **Management Metrics** - List and describe the key and specific metric used to measure and assess the success of each management and hiring activities. In **Exhibit 34 – Key Management Metrics** on page 179 are examples.

Exhibit 30 – The Management Plan

MANAGEMENT PLAN

Personnel

Who are the company's principals, managers, key persons and employees? What positions do they hold? Describe their specific duties and responsibilities. Which departments, employees will each principal, manager or key person or employee be responsible? Describe the applicable experience they have in the industry? Include résumés or curriculum vitae.

Describe hiring practices (e.g., recruitment, orientation, aptitude testing, physicals, drug testing, assessing fitness for hire, background checks, credit checks, security clearances, etc.). How will staffing be affected during slow periods? How will layoffs or furloughs be conducted when necessary? Prepare staffing model. Will employees have union representation? If so, which union(s)?

What level of skill or education is required to manufacture/produce these products/services? What type of training will be available for employees? Discuss employee evaluation procedures and promotions. Will employees be able to cross train for new positions or to stand in in an absence? What performance measures will be used? How often will employee performance evaluations be conducted?

Are there Equal Employment Opportunity (EEO) and Affirmative Action (AA) plans in place? Is an employee handbook available for each employee? Who and how will updates, changes, etc. be made to the handbook? Discuss employee grievance policies. Will grievances be handled in-house or by an independent organization?

Compensation & Benefits

Discuss compensation (e.g., salary, hourly wage, commission, other). Will pay be commensurate with experience or according to industry rates? What, if any, medical, dental, retirement, investment benefits will be offered? Discuss fringe benefits (e.g., vacation, sick leave, personal leave, family leave, short- or long term-disability, etc.). Discuss other incentives (e.g., bonuses, salary increases, auto allowances, higher education allowance, outside training and development, expense account, health club, day care, etc.). How are compensation and benefits determined for each level employee? Describe any separation plan (e.g., severance pay, golden parachutes, etc.).

Outside Professional Services

What outside professional services will be used (e.g., accountants, attorneys, bankers, insurance, business consultants, financial planners, publicists, subcontractors, etc.)? Where are they located? What will the relationship be with the outside services (e.g., consultant, contractor, subcontractor, retainer, full time)? Discuss the details of each contracting agreement, including compensation.

Advisory Board/Board of Directors

Who are the advisory board members (for sole proprietorships or partnerships)? Who are the board of directors (for corporations and not-for-profits)? What are their qualifications? What special talents do they bring to the business? What significant achievements and professional expertise do they each have? What role is each advisor/board member expected to play in the company? What compensation or benefits will each receive? Include résumés/CVs.

Consultant/Contractor/Subcontractor Agreements

Describe the terms and conditions of each consultant/contractor/subcontractor agreement. What are the specific responsibilities? What are the payment terms? What is the duration of the agreement?

Organizational Structure

How is the organization structured? What does the organization look like on an organizational chart? Describe and show the chain of command. Provide a staffing plan to show how the organization is staffed throughout the year.

Management Metrics

What metrics will be used to measure and assess management performance? List and describe each metric used. Why were those metrics used? What does each metric intended to tell you about your management efforts? How is each metric constructed? What is the output of each metric (e.g., content, dollars, numbers, percentage, rating, etc.)?

What are the success factors? What rationale will be used to determine what success looks like in each metric? How will metrics that are not reaching the level of expectation be handled? How will it be determined that other measurements should be used? At what point will these determinations be made?

The Organizational Chart

An organizational chart is used to graphically show relationships of all employees or members of a business or organization. With an organizational chart, you can quickly identify the decision-making authority from the board of directors to line employees.

Even if the legal structure of your business is a sole proprietorship with no employees, an organizational chart can serve to identify the area(s) where one or more consultants perform major functions. If the legal structure of your business is a partnership or corporation, then an organizational chart is even more beneficial in delineating the functions of each employee, consultant, partner or stockholder.

The chain of command in any company/organization can be either vertical or horizontal. The vertical structure is where the organization is a tall structure with a CEO at the top that delegates authority down. With a horizontal chain of command, the organization is flat, meaning there are no middle managers and high-level managers are closely involved in the day-to-day operations of the company.

A typical company/organization depending on its legal structure has the following vertical (top down) structure:

- Board of Directors
- President/Chair
- Vice President/Vice Chair
- Executives
  - o Sales & Marketing
  - o Finance & Accounting
  - o Human Resources
  - o Research & Development
  - o Information Technology
- Division managers
- Department managers
- Department supervisors
- Clerical and technical
- Line employees, union

Exhibit 31 – Organizational Chart on page 174 is an example of an organization with a vertical structure.

Exhibit 31 – Organizational Chart

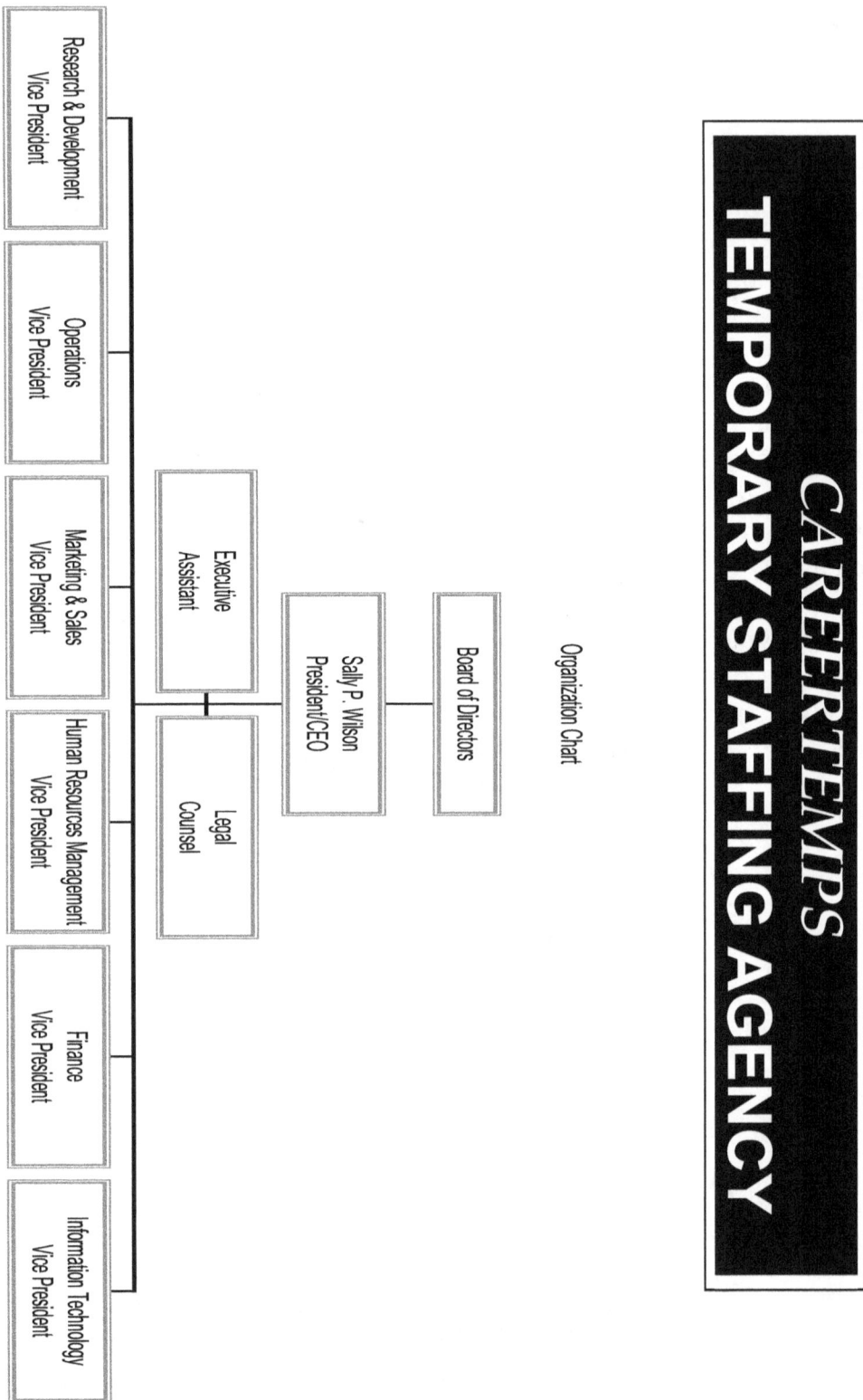

CAREERTEMPS
TEMPORARY STAFFING AGENCY

Organization Chart

- Board of Directors
- Sally P. Wilson President/CEO
  - Executive Assistant
  - Legal Counsel
  - Research & Development Vice President
  - Operations Vice President
  - Marketing & Sales Vice President
  - Human Resources Management Vice President
  - Finance Vice President
  - Information Technology Vice President

The Staffing Plan Chart

A staffing plan is a map outlining staffing requirements for your company at a certain period. It will help you identify and organize your staffing needs. When changes in business occur, staffing must also change. These changes can occur for any of the following reasons:

- Business growth or decline (e.g., seasons, supply, demand)
- New competitors enter the market
- New products enter the market
- Retirement of employees
- Budget restraints requiring layoffs
- Need for a new knowledge or skill

Hiring, promoting or even laying off should always be based on the needs of the company. Developing a staffing plan and strategy for either of these functions is critical in determining which should be done and when.

By creating a staffing plan chart, you can determine what level and the number of employees you will need to meet your company/organization, mission, deliverables and goals at a particular time. **Exhibit 32 – Staffing Plan Chart** on page 176 is an example of a staffing plan chart including position, number of staff needed in each position, whether to use full- or part-time, permanent or temporary, consultants, and the months needed throughout the year.

Once you have determined what your staffing needs will be, you will need to develop the plan. In your plan, include responses to the following, but limited to:

- For what position(s) are you hiring?
- Why is/are the position(s) necessary?
- What is the job description for each hire?
- Who will the hire(s) report to?
- How will the company benefit from the hire(s)?
- Will the position(s) be full-, part-time, temporary or permanent?
- How many hours per week?
- What will be the rate of pay? Annual cost?
- How does this cost affect the company bottom line?

Exhibit 32 – Staffing Plan Chart

Position	Jan	Feb	Mar	Apr	May	Jun	Jul	Aug	Sep	Oct	Nov	Dec	Remarks
			CAREERTEMPS TEMPORARY STAFFING AGENCY STAFFING PLAN For the year 20XX										
Executive	1	1	1	1	1	1	1	1	1	1	1	1	Full time permanent
Management	1	1	1	1	1	1	1	1	1	1	1	1	Full time permanent
Professional	0	0	0	1	0	0	1	0	0	1	1	1	Staffed at quarter end
Technical	1	1	1	1	1	1	1	1	1	1	1	0	Full time permanent
Union/hourly	1	1	1	0	0	0	0	0	0	0	0	0	First quarter only
Clerical/Technical	2	2	2	2	2	2	2	2	2	2	2	2	Full time permanent
TOTAL	6	6	6	6	5	5	6	5	5	6	6	5	

The Résumé/or Curriculum Vitae

The submission of a résumé versus a curriculum vitae (or "CV") to a respective employer is dependent on whom the document is being submitted to. There sometimes may not be a choice. The recipient may specifically request one over the other. In business, CVs are required when submitting a proposal for a professional services contract. On the hand, when hiring for a non-professional position, a résumé is the preferred document.

A résumé is the most familiar of the two document types. It is a concise introduction of your experience and skills relative to the position you are seeking. Therefore, when preparing a résumé, it must change depending on the required qualifications and experience of the position. Also, a typical résumé is usually fewer than three pages in length and generally includes:

- Name and contact information
- Education
- Work history
- References (sometimes upon request)

A CV on the other hand, is a detailed overview of one's life accomplishments, particularly in the world of academia. Because a CV is intended to show a complete work and educational history (relevant and non-relevant), it is usually lengthy, five pages up to double-digit pages and includes:

- Name and contact information
- Summary of accomplishments
- Areas of interest
- Education
- Honors and awards
- Publications and presentations
- Employment and experience
- Scholarly or professional memberships

Exhibit 33 – Résumé/Curriculum Vitae on page 178 is just one example of a résumé and curriculum vitae.

Exhibit 33 – Résumé/Curriculum Vitae

JANE WALKER
222 Amhurst Street
My Town, IL 69478
Phone: 321-789-5543
Email: jwalker@careertemps.com

SUMMARY
Opening statement to include current position, major accomplishments and career objectives. Emphasize contributions to be made to the organization based on related past experience.

EXPERIENCE

Month/Year   Name of company – Department
                    Position held

Individually list only the most relative and significant positions held. Start with the last position held and work backwards. Be sure to cover employment history spanning not more than 10 years. Ignore positions held for less than 6 months, especially those that are unrelated. Include all supervisory tasks and any major responsibilities.

EDUCATION & TRAINING
Name of institution – Graduation date
Degree obtained
Field of study

Start with the highest education or most recent training. Discuss any papers or articles written, research findings, other applicable information regarding studies, training, workshops or seminars attended.

LICENSES & CERTIFICATIONS
List and describe all applicable licenses, permits, registrations and certifications. Include institution(s) where attained, date issued and expiration.

AFFILIATIONS
List each club and/or professional membership organization most applicable to your position or business. List honors, awards or scholarships received.

REFERENCES
Refer to persons in professional positions only. Include name, company, position, address, phone and capacity in which you worked with each person. Reference letters or letters of recommendation should be included here or in the Appendix.

Exhibit 34 – Key Management Metrics

METRIC	KEY INDICATOR	CONSTRUCTION	INPUT/OUTPUT
Productivity	Amount of output per person, per day	Amount of output / number of hours worked for the output	Improvement or decrease in productivity over a period of time
Quality of work	Amount of work accepted versus rejected	Amount of output / the amount of work rejected	Percentage of quality work versus total output
Retention and attrition rate	Amount of turnover in an organization	Number of employees leaving / the number of employees retained over a certain period of time	Percentage of employees retained over a certain period of time
Workforce cost	Amount of money it cost for a workforce over a specific period of time	Total of all workforce-related costs	Dollar amount paid on employee-related issues over a period of time
Compliance	Number of sanctions against a company for non-compliance	Total number of responses to sanctions	The number of sanctions over a period of time
Customer satisfaction	Rating of how customers view employee performance	Use of scorecard with 1 to 5 or 1 to 10 measurements	Overall score of performance based on customer comments
Employee satisfaction	Rating of how employees view their own performance	Use of scorecard with 1 to 5 or 1 to 10 measurements	Overall score of performance based on employee comments

The Financial Plan

The Financial Plan is vital to your business whether or not you're seeking outside financing. It gives you and your potential lenders or investors a clear picture of your company's financial strength. Even in large corporations presidents and board of directors rely heavily on the "bottom line" in their decision making. This is important to note because many of the financial decisions that need to be made by small businesses are similar to that of large businesses.

If finance and accounting aren't one of your strengths, it's critical that you hire a bookkeeper or accountant as early as possible. But whatever choice you make, understanding the principles of bookkeeping and accounting are essential for your business success. This especially holds true in this time of economic uncertainty. Pages 183 to 186 are samples of financial statements most often used in business. **Exhibit 40 – Key Financial Metrics (Terms, Ratios & Formulas)** beginning on page 190 lists and defines key financial terms for use in understanding financial statements and formulas.

Purpose of Financial Planning

Because financial planning takes years of study and practical experience to master, this section was created to simply give you an idea of what it entails. The purpose of financial planning is to aid you in:

1. understanding your company's present and anticipated financial position;

2. making sound financial decisions (e.g., major purchases, hiring additional staff, etc.);

3. creating and managing budgets;

4. determining how much money, if any, you will need to borrow;

5. determining how the money will be used and when it'll be repaid or the return on investment;

6. filing tax returns;

7. passing financial audits;

8.   settling legal matters;

9.   measuring business success for failure; and

10. reporting.

How Financial Planning Begins

The financial planning process begins with a reliable accounting system. The importance of accurately recording all transactions affecting a company's financial position cannot be overemphasized. The major components of every accounting system include:

1.   **Source documents** – original documents, usually a sales slip, invoice, time card or check;

2.   **Journalizing** – the manual or electronic processing of any source document into various journals;

3.   **Posting** – transferring data from the journals to the general ledger; and

4.   **Trial balance** – listing of all accounts, their titles and all debits and credits in the order in which they appear in the general ledger.

Once all transactions have been posted to the general ledger, a trial balance is prepared. From the trial balance, an account balance is taken (i.e., total debits and total credits) which is used to prepare the income statement (profit and loss [P&L]), balance sheet and other financial statements. Closing entries are then made to both the general journal and the trial balance (usually at month end). From there financial statements are interpreted and financial decisions are made.

Establishing a Financial Accounting System

No matter where you do business in the world, there are rules and guidelines that accountants and bookkeepers follow for recording all business transactions. The Financial Accounting Standards Board (FASB www.fasb.org) is the independent body in the U.S. that governs what we call generally accepted accounting principles (GAAP). GAAP (pronounced "gap") is essentially the uniform way in which financial statements are prepared or presented.

When setting up your accounting system, you must determine whether you will use an accrual based or cash based accounting system. With an accrual-based system, a customer could buy your product/service in August, but cash may not exchange hands until September. Even though the sale is made prior to payment, the revenue is recognized upon delivery as opposed to when payment is actually received. With the cash based system, however, revenue is recognized at the time payment is made. For credit card sales, the revenue is recognized when payment is received. Regardless of the type of system you implement (specially-designed or commercially-marketed), it should be tailored to meet the specific needs of your business.

General Accounting/Financial Information

Other general accounting and financial information that's important to know about your company includes:

- How much has been invested in the company by each owner?

- When was/were the investment(s) made?

- What is the percentage ownership for each owner?

- How is the value of the company calculated?

- What was the valuation based on the latest round of investing?

- How much debt is on the company?

Pro Forma Statements

Pro forma financial statements are projected financial statements, information before the fact. In preparing pro forma statements, assumptions and estimates are made based on current and historical business strategies (e.g., marketing, sales, operating, management, etc.) derived from business operations. Financial institutions rely on this information to assess a firm's expected financial situation. These statements provide bankers and investors an idea of what is possible using various scenarios of what could happen in the business under a variety of circumstances (e.g., changes in trends in the industry, changes in products/services, changes in competition, etc.)

Components of the Financial Plan

Documents typically in the Financial Plan include:

1. **Cover letter** – The cover letter simply identifies the financial plan and describes the documents included and the purpose for submission.

2. **Balance Sheet** – Sometimes called the Statement of Financial Condition or Statement of Financial Position, this statement is used to show a company's financial position at a particular date. It's called a "balance" sheet because total assets invested in the business at any time are matched by the sources of these assets. **Exhibit 35 – Balance Sheet** on page 185 is an example.

3. **Income Statement** – Sometimes called the Operating Statement or Profit and Loss Statement (P&L), is used to list revenues and the costs and expenses charged against them for a specific period of time. **Exhibit 36 – Income Statement** on page 186 is an example.

4. **Cash Flow Analysis** – Used to show the changes in assets (especially cash, accounts receivable, inventory and working capital) and liabilities (payables). **Exhibit 37 – Cash Flow Analysis** on page 187 is an example.

5. **Operating Budget** – This statement provides an estimate of sales and expenses for one year. Using historical data, you can project economic trends, inflationary increases and anticipated business changes (e.g., capital expenditures, increases/decreases in staff, production, etc.). **Exhibit 38 – Operating Budget** on page 188 is an example.

6. **Estimated Projections & Forecasts Statement** – This statement uses historical information to project the future. It provides information to predict what could happen under various circumstances. Projections should be made for an entire year. **Exhibit 39 – Estimated Projections & Forecasts Statement** on page 189 is an example.

7. **Assumptions** – This is a supposition that facts or ideas would be true under an arranged set of circumstances. For instance, pro forma (information before the fact) statements are prepared under the assumption that certain planned activities will yield the anticipated result. Some examples of financial assumptions are:

1 – Number of applicants in the database should rise 10% by 2ⁿᵈ quarter 20XX.

2 - Opening of new Fortune 10 company in the area will require 100 temporary warehousing employees.

3 – A local call center is anticipating a need for 25 customer service clerks for the holiday season.

8. **Notes to Financial Statements** – Numbers alone don't always paint a complete picture of a company's financial position. For this reason, accounting notes are prepared to explain, in detail, what the numbers actually mean. For example, notes can state what accounting rules applied to the financial statement or discuss other information not included in the financial statements.

If accounting notes are required, the following statement should be centered at the bottom of each page containing the data for which the notes are written:

"See accompanying accountant's review report and notes to the financial statements."

The Notes page should be formatted in such a way that notes are clearly identified and defined as shown in the following example:

CareerTemps **Temporary Staffing Agency**
Notes to Financial Statements
Year ending December 31, 20XX

Accounts Receivables
Receivables of $150K from top two customers are included in balance sheet, however, will be discounted if paid within 30 days.

Depreciation of Equipment
The calculation for depreciation of new computer lab equipment will be taken using "sum of the year digits."

---

9. **Key Financial Metrics (Terms, Ratios & Formulas)** – Most common terms, ratios and formulas used in financial accounting and in pricing your products or services.

184

Exhibit 35 – Balance Sheet

CAREERTEMPS TEMPORARY STAFFING AGENCY BALANCE SHEET At December 31, 20XX		
ASSETS		
Current assets:		
Cash	$ 45,000.00	
Accounts receivable	$ 12,000.00	
Inventory	$ 3,300.00	
Prepaid expenses	$ 850.00	
Total current assets		$ 61,150.00
Fixed assets:		
Machinery & equipment	$ 12,000.00	
Furniture & fixture	$ 6,000.00	
Less depreciation	$ (1,250.00)	
Total fixed assets		$ 16,750.00
TOTAL ASSETS		**$ 77,900.00**
LIABILITIES & STOCKHOLDERS' EQUITY		
Current liabilities:		
Accounts payable	$ 4,500.00	
Notes payable	$ 3,400.00	
Federal & state taxes payable	$ 2,800.00	
Wages payable	$ 14,000.00	
Loans	$ 6,400.00	
Total current liabilities		$ 31,100.00
Long-term debt	$ 10,000.00	
Total liabilities		$ 10,000.00
Capital:		
Capital/owner's equity/draw	$ 8,500.00	
Retained earnings	$ 28,300.00	
Total capital		$ 36,800.00
TOTAL LIABILITIES & CAPITAL		**$ 77,900.00**

Exhibit 36 – Income Statement

CAREERTEMPS TEMPORARY STAFFING AGENCY INCOME STATEMENT (Pro forma) For the month ending JANUARY 31, 20XX		
REVENUE		
Sales		$50,000
EXPENSES		
Cost of goods sold	$2,600	
Advertising	$1,500	
Depreciation	($575)	
Business insurance	$1,200	
Health insurance	$6,200	
Rent	$2,200	
Salaries	$14,000	
Professional fees	$950	
Supplies	$500	
Utilities	$425	
Miscellaneous expense	$650	
Total Expenses		$29,650
NET INCOME (LOSS)		**$20,350**

Exhibit 37 – Cash Flow Analysis

CAREERTEMPS TEMPORARY STAFFING AGENCY
CASH FLOW ANALYSIS
January 1, 20XX thru December 31, 20XX

	Jan	Feb	Mar	Apr	May	Jun	Jul	Aug	Sep	Oct	Nov	Dec	Total
Beginning balance	$22,000	$42,350	$44,051	$37,024	$32,655	$29,110	$30,134	$35,615	$36,839	$32,324	$26,704	$21,765	$390,571
Projected receipts:													
Cash sales	$22,000	$15,000	$12,000	$16,200	$18,000	$21,650	$25,000	$27,000	$18,000	$15,600	$16,250	$19,825	$226,525
Credit sales	$28,000	$16,000	$9,000	$7,550	$7,235	$12,000	$13,500	$8,500	$6,300	$6,590	$5,500	$4,500	$124,675
Loan proceeds	$0	$0	$0	$0	$0	$0	$0	$0	$0	$0	$0	$0	$0
Other income	$0	$0	$0	$0	$0	$0	$0	$0	$0	$0	$0	$0	$0
Total cash in	$50,000	$31,000	$21,000	$23,750	$25,235	$33,650	$38,500	$35,500	$24,300	$22,190	$21,750	$24,325	$351,200
TOTAL CASH	$72,000	$73,350	$65,051	$60,774	$57,890	$62,760	$68,634	$71,115	$61,139	$54,514	$48,454	$46,090	$741,771
Projected cash payments:													
Raw materials	$2,100	$1,800	$1,250	$965	$1,500	$2,585	$2,245	$3,200	$900	$845	$750	$500	$18,640
Merchandise	$500	$150	$200	$150	$575	$275	$300	$350	$275	$95	$75	$55	$2,500
Administrative salaries	$6,000	$6,000	$6,000	$6,000	$6,000	$6,000	$6,000	$6,000	$6,000	$6,000	$6,000	$6,000	$72,000
Employee salaries	$5,000	$5,000	$5,000	$5,000	$5,000	$5,000	$5,000	$5,000	$5,000	$5,000	$5,000	$5,000	$60,000
Administrative fees	$1,500	$1,500	$1,500	$1,500	$1,500	$2,750	$2,750	$2,750	$1,500	$1,500	$1,500	$1,500	$21,750
Payroll & other taxes	$5,600	$5,600	$5,600	$5,600	$5,600	$6,250	$6,250	$6,250	$5,600	$5,600	$5,600	$5,600	$69,150
Professional fees	$950	$950	$950	$950	$950	$950	$1,025	$1,025	$950	$950	$950	$950	$11,625
Rent	$2,200	$2,200	$2,200	$2,200	$2,200	$2,200	$2,200	$2,200	$2,200	$2,200	$2,200	$2,200	$26,400
Utilities	$425	$352	$325	$124	$432	$322	$345	$434	$213	$121	$341	$123	$3,557
Telephone	$275	$253	$124	$323	$241	$285	$198	$132	$231	$313	$225	$186	$2,786
Advertising	$304	$647	$126	$589	$645	$865	$1,200	$950	$1,189	$653	$452	$395	$8,015
Selling & commission expense	$3,000	$3,000	$3,000	$3,000	$3,000	$3,650	$3,965	$4,500	$3,252	$3,125	$2,150	$2,215	$37,857
Interest	$96	$96	$96	$96	$96	$96	$96	$96	$96	$96	$96	$96	$1,152
Insurance	$1,200	$1,200	$1,200	$1,200	$1,200	$1,200	$1,200	$1,200	$1,200	$1,200	$1,200	$1,200	$14,400
Miscellaneous	$500	$551	$456	$422	$341	$123	$245	$189	$209	$112	$150	$176	$3,474
Total cash out	$29,650	$29,299	$28,027	$28,119	$28,780	$32,626	$33,019	$34,276	$28,815	$27,810	$26,689	$26,196	$353,306
NET CASH INCR (DECR)	$42,350	$44,051	$37,024	$32,655	$29,110	$30,134	$35,615	$36,839	$32,324	$26,704	$21,765	$19,894	$388,465

Exhibit 38 – Operating Budget

CAREERTEMPS TEMPORARY STAFFING AGENCY
OPERATING BUDGET
January 1, 20XX thru December 31, 20XX

	Jan	Feb	Mar	Apr	May	Jun	Jul	Aug	Sep	Oct	Nov	Dec	Total
SALES	$50,000	$50,000	$50,000	$50,000	$50,000	$65,000	$65,000	$65,000	$45,000	$45,000	$45,000	$45,000	$625,000
Cost of Goods Sold:													
Raw materials	$2,100	$2,100	$2,100	$2,100	$2,100	$2,500	$2,500	$2,500	$1,800	$1,800	$1,800	$1,800	$25,200
Direct labor	$5,000	$5,000	$5,000	$5,000	$5,000	$5,300	$5,300	$5,300	$4,500	$4,500	$4,500	$4,500	$58,900
Indirect labor	$6,000	$6,000	$6,000	$6,000	$6,000	$7,500	$7,500	$7,500	$5,500	$5,500	$5,500	$5,500	$74,500
Insurance	$1,500	$1,500	$1,500	$1,500	$1,500	$1,800	$1,800	$1,800	$1,500	$1,500	$1,500	$1,500	$18,900
Payroll & other taxes	$1,500	$1,500	$1,500	$1,500	$1,500	$1,800	$1,800	$1,800	$1,500	$1,500	$1,500	$1,500	$18,900
Depreciation	($600)	($600)	($600)	($600)	($600)	($600)	($600)	($600)	($600)	($600)	($600)	($600)	($7,200)
Total Cost of Goods Sold	$15,500	$15,500	$15,500	$15,500	$15,500	$18,300	$18,300	$18,300	$14,200	$14,200	$14,200	$14,200	$189,200
Gross Profit	$34,500	$34,500	$34,500	$34,500	$34,500	$46,700	$46,700	$46,700	$30,800	$30,800	$30,800	$30,800	$435,800
Operating Expenses:													
General & administrative	$17,000	$17,000	$17,000	$17,000	$17,000	$17,000	$17,000	$17,000	$17,000	$17,000	$17,000	$17,000	$204,000
Salaries & commissions	$3,000	$3,000	$3,000	$3,000	$3,000	$5,000	$5,000	$5,000	$3,000	$3,000	$3,000	$3,000	$42,000
Advertising	$500	$500	$500	$600	$600	$600	$600	$500	$500	$500	$500	$500	$6,400
Interest	$100	$100	$100	$100	$100	$100	$100	$100	$100	$100	$100	$100	$1,200
Miscellaneous expense	$500	$500	$500	$500	$500	$500	$500	$500	$500	$500	$500	$500	$6,000
Total Expenses	$21,100	$21,100	$21,100	$21,200	$21,200	$23,200	$23,200	$23,100	$21,100	$21,100	$21,100	$21,100	$259,600
Net income before taxes	$13,400	$13,400	$13,400	$13,300	$13,300	$23,500	$23,500	$23,600	$9,700	$9,700	$9,700	$9,700	$176,200
Income tax expense	$5,360	$5,360	$5,360	$5,320	$5,320	$9,400	$9,400	$9,440	$3,880	$3,880	$3,880	$3,880	$70,480
Net income	$8,040	$8,040	$8,040	$7,980	$7,980	$14,100	$14,100	$14,160	$5,820	$5,820	$5,820	$5,820	$105,720

Exhibit 39 – Estimated Projections & Forecasts Statement

CAREERTEMPS TEMPORARY STAFFING AGENCY
ESTIMATED PROJECTIONS & FORECASTS STATEMENT
January 1, 20XX thru December 31, 20XX

	Jan	Feb	Mar	Apr	May	Jun	Jul	Aug	Sep	Oct	Nov	Dec	Total
Gross Receipts	$50,000	$50,000	$50,000	$50,000	$50,000	$65,000	$65,000	$65,000	$45,000	$45,000	$45,000	$45,000	$625,000
Merchandise Cost	$2,100	$2,100	$2,100	$2,100	$2,100	$2,500	$2,500	$2,500	$1,800	$1,800	$1,800	$1,800	$25,200
Gross Profit	$47,900	$47,900	$47,900	$47,900	$47,900	$62,500	$62,500	$62,500	$43,200	$43,200	$43,200	$43,200	$599,800
Expenses:													
Salaries	$14,000	$14,000	$14,000	$14,000	$14,000	$17,800	$17,800	$17,800	$13,000	$13,000	$13,000	$13,000	$175,400
Professional fees	$950	$950	$950	$950	$950	$1,025	$1,025	$1,025	$950	$950	$950	$950	$11,625
Advertising	$304	$647	$126	$589	$645	$865	$1,200	$950	$1,189	$653	$452	$395	$8,015
Payroll & other taxes	$5,600	$5,600	$5,600	$5,600	$5,600	$6,250	$6,250	$6,250	$5,600	$5,600	$5,600	$5,600	$69,150
Rent	$2,200	$2,200	$2,200	$2,200	$2,200	$2,200	$2,200	$2,200	$2,200	$2,200	$2,200	$2,200	$26,400
Utilities	$425	$352	$325	$124	$432	$322	$345	$434	$213	$121	$341	$123	$3,557
Telephone	$275	$253	$124	$323	$241	$285	$198	$132	$231	$313	$225	$186	$2,786
Supplies	$500	$551	$456	$422	$341	$123	$245	$189	$209	$112	$150	$176	$3,474
Interest	$96	$96	$96	$96	$96	$96	$96	$96	$96	$96	$96	$96	$1,152
Repayment of loan	$0	$0	$0	$0	$0	$0	$0	$0	$0	$0	$0	$0	$0
Maintenance & repairs	$0	$0	$0	$0	$0	$0	$0	$0	$0	$0	$0	$0	$0
Insurance	$1,200	$1,200	$1,200	$1,200	$1,200	$1,200	$1,200	$1,200	$1,200	$1,200	$1,200	$1,200	$14,400
Miscellaneous*	$500	$551	$456	$422	$341	$123	$245	$189	$209	$112	$150	$176	$3,474
Total	$26,050	$26,400	$25,533	$25,926	$26,046	$30,289	$30,804	$30,465	$25,097	$24,357	$24,364	$24,102	$319,433
Net Profit	$21,850	$21,500	$22,367	$21,974	$21,854	$32,211	$31,696	$32,035	$18,103	$18,843	$18,836	$19,098	$280,367
Less income taxes (at 14%)	$306	$301	$313	$308	$306	$451	$444	$448	$253	$264	$264	$267	$3,925
Net Profit After Taxes	$21,544	$21,199	$22,054	$21,666	$21,548	$31,760	$31,252	$31,587	$17,850	$18,579	$18,572	$18,831	$276,442

*Itemize if numerous

Exhibit 40 – Key Financial Metrics (Terms, Ratios & Formulas)

TERMS & DEFINITIONS	RATIOS & FORMULAS
Accounting Equation *What the company owns is equal to what the company owes plus the owner's equity.*	Assets = Liability + Owner's Equity
Accounts Receivable Aging *Measures the length of time an account receivable has been outstanding divided by the number of days.*	Net accounts receivable / Net sales x 365
Accounts Payable Aging *Measures the length of time an account payable has been outstanding divided by the number of days.*	Net accounts payable / Net sales x 365
Accounts Receivable Turnover *Number of times its takes to turn accounts receivables into cash.*	Credit sale / Average accounts receivables
Average Collection Period *Time required to collect money due.*	Average accounts receivable / Average daily sales
Average Fixed Cost *Fixed costs divided by the number of units produced.*	Fixed costs / Number of units produced
Average Total Cost *Total cost divided by the number of units produced.*	Total cost / Number of units produced
Average Variable Costs *Total variable costs divided by the number of units produced*	Variable costs / Number of units produced
Breakeven Point *Number of sales to be made before costs are covered.*	Total fixed costs / Selling price per unit – variable unit cost
Cash Ratio *Percentage of cash to liabilities.*	Cash / Current liabilities
Conversion Rate *The percentage of visitors who take action.*	Number of visitors / the number of times they take specific actions
Cost of Goods Sold *Total original purchase price of merchandise sold during a fiscal period.*	Beginning merchandise inventory + purchases / Total merchandise available for sale - end merchandise inventory
Current Assets *The sum of assets that will convert to cash in less than 12 months.*	Cash, accounts receivable, inventory, prepaid expenses
Current liabilities *Bills due within 12 months.*	Accounts payable + accrued expenses + current portion of debt + income + taxes payable
Current Ratio *Cash or assets which can be converted into cash within 12 months.*	Current assets / Current liabilities

TERMS & DEFINITIONS	RATIOS & FORMULAS
Debt Ratio *Proportion of total assets provided by the firm's creditors.*	Total liabilities / Total assets
Debt-to-Equity Ratio *The amount of debt being used to finance assets relative to the shareholders' equity.*	Total liabilities / Shareholders' equity
FIFO (First in, First out) *Inventory pricing method.*	Units acquired first, sold first
Fixed costs *Costs that remain regardless of the number of units produced.*	Rent, taxes, salaries
Gross Margin *Amount remaining after cost of goods sold are taken away from net sales.*	Net sales – cost of goods sold
Gross Profit Margin *Percentage of each sales dollar remaining after the firm has paid for its goods.*	Sales – cost of goods sold / Sales
Inventory Turnover *Number of times the average level of inventory is sold.*	Cost of goods sold / Average inventory
LIFO (Last in, First out) *Inventory pricing method.*	Units acquired last, sold first
Marginal Cost *Change in total cost that arises when quantity produced in increased by one unit.*	*Cost of producing each additional unit; indicates the minimum extra revenue that should be generated by each additional unit.*
Mark-up Amount *Percent covering all operating expenses plus providing margin of profit.*	Unit cost **x** mark-up percentage
Net Fixed Assets *Book value of fixed assets.*	Fixed assets at cost – Accumulated depreciation
Net Income *All income less total expenses and costs.*	Income from operations **+** interest income **–** expenses **+** income taxes
Net Loss *Deficit after all expenses are paid.*	(Revenue) – expenses = (net loss)
Net Worth *Capital belonging to the owners as opposed to lenders or others.*	Total assets – total liabilities
Operating Expenses *Expenses paid to develop and sell products/services.*	Sales & marketing **+** research & development **+** general and administrative
Operating Income *Net profit from products or services sold.*	Gross margin – operating expenses

TERMS & DEFINITIONS	RATIOS & FORMULAS
Overhead Rate *Percentage or hourly rate overhead costs are allocated to each product/service.*	Total overhead cost / Total direct labor cost
Quick Ratio/Acid Test Ratio *Showing how much and how quickly can be found.*	Current assets – inventory / Current liabilities
Return on Capital *Net profits computer on the basis of capital in the company instead of sales.*	Net profit / Tangible net worth
Return on Equity *Return earned on the owners' investment.*	Net profits after taxes / Stockholders' equity
Return on Investment *Profits generated with available assets.*	Net profit after taxes / Total assets
Selling Price *Cost of goods sold plus mark-up.*	Unit price + mark-up amount
Shareholders' Equity *Value of the company to its owners. Also call net worth.*	Capital stock + retained earnings
Total Asset Turnover Ratio *Firm's ability to use its assets to generate sales dollars.*	Sales / Total Assets
Total Cost *Sum of total fixed and variable costs for a specific quantity produced.*	Total fixed costs + variable costs
Total Liabilities & Equity *Total liabilities of the company plus worth of the company.*	Current liabilities + long term debt + shareholders' equity
Turnover in Working Capital *Complete replacement of working capital using available funds.*	Net sales / Current assets – current liabilities
Variable Costs *Costs directly related to production.*	Material costs, sales commissions

Key: **/** - Divided by   **X** – Multiplied by   **-** - Minus (or less)   **+** - Added   **=** - Equals

The Strategic Plan

Strategic planning (sometimes interchanged with long range planning, but is not the same) is as crucial for start-ups as is for existing businesses. It focuses specifically on the major direction of the company. Long range planning, on the other hand, is conducted only after strategic planning is completed, and is used simply to carry out prescribed strategies over a set period of time (usually 2 to 5 years).

The purpose of strategic planning is to establish goals and objectives and their priority level necessary for growth, expansion, acquisition, merger and exit. As part of the business planning, strategic planning should be conducted annually, at a minimum. This is particularly important in industries that experience frequent and major change. But if it's for the purpose of developing a new venture, creating a new department or introducing a new product/service, it should be conducted at that specific time.

Considerable time and effort are necessary in preparing a strategic plan. Without taking the time to construct one, you may very well encounter difficulty in growing, expanding or exiting your business and being profitable. Included in the strategic planning process are the organizational goals to be achieved, resources needed to achieve those goals and the funding needed to obtain those resources.

Your strategic plan should focus on every aspect and each independent function and unit of your company. It does, however, begin with taking stock of how the company is structured and managed. A few of these areas include, but not limited to, addressing performance in the following key areas:

- **Company structure**
  - Is the current legal structure functioning well?
  - Should the legal structure be changed?
  - What is the current ownership breakdown?
  - What are the plans to change the ownership in any way?

- **The business**
  - What is the mission of the company?
  - What is the vision of the company?
  - What is the value of the company?
  - How well is the current business model working?
  - What are the company's core competencies?
  - Has the company been profitable in the past few years?
  - Is the company sufficiently capitalized?
  - Are the accounting systems in place working?

- o Is financial reporting done on a monthly basis?
- o Are all taxes paid on time?
- o Are debts paid on time?
- o Does the company maintain a good credit rating?

- **Products/services**
  - o How are current products/services performing?
  - o Are all products/services sales goals met?
  - o Are materials and supplies available when needed?
  - o Are there products/services that are obsolete?
  - o What, if any, are the areas that have sales declines?
  - o Is production up to par?
  - o Are inventory levels sufficient?
  - o What are the plans for adding or deleting products/services?
  - o What process improvement measures are being taken?

- **Company leadership**
  - o How well does the leadership understand the company and its business?
  - o Is the leadership in alignment with every member of the organization?
  - o Does the leadership recognize when operational performance improvements are necessary?
  - o Does leadership take full responsibility and is held accountable for results?
  - o Does the leadership encourage teamwork at all levels?
  - o Are communications vehicles sufficient and in full reach of all employees, customers and other relevant entities?
  - o Is there a level of trust that exists among company leadership and employees?
  - o What vehicle is used to gauge employees' attitudes towards the company, its leadership and their positions?
  - o What process or steps are taken to resolve issues that arise?

- **Company culture**
  - o What is the prevailing culture of the company?
  - o Do employees believe they matter and are cared about?
  - o Do employees believe that the company takes a sincere interest in their families and lives?
  - o Is there an open- or closed-door policy for employees to communicate with management at all levels?
  - o Is the customer or the business the central focus?

- o Are independent ideas, thinking or pursuits encouraged or discouraged?
- o Is "process" strictly adhered to? Is it embraced or challenged?
- o Is change embraced or challenged?
- o In which ways are employees shown appreciation or commended for their good work?
- o How are employee-to-employee "relationships" handled? Are they discouraged?

- **Company environment**
  - o Is the physical location of the company adequate?
  - o Is the working environment clean and organized?
  - o Is the office décor pleasant, comfortable, sufficiently lighted, well furnished, adequately sized, colorful, etc.?
  - o Are employees provided the proper equipment and materials needed to work efficiently and productively?
  - o Is the company concerned with employees' health and well-being?
  - o What are the attitudes of employees towards the company?
  - o What are the attitudes of employees towards management?
  - o Does the company show interest in making the work environment better for employees?
  - o Is there a level of trust that exists among employees with their fellow workers?

- **Employee performance**
  - o Are performance measurements in place to review (and reward) good performance (e.g., scorecard, annual reviews, etc.)?
  - o Are employees given incentives for new ideas, processes or procedures implemented that yield cost savings or improved production?
  - o How are the various units of the company aligned?
  - o Is cross-training encouraged or discouraged throughout the company or in specific areas?
  - o Are employees challenged with projects that can help them expand their skill sets?

- **Retention**
  - o Does the company focus on employee retention?
  - o What incentives are put in place to retain employees?
  - o Does the company have a sense of why employees stay or why employees leave?

o How does the company identify necessary talent when needed?

- **Employee perks**
  - o What types of perks (e.g., free coffee, free snacks, gym, etc.), does the company offer that makes employees feel appreciated?
  - o Are employees allowed to work from home? What is the protocol for working from home?
  - o Are employees offered flexible or staggered work hours?
  - o Does the company offer day care?
  - o Is there unlimited vacation time off for vacation, illness, personal or bereavement?
  - o Are employees offered paid time off for volunteer work (e.g., company sponsored or personal)?
  - o Does the company provide education assistance or training?
  - o Are there nap rooms or quiet space to employees to rest?
  - o Does the company offer gifts (e.g., tickets to ballgames or shows, raffles, dinners, vacation packages, plaques, etc.)?

- **Future of the company**
  - o What are the future plans for the company?
  - o Will it continue? For how long?
  - o Will it be sold, liquidated, merged or acquired or liquidated? When will either of those things happen?
  - o How will the decision be made?
  - o How will either of those situations be handled?
  - o What will happen to the company if necessary changes are not made?
  - o What will be the rewards or consequences of making the necessary changes?

What are Goals and Objectives?

Goals and objectives are the measurements for business success. For clarification, these very important terms used in strategic planning are defined as:

Goal – *the end toward which effort is directed*

Objective – *something toward which effort is directed*

Priority – *Level of importance*

196

Strategic (strategy) – *carefully or methodically planned activity for achieving a result*

Task – *an assigned piece of work to be completed within a certain timeframe*

Project Plan

If the strategic plan is prepared as a separate document for a specific purpose, it should be developed in much the same way as your business plan as a project plan, and contain the following documents:

1. <u>Cover page</u> – Refer to **Exhibit 11 – Cover Page** on page 128.

2. <u>Table of Contents</u> – Refer to **Exhibit 13 – Table of Contents** on page 133.

3. <u>Authorizations page</u> – Refer to **Exhibit 14 – Authorizations** on page 135.

4. <u>Executive Summary</u> – Refer to **Exhibit 15 – Executive Summary** on page 138.

5. <u>Organizational description</u> – Describe the history of the organization, its major products and services, significant events in the industry and accomplishments. Refer to **Exhibit 31 – Organization Chart** on page 174 and **Exhibit 32 – Staffing Plan**, on page 176.

6. <u>Mission, Vision and Value Statements</u> – Refer to **Exhibit 15 – Executive Summary** on page 138.

7. <u>Goals and Objectives</u> – Refer to **Exhibit 42 – Goals & Objectives** on page 209.

8. <u>Appendix</u> – Confidential, specific and detail-oriented information to include:

   a. <u>Action Plan</u> – Specific objectives, assumptions, major activities, responsibilities and timelines;

   b. <u>Description of Process Used</u> – How plan was developed, each participant, meetings held, lessons learned to improve processes in the future;

c. **Internal and External Analyses Data** – Any information compiled from all areas and functions of the company to include statistics, reports, tests, SWOTs, etc.

d. **Goals for Management and Above** – Should be directly aligned with overall company goals and used as a basis to evaluate performance.

e. **Budget Plan** – Use of financial resources and funding needed to achieve strategic goals.

f. **Financial Reports** – Most current balance sheet, income statement, operating budget with estimated expenses and actuals. Refer to the **Financial Plan**, beginning on page 177.

g. **Strategic Implementation Plan** – Criteria for monitoring and measuring implementation of the plan. Refer to **Exhibit 45 – Strategic Implementation Plan** beginning on page 212.

h. **Communications Plan** – Actions for communicating plans and to whom. The types of communications vehicles used and how information will be disseminated

i. **Key Strategic Plan Metrics** - List and describe the key and specific metrics used to measure and assess the success of each area of strategic planning. Refer to **Exhibit 47 – Key Strategic (Long Range) Plan Metrics** on page 214.

How Strategic Planning Begins

The strategic planning process begins by first understanding your business, its industry, where you are and where you want to go. Many companies have the luxury of having long range planning retreats. Top level and other critical persons in the company are invited to off-site locations, usually a hotel resort of some kind. There, they spend several days going through an agenda prepared in advance designed to help them look at the company as it currently exists, then collaborating and working through strategies designed to help grow or improve it.

With a full agenda and other supporting information and supplies, the planning sessions begin by reviewing, developing or updating the mission (or purpose) using the customer's point of view. In other words, your mission statement must reflect your response to customers' needs and wants. Developing a mission will enable you to effectively and efficiently guide your company, focus on key success factors and direct the appropriate resources and energies. It should describe with absolute clarity:

1. the purpose of your business;

2. what the business stands for; and

3. the future goals.

Setting Goals & Objectives

Setting measurable goals and objectives is a critical aspect of the strategic planning process. If you don't have goals or objectives to meet them, you are just moving along without any real direction. In doing so, remember to keep the commonly-known and - used acronym "S. M. A. R. T." at the forefront of the discussion:

S - **Specific** and can invoke action
M - **Measurable** to let you know when your goals have been met
A - **Attainable** steps that will enable you to reach your goal
R - **Relevant** and fits your need
T - **Timeline** for which goal is targeted for completion.

Use **Exhibit 42 – Goals & Objectives** on page 209 to identify goals and objectives.

Identifying Key Results Areas (KRAs)

Prior to setting objectives for meeting goals, each key person or manager must identify his own key results areas. KRAs are defined as highly selected areas of a manager's or key person's job where results must be achieved to be most successful. These areas include, but are not limited to, operations, marketing, human resources, capital resources and profitability. This activity is intended to assist each manager in directing his individual resources that will contribute to the overall success of the company. **Exhibit 43 – Key Results Areas** on page 210 will be helpful.

Problem Solving to Reach Goals

Inevitably problems will arise during the course of business. It's not necessarily because of poor planning or no planning at all. Sometimes issues arise that are beyond the control of the business owner. Legislative, environmental, material shortages, problems with suppliers, etc. are just a few reasons why things go wrong. Problem-solving skills are a vital skill set for business owners to get back on track after issues arise.

Here are just a few steps for problem solving:

1. **Identify the specific problem.** Be sure the problem is clear and understood. The only way to solve a problem is to understand exactly what it really is.

2. **Assemble the appropriate persons to help provide solutions.** Solicit input from all relevant parties so that every option in resolving issues can be considered and all available resources are employed.

3. **Settle on a mutually-agreed upon solution.** The more input and buy-in from the relevant parties, the more likely a solution can be found.

4. **Implement the solution.** Not everything that works in theory works in fact. So whatever the outcome of the planning is, it must be implemented.

5. **Review, measure and revise.** Once the new process is in place, it must be reviewed, measured for effectiveness and then revised if necessary.

Knowing that problems will always occur (hopefully less often than so), there always needs to be a process in place to mitigate them as they occur and devise a plan to ensure they don't recur. Obviously some issues will require more time to resolve than other issues, but the basic steps for resolution are outlined above. These are the initial steps for resolving any issue at any time.

Embracing challenges is also a means of resolving them. It's difficult to face challenges head on, but the way they get resolved is to do exactly that. So often problems look much bigger and greater than they actually are. Once you have decided that you are confronted with an issue that could potentially destroy or at least derail your business, figuring out how to solve the problem will keep you moving forward. The old adage, "you only fail if you quit" is a very valid statement.

As you continue to work towards a resolution to any problem that may arise in your business, you should not consider this a defeat. Even if a problem is the result of a bad decision made by you or top-level people in your company, it's not the end of the world. But when it happens, you should immediately:

1. Take ownership of the problem.

2. Be transparent about what happened and your role.

3. Apologize for your mistake.

4. Take whatever criticism that is given.

5. Devise and implement a plan to mitigate any damages.

6. Employ all necessary resources available.

7. Move forward.

Strengths, Weaknesses, Opportunities or Threats (SWOTs)

A clear understanding of strengths, weaknesses, opportunities or threats is essential to capitalize on new directions or new opportunities when they present themselves. It will also signify your company's ability to compete in whatever environment it exists. Not even Fortune 500 companies function perfectly at all times. And as a small business owner, you are not expected to be any different.

Use **Exhibit 44 – Strengths, Weaknesses, Opportunities & Threats** on page 211 to identify each SWOT.

Components of the Strategic Plan

Information contained within the Strategic Plan includes:

1. **Analyzing Current Situation** – Internal & External Factors – Each owner or key person must examine and prepare a written analysis of both internal and external factors that have or could have a significant impact on the company. This information will be used to develop the overall strategic plan.

2. **Planning Session Preparation** – If possible, secure an offsite meeting location that would be conducive to uninterrupted and relaxed brainstorming, reflection and problem solving. The room should be properly stocked with equipment and supplies. Participants should include representatives from key areas of your company, and where necessary, outside professionals.

3. **The Planning Session** – Begin by first reviewing the mission and vision of the company to determine whether everyone is in agreement with the company's intended mission or purpose. This should be followed up with identifying goals and objectives, key results areas, SWOTs, and the implementation (tactical objectives).

4. **Contingency Planning** – Decide early on the "what ifs" and map out a detailed plan so you will be ready in the event something goes wrong (e.g., personal or family tragedy, illness, disability, withdrawal of an owner or key employee, lawsuits, buy-outs, takeovers, unavailability of materials or supplies, increase in competition, customer decline, etc.).

5. **Integration of Budgeting into the Strategic Plan** – Create a budget allocating the funds required to carry out strategies. Refer to **Exhibit 38 – Operating Budget** on page 188.

6. **Business Plan Coordination** – Update the business plan in accordance with the newly-created goals.

7. **Strategic Implementation Plan** – Steps taken to carry out all strategies and individuals responsible. **Exhibit 45 – Strategic Implementation Plan** on page 212 will be helpful.

8. **Status Report** – **Exhibit 46 – Status Report** on page 213 will help you evaluate the progress of each responsible person to ensure that targets are met and if not, provide a heads up so that issues can be mitigated at the earliest possible time.

9. **Strategic (Long Range) Planning Metrics** - List and describe the key and specific metrics used to measure and assess the success of each area of strategic planning. Refer to **Exhibit 47 – Key Strategic (Long Range) Plan Metrics** on page 214.

Exhibit 41 – Strategic Plan

ANALYZING CURRENT SITUATION

Internal and External Factors

Describe the current state, use, changes, associated risk factors, effectiveness or value in each of the following areas. Discuss the impact of political, technological, geographical, social, environmental and economic events on a local, regional, national or global level as applicable.

1. The Business
    - Mission, vision and value statements
    - Nature of the business from the original plan
    - The business model
    - Entrance strategy
    - Company name
    - Business location(s)
    - Legal structure
    - Insurance coverage
    - Quality certifications
    - Business and/or professional licensing
    - Risk assessments

2. Operations
    - Each product/service
    - Manufacturing or production facilities
    - Administrative functions
    - Use of technology
    - Manufacturing and production processes
    - Process improvements
    - Economies of scale
    - Equipment, machinery and supplies
    - Research and development
    - Management information systems
    - Information management systems
    - Product packaging and delivery
    - Expansion and improvement
    - Warranties and guarantees
    - Franchising the business

3. Marketing
    - Industry outlook
    - Brand image
    - Social media
    - Customer needs

- Sales objectives
- Advertising and promotion
- Competition
- Customer service
- Customer relationship management
- Service contracts
- Use of technology

4. Management
   - Leadership
   - Personnel
   - Company culture
   - Compensation and fringe benefits
   - Retirement planning
   - Outside professional services
   - Advisory board/board of directors
   - Consulting services
   - Contracts and agreements
   - Use of technology

5. Finance and Accounting
   - Financial management
   - Budgets
   - Capital spending
   - Projections
   - Taxes
   - Financial statements
   - Audits
   - Use of technology

6. Strategic and Long Range Plan
   - Internal and external factors
   - Defining/redefining mission and vision
   - Contingency plan
   - Integrating budgets into strategic plan
   - Business plan coordination
   - Implementation
   - Monitoring and measuring progress
   - Use of technology
   - Exit strategy

7. Succession
   - Goals and objectives
   - Consulting with professionals
   - Compensation of owners/key persons

- Training and development of successors
- Training and development options
- Transfer of ownership
- Business continuation
- Use of technology

PLANNING SESSION PREPARATION

Organizing Strategic Planning Sessions

Strategic planning is most successful when it's a participative process. Therefore, it's essential that all critical areas of the company be represented. This way each area can contribute and will be more likely to "buy in" to the goals ultimately set.

1. Organize a meeting with key persons within and without the company who represent each key area.

    - Owners, officers, key personnel, outside professionals, consultants
    - Operations
    - Marketing
    - Human Resources
    - Finance
    - Legal

2. Choose an off-site location (hotel or resort) for approximately two days that's free from distractions and interruptions, and where meals (breakfast and/or lunch) can be brought in each day.

3. Structure the meeting in advance by:

    - Establishing guidelines where creativity is encouraged and participants will understand that no idea will be immediately discarded as impractical or undesirable.

    - Preparing an agenda for each day of the session to include:

        o Title of the session
        o Dates and times
        o Location
        o Each topic to be covered
        o Person responsible for each topic

    - Appointing a facilitator who will be impartial enough to see potential merit in the ideas of others.

    - Setting up the room in a format most conducive to interacting (e.g., classroom style, theatre style, rounds of 10, etc.), and making sure it is a comfortable temperature (70 degrees seems comfortable for most).

THE BUSINESS PLANNING PROCESS

- Equipping the room with necessary equipment supplies to include, but not limited to:

  o Laptop computer with spreadsheet, database, presentation and word processing software
  o LCD or overhead projector
  o DVD (or VCR) and television monitor
  o Conference or speaker phone
  o White board
  o Video or still camera, if appropriate
  o Felt and dry erase markers
  o Easel and flip charts
  o Writing instruments
  o Note pads, scratch paper, sticky notes
  o Masking tape, cellophane tape, thumb tacks
  o Copy machine
  o Refreshments, water, pastries
  o Lunch
  o Afternoon snacks

THE PLANNING SESSION

Mission, Vision and Value Statements

Establish or revisit your mission, vision and, if applicable, value statements. Why does the company exist? What are the company's core competencies? What are the products and services offered? Who are the customers served? What geographic territory is covered?

Setting Goals and Objectives

Always remember the "S.M.A.R.T." acronym when setting goals. Give a specific description of each goal (e.g., reduce production times by "x" days, eliminate or increase products by "x" number, increase services revenue 30%). What is the priority of each goal? What objectives would accomplish these goals? Describe each task for meeting each objective. Discuss the assumptions for which each objective is based (e.g., improved industry growth trends, less competition, etc.).

What will be the measurable targeted result for each (e.g., cost or percentage savings or increase in defect elimination, reduction in production time)? How do these goals and objectives fit the company's overall mission? What strategies will be employed to meet these goals? What are the deadlines or timeframes for accomplishing each goal? What measure is used to determine when it's time to grow? What performance metrics are used to determine whether goals have been met?

Key Results Areas (KRAs)

What are key results areas (KRAs) for each manager? What are the primary objectives needed to be met? What role will each key person or manager play in meeting objectives? What strategies must be employed to reach stated objectives? What resources are needed? How will new strategies change risk exposure in each area? How can processes be improved? How will new processes improve performance?

<u>Strengths, Weaknesses, Opportunities & Threats (SWOTs)</u>

Using the key results areas prepared by each participant, identify each SWOT. You will want to discuss the impact on the following in each item listed as they relate to:

1. Improving the company's financial position;

2. Capitalizing on emerging trends in the industry;

3. Improved technology in the manufacture or production of products and services;

4. Improved information and equipment technology;

5. Implement and improve on social media presence using marketing campaigns;

6. Develop a more robust website

7. Keeping pace with the competition;

8. Improving supplier relationships (supply chain management);

9. Customer relationship management (CRM); and

10. Improving internal and external communications

<u>Tactical Objectives</u>

In each of the areas, determine what tactical objectives must be established to support each strategy. What are the priorities for employing each tactic? Who is the responsible person? What is the process for meeting each tactical objective? What are the target dates for completion? How will success be measured?

CONTINGENCY PLAN

What events would necessitate deviation from the original plan (e.g., natural disaster, withdrawal of key person, etc.)? At what point will there be a deviation in the plan? What steps will be taken if goals and objectives are not achieved according to the specified timelines? What is the process for revising stated goals, objectives and timelines? Will priorities be changed to ensure goals are achieved? What corrective actions will be put in place for each objective in the event it can't be met?

INTEGRATING BUDGET INTO STRATEGIC PLAN

Each manager should provide an estimate of expected revenue, costs, expenses, rates of return or capital required to meet objectives. A consolidated budget is then prepared. Review **Exhibit 38 -**

THE BUSINESS PLANNING PROCESS

Operating Budget on page 188. Once the budget is approved, resources are allocated and made available at the targeted dates.

BUSINESS PLAN COORDINATION

Who will be responsible for coordinating the update of the business plan? What key persons or managers will be responsible for submitting information? What type of information will be collected (internal and external)? How will information be collected? In what format will information be requested? What will be the target date for submission? What will the review process entail? How will the details of the final document be communicated?

STRATEGIC IMPLEMENTATION PLAN

Who will be involved in the implementation of the plan? What will be their roles and responsibilities? Will there be an action plan developed to guide the implementation? Who will develop and monitor it? How often will the action plan be reviewed to ensure all activities are being performed as expected? Discuss the schedule of activities. How will feedback be handled? How will implementation progress be communicated?

MONITORING & MEASURING PROGRESS

What performance metrics and success indicators will be used to determine whether objectives have been met? What measures will be put in place for each manager to ensure objectives are met? What are the early warning signs that will show whether objectives are on target? How will results and progress be reported? How often will feedback be requested? Has a scorecard been developed to measure performance?

STATUS REPORT

List each objective. Who is the responsible person? What is the current status of each objective? Is this objective in line to be completed as planned? If not, why? What is the revised estimated time of completion? What changes need to be made to ensure that revised completion dates can be made? What changes in resources or activities would be necessary for completion?

STRATEGIC (LONG RANGE) PLANNING METRICS

What metrics will be used to measure and assess goals and objectives? List and describe each metric used. Why were those metrics used? What does each metric intended to tell you about your strategic planning efforts? How is each metric constructed? What is the output of each metric (e.g., content, dollars, numbers, percentage, rating, etc.)?

What are the success factors? What rationale will be used to determine what success looks like in each metric? How will metrics that are not reaching the level of expectation be handled? How will it be determined that other measurements should be used? At what point will these determinations be made?

Exhibit 42 – Goals & Objectives

CareerTemps **Temporary Staffing Agency**
20XX Goals and Objectives

Goals	Objectives	Assumptions	Strategy	Tactics
Rank 3 or higher in revenue for staffing agencies in region by year end 20XX	Incrementally increase sales 10% each quarter for the year 20XX by attracting applicants in the fields of technology, medical and education.	Economy is in a recovery mode including the jobs market. Employers in the region are using more temporary staffing.	Secure mid- to large-sized business accounts to provide temporary staffing in the fields of technology, medicine and education.	• Contact human resources in local mid- to large-sized businesses in the region • Create a specific presentation for HR managers
Build a social media following of 10,000 on both Facebook and Twitter platforms by year end 20XX	Open Facebook and Twitter social media accounts in 1st quarter 20XX	Social media is the best platform for communicating and doing business today.	Use social media to drive traffic to the CTSA website and sign up new applicants	• Open social media accounts • Post at least 2 times per week • Respond to posts daily
Place 100 job seekers in technical positions each quarter for the year 20XX	Promote available technology positions throughout region for job seekers	There is a need for technology experts in the region due to the arrival of new businesses opening.	Develop new promotion campaign specifically for technology, medical and education	• Place ads in local papers • Attend job fairs and business fairs • Create new solicitations on website
Secure at least 5 staffing contracts per quarter with regional corporations to meet temporary staffing needs	Hire sales 3 sales associates to secure new business	A sales force needed to focus on securing new business could assist with identifying the needs in the.	Develop a sales force to focus on securing contracts with mid- to large-sized businesses.	• Develop solicitation to hire sales team • Interview applicants • Hire and train
Upgrade website to accept job applications by 20XX	Develop the CTSA website to make more robust for application processing	Job searches have become more sophisticated. More job seekers are applying online.	Work with web developer to enhance website by adding more features.	• Identify all new needed features • Develop online application • Train staff to access and process applications

Exhibit 43 – Key Results Areas (KRAs)

**CareerTemps Temporary Staffing Agency
20XX Key Results Areas**

Key Results Area	Job Responsibilities	Responsible Person(s)
Incrementally increase sales 10% each quarter for the year 20XX	• Develop new business through sales force • Develop new business through website • Manage marketing efforts to solicit applicants	Human Resources Manager
Open Facebook and Twitter social media accounts in 1st quarter 20XX	• Open Facebook and Twitter accounts • Post to Facebook at least 3 times per week • Post to Twitter at least 1 hour per day	Information Technology Manager
Promote technology positions throughout region for job seekers	• Attend regional job fairs • Create new social media campaigns targeting technology, medical and education applicants • Place ads in local newspapers soliciting applicants	Business Development Manager Social Media Manager
Hire sales 3 sales associates to secure new business	• Develop new campaigns targeting mid- to large-sized businesses in the region • Develop a sales strategy for those businesses • Establish relationships to secure contract for staffing	Business Development Manager
Upgrade website for applicants to apply online and receive information on interviewing techniques, hiring practices, resume writing	• Add new features to website • Design online application • Create new helpful information and training materials for job seekers • Train staff on accessing and uploading information	Human Resources Manager Information Technology Manager

Exhibit 44 – Strengths, Weaknesses, Opportunities & Threats (SWOTs)

CareerTemps Temporary Staffing Agency
20XX Strengths, Weaknesses, Opportunities or Threats

Present		Future	
Strengths	Weaknesses	Opportunities	Threats
CTSA is the 6th largest staffing agency in the region	There are 5 agencies that are more established	Job seekers are looking for something new and different, particularly if they have used the more established agencies	The businesses in the region are loyal to the more established agencies
CTSA has office space conducive to providing training and other resources for job seekers	Cost for commercial space is high. To grow the training and resources of the agency, more space is needed.	Economy in a steady recovery mode. CTSA has an opportunity to increase revenue and develop strategy for acquiring more space	Space may not be available at current location. Building is currently at 60% capacity.
CTSA staff are experienced in growth industries in the region (e.g., technology, medical, education)	Job seekers have several options of agencies with experience in the region	Employers are beginning to a hire a large number of temporary staff	The larger staffing agencies also have staff experience in the same growth industries
CTSA has developed state-of-the-art materials and resources job seekers can access to upgrade their current skills and learn new skills	Training can only be conducted with 10 job seekers at a time because of the limited number of computers and space	CTSA has copyrighted materials that are a step ahead of the competition	Competitors can replicate if they are made aware of the materials
CTSA currently has 500 applicants in the database ready, willing and able to take an assignment	Only 65% of the available workers are experienced in the high growth areas	With the new companies coming to the region, CTSA has enough applicants to fill temporary positions	Larger agencies have more applicants to send on assignments meaning potentially lost revenue for CTSA
CTSA is continuously seeking new ways to meet the needs of employers	Does not have as many applicants available as the larger agencies	Able to meet a great need for employers at a comparable price	Employers reticent about contracting for additional workforce versus paying overtime to current workforce

211

Exhibit 45 – Strategic Implementation Plan

CareerTemps **Temporary Staffing Agency**
20XX Strategic Implementation Plan

Tactic	Responsible person	Process/Resources	Timeline
Hire 3 sales persons focused on mid- to large- business contracts for temporary staffing services	Human Resources Manager	• Advertise positions • Interview and hire desired applicants	Begin January 15, 20XX Hire by January 31, 20XX
Develop sales presentation	Business Development Manager	• Identify key person in each company targeted • Contact by phone to schedule visit	Begin February 1, 20XX Complete by February 15, 20XX
Contact human resource managers at target companies	Sales Team Members	• Introduce company and provide information on core competencies	Begin February 28, 20XX Indefinite
Open Facebook and Twitter social media accounts	Information Technology Manager	• Begin organically building following • Post on Facebook 2 times weekly • Respond to posts daily • Post on Twitter at least 2 hours per day	Begin January 15, 20XX Indefinite
Upgrade and enhance CSTA website	Information Technology Manager	• Upgrade website with new features • Develop an online application and process • Create new resources and tools	Beginning January 15, 2015 Indefinite
Update in-house and online resources and training materials	Information Technology Manager Human Resources Manager	• Review current resources • Revise and update	Beginning January 3, 20XX Finalize by March 1, 20XX

Exhibit 46 – Status Report

CareerTemps **Temporary Staffing Agency**
20XX Status Report

For period of 1st Quarter 20XX

Responsible person   Information Technology Manager

Department/Section   Information Technology

Objective	Current Status	Estimate completion date
Open Facebook and Twitter social media accounts	Accounts opened. Currently 200 new friends on Facebook and 150 new followers on Twitter	Accounts opened January 15, 20XX
Upgrade and enhance CSTA website	Upgrade process has begun. New application software is being developed. New features are being reviewed	First review January 31, 20XX Final review February 15, 20XX Launch February 28, 20XX
Upgrade online resources and training materials	Research is currently being conducted to develop new materials and tools. Each item is being coded for placement on the website. In-house materials and tools are being designed. Currently seeking quotes from printers to create hard copies of materials.	First iteration due January 31, 20XX Contractor to print selected by February 5, 20XX Edits and revisions due February 15, 20XX Final review and edits due February 28, 20XX Copy to print contractor by March 10, 20XX Materials delivered by March 20, 20XX

Exhibit 47 – Key Strategic (Long Range) Plan Metrics

CareerTemps Temporary Staffing Agency
20XX Key Strategic Plan Metrics

METRIC	KEY INDICATOR	CONSTRUCTION	INPUT/OUTPUT
Sales goals	Change in sales	Sum of revenue gains or losses	Revenue in dollars gain or loss
Gross margin	Amount remaining after applicants and overhead have been paid	Net sales – cost of goods sold	In dollars
Market position	Rise from position 6 to higher market position in the region	Surpass sales revenue of competition	Amount of revenue earned to improve market position
Customer satisfaction	Responses from clients on applicant performance	Scales from 1 to 10 on a scorecard	Weighted average of scores
Social media	Number of Facebook friends and Twitter followers	Number increase in friends and followers	Total number of friends and followers
Recruitment	Number of job seekers applying at CTSA	Number increase in new applications received online and in person	Total number of new applications received
Placements	Increase or decrease of applicants placed	Sum of applicants placed	Total number applicants placed
New hires versus promotions	Replacing or filling new company positions	Number of higher-level positions available / number promoted in-house or number hired from outside	Percentage of new hires versus employees promoted within
Company employee retention	Are there hires because of company growth or are employees leaving	Number of employees at a specified time / the number of employees at the end of a specified time	Percentage of employees retained at or leaving at a specific time

The Succession Plan

Death, disability, divorce or retirement of owner(s) or key person(s), and transferring a business is a fact of life. Decisions relating to how or if the business will continue, be transferred, sold, merged, acquired or liquidated when either of these events occur should be addressed at the start of the business planning process. This is known as succession planning and is designed to plan for an exit when closing or transferring a business, and to mitigate conflicts that can arise when it becomes necessary to do so.

Just as strategic and long range planning are vital to the future success of your business, succession planning is equally important in that it provides for an exit that will not leave heirs saddled with a huge tax bill or will keep your business moving forward. No business plan is complete without a succession plan. Unfortunately, many business owners fail to recognize the significance of what could happen in the absence of an owner or key person. No one likes to think in terms of when it will end, but at least being prepared helps to ease the pain.

In addition, succession can be the determining factor as to whether a loan or funding is granted. Many lenders and investors want to see a succession plan as part of the financial package. The reason is that they want to know how they will be repaid or receive a return on their investment in the event transfer, sell, merger, acquisition or liquidation of the business is necessary.

Whether the business is to be transferred or it continues, there are laws and regulations that dictate how that can be done. Here is another example of where the expertise of an attorney, insurance agent and accountant can be invaluable. They can advise you on the best way to handle the transfer or the continuation when the need arises from both a legal and financial standpoint.

Business Continuation

Most business owners don't prepare a continuation plan (which is part of business succession) because they don't like to think about their own mortality. In the unlikely event either of these facts of life listed above occur, it's not always necessary for the business to close. But if the business is to continue following the departure of an owner or key person, there must be plan to detail how that will happen.

Failing to prepare a business continuation plan can have a devastating effect on those left behind to manage the operations. Remaining owners of the company are put in a position of trying to figure out what the future of the company will be while dealing with a distressing loss when these issues should have been thought out in the beginning.

As part of the plans for continuation, decisions need to be made as to how the business will continue. This requires consideration of how the ownership interest of the departing owner will be handled, what will be the source of income for their family, and what is the direction for the company. These decisions should include, but not be limited to:

1. What funding vehicles will be used for the buy-out of their ownership interest?

2. What is the fair value of their ownership interest?

3. Who in the company will take control of the affairs of the departed owner as it pertains to their ownership interest in the company?

4. What are the plans for working with family/heirs to their ownership interest, and how they will receive income from the business?

5. What are the details in the agreement for continuing the business?

6. How will the company be restructured, if at all?

7. Will the company be sold, merged, acquired or liquidated? If so, what will be the timeframe?

Transfer of the Business

Understand that the legal structure of the business will dictate how the transfer will be carried out. If the business is a sole proprietorship, the business may be transferred to a capable family member as a gift through provisions in the proprietor's will or by a sale provided through a prearranged purchase agreement effective at death. If neither of these are an option, then the business must be sold, merged, acquired, or liquidated.

If the business is a partnership, unless there is a written agreement to the contrary, the death of a partner automatically dissolves the business. In the absence of a partner, the surviving partners have no rights to the purchase of the deceased partner's interest. The surviving partners may then act as liquidating partners. Another option would be for the surviving partners to reorganize the partnership by taking heirs into the partnership, having heirs accept a new partner, selling the deceased's interest to the heirs or buying out the heirs.

And finally, if the business is a corporation where the deceased has been active in the operation (pertains to a closely-held corporation), the family may retain stock interest. If the heirs have a majority interest, they may choose to become personally involved in the management in order to receive income.

Preparing the Succession Plan

Once the need arises, you will need to consult with the appropriate legal, accounting or financial and insurance professionals. Depending on your level of expertise, budgetary constraints and the size and type of your business, you may be able to handle these functions yourself. Numerous books and a multitude of information exists that can help. But know your limitations, and for all else, consult an attorney.

Phase I of the succession plan will focus on developing succession strategies in the event of death, disability, divorce or retirement of any owner or key person. Phase II of the plan focuses on choosing a successor. This is done by identifying someone externally (possibly an heir or other individual) or by cross-training other key persons internally. Employees (not just family members) should be afforded an opportunity to cross train. Employee training and development programs can eliminate minor disruptions that could occur in the day-to-day operations of your business. Training would not only increase employees' worth to the company, but would also allow them to step in and effectively assume the responsibilities in the absence of other employees.

Components of the Succession Plan

Information contained within the Succession Plan includes:

1. **Phase I – Initial Planning** – Succession strategies determining what will happen to the business, business valuation, hiring a successor and transferring assets.

2. **Phase II – Cross Training & Job Diversification** – Provides options and incentives for training a successor whether they are selected internally or externally.

3. **Succession Planning Metrics** - List and describe the key and specific metric used to measure and assess the success of each area of succession planning. **Exhibit 49 – Key Succession Plan Metrics** on page 222 is an example.

Exhibit 48 – Succession Plan

PHASE I – INITIAL PLANNING

Preparation for Succession

Will the legal structure of the company change? What will happen to the business (i.e., will it be transferred, sold, merged, acquired or liquidated)? When will this change take place? How will the transfer, sell, merger, acquisition or liquidation be handled? Will it be handled by the owners, in-house or by an outside entity? Who will continue in the leadership role during the transition? What will their role be? What authority will they have?

What is the company's current financial position? What is the company's current value? How will the transition affect the strategic plan for growth and prosperity? Will there be any changes in the products and services the company currently provides? What will those changes be? Does the company anticipate making any mergers or acquisitions? What manpower changes will take place? What new positions will be added? What level of expertise will be required?

Consult with Professionals

- **Attorney** – To discuss and advise on legal issues and to execute all legal filings, agreements and contracts

- **Accountant** (particularly with previous IRS [Internal Revenue Service] experience) – To discuss the company's current and anticipated financial position, determine the value of the company and advise on tax consequences, capital gains in particular

- **Insurance agent** – To implement funding vehicles (usually insurance policies) for the transition

Compensation of Owner(s) or Key Persons

What ownership stake, if any, will owners or key persons maintain if the business is transferred, sold, merged, acquired or liquidated? Will the owner(s) be given or maintain stock options? What is/are the owner(s) compensation requirements?

Selecting a Successor

Who will take over in the leadership position temporarily or permanently? What leadership qualities or business acumen would be required? What are their qualifications for taking over a part of the business?

How will their ownership interest be obtained (e.g., contribution of cash, equipment, expertise, inheritance, gift, etc.)? What, if any, control will owner(s) be relinquishing or retaining? What and for how long will compensation continue for any disabled owner?

Business Continuation

How will the business continue? Are the surviving owners or key persons able to make those decisions? What are the arrangements between the owners for the business to continue? What funding vehicles are in place to buy out the heirs of the departing owners? How will ownership interests be handled? How will the management structure change?

What are the plans for the future of the company? How will product/service lines change? What are the goals and objectives for the future of the company (e.g., 5 to 7 years out)?

Transferring the Business

If the business is to continue, some or all of the following documents and/or agreements must be prepared with explicit details of how the transfer will be executed:

1. **Covenant of Non-compete** – Prohibits the transferor or shareholders of the company from competing with the transferee.

2. **Consulting Agreement** – Agreement between the company and transferor to provide consulting services on a full- or part-time basis.

3. **Employment Agreement** – An agreement for full- or part-time employment with salary and benefits.

4. **Confidentiality Agreement** – An agreement in which transferor/seller agrees to disclose certain confidential information relating to the company to the buyer.

Selling the Business

If your plan is to sell the business or your interest in the business, to whom will it be sold (e.g., remaining owners, family members, employees, others)? What is the value of the company? What method of valuation is used: net asset value, historical cash flow, future cash flow, profitability, liquidation)?

If the owner wishes to sell the company in whole or in part, the following agreements should be executed:

- **Agreement for Purchase & Sale of Assets** – Agreement in which the owner agrees to sell some of its assets and retain others.

- **Agreement to Purchase Shares** – An agreement in which the seller agrees to transfer or sell all the issued and outstanding shares of stock.

If financing is required in the sale of the business, some or all of the following documents should be executed:

- **Buy/Sell Agreement** – An agreement by which the seller agrees to sell and the buyer agrees to buy the shares of the company as set forth.

- **Promissory Note** – An agreement between the buyer and seller identifying specific amounts (including interest) to paid over a specific period of time.

- **General Security Agreement** – An agreement between the seller and buyer by which the seller has a secured interest (as defined by the Uniform Commercial Code) and all personal property and tangible assets for the purpose of securing the promissory note.

- **Guaranty Agreement** – An agreement between the seller and buyer in which the buyer agrees to make all payments on time and in full.

- **Buy-back Agreement** – An agreement between partners by which terms and conditions of how to handle a partner's share if termination of the partnership is desired.

- **Carry-back Agreement** – An agreement between buyer and seller where the seller carries a percentage of the sell of the business until buyer is able to pay for shares in full.

Merging the Company

Are there plans to merge the company with another? What type of merger would it be (e.g., conglomerate, horizontal merger, vertical merger, product extension or market extension? What type of company would be considered to merge with? What industry is the merged company associated with? Is the company local, national or international? What will options for retaining current management or line employees be?

Company Being Acquired

Will the company be acquired? What company will be considered to acquire it? What industry is the acquiring company associated with? What products or services does the acquiring company sell? Is the company local, national or international? What will options for retaining current management or line employees be?

Liquidating the Business

Bankruptcy or selling all assets of the business are the two most common forms of liquidation and may become necessary if money is needed to pay off heirs, debts, taxes or other liabilities. Forms of liquidation are described as:

- **Bankruptcy** – Controlled by the federal government, the Federal Bankruptcy Act was created for the purpose of relieving the honest debtor from the weight of oppressive indebtedness and to permit a fresh start. The four forms of bankruptcy include:

  o Chapter 7 – Releases the debtor from personal liability for debts incurred before the date the bankruptcy petition is filed; and

  o Chapters 11, 12, 13 – Debt reorganizations in which a trustee is assigned to collect the non-exempt property of the debtor, convert the property to cash and distribute the cash to creditors.

- **Selling all Assets** – Tangible and fixed assets (i.e., buildings, other property, equipment, machinery, materials, inventory, supplies, etc.) are sold for pennies on the dollar.

PHASE II – CROSS-TRAINING & JOB DIVERSIFICATION

Training & Development of Successors

What is the process for selecting a successor? Will an outside person be selected without consideration of a current employee? What recruitment steps will be taken? Will there be a local or national search? What is the preferred level of education? How much experience will be required? What will their compensation package include? Will current employees be considered as successors? If current employees are not considered as successors, why?

Training & Development Options

What training options will employees be afforded? What criteria will be used to determine whether an employee is eligible for training? How will training be conducted? Evaluate the current skill level of each employee. Where are the gaps between where they are and where they need to be? In what areas specifically should each employee be trained? Who will provide the training? Some training options may include:

- In-house training and cross-training involving owners, managers and other employees

- Video-based, web-based, computer assisted

- Tuition assistance for college or extension courses, seminars

- Outside courses or seminars conducted by professional technical societies

SUCCESSION PLANNING METRICS

What metrics will be used to measure and assess performance? List and describe each metric used. Why were those metrics used? What does each metric intended to tell you about your succession planning efforts? How is each metric constructed? What is the output of each metric (e.g., content, dollars, numbers, percentage, rating, etc.)?

What are the success factors? What rationale will be used to determine what success looks like in each metric? How will metrics that are not reaching the level of expectation be handled? How will it be determined that other measurements should be used? At what point will these determinations be made?

Exhibit 49 – Key Succession Plan Metrics

CareerTemps **Temporary Staffing Agency**
20XX Key Succession Plan Metrics

METRIC	KEY INDICATOR	CONSTRUCTION	INPUT/OUTPUT
Legal structure	Whether current legal structure worked	Making other legal and other business decisions based on current structure	Decision as to whether the legal structure should be changed
Current value of the company	Whether the value of the company has increased or decreased based on revenue, assets, new business, etc.	Difference in the value in the past 12 months has increased or decreased	Dollar and percentage change in value
Balance Sheet	Change in company's financial position	Owner's equity = assets - liabilities	Book value of the company
Operating Statement	Revenues and the cost and expenses charged against them	Revenue – expenses = net income or (loss)	Net income or (loss) in the company
Retention of key persons	Frequency key persons change	Number of days difference between the start	Length of time a key person fills a position
Filled positions	Promoting internally or hiring externally	Number of promotions / number of new hires	Number of times positions are filled in-house versus hired
Recruiting costs	Hiring expenditures	Total cost of hiring externally	Dollar amount spent to hire talent
Time to fill open position	Length of time it takes to hire or promote	Number of days position remains vacant	Amount of time it takes to fill open positions
Training	Number of employees receiving training	Cost of training	Effects of training provided to candidates

The Appendix

The Appendix or Appendices are used to supplement information contained in the business plan. They usually include, but are not limited, to:

- Affiliates
- Annual reports
- Articles of incorporation
- Bonding policies
- Branding
- Brochures
- Business licenses
- Business model
- Buy-back agreements
- Buy-sell agreements
- By-laws
- Certifications
- Charts
- Consultant agreements
- Contracts (current and past)
- Copyrights
- Curriculum vitae
- Current and previous contracts
- Customer contracts
- Educational documentation
- Employment agreements
- Employment policies
- Executed contracts
- Financial information
- Forms
- Franchise agreements
- Graphs
- Guarantees

- Historical information
- Incorporation documents
- Insurance policies
- Lease agreements
- Letters of intent
- Licenses, other
- News articles
- Non-compete agreements
- Notice to Proceed
- Organizational charts
- Organizational plans
- Ownership agreements
- Partnership agreements
- Patents
- Photographs of key personnel
- Professional licenses
- Purchase agreements
- Quality certifications
- Questionnaires
- Rental agreements
- Resumes
- Research data
- Stock certificates
- Surveys
- Trade references
- Trademarks
- UCC filings
- Warranties
- White papers

List and describe each document included in the business plan with page numbers. **Exhibit 50 – Appendix** on page 224 is an example of an appendix list and a few of the documents that might be included.

Exhibit 50 – Appendix

APPENDIX 1
List of Appendices

Articles of incorporation	x
Brochures	x
Business and professionals licenses	x
Business model	x
Buy-back agreements	x
Buy-sell agreements	x
By-laws	x
Charts, graphs, schematics	x
Copyrights	x
Customer contracts	x
Executed contracts	x
Forms	x
Franchise agreements	x
Guarantees	x
Insurance and bonding policies	x
Lease agreements	x
Letters of intent	x
Licensing agreements	x
News articles	x
Notice to proceed	x
Partnership agreements	x
Patents	x
Purchase agreements	x
Quality certifications	x
Questionnaires	x
Research data	x
Surveys	x
Trademarks	x
Warranties	x

The Glossary of Terms

Terms have different meanings depending on the industry in which they are associated. For this reason they can easily confuse your reader. The purpose of a glossary is to define terms that may be unique to your business or industry. Never assume that the individual reading your business plan understands each term. **Exhibit 51 – Glossary of Terms** below is a sample glossary of just a few terms as they are defined in the temporary staffing industry.

Exhibit 51 – Glossary of Terms

GLOSSARY OF TERMS

Client - *A person who engages the professional advice or services of another (including an applicant seeking temporary employment)*

Customer – *One who is a patron or uses the services (including the company or business needing temporary staffing)*

Database –*Information bank compiled and inputted into a computer program for later retrieval*

Information retrieval – *Techniques of storing, retrieving and often disseminating recorded data especially through the use of a computerized system*

Model – *A description or analogy used to help visualize something (e.g., specific type of employee needed for company and position)*

Operational – *Ready for or in condition to undertake a destined function*

System – *An organized set of doctrines, ideas or principles in which applicants are screened, tested and prepared for temporary employment*

PART IV

THE BUSINESS CENTER

CHAPTER 4

ACCESS
TO
MARKETS

Accessing Your Market

Accessing the best and appropriate market(s) that will purchase your products/services is what doing business all about. Success is predicated on identifying and reaching your target customer at the right time, in the right place at the right price. This section is intended to provide more specificity on various markets and how to present your products/services within those markets and to garner market share. You will need to determine:

1. current needs to be met in the marketplace;

2. the demand for each need;

3. how current products/services meet the needs;

4. which markets are best suited for your products/services, which ones are not and why;

5. what marketing strategies will be used to penetrate these markets;

6. which contracting or procurement opportunities within those markets would meet sales, profit and return on investment objectives; and

7. what is your competitive advantage in each market.

It's a fact that business success hinges on your ability to identify and access the markets best suitable for you to sell and deliver your products or services. It's important to note that there are barriers to entry in most industries, including any area of government. In other words, there are limitations that can inhibit a business' ability to enter a particular market. Limitations such as finances, expertise, size, scale, competition, relationships and capital equipment resources top the list.

Which Markets Do You Choose

Generally speaking, it's not possible for any business to successfully capture a large share in all markets. Therefore, you must decide which markets can provide opportunities that best match your company's resources and objectives. If you sell to retailers or distributors, keep in mind that your customers will always be looking for products/services that can add value to their core competencies and make them more competitive. If you sell to end users, your customers will be looking for the right product/service at the right price.

There are four roads to explore when determining the best markets for you to pursue. They are:

1. **Public sector** – federal, state and local government agencies, transportation agencies (e.g., airlines, rail, light rail, bus, etc.), quasi-government (e.g., water districts, state universities, community colleges, school districts, etc.)

2. **Private sector** – end users, retailers, distributors, private corporations, other businesses, utility companies, franchises, consumers, distributors, Internet, etc.

3. **Not-for-profits** – the most common are 501(c)3, 501(c)4 and 501(c)6

4. **International markets** – doing business around the globe (e.g., Europe, Asia, Africa, South America, Australia, Canada)

Research Resources

Before moving into any market, the first step is to research it thoroughly. An infinite amount of market information exists on every kind of business, industry, product, service, etc. to assist you in the development, growth or expansion of your business and help you compete. Demographic and geographic information can aid you in locating your customer, understanding buying habits and identifying your competitors. These resources include:

1. **The Internet** – Using a search engine such as Google, Bing, Yahoo!, Ask, or Aol to name a few, is a quick and simple way of researching any type of information via the Internet.

2. **Bureau of Labor Statistics** – The principal fact-finding agency in the broad field of labor economics and statistics that collects, processes, analyzes and disseminates essential statistical data to the American public, Congress and other federal, state and local governments and businesses.

3. **ESRI Business Information Solutions** – Geographic Information Systems (GIS) Technology - An organization that helps industry, government and not-for-profits understand customers, analyze site locations, visualize and map marketing and demographic data, and identify untapped market potential.

4. **LexisNexis** – Provides information to legal, corporate, government and academic markets and publishes legal, tax and regulatory information online, hardcopy and CD-ROM.

Qualifying as a Supplier

There are minimum qualifications a prospective supplier must meet prior to engaging in a business relationship with a government agency or corporation. As long as the business meets the specific needs of the agency or organization, there exists and opportunity to provide products and services. These qualifications include, but are not limited, to:

1. being an established business;

2. have and can deliver products and services to specification, on time and at a fair price;

3. having financial stability as reported by Dun & Bradstreet;

4. having full insurance coverage compatible with the risks of the business;

5. having adequate tracking systems;

6. meeting quality standards; and

7. demonstrating skills and abilities in core areas.

Understanding Your Competitive Advantage

Your competitive advantage is the one element that separates you from your competition. It focuses on the attributes that make your products or services stand above everyone else's. It could entail having:

1. intangible assets such and knowledge and/or skills in areas unmatched by the competition;

2. a patented product that's new, innovative and unmatched;

3. relationships in the industry or with a customer that the competition doesn't have equal access; and

4. technical expertise in providing continuous innovation not easily or efficiently replicated.

Common Mistakes Business Owners Make

We know that being in business comes with a multitude of challenges, and consequently many mistakes are made. The single most common mistake you can make is in believing that you can be all things to all people. This philosophy has proven disastrous to every business that employs it. That's why having a marketing plan is critical. The second most common mistake is not having, not implementing or not adhering to an established marketing plan.

To avoid these pitfalls, be sure to:

1. have a thorough understanding of who needs, wants and can benefit from your products/services;

2. have sufficient knowledge of the core competencies of your potential customer and their customers;

3. have sufficient knowledge of their competition; and

4. have a marketing strategy that details your business, financial position, specific products or services you're offering to each customer.

Choosing the Best Market – The Public Sector

Federal, state and local governments, as well as quasi-government agencies (e.g., water and sewer companies, gas and electric utility companies, cable, telecommunications companies, etc.), purchase any and every kind of product/service imaginable. The government is comprised of hundreds of departments and agencies, and each has unique purchasing needs. They buy everything in the world from livestock to baby car seats.

To be a successful contender in the government market, you must first know your business and second, know how the government procurement process works. Part of that is knowing when the fiscal year of the agency ends (usually June 30, September 30 or December 31). This is because monies are usually appropriated in a particular year for a particular purpose. Once they have been allocated, chances are no more will be spent for that purpose in that year.

Marketing to the federal government is quite different from marketing to private corporations. Instead of developing advertising or promotion pieces for those markets, you must contact the buying agency directly. The U.S. federal government is the world's largest purchaser with over $500 billion in goods and services per year, and more than $75 billion goes to small, minority, women, veteran and service disabled veteran business enterprises.

Government Contracting Rules and Regulations

Basic federal government contracting rules are set forth in the Federal Acquisition Regulation (FAR) which can be found at on the web at https://www.acquisition.gov/. Other agencies have a FAR supplement such as Department of Defense (DFAR), Department of Energy Acquisition Regulation (DEAR). And still more such as the Army, Navy, Air Force and NASA. While the needs for each government entity may be different, the process for doing business with any of them is basically the same.

While each agency, sub-agency, administration, or department of the federal government can impose unique requirements on suppliers, they cannot supersede or delete FAR requirements. It's not necessary that you memorize the FAR in its entirety. However, it's important that you familiarize yourself with what they are and how they apply to contracts you will be bidding on.

But before you can register and participate in any government contracting, you will need to have available the following:

- **DUNS** (Data Universal Numbering System) number
  http://www.dnb.com/

- **Small Business Size Standards**
  https://www.sba.gov/sites/default/files/files/Size_Standards_Table.pdf

- **NAICS (North American Industry Classification System)**
  http://www.census.gov/eos/www/naics/

- **TIN or EIN (Federal Tax Identification Number)**
  https://www.irs.gov/Businesses/Small-Businesses-&-Self-Employed

- **Product Service Code (PSC)**
  https://www.acquisition.gov/sites/default/files/page_file_uploads/PSC%20Manual%20-%20Final%20-%2011%20August%202011.pdf

- **Commercial and Government Entity (CAGE) Code**
  https://www.sam.gov/portal/SAM/##11
  (Assigned 4 – 5 business days following SAM approval)

- **Federal Supply Classification (FSC) Code**
  https://www.fbo.gov/index?s=getstart&mode=list&tab=list&tabmode=list&static=faqs#q4

Federal Contracting Opportunities

While securing a government contract can be quite lucrative and give your business the type of credibility and financial strength it needs to grow and prosper, getting through the bureaucracy can be overwhelming. Recognizing this, in October 1994, President Bill Clinton signed into law the Federal Acquisition Streamlining Act (FASA). This Act allows for less complicated purchasing procedures for procurements up to $100,000. Information on FASA can be found at www.dol.gov/oasam/regs/statutes/fasa1.htm.

The best source for obtaining information on federal government procurements is the *FedBizOpps* at www.fedbizopps.gov. At this site are all federal government buying agencies are required by the FAR to synopsize proposed competitive contracts expected to exceed $25,000, non-competitive contracts expected to exceed $10,000 and any contract awards in excess of $25,000. In addition, it has contract awards, special notices, foreign government standards and surplus property sales.

Registering for Government Contracting Opportunities

There are several ways to identify or receive notification of contracting and procurement opportunities in the Federal Government. These sources include:

1. **System for Award Management (SAM)**, (formerly Central Contractor Registration [CCR]/ProNet)
   SAM is now the official U.S government system that consolidated the capabilities of CCR/FedReg, ORCA and EPLS. To register for SAM, visit the website at https://www.sam.gov/.

2. **Office of Small & Disadvantaged Business Utilization (OSDBU)**
   Assists small, disadvantaged, women, 8(a), HUBZone, veteran, service-disabled veteran businesses in obtaining contracts and subcontracts with all federal government agencies and its prime contractors. For more information, see **CHAPTER 8, BUSINESS RESOURCES**, in the **"FEDERAL AGENCIES"** section beginning on page 336.

General Services Administration (GSA) Schedules

The General Services Administration (GSA) establishes policies for and provides economical and efficient management of government property and records, including:

1. construction and operation of buildings;

2. renovation and rehabilitation of buildings, parks, recreation centers, public safety buildings, etc.;

3. procurement and distribution of supplies;

4.   utilization and disposal of real and personal property;

5.   transportation, traffic, and communications management; and

6.   management of the government-wide automatic data processing resources program.

The GSA Schedules Program (also referred to as Multiple Award Schedules and Federal Supply Schedules) establishes long-term government-wide contracts with commercial firms to provide access to over four million commercial products and services that can be ordered directly from GSA Schedule contractors or through the GSA Advantage!® online shopping and order system. In addition, the Office of Enterprise Development (OED) focuses on programs, policy and outreach to assist the small business community nationwide in doing business with GSA. For more information contact GSA online at www.gsa.gov/.

Technical Assistance

Understanding all the ins and outs of government contracting can be a difficult task. The Procurement Technical Assistance Program (PTAP) was established to expand the number of businesses capable of participating in government contracting. Procurement and Technical Assistance Centers (PTACs) have a local presence in all 50 states, the District of Columbia, Puerto Rico and Guam to assist businesses interested in contracting with federal, state and local government. For more information visit the Defense Logistics Agency (DLA) online at http://www.dla.mil/HQ/SmallBusiness/PTAP.aspx to locate an office near you.

State, Local and Quasi-Government Agencies

If your objective is doing business with state and local government agencies, you will need to contact each agency individually (including schools, universities and quasi-government agencies, to include water districts and utility companies). Regardless of their size, they have similar contracting and procurement processes. However, advertisements for contractor and procurement opportunities vary from agency to agency and state to state. You will then need to:

1. **Visit the agency or their website** – Download and print out any purchasing information they may have (e.g., supplier profile forms, purchasing procedures and processes, etc.). It'll be important to familiarize yourself with their new vendor processes prior to making any contact by phone, in person, by mail or e-mail.

2. **Follow instructions carefully** – Make sure all forms are complete and thorough, and all documents requested are included. Depending on the agency's procurement processes, you may be able to apply as a new vendor online. If not, it's imperative that you send a complete package to the appropriate person.

3. **Identify the individual responsible for purchasing the types of products or services you provide** – Purchasing agents are inundated with calls and emails everyday with interested vendors. You may also want to contact the end user in the agency. This information may be available on their web site as well.

4. **Upload, e-mail or mail all pertinent information** – With your submission, include a cover letter (refer to **Exhibit 12 – Cover Letter of Introduction** on page 131).

5. **Follow up with a phone call or e-mail** – The date they can expect to hear from you should be stated in your cover letter. Request or suggest a date and time to meet with the buyer and any other members of the agency that may be appropriate. You may need to be persistent, but try not to be a nuisance.

Choosing the Best Market – The Private Sector

Many similarities exist in doing business in the private sector as in the public sector. It, too, entails making contact, submitting the proper documentation, adhering to a prescribed procurement process, follow-up, and of course, relationship building. The good news is that doing business with private corporations can be slightly simpler. Many opportunities with private-sector companies are for government contracts. Once the previous steps have been satisfied, to do business in the private sector, you must:

1. Visit and review their web site or other company information;

2.   Download the proper information;

3.   Identify an internal contact;

4.   Submit documentation;

5.   Follow-up with phone calls or e-mails; and

6.   Build and nurture relationships.

Choosing the Best Market – Not-for-profit Organizations

As for-profits and government agencies have purchasing needs, so do not-for-profit organizations. While most of them don't have budgets as large as government agencies and private corporations, they are a viable market as well. But if your products and services can be utilized by not-for-profit organizations, you will need to contact them individually.

Associations and Foundations

The most comprehensive sources for locating not-for-profit organizations are the *Encyclopedia of Associations* and the *Foundation Directory*. The Encyclopedia of Associations lists more than 23,000 national and international organizations in the following categories:

1.   Trade, Business and Commercial

2.   Environmental and Agricultural

3.   Legal, Governmental, Public Administration, Military

4.   Engineering, Technological and Natural and Social Sciences

5.   Educational

6.   Cultural

7.   Social Welfare

8.   Health and Medical

9.   Public Affairs

10. Fraternal, Nationality and Ethnic

11. Religious

12. Veterans' Heredity and Patriotic

13. Hobby and Avocational

14. Athletic and Sports

15. Labor Unions, Associations and Federations

16. Chambers of Commerce and Trade and Tourism

17. Greek letter and related organizations

18. Fan clubs

For more information on associations and foundations, contact the Gale Group, Inc. online at http://find.galegroup.com/.

The *Foundation Directory* lists the nation's 10,000 largest grantmaking foundations. Information is based either on reports received directly from the foundations or most current records available. The *Foundation Directory* names four types of foundations:

1. **Independent foundations** – Established to aid social, educational, religious or other charitable activities.

2. **Company-sponsored foundations** – Legally and independent grantmaking organization with close ties to the corporation providing the funds.

3. **Operating foundations** – Organizations that use its resources to conduct research or provide a direct service.

4. **Community foundations** – Publicly-sponsored organizations that make grants for social, educational, religious or other charitable purposes in a specific community or region.

The Foundation Center offers free access to information resources and education programs at operating library/learning centers in five locations; New York City, New York; Washington, DC; Atlanta, Georgia; Cleveland, Ohio; and

San Francisco, California. To order publications or electronic products, contact The Foundation Center online at http://foundationcenter.org/about/index.html

Choosing the Best Market – International Markets

Doing business internationally is not for all businesses. Deciphering foreign regulations and standards, and securing certifications can be a painstaking endeavor. If doing business abroad is your desire you must decide the way in which you want to get involved. This can be accomplished in one of two ways:

1. fill orders for domestic buyers from vendors abroad; or

2. export domestic products to international markets.

Is Your Company Export Ready?

Before you begin, there are number of considerations that must be taken into account to determine whether your company is export ready. Developing a detailed and thorough strategy should be your first step and should show you:

1. whether your company has adequate capabilities and resources;

2. whether there is really a market for your products;

3. what steps to take and when to take them; and

4. what the costs will be in terms of time and money.

This strategy must include:

1. evaluating your product to assess its export potential;

2. determining whether you have a true commitment companywide to exporting;

3. researching your market abroad thoroughly;

4. evaluating and establishing the best distribution system;

5. determining export prices, payment terms, methods and techniques; and

6. familiarizing yourself with exporting laws and regulations, shipping methods, documentation procedures and other export requirements.

Risks of Doing Business Abroad

Business in general has a great number of challenges. If you're doing business abroad the challenges are even greater. There are many issues we take for granted when doing business in the U.S. that seem simple, however, trying to apply the same principles abroad presents a whole new set of issues. While you're preparing your strategy for importing and exporting, the following are potential risks that should be considered:

1. **Communications barriers** – Understanding the language and culture;

2. **Credit risk** – Knowing when and when not to extend credit;

3. **Political risk** – Foreign government policies that might impact the country's economic future;

4. **Foreign exchange** – The ability and willingness of the foreign government to make enough foreign exchange available to its citizens, foreign residents, public and privately-held companies and government owned agencies.

Technical Assistance

The Trade Information Center (TIC) within the U.S. Department of Commerce is one of the best resources available to you. TIC trade specialists will provide assistance in:

1. locating and using government programs;

2. guiding you through the export process;

3.   directing you to market research and trade leads;

4.   providing information on domestic and overseas trade events and activities;

5.   explaining sources of public and private export financing;

6.   helping you locate reports and statistics on trade; and

7.   referring businesses to state and local trade organizations that can provide additional assistance.

In addition, the TIC provides export counseling for the Western Hemisphere (including NAFTA), Western Europe, the Middle East, Africa and Asia to include:

1.   import tariffs, taxes and customs procedures;

2.   standards, intellectual property rights, government procurement, and other commercial laws, regulations and practices;

3.   distribution channels, business travel and other market research, access and compliance information;

4.   opportunities and best prospects for U.S. companies in individual markets;

5.   difficulties encountered on specific commercial transactions; and

6.   credit risks of foreign customers.

The International Trade Administration (ITA) works to improve the global business environment by helping U.S. organizations compete at home and abroad. The ITA is organized in three unique, but complementary business units to include:

1.   **Global Markets Unit** - Combines ITA's country and regional experts, overseas and domestic field staff, and specific trade promotion programs to provide U.S. firms with the full suite of country-specific

export promotion services and market access advocacy, while promoting the United States as an investment destination.

2. **Industry and Analysis (I&A) Unit** - Brings together ITA's industry, trade, and economic experts to advance the competitiveness of U.S. industries through the development and execution of international trade and investment policies and promotion strategies.

3. **Enforcement and Compliance Unit** - Enhances ITA's responsibilities to enforce U.S. trade laws and ensure compliance with trade agreements negotiated on behalf of U.S. industry.

For information and to obtain import and export assistance online, visit the following:

- **Trade Information Center (TIC)**
  http://www.export.gov/exportbasics

- **International Trade Administration (ITA)**
  http://www.trade.gov/about.asp

- **United States Export Assistance Centers**
  https://www.sba.gov/managing-business/exporting/us-export-assistance-centers

E-business – Marketing on the Internet

The use of the Internet for commerce is the fastest growing sales and marketing channel in the world. Both e-commerce and online advertising spending have increased exponentially year over year, and advertisers are now beginning to see a profit. Companies such as e-Bay and Amazon.com, for example, have business models that have revolutionized doing business on the web.

In the past, banner advertisements were predominately used to promote products and services. Today new direct interactive marketing technologies have dramatically increased Internet marketing demand, and have reduced the cost of promoting products and services. Through the use of segmented customer-targeting techniques, businesses have seen a vast improvement in sales and marketing performance.

With segmented target advertising, one of the most effective customer-targeting techniques is the positioning of an online ad near a related editorial comment. An example of this technique entails placing an ad for securing a small business loan near editorial on the purchase of capital equipment or other fixed assets. Other segmented targeting methods include using geographic and demographic information to target customers in specific locations (e.g., zip codes, area codes, regions, etc.) and customer type (e.g., age, income level, education, sex, lifestyle, etc.).

Keyword searches on major portals such as Yahoo!, AOL and Alta Vista is yet another very effective marketing technique, but can range in cost in the millions. And one other of the many marketing techniques is Amazon.com's affiliate network model that enables marketers to cover niche market segments through the more than 450,000 partners in their network. Additionally, there is permission-based e-mail direct marketing where customers can elect to receive marketing information by simply "opting- in." The most popular email marketing companies today include iContact, Benchmark Email, Pinpointe and Constant Contact.

Independently-published, on-line newsletters are a low-tech, low-cost approach to effective business-to-business advertising. These newsletters help marketers target niche interest groups and communities all over the world. There are currently thousands of them on the Internet and are devoted to a wide range of subjects. Some have small circulations, but a large number have millions of subscribers.

Reverse Auctions

Government agencies as well as private corporations have begun to incorporate reverse auctions as another alternative in their procurement activities. Affectionately called "e-Bay in reverse" this process uses the Internet to procure direct and indirect goods and services such as plant equipment, raw materials, component parts, food products, packaging, marketing, printing and the list goes on.

As much as 10% to 15% cost savings have been reported amounting to millions of dollars. But equally important is the short time cycles as compared to the traditional bid process that generally takes weeks. Using reverse auctions takes only 30 to 45 minutes and enables bidding to be conducted across multiple countries in multiple currencies.

The way the process works is the buying agency pays an online auction provider to use their technology. Buyers invite pre-qualified bidders to participate. Each bidder is then provided with the software, log-in and password. Vendors compete real time in an open and interactive environment. The transparent nature of this process allows bidders to see others' bids, but not their identity.

Buying agencies are not held to the lowest bid because vendor selection is based on best value. But because competitors' bids are shown, vendors are given the opportunity to offer the absolute lowest price. The single requirement for buyers, however, is that they must select one of the bidders or they can elect to reject them all. This process may not work for all procurements. Generally, it's used for procurements of $1 million or more, though it can be used for smaller procurements.

Building Customer Relationships

Whether your customer exists in the public sector, private sector, , not-for-profit, internationally or some combination thereof, the key to success is building strong business relationships. Once you've targeted your prospective customer you must learn as much about them as you can. The more you know, the better you will be able to determine which of your products or services best meet their specific needs, provides them with solutions, while at the same time, making a profit.

Some of the most helpful sources of information about any company are their annual report, website, news articles, television news and commercials, printed ads (including outdoor), etc. However, companies such as Hoover's and the Library of Congress Business Reference Services provide information on companies. From these sources, and others, you will need to ascertain:

1. who are the corporate board members and leaders;

2. the core business of each prospective customer;

3. how they're performing in their industry;

4. whether they're developing new products or services;

5.   whether they're in an introductory, growth, expansion or decline mode; and

6.   who their customers are.

What every organization or corporation seeks in building a partnership with any supplier is to develop a long-term, mutually-beneficial relationship that would give them a competitive advantage. Potential suppliers and partners must be capable of providing quality products and services that bring value to include:

1.   innovative and creative ideas that reduce cost and inventory;

2.   on-time delivery;

3.   highest quality;

4.   providing large quantities over a long period time, sometimes for 5 to 10 years;

5.   competitive pricing with the lowest possible cost of ownership with the highest possible value;

6.   availability and flexibility to absorb lead times and unexpected scheduling changes;

7.   communication and interaction with technical, procurement or other authorized personnel; and

8.   continuous process improvements to increase value to the company.

Customer Relationship Management

Customer relationship management (CRM) is a crucial part of sustaining business relationships. CRM systems are designed to automate customer-facing processes, and make those processes more efficient and effective with costs savings and no sacrifice to customer satisfaction. It assists in understanding and analyzing customer behavior and preferences, and making sure that products and services are aligned with customer needs and preferences.

Because of today's immensely competitive environment, CRM is critical to the success and long-term profitability of every company. Each year U.S. corporations spend over $10 million for CRM solutions. Their goal is to use this technology to build long-term relationships and increase customer loyalty and generate higher margins. Hundreds of CRM software solutions can be found online. To find the best solution for your business, just put "customer relationship management" in your preferred search engine. There you will find thousands of options from which to choose.

Supplier Development Initiatives

Government agencies and private corporations have supplier development initiatives to assist their suppliers in growing and developing their businesses. The benefits are two-fold. Once an agency or corporation establishes a relationship with a supplier, the supplier essentially becomes an integral part of the agency's or corporation's operation. The development that takes place is designed to provide the agency or corporation with the reliability and cooperation from the supplier that enables the two entities to maintain a long-term, productive and profitable relationship.

Supplier Development

Corporations institute supplier development initiatives to assist current and potential suppliers in identifying and developing business opportunities with their companies. This development process helps in the growth and expansion of a supplier, and is implemented in one of three ways:

1. **Partnering** – forming a strategic alliance with a Tier 1 supplier or corporate sourcing or procurement specialists;

2. **Joint venturing** – forming a separate and legal entity and combining independent human and financial resources, capital and expertise for the purpose of taking on other projects, usually larger;

3. **Mentoring** – developing a mentor-protégé relationship; and

4. **Incubation** – providing on-site, full management and technical support.

Supplier Diversity

The most notable supplier development initiative in the private sector is supplier diversity. Either by government or corporate mandate, corporations institute supplier diversity initiatives to promote the integration and retention of certified minority, women and service disabled veteran business enterprises (S/D/M/W/V/DVBEs) in corporate-wide contracting and procurement. These firms are provided a vehicle to expand their present capacity, and for less experienced ones, the training and assistance needed to grow.

Supplier diversity initiatives have served to increase the competitive advantage of corporations in the marketplace. It's believed that diverse firms provide innovative business solutions, improve bidding advantages, as well as promote an increased diverse customer base. Corporations actively seek to integrate their supply chain to reflect the markets they serve through the development and implementation of a supplier diversity program.

If you are certified, you are eligible to participate in a corporate supplier diversity program. Visit the web site of the corporation you're interested in developing a business relationship. Search for the supplier diversity, corporate sourcing, purchasing, emerging business office (or the like) for more information. If you are interested in becoming a certified S/D/M/W/V/DVBE certification, see **CHAPTER 8, SMALL, DISADVANTAGED, MINORITY, WOMEN, VETERAN-OWNED AND SERVICE-DISABLED VETERAN BUSINESS ENTERPRISE DEVELOPMENT** beginning on page 319.

Strategic Alliances

A strategic alliance is defined as a partnership between two or more companies. This form of business has become a more viable, cost effective and efficient way to meet internal growth objectives. More and more companies are relying on strategic alliances as opposed to mergers or acquisitions. The purpose of forming an alliance includes, but is not limited, to:

1. revenue growth by gaining entrance into new markets at less cost and greater speed;

2. cutting costs in current operations;

3. accessing new distribution channels and geographical areas; and

4.   sharing risks in new growth ventures.

While this form of business growth has been proven successful in many instances, implementation doesn't come without difficulties. Research and planning are key critical elements that can mitigate problems that may arise. But to achieve success, you must begin by:

1.   having clear goals and objectives;

2.   obtaining strong commitment of senior management;

3.   screening partners carefully;

4.   structuring solid agreements; and

5.   setting measurable performance goals.

Mentor-Protégé Programs

Mentor-Protégé programs are designed to enhance the capabilities and improve the abilities of small businesses to successfully compete for and receive public and private contracts. The benefits of participating in a mentor-protégé program may include, but is not limited, to:

1.   an opportunity for the protégé to joint venture with the mentor;

2.   mentor making its expertise, resources and capabilities available to the protégé; and

3.   mentor aiding the protégé financially.

Program eligibility and criteria vary by organization. But in most instances, participants receive management and technical contract assistance, financial aid and subcontract support. Requirements of mentors and protégés include:

Mentor
- can be a large or small business concern;
- must show commitment and ability to assist;

- business has shown profitability over time;
- must provide valuable support; and
- has knowledge of contracting guidelines.

Protégé
- must be a small business concern as defined by the Small Business Administration;
- must be in business for specified length of time as required by the agency or corporation; and
- must have demonstrated knowledge of their business and capabilities.

As with any other business relationship, a mentor-protégé relationship begins with a written agreement. The agreement is intended to specify the responsibility of the mentor and protégé, as well as, provide a mechanism for monitoring the overall relationship. The most critical aspect of forming a mentor-protégé relationship is that roles are specifically understood by both parties and the relationship does not turn in to one where the protégé becomes an "employee" of the mentor. The agreement must include:

1. an assessment of the protégé's needs;

2. specific assistance needed from the mentor to address those needs;

3. roles and responsibilities of all involved;

4. terms and conditions;

5. the time limits of the agreement; and

6. conditions under which the agreement can be terminated.

Federal government agencies such as the Small Business Administration, Department of Defense, Department of Transportation and Department of Treasury all have mentor-protégé programs. Even your local SCORE office can arrange a mentor your business. You can obtain more information online at:

1. **Small Business Administration Mentor-Protégé Program**
   https://www.sba.gov/content/mentor-protege-program

2. **U.S. Department of Defense Small Business Programs**
   http://www.acq.osd.mil/osbp/sb/programs/

3. **U.S. Department of Transportation**
   https://www.transportation.gov/osdbu/procurement-assistance/mentor-protege-pilot-program

4. **U.S. Department of the Treasury Mentor-Protégé Program**
   https://www.treasury.gov/resource-center/sb-programs/Pages/dcfo-osdbu-mentor-protege-index.aspx

Many private corporations offer mentor-protégé programs as part of their overall supplier development initiatives to help grow their small business partners. These programs vary in size and scope depending on the company's interest in small business development. However, they are not widely broadcasted so you will need to visit their websites to obtain specific information on their individual programs.

Preparing Bids & Proposals

The Competitive Bid and Proposal Process

Preparation of bids and proposals can be a complex and time-consuming task. Bidders and proposers must have a clear understanding of the bid and proposal process, scope of work, scheduling and total involvement of the appropriate staff. This includes the technical expertise required to perform, the facilities necessary to support the technical personnel, and administrative and financial personnel familiar with government contracting and cost performance.

The bid and proposal processes begin with a need. In order for that need to be fulfilled, an Invitation for Bid (IFB), Request for Proposals (RFP) or a Request for Qualifications (RFQ) is issued. These opportunities are made public through some type of advertising medium (e.g., local newspapers, contracting offices, *FedBizOpps*, company web sites, etc.). Unsolicited proposals are those submitted to an agency, corporation or organization where there has been no advertisement for a product/service.

Once a solicitation of any kind has been let, it is imperative that the bidder/proposer carefully read each and every page in the packet. This is important because the language in a solicitation can be overwhelming and confusing. Terms like "compliance", "deliverables", "severability", "waiver", "indemnity", "default", "termination", "general provisions", "special conditions", "exceptions" and "change orders" are but a few of the many terms that must be understood and accurately interpreted as defined in the bid/proposal package.

When provided with the opportunity to do so, send questions to the agency to get clarity where needed. Agencies generally have a deadline and a contact person for submitting questions to items in the solicitation who will respond in writing and send to all bidders/proposers.

You should also find out whether a pre-bid or pre-proposal conference has been scheduled for the solicitation. Depending on the nature of the bid/proposal, these conferences could be mandatory, not mandatory, in person, via conference call or any combination of these methods. The purpose of attending this type of event is for bidders/proposers speak directly with agency personnel who are responsible for the bid/proposal.

Also, at times errors are made in the solicitation by the issuing agency that are they sometimes not aware of until mentioned by bidder/proposer. In that case, an addendum is developed. It too must be read very carefully in that it may require additional or less documentation not stated in the original solicitation. You may be required to demonstrate you've seen and read it.

An IFB is issued when there is a need to procure a specific product/service. This sealed bid process states exactly what is to be procured so all bidders are bidding on the same requirements and competing at the same level. Typically items such as commodities, minor services and minor construction projects are procured through this process. Because these types of procurements are usually very specific, the process is relatively simple. However, it is critical that each bid specifically address what is called out for and must be submitted by the deadline or it will be rejected.

RFPs and RFQs (solicitations usually for professional services) are issued by a government agency or corporation when products or services being procured cannot be defined well enough in an IFB and negotiation may be necessary. This process enables the proposer to expound on their capabilities and offer an approach or methodology for accomplishing specific tasks. Submissions are then delivered to the agency or corporation in the form of a proposal.

Bid Preparation

Bids are generally publicly advertised online or in a local newspaper by each issuing agency. The process entails obtaining a bid package for a project, thoroughly completing it and submitting it on or before a set date. A typical bid package contains:

1. title, issuing agency, bid number, submission date and time, bid opening date;

2. requirements as to how the bids should be submitted;

3. when and how the awards will be made;

4. contact persons for purchasing, technical, payment, etc.;

5. specifications for each product/service needed; and

6. bid form stating the cost and authorized signatories.

Writing a Proposal

If you're still interested in pursuing contract opportunities, writing a proposal is inevitable. A proposal is intended to demonstrate a company's best technical and management abilities. Much like a business plan, there are several ways to write a proposal. Each agency or corporation will have a specified format to be followed to the letter. The RFP or RFQ will outline categories and contain documents that will need to be completed and signed. But regardless of the format used, the basic components include:

I. **Cover letter** - On company letterhead, addressed to agency contract officer, name of project, project number, bid-proposal date, list of documents within the bid/proposal package, contact person with phone number, and other information as applicable. Refer **to Exhibit 12 – Cover Letter of Introduction** on page 131.

II. **Cover page** - Displays company name, address, phone number, web address, logo, document name, project name, project number, contact person with title and date. Refer to **Exhibit 11 – Cover Page** on page 128.

III. <u>Table of Contents</u> - List all documents with pages numbers contained within the proposal. Refer to **Exhibit 13 – Table of Contents** on page 133.

IV. <u>Authorizations Page</u> - Signatures of appropriate board members, executives or other applicable parties demonstrating their approval and support of the document being submitted. Refer to **Exhibit 14 – Authorizations Page** on page 134.

V. <u>Technical Proposal - Introduction or Executive Summary</u> - Summarize all major information and details contained within the proposal. Outlines program scope, expected results, staffing, resources and a brief methodology. Refer to **Exhibit 15 – Executive Summary** on page 138.

VI. <u>Project Approach</u> - Detailed methodology, production plans, production schedule, quality control plans, reliability testing. Include graphs, charts, tables, schedules, drawings, illustrations, reference material, supporting statistical and narrative data, etc.

VII. <u>Management Proposal</u> – Résumés or CVs of all officers and key persons involved with the project. Details of expertise, training, education, licensing and certifications. Equal opportunity/affirmative action and subcontractor information, if applicable. Details of company's past experience and performance on similar projects or projects of equal or similar magnitude. Refer to **Exhibit 33 – Résumé/Curriculum Vitae** on page 178.

VIII. <u>Financial Stability</u> - Supporting documentation of a firm's and its subconsultant's financial stability and ability to perform the contract to include audited financial statements for the past three years and information pertaining to past bankruptcy, contract defaults, and violations of any regulatory acts. Refer to **Exhibits 35 to 40** on pages 185 thru 192 for sample financial statements and financial metrics.

IX. <u>Price/Cost Proposal</u> - Include detailed data on direct and indirect labor costs, taxes, travel, research and development (R&D) expenditures, pricing terms, payment terms, etc.

X. **Table of Exceptions** - A statement of whether or not a firm fully complies with the requirements as defined in the RFP and a detailed list of expectations, usually in a table format.

XI. **Applicable Forms** - Complete all forms presented in the original, RFQ, IFB or RFP. Place them wherever appropriate in the proposal or in the Appendix.

XII. **Appendix** - Any attachments to include forms, documents listed in the technical proposal and other supporting documents as applicable. Refer to **Exhibit 50 – Appendix** on page 224.

XIII. **Definition of Terms** - Definitions of all technical terms or terms which may be unclear or confusing. Refer to **Exhibit 51 – Glossary of Terms** on page 225.

Because proposal evaluators read so many proposals in response to any one RFP, IFB or RFQ solicitation, they exercise their option to eliminate as many as possible on the basis of non-responsiveness. This could include the proposer:

1. not following submission instructions to the letter, including not signing it;

2. omitting any forms or documents requested.

3. not answering questions properly or fully.

4. submitting a proposal that is sloppy, disorganized, incoherent or late.

5. unethically trying to gain an unfair advantage in the process.

Offer and Acceptance of Bids/Proposals

Once all bids/proposals have been received, a team of reviewers evaluates each proposal, rejecting those that are non-conforming, non-responsive or late. Openings can either occur publicly (e.g., construction related bids) or privately (e.g., professional services proposals). With all things being equal, more often than not, an award is made on lowest price. There are, however, many exceptions to this practice. Sometimes a bidder/proposer may have a higher price, but because of their reputation or their relationship, they could receive the award.

Contract Performance

Being awarded a contract is an amazing event. But the award is just the beginning. Successful bidders are expected to deliver products/services with the highest degree of skill, care and diligence using the highest professional standards. Meeting the schedule of deliverables set forth in the proposal is paramount. Once all obligations of a contract have been met completely and exactly (even if there are modifications) the contract is then discharged. However, contracts can be discharged for other reasons:

1. **By agreement** – where either party terminates their contract by written agreement.

2. **For breach** – where one party does not adhere to their duties or responsibilities, then the non-breaching party may terminate the contract.

3. **Doctrine of frustration** – when an unforeseen event undermines a party's principle purpose for entering into a contract.

4. **Doctrine of impossibility** – when non-performance of duties under a contract occurs based on a change in circumstances or the discovery of pre-existing circumstances.

In the event a successful bidder defaults on a contract, the contracting agency may without prejudice terminate the contract and/or the bidder's right to perform contracted services. The agency will then finish the contract using any method it deems expedient and in their best interest. If damages occur, the agency can borne any costs and expenses on the bidder in default.

Many contracts also have a liquidated damages clause. They are agreements especially common in construction contracts. The purpose of a liquidated damages agreement is to ensure that one party is not damaged by the failure of the other party. It establishes a predetermined sum that must paid if a party fails to perform as promised.

CHAPTER 5

EMAIL, SOCIAL MEDIA, EMAIL MARKETING & USING YOUR WEBSITE

Email and Social Media: The Science

Email, social media, email marketing and the development and use of a website is practically a science in this day and age. Volumes and volumes of information have been written and published in books, magazines and on the Internet about this communications phenomenon. In this chapter, we have provided just a brief overview of what this medium entails.

Email: The First Social Media

When we think of email, we don't necessarily associate it with social media. However, email, in fact, was the very first social media platform. Dating back to 1969, ARPANET (Advanced Research Project Agency) developed the first operational switching networks which ultimately became the Internet which was used by research laboratories and universities as a means of electronic communications, email.

Shortly thereafter, the use of email was internal to companies and organizations to send messages to colleagues working within the same network, from one computer to another. According to a 2013 report from The Radicati Group, Inc., "The total number of worldwide email accounts is expected to increase from nearly 3.9 billion accounts in 2013 to over 4.9 billion accounts by the end of 2017."

Email is the most widely-used and cost effective form of communications today. It has basically taken the place of the telephone. No longer is it necessary for a person to be personally or even physically available for them to get a message or receive documents for that matter. As long as an Internet connection is available, anyone can receive any kind of message or attachment anytime, anywhere in the world on a computer, phone, and now on a watch.

Unwanted and Unsolicited Email Messages

Nearly everyone receives unsolicited email at some time or another. Someone may have gotten your email address from a list you may have knowingly or unknowingly been added to, from a purchase you've made online or maybe from someone who knows you. Worse, hackers or spammers may have gotten it after trolling the Internet and found it because your computer is unprotected. They then try to get you to install "malware" so that they can control your computer remotely.

Either way, unwanted and unsolicited email (considered "junk mail" also known as SPAM) can be a nuisance. And opening SPAM or junk mail can ruin your computer and easily allow hackers to send unwanted messages to your contacts as though it were you. But if your computer has ever been hacked, there are ways to fix it and prevent it from happening again.

1. **Use security software that updates automatically.** Microsoft Security Essentials is free product that can protect against viruses, spyware, and other malicious software. You can also purchase antivirus software such as McAfee and Norton for a fee.

2. **Use extreme caution when opening attachments or downloading files received in an email.** Unless you are familiar with the sender, don't open attachments you are not expecting or that you believe could be dangerous to your system.

3. **Download only free software that you know and trust.** Free software (particularly for games, file-sharing and custom toolbars) can and obtain contain malware.

4. **Report SPAM.** You can forward unwanted or deceptive messages to the Federal Trade Commission (FTC) at spam@uce.gov. Be sure to include:

   - The complete email
   - Your email provider
   - That you are complaining about SPAM
   - If you are unable to unsubscribe to the email list and your request is not being honored

You can also file a formal complaint with the FTC online at https://www.ftccomplaintassistant.gov/#&panel1-1. Diligence is key. Always watch for warning signs that your computer has been hacked. If you find messages from you that you did not send, or your computer is running slow or inefficiently, or family, friends or customers alert you of messages that seem strange or uncharacteristic of you, then you may have been a victim of a computer hack. If this happens:

1. Locate the Microsoft Safety Scanner online. Download the scanner at http://www.microsoft.com/security/scanner/ and follow the instructions. This free online scanner can help you identify and remove viruses, clean up your hard drive, and in some instances, improve your computer's performance.

2. If you can't get to the Internet, restart your computer in Safe Mode with networking enabled. Repeatedly press the "F8" key until the "Advanced Boot Options" screen appears.

3. Use the arrow keys to highlight "Safe Mode with Networking", then press "Enter."

4. Log on to your computer with the user account with administrator rights.

5. Follow the instructions above using the Microsoft Safety Scanner online.

There is a plethora of information online regarding removing computer viruses. Just do a little research and you will find free and paid solutions to protect your computer.

Creating Effective Email Messages

Email is a prevalent force in the world today. Without it, businesses would be unable compete in this global economy. The general public would be unable to communicate at the speed of light. Now that we understand email and its significance in our society (for both business and personal use) it's important to know how to construct a proper email.

Conforming to email etiquette is important when reaching out to family, friends, and current and potential business associates. As with speaking, the "way" you say something via email is equally as "how" and "what" you say. And because it is so prevalent in our society, the term "Netiquette" (net etiquette) has been coined in reference to the use of decorum when creating and responding to emails.

When composing an email, the recipient is the first consideration when determining how and what will be stated. Using inappropriate statements, unsuitable language, poor grammar and typographical errors can be embarrassing when composing an email for business purposes. Even the use of all capital letters has standards. However, when the email is for a friend or family member, rules are not so stringent, but always remember that once you hit "send" it is out there for anyone on the planet to see it.

The table below provides a guideline as to how email should be used in both personal and professional environments:

EMAIL TOPIC	PERSONAL EMAIL	PROFESSIONAL EMAIL
Personal email address	Should generally be used for personal emails to family and friends.	Should not be used when sending emails to business associates. However, can be used when sending email for personal reasons to a company or organization.
Business email address	Should not be used for personal email.	Should always be used for business email because it adds credibility to the message.
Subject line	Can be casual depending on the recipient. For example, "Yo, let's hook up 'bout 6. CU ltr."	Should be clear and direct. Let recipient know specifically the purpose of the email. A good is example, "January Sales Goals On Target."
Proofreading	Proofreading is always a good idea, especially if you are sending an email and auto-correct is enabled. However, if your grammar and spelling are not quite up to par, your friends and family will understand.	Proofreading is critical when sending a professional email. Never rely on spell check or auto correct. You could very easily end up using a term that is misleading, incorrect or improper. PROOFREAD. PROOFREAD. PROOFREAD.

EMAIL TOPIC	PERSONAL EMAIL	PROFESSIONAL EMAIL
Reply or Reply All	If for more than one person, be sure you want everyone to see your response and the response from others. If you receive an email in error, let the sender know.	It's always a good idea to reply to an email. It lets the sender know that you received the email, even if you don't have anything to contribute to the conversation. It's not always necessary to "Reply All." Email threads can get lengthy, and most people don't need that much information.
Email greeting	Greetings such as "hey there", "what's up" and the like are fine for friends and family.	Always use an appropriate salutation such as Mr., Mrs., or Hi or Hello unless you know the individual prefers to be called.
Punctuation and capitalization	Overuse of exclamation points or capital letters can give a sense you are yelling. Unless that is your intent, less is better.	It's never a good idea to use exclamation points (especially several) in a professional email. And as a general rule, all caps, again, give the sense that the sender is yelling.
Emoticons	Emoticons are fun and totally acceptable in personal emails. However, there are some that are meant to be offensive.	Almost never a good idea to use emoticons in a professional email. However, it the recipient is a very close business associate/friend, limited use of emoticons is acceptable.
Addressee/recipient	Check and check again your email address. Some ISPs auto load email addresses and you wouldn't want your email to go to the wrong person with the same name as the intended recipient.	Sending an email to the wrong recipient could be damaging. Particularly is the wrong person receives private or critical information.
Humor	Family and friends use humor all the time in email. As long as the recipient is not offended, it's okay.	It's rarely a good idea to use humor in an email. Because the recipient can't "hear" you, it's easy for the joke to lose something in translation.

261

What is Social Media?

Social media is an instant and free form of communication used by individuals and businesses worldwide to engage in conversation with millions, providing the visibility and connectivity individuals use to communicate and businesses use for branding. Social media is defined by Wikipedia as:

> ". . . computer-mediated tools that allow people to create, share, or change information, career interests, ideas and pictures/videos in virtual communities and networks."

More simply put, social media is the way in which human beings use technology to communicate with others, far and wide, and in real time. Not since the telegraph and telephone were invented in 1875 and 1876, respectively, have people been able to connect so quickly and easily for personal or business reasons. While the functions of telephone and telegraph pale in comparison to today's communications technology, both were, in fact, that period's state-of-the-art communications tools.

In this new information economy, through the use of social media, we can communicate, share, and most importantly, build trust with one another with speed and proficiency like never before. Whether it's via Facebook, Instagram or others where we connect with family and friends online with comments, pictures and videos or via Pinterest where we share our hobbies and interests through posting images and pictures, people want to share their good and bad experiences with the world.

After identifying the appropriate social media tool, you'll need to open an account, build a profile and then begin your journey connecting with the world. The key to successful use of social media is participation. You want to locate or create a group, participate in the discussion, and provide great content. If you are using social media for personal reasons, then regular participation is not necessary.

On the other hand, if you are using social media to build a business, frequent and consistent participation is not only necessary, it's required. In addition to use as a means of communicating internally and externally, social media is used in marketing, sales, customer service and public relations. According to the Social Media Examiner, in 2014, 97% of marketers are currently participating social media though "aren't sure what social media tools are the best to use."

Time and again the use of social media has been proven to dramatically increase sales for many businesses. Both large and small businesses do an amazing job of incorporating social media in their day-to-day marketing efforts. If your business is not using any form of social media, you are being left behind. You can believe your competitors are using social media in some or all of the following ways by:

1. disseminating your product and/or company information.

2. educating customers and followers by providing company and other relevant facts.

3. inexpensively responding to current customers and reaching out to new customers.

4. increasing brand recognition that leads to brand loyalty.

5. quickly converting customer inquiries into sales.

6. receiving customer comments about products and services.

7. networking and relationship building with similar and sometimes dissimilar businesses, individuals and organizations.

8. entertaining via music, movies and videos.

Social media, like a website, can show your customer or potential customer that your business is real and offers real products or services. The online discussions about your company inform the public that you are a real organization, even if the discussion is negative. Using and accessing social media is just the validation individuals need to determine whether they should do business with any company.

Social Media Platforms

A significant impact in reaching out to others across the globe has been made through the use of social media. Over the past few years, many platforms and tools have been developed to aid in this phenomenon. While they serve different purposes, for the most part all are created to share, interact and educate through the use of commentary, photos, images, audio and video.

The key to using social media successfully is in determining which social media platform is the best for your type of business. Over the past few years, a multitude of social media tools have been developed and are now gone. Today, some of the most popular social media platforms and their purpose include those listed in the following table:

SOCIAL NETWORK	ESTIMATED USERS	TYPE OF SOCIAL MEDIA USE	TARGET POST FREQUENCY
Facebook www.facebook.com/	1.28 billion	Social network leader focused on interaction with friends and family, and now business. Messages, photos, videos and website links can be posted.	2 posts per day
Twitter www.twitter.com	255 million	Microblogging with short messages (maximum of 140 characters to keep up to date with day's events.	One "tweet" per hour
LinkedIn www.linkedin.com	300 million	For building professional connections to aid in career development.	Any time during work week 2 to 5 posts
Google+ www.plus.google.com	1 billion	Social network product of Google with a heavy visual focus.	One post per day
Pinterest www.pinterest.com	70 million	A platform that allows "pinning" of pictures of individual interests just like on a bulletin board. It is a tool for collecting and organizing images, videos or webpages that are personal or from the Internet.	Pin 3 to 4 times per week
Instagram www.instagram.com	300 million	Platform for sharing visual content using mobile devices Used for taking, editing and sharing photos and videos on a mobile device.	Post 1 to 2 per day
YouTube www.youtube.com	1 billion	Platform for hosting and sharing video content. Helps to keep with favorite video bloggers (vloggers)	Helps one keep up to date with favorite video bloggers (vloggers).
Foursquare www.foursquare.com	45 million	Focused on geolocation based interaction	N/A

SOCIAL NETWORK	ESTIMATED USERS	TYPE OF SOCIAL MEDIA USE	TARGET POST FREQUENCY
Snapchat www.snapchat.com	100 million	Microblogging platform where images and videos can be sent, but don't remain on devices.	N/A
Blog Uses the feature from your website or a blogger application	150 million	A web log used in business and as personal journals on virtually every topic in in the world. One of the many platforms where anyone can discuss hobbies, interest, life, travel, etc.	3 posts per week
Reddit www.reddit.com	20 million	Platform for what's new and popular on the Internet where users post stories, links and media, and other users vote and comment on the posts.	N/A
Yelp www.yelp.com	142 million	Helps people find local businesses such as restaurants, events, hair stylists, medical professionals. Users can post reviews on their experiences.	N/A

Social Media Planning

With a clear understanding of what social media is, we now need to discuss what social media does. As a business owner, marketing is a major function regardless of the business or industry. Through the use of social media, companies can literally watch their sales grow astronomically instantaneously following the release of a product through social media marketing. The first step is to develop a social media marketing plan. In doing so you must ascertain:

1. Who is customer/audience? (e.g., men, women and/or children, animals, others)

2. What is their profession or interests? (e.g., doctors, teachers, artists, musicians, cooks, etc.)

3. Where is your customer or audience located? (e.g., local, national, global)

4. What social media tools does you customer/audience use most?

5. What is your mission statement for the use of each social media platform to reach your customer/audience?

6. What is your outreach goal for the use of each social media platform? (e.g., 100 new followers per month, increase sales $1000 in new business or new subscribers, etc.)

7. What is your strategy for providing your new customer/audience content? (e.g., number of new postings each week, postings that coincide with major holidays, local or national events, etc.)

Once you have determined the best social media platform(s) for your business, devising a plan for use is your next step. Social media planning is much like long range or strategic planning as outlined in **CHAPTER 3, STRATEGIC (LONG RANGE) PLAN** beginning on page 193. Your social media plan should entail the following:

1. **Assess your current social media and marketing situation**
   Review how you are currently using social and other marketing methods. Assess how and if they are effective, taking note as to how much your following has increased/decreased and how that change affected sales or participation.

2. **Set goals and objectives**
   Establish your goals and objectives for social media. This will help you gauge whether your social media campaign(s) is/are meeting your overall marketing goals and objectives, and determine your return on investment.

   One example of a social media goal and objective would be:

   Social Media Goal: To increase online sales 5% every month using Instagram.

   Social Media Objective: To create two videos each month to increase followers by 200 each month.

3. **Devise steps to improve your social media presence**

In preparing your social media plan, referring to your stated goals and objectives, you will need to create a document to include:

- **Introduction** – What are the social media issues?

- **Background** – How has social media been handled in the past?

- **Strategy** – What is the strategy for improving the current social media plan?

- **Implementation** – What steps will be taken to meet the strategy?

- **Opportunity** – What opportunities exist with implementing a new social media strategy?

- **Measuring & Reporting** - How will results be measured and reported? What metrics and analytics will be used?

- **Conclusion** – What do the results of the final plan look like?

4. **Determine the type of content for your social media marketing.**

In the world of social media and publishing, content is KING! Devise a plan to create content and a schedule for posting. You may want to create and schedule postings for several weeks at a time. This will enable to you post content regularly. Your content plan should include:

- The type(s) of content you intend to post and promote
- The frequency you will post
- The intended audience for each post or promotion
- Who will create the content – in-house or out-house
- A plan for promoting the content
- A plan for responding to comments
- Measuring results of social media marketing

5. **Test campaign, track progress, analyze results and modify your plan**

Not every campaign or plan works out after its launch. So it is important that you know what is working and what's not. Sales, comments, reposting, etc. are signs that your campaign is working. But in either case, you should always be looking to make any adjustments to test different audiences and customers.

A great tool for managing your social media accounts is Hootsuite. Launched in 2008, Hootsuite is a social media management system that helps keep track and manage many social media network channels simultaneously. You can view streams from multiple networks such as Facebook, Google+, Twitter Instagram, LinkedIn, Foursquare, WordPress and Vimeo.

Remember, your social media plan, as with your business plan for which your social media plan is a part, it is a working document. It should reviewed regularly and revised as necessary. Pay close attention to how and what social media tools are working and which ones are not.

Email Marketing

Email marketing is exactly what its namesake suggests, marketing via email. The purpose of email marketing is to send direct promotional information to increase business from existing customers and acquire new customers. The beauty of using email marketing is the ability to track your return on investment (ROI), that it's significantly less expensive than traditional mail, there's are no printing, and no addressing or mailing costs associated with any campaign.

Email marketing takes the form of advertisements, newsletters, invitations, announcement, special offer or educational information. One of the benefits of this type of email marketing is that you can literally send thousands of emails to your contacts simultaneously. This is one of the most cost-effective methods of sending your messages to large numbers of recipients.

The one differentiator of email marketing from any other email marketing is that email marketing is permission based. That means the sender MUST have permission from the recipient to send them an email via this platform. Without permission, the email is considered SPAM and can cause your email marketing account to be shut down.

Some of the more popular email marketing companies include:

- **Constant Contact**
  https://login.constantcontact.com

- **GetResponse**
  http://www.getresponse.com

- **IContact**
  https://www.icontact.com

- **MailChimp**
  http://mailchimp.com/

- **Pinpointe**.
  http://www.pinpointe.com/

When using email marketing, it's important to know whether a program violates any spam laws such as the United States' Controlling the Assault of Non-Solicited Pornography and Marketing Act of 2003 (CAN-SPAM) which can be found online at the FTC https://www.ftc.gov/tips-advice/business-center/guidance/can-spam-act-compliance-guide-business.

Marketing Using Your Website

Let's begin by defining the obvious, "what is a website?" Wikipedia defines website as,

". . .a set of related web pages typically served from a single web domain. A website is hosted on at least one web server, accessible via a nework such as the Internet or a private local area network (LAN) through an Internet address known as a uniform resource locator (URL)."

A website is very important to your business because it serves as the voice for your business that "speaks" 24 hours a day, 7 days a week, 365 days a year. Having an online presence allows your customers to conveniently and instantly locate your company. If your site is well-constructed, easy to navigate and contains great content, your customers will purchase your products/services, and visit your site often.

Another benefit of having a website is that it alleviates the need for brick and mortar. Billions of dollars in goods and services are sold each year online. No longer do customers have to spend time going from store to store. They can let their fingers do the walking and find more on the web than they can letting the feet do the walking. In addition, the cost benefit to you is not having to pay rent in commercial space.

A well-constructed website should:

1. Have a masthead with your logo. Visitors need to know that they have reached the desired site.

2. Easily navigate from page to page. All pages should be appropriately titled and load quickly.

3. Have a clear message of what your company is and does. The language should be clear enough for a child to comprehend.

4. Have a mission statement that lets your visitors know who you are and what you are doing.

5. Be clutter-free from a lot of visuals. People are drawn to white space.

6. Have useful content. Providing information of value will not only bring visitors back to your site, but could also increase sales of your products and services. In addition, people love to share good information.

7. Help build a community of visitors with the use of your social media.

8. Create a blog. A good conversation will always keep people returning to your site.

Creating Your Blog

Maintaining a blog, either on a website or by use of blogging applications, has become a major online media for personal use and in the world of business. While social media such as Facebook and Twitter hold the top spots in social media use, the use of blogs continues to grow year after year. In fact, more CEOs, college professors, journalists and political figures use blogs as a means of reaching their constituents on a daily basis.

So what exactly is a blog? Its name comes from the amalgamation of the terms "web" and "log." It makes up in the Internet what's referred to as the "blogosphere." A blog is defined by Wikipedia as:

". . .a discussion of informational site published on the world wide web consisting of discrete entries ("posts") typically displayed in reverse chronological order."

While blogs can be added to any website, it's a little different from a website. A blog is generally a single page of posts. Each post is displayed in reverse chronological order, meaning the latest post is first. Each entry is composed by one author. The author writes a short commentary about any topic which can include links, images, photos, audio, video, etc. Others viewing the post can then share or comment on the post. It's that simple.

Blogs provide commentary on current events, news or just something of interest to the author. To others, blogs serve as a personal journal containing thoughts, ideas or opinions. As a communications vehicle for businesses, blogs are used for sales, marketing, public relations or internal communications. Through stream of consciousness, blogs created by individuals discuss areas of interest to include vacations, family, recipes, or just gossip.

A similar communications vehicle used by corporations is called a "qlog" (questions blog). With it, readers submit questions to be answered by designated persons within the company. And then there's the "vlog" (video blog). This media used to post videos. As with a normal blog, a vlog is a post from a single author on any topic, however instead of being composed with text, images, photos, etc. it's actually a video. Once footage is completed, it can be uploaded to a YouTube channel for viewing.

Considering the use of a blog on your website is good step in communications sharing with your visitors. A blog can provide your visitors with rich content that can educate, entertain, and serves as a means of exchanging thoughts and ideas. Whether you post text, audio and/or video, your visitors can learn a tremendous amount about you and your company. And creating good content will keep them coming back for more.

As with all other media, there is a multitude of blogging applications available today. Many are free and others are fee based and offer additional features. Some of the top blogging applications include:

- **WordPress.com** (free and fee based)
  https://wordpress.com/

- **Blogger** (free)
  www.google.com

- **Typepad** (fee based)
  www.typepad.com

- **Copyblogger** (free)
  www.copyblogger.com/blog/

- **Tumblr** (free)
  www.tumblr.com

- **Movable Type** (fee based)
  https://www.movabletype.com/

It's important to look at all the available options for your blog before settling on one. Definitely using the blog application in your website is a great choice. However, if you chose to use a separate application like one of those listed above, do your homework. The free applications may suffice, but depending on your plans for your blog, you may need the additional features a paid application offers, such as plug-ins and full control of your content. Free platforms won't necessarily provide everything you need.

After selecting your blogging platform (or using your website), you are well on your way to becoming a part of the blogosphere. Any platform you select will provide you with step-by-step instruction (with video and/or text) on setting up your page. It will also provide you with technical support via phone or chat.

Maintaining a blog requires an extreme amount of dedication in posting if it's to attract and retain readers. An ongoing stream of traffic and interaction can also earn a business a lot of money. One to two quality posts per day can keep readers coming back. A few ways to keep up a quality blog include:

1. Find unique and interesting topics to post. You don't need to do what everyone else is doing.

2. Make sure your headlines are attention getters. A great headline is usually the one thing that will make a visitor to your blog take notice.

3. Provide honest content to readers. No one wants to be lied to or misled. Your readers want to follow someone who they trust.

4. Make your content easy to understand and worth sharing. In the case of content sharing, imitation is the greatest form of flattery.

5. Be generous with information. Not everything is obvious to everyone.

6. Respond to your readers. This will help keep the conversations alive and lively. This is especially important when receiving negative comments on a post.

7. Provide comments on other blogs as often as possible. Make sure to give the same care and relevant content as you do for your own blog.

8. Build an email list. This will enable you to promote new ideas to readers.

9. When possible, include a call to action (e.g., sign up for a newsletter, purchase a product, follow you on social media, etc.).

10. Find your own voice. Your readers need to get to know the real person behind the words, pictures, images and videos.

11. Be patient. A large following definitely doesn't come over night. Good content, consistency and patience will bring the numbers you desire.

A great website/blog resource is Mashable (www.mashable.com). It is a news blog that publishes thousands of articles and videos on current news and events, social media, small business, entertainment, and the newest innovations in technology. Mashable was created to inform, inspire and entertain the digital generation. In their own words, ". . . *redefining storytelling by documenting and shaping the digital revolution in a new voice, new formats and cutting-edge technologies to a uniquely dedicated audience. . ."*

This powerful resource for information, Mashable has over 45 million monthly unique visitors and over 26 million social media followers. Mashable can be followed on RSS (really simple syndication) feed, email, Twitter or Facebook. Because massive amounts of information are generated daily, it's possible to subscribe to just a few individual channels to avoid being overwhelmed with content.

Other helpful resources include blog indexes for bloggers to promote their blogs or identify blogs with content relevant to their business or interests. Some blog indexes include:

- **The Blog Index**
  http://www.theblogindex.net/

- **Blogs Index Web Directory**
  https://sites.google.com/site/blogsindex/web-directory

RSS (Really Simple Syndication) Feed

An RSS (really simple syndication) feed is the way to automatically share your website content and keep track of new content on your favorite websites. Instead of "bookmarking" selected websites to receive updates, an RSS feed will automatically update your feed when new information is posted. With bookmarking you would have to regularly check the websites you follow. If you're tracking a number of them, it could get tedious and you could miss new postings.

By going to your favorite website, blog or news site, locate the RSS button and select your feed reader. A feed reader, sometimes call an "aggregator" is a program or website that will check and continuously search for new content on all the blogs, news and websites that you have subscribed to, and feed that information to you on your website.

Some of the top RSS reader services include:

- **Feedly**
  https://feedly.com/

- **Feedbin**
  https://feedbin.com/

- **Newsblur**
  https://newsblur.com/

- **Feed Wrangler**
  https://feedwrangler.net/welcome.html

Search Engine Optimization (SEO)

There are nearly one billion websites in the world today and the number increases by the second. A single search on any topic can return millions of results. This is why it's so important that your website rise to the top of list. Search engine optimization or SEO is the methodology of the strategies, techniques and tactics used to rank content based on the number of visitors to a website in the search results page of a search engine improving the site's visibility.

How SEO Works

As explained by Google, SEO uses three key processes in delivering search results: 1) crawling; 2) indexing; and 3) serving. Using huge set of computers, a Googlebot (also known as a robot, bot, or spider) program "crawls" billions of pages on the web. An algorithmic process using computer programs determines which sites to crawl, how often and how many pages to fetch from each site beginning with a list of web page URLs generated from previous crawl processes, augmented with sitemap data provided by webmasters.

Next, a massive index of all the words and their location on each page is compiled. This includes most content types such as key content tags and attributes, but may exclude some rich media files or dynamic pages. During a query, the system searches the index for matching pages and returns what is considered the most relevant results.

For a website to rank high in search results, Google must be able to crawl and index the site correctly. There are Webmaster Guidelines that can be found at https://support.google.com/webmasters/answer/35769 and provide very important information on SEO for your website. These guidelines will help Google find, index and rank your site. To avoid being removed from the Google index, be sure to adhere to quality guidelines.

Affiliate Marketing

Affiliate marketing is a way website owners earn commissions by promoting online businesses' products on their sites. An affiliate program is designed to build partnerships between merchants (online sellers of goods and services) and publishers (website owners). Some of the top affiliate programs pay anywhere from 25% to 50% in commission.

There are literally thousands of affiliate programs to join. Members of these affiliate programs include Macy's, Amazon, Fingerhut, Home Goods, JCPenney, Walmart and Barnes & Noble just to name a few. The benefits of being an affiliate marketer include:

1. No cost to join and there are no start-up costs.

2. Receiving pay per sale, pay per lead and pay per click commission based on visitor response to their site.

3. Building a lucrative business for anyone willing to put in the time and effort to build a following by consistently driving traffic to their site.

4. Working for companies selling products of the affiliate's choice.

5. Affiliate site visitors can provide valuable information on the latest trends.

The benefits of being a merchant include:

1. Building an online sales team that drives customers their sites.

2. Free advertising space on affiliate websites.

3. Receiving new traffic they may not have otherwise received via their normal advertising methods.

4. More effective use of advertising dollars.

5. Tracking sales, click-throughs and views are easy.

As with all online business dealings, there have also been scams reported regarding affiliate marketing. Both the merchant and the affiliate must exercise complete discretion when determining which sites to advertise on and which merchants to partner with, respectively.

If an affiliate puts false or misleading information on their site, it could seriously damage the reputation of the merchant. And on the other hand, affiliates must be careful about the program they select because merchants have been known to discontinue their programs without paying commissions to the deserving affiliates.

If affiliate marketing is something you are interested in, be sure to do your homework. Due diligence is key to a successful affiliate relationship. Below are list of the top affiliate marketing programs to consider:

- **Rakuten Linkshare**
  http://marketing.rakuten.com/affiliate-marketing

- **CJ by Conversant**
  www.cj.com

- **Amazon**
  https://affiliate-program.amazon.com/

- **Avangate**
  http://www.avangate.com/

- **Ebay Partner Network**
  https://www.ebaypartnernetwork.ebay.com/

Social Media Metrics

To ensure that your social media plan and individual campaigns are working according to established goals, you will need track, monitor and measure activities. There are some social media activities that are more important and more relevant to your business than others may be. Whatever the case, at a minimum, you will always want to analyze the following data:

1. **Reach** – The growth rate of your audience. This includes new followers.

2. **Visits and unique visits** – Visits are the number of times each person visits your website. Unique visits are counted only once.

3. **Engagement** – The rate of how much your followers/audience are engaged in responding to posts. This includes "likes", "shares", and comments on any post.

4. **Acquisition** – The number of visits that come from other social media platforms.

5. **Conversion** – The desired results from a post. This includes sales, signing up for a newsletter or coupon, completing a form, etc.

6. **Leads** – Visitors with the need or interest in your product/service.

7. **Impressions** – The number of visitors who saw your post.

8. **Bounce rate** – The number of visitors to your page, but leave without viewing other pages on your site.

9. **Exit rate** – The rate at which people leave your site at a given page.

10. **Time on site** – The length of time visitors stay on your site before exiting.

11. **Inbound links** – The number of sites linking back to your website or page.

12. **Response rate** – The speed at which comments and replies are made on social media, and how quickly marketing and sales leads are followed up on.

13. **Amplification rate** – The number of reshares or retweets on average for each post.

One of the most popular analytics tools is Google Analytics. It reports most all activity about your website and traffic, including all necessary social referrals for which you're interested. With it you can create custom dashboards for the metrics that are most important to you only. For more information on Google Analytics, visit their website at https://www.google.com/analytics/.

Social Media Marketing ROI (Return on Investment)

While we consider ourselves business people, we're not necessarily financial people. For the non-financial person, performing business calculations can be extremely challenging. But some degree of understanding financials is very important to your business in many aspects. To know whether your company's investment in social media marketing (as well as other marketing and promotion campaigns) has generated a profit, you must know and understand how to calculate your return or investment or ROI.

Return on investment is the measure in a percentage of net profit over the investment needed to generate that profit. The basic formula for calculating social media marketing ROI is:

<u>**Gross Profit – Marketing Investment = Net Profit**</u>
Marketing Investment

1. Determine the gross profit - generally total sales
2. Subtract the marketing investment – costs paid
3. That equals the net profit
4. Divide the marketing investment by the net profit

Setting an ROI goal on each marketing campaign (as well as an overall marketing goal) will guide your decisions on the types of campaigns and the resources needed to carry them out. The ROI metric will let you know which campaigns are working, which ones are not, and where you should dedicate marketing resources. For these reasons primarily, it's critical to track your ROI to know whether you are spending marketing dollars effectively and that they produce the best rates of return.

Another reminder to have an accountant (not just a bookkeeper) on your team to help you perform all the necessary calculations needed to understand whether your business is profitable. This may seem like a big expenditure, however, losing money, misallocated resources, and other financial missteps are even more costly.

CHAPTER 6

ACCESS
TO
CAPITAL

Understanding Financing Needs

Successful borrowing is more than just seeking financing. In fact, borrowing money is much like a science and requires a significant amount of planning. Those who lack experience and knowledge of what financing entails will ultimately find themselves in a situation much worse than they would have by not obtaining financing at all.

The ability to secure financing when you need it is as critical to the operation of your business as a good location, the right equipment, reliable sources of materials and supplies and an adequate labor force. When seeking financing to start a business, acquire a business or expand your current operation, you will need to decide:

1. What will the money be used for?

2. How much money do I need?

3. When will I need the money?

4. Where will the money come from?

5. What is my plan for repayment or return on investment?

In order to realistically answer these questions, you will need to make an assessment of your current business situation. This is done by writing a business plan or reviewing every aspect of your current one. Both the financial and marketing sections of your business plan can provide you with projections and assumptions that will support your funding needs.

Types of Financing

There are two types of financing; debt financing and equity financing. Debt financing is money borrowed from an outside source. With debt financing, lenders don't have an ownership interest in the business; the loan must be repaid with interest, collateral may be required and the financial relationship terminates upon repayment of the loan. Sources of debt financing include term lenders such as banks, credit unions commercial lenders, insurance, trust and mortgage companies, as well as government agencies.

Equity financing on the other hand, is money provided by investors for an ownership interest in the company. With equity financing, the money doesn't have to be repaid, collateral isn't necessary and there is no interest or fees associated. However, profits must be shared with investors, they may exercise some control of the company, and dividends paid to investors are not tax deductible. Sources of equity financing include venture capital and subordinated or mezzanine debt.

Depending on your capital needs, one source of financing may work better than another. For instance, if money is needed to make minor purchases, finance receivables, or is needed for only a short period of time, then debt financing is the best option. If a large amount of money is needed for an extended amount of time, equity financing is the obvious choice.

Selecting the Best Source of Capital

Funding requirements for new businesses are similar to those for established ones. The only exception is that for the established business with a good financial track record, obtaining capital can be a simple and painless undertaking. Both traditional and non-traditional sources of financing are viable options. Unfortunately, this doesn't hold true for the start-up or inexperienced borrower. Traditional forms of financing are usually not an option. This is simply because they:

- lack the assets necessary;

- have not yet established a relationship with their banker; or

- have not yet developed a financial track record.

Preparing the necessary documentation for a new business can sometimes be a great challenge. This is because all information presented is based on projections as opposed to actual historical data presented by an existing business. This is what makes funding new businesses a greater risk.

Sources of Capital

The following lists and describes just a few of the many debt and equity capital sources available to both new and existing businesses. Depending on the length of time in business, the type of business, or the reason for securing capital, some of these resources may or may not be the best option for your business. However, it would be worth the while to consider each option. Also, working with your accountant will prove valuable when making your financing decisions.

Debt Capital

Private

- **Personal accounts, friends, business associates and relatives**
  This is the most common way businesses are financed. Some of the vehicles used include personal savings, credit cards, insurance and pension. This type of financing is the least expensive from a financial standpoint, but can be costly from a relationship standpoint.

- **Partners**
  Can provide an important element to your business. Just be sure to select those who can supplement areas where you may be weak and provide complementary experience. Additionally, have a written partnership agreement that includes a provision for dissolution or buyout.

- **Employees**
  Employees who are loyal and have some tenure may be open to investing in the business under an employee stock option program (ESOP). While their contribution may not be significant and extended terms and favorable prices may be necessary, every dollar invested counts. Just be sure to always have written buy-back provision. If possible, keep employees' ownership below 20%.

<u>Term Lenders</u>

- **Banks and Credit Unions**
  This traditional lending source provides short-term lending for day-to-day operating capital, lines of credit, leasing, mortgages, letters of credit, credit references and other financial services.

- **Commercial Lenders**
  In addition to banks, this includes primarily acceptance companies and finance companies. They lend on commercial assets to include land, buildings and equipment.

- **Insurance, Trust and Mortgage Companies**
  These institutions lend on mortgages for land and buildings for longer term, usually 15 years and more.

- **Subordinated Debt**
  Subordinated debt or mezzanine debt is debt that is subordinate to senior debt, giving it a second claim on a company's assets, much like a second mortgage on a home. It is generally provided from insurance companies, finance companies and subordinated debt funds, and is raised with public offerings of high-yield or "junk" bonds sold to the investors.

  To meet a number of business objectives, subordinated debt can be used to meet balloon payment obligations, secure lower interest on current interest rates, complete a management or employee buy-out or finance a turnaround. Interest costs can be anywhere from two to eight percentage points higher than senior debt.

  To find out more about subordinated or mezzanine financing, contact a local investment banking or capital asset management firm such Hewitt, Fleet Capital, Prudential and JP Morgan Chase/Bank One. They can provide you with the information and assistance you will need.

Government Financing

<u>Federal Government</u>

- **The Small Business Administration (SBA)**

  There are three basic types of SBA lending programs available: the 7(a) Loan Guarantee Program, the 7(m) Microloan Program and the 504 Certified Development Company Loan Program.

  The SBA is not a direct lender. However, under the SBA's loan guarantee programs, the borrower applies to a lending institution. If it's determined that the borrower needs a guarantee, the lender then applies to the SBA for the guarantee through either Standard, Certified Lenders, Preferred Lenders, SBA*LowDoc*, SBA*Express* Community*Express*, and CAPlines (Seasonal, Contract, Builders).

  You can find out more by contacting the local SBA office in your state or online at https://www.sba.gov/loanprograms.

- **Department of the Treasury**

  Under the Department of the Treasury, the Community Development Financial Institutions (CDFI) Fund was created to expand the availability of credit, investment capital, and financial services in distressed urban and rural communities. CDFIs include community development banks, credit unions, loan funds, venture capital funds and microenterprise loan funds to name a few.

  Their wide range of financial services include mortgage financing for first-time homebuyers, financing for community facilities, commercial loans and investments to start or expand small businesses, loans to rehabilitate rental housing, and financial services needed by low-income households and local businesses.

  For more information on CDFI funding, visit the website at https://www.cdfifund.gov/Pages/default.aspx.

- **Housing & Urban Development (HUD)**

  As the nation's community development agency, HUD is dedicated to assisting communities attract new private-sector investments and jobs through support for locally-driven economic development efforts in our nation's most economically distressed communities.

HUD's Office of Economic Development (OED) is responsible for community planning and development (CPD) programs that provide technical assistance grants to for-profit, not-for-profit and government agencies that have demonstrated their expertise and capability to provide the guidance and training that participants can use.

For more information, contact the HUD office in your area or online at www.hud.gov.

- **U.S. Department of Agriculture (USDA)**

The USDA is the country's largest conservation agency, encouraging voluntary efforts to protect soil, water and wildlife in the 70% of America's privately-held lands. Among their many responsibilities they are the research leader in everything from human nutrition to new crop technologies, the federal anti-hunger effort with food stamps, school breakfast and lunch programs, WIC (Women, Infants & Children), and the safety of meat, poultry and egg products programs.

In an effort to carry out their mission of providing leadership on food, agriculture, natural resources and related issues based on sound public policy and the best available science and efficient management, the USDA has established several business and cooperative grant and loan programs. These programs are created to provide financial backing in rural economies for creating jobs, financing business facilities, facilitating development of small and emerging private businesses and financing electric and telephone utilities.

For more information about USDA programs, visit online at www.usda.gov.

- **U.S. Department of Commerce (DOC)**

Economic Development Administration (EDA)

The EDA was created within the DOC to provide financial assistance to meet the economic development needs of distressed communities throughout the U.S. Its mission is to assist states, regions and communities in creating wealth and minimizing poverty by promoting a favorable business environment to attract private capital investment and higher-skill, higher-wage jobs.

To assist in providing direct grants on a cost-share basis for projects that will create and retain private-sector jobs and leverage public and private investment, EDA created community and regional economic development assistance programs. They include public works, economic adjustment assistance, research and national technical assistance, partnership planning, university center, and trade adjustment programs.

For more information, contact them online at www.eda.gov

Minority Business Development Agency (MBDA)

MBDA is the only federal agency created specifically to foster the establishment and growth of minority-owned businesses in America. MBDA is an entrepreneurially focused and innovative organization committed to wealth creation in minority communities. While MBDA is not a funding source and does not give grants, it does, however, provide referrals and assistance to minority businesses to obtain capital for their businesses.

To access capital, the entrepreneur needs to prepare and understand basic credit guidelines and resources available using MBDA's portal. As a part of the portal, the Resource Locator lists organizations that specialize in starting, operating, financing and expanding a business. For more information, contact MBDA online at www.mbda.gov.

• Overseas Private Investment Corporation (OPIC)

OPIC was established as a development agency of the U.S. government to help U.S. businesses invest overseas, foster economic development in new and emerging markets, complement the private sector in managing risks associated with foreign direct investment and support U.S. foreign policy. In addition, OPIC-supported projects can encourage political stability, free market reforms, U.S. best practices, and support American jobs and exports.

The new Small and Medium Enterprise Department and OPIC's Small Business Center (SBC) were established to address the needs of small and medium-sized American companies in an effort to ease their entry into new markets. Lack of resources, concerns over political risks or the inability to find private-sector support has prevented U.S. small businesses from expanding overseas. The SBC helps to meet these needs by providing financing and political risk insurance to eligible small businesses.

For more information on OPIC programs, visit them online at https://www.opic.gov/.

- **Export-Import Bank (Ex-Im Bank)**

  Ex-Im Bank of the United States is the official export credit agency whose mission is to assist in financing the export of U.S. goods and services to international markets. Ex-Im Bank enables large and small U.S. companies turn export opportunities into real sales that help maintain and create U.S. jobs and contribute to a stronger national economy.

  Ex-Im Bank provides working capital guarantees (pre-export financing), export credit insurance (post-export financing), and guarantees and direct loans (buyer financing). Some of the benefits offered include enabling international buys, obtaining loans from lenders, covering 100% of commercial and political risks, flexibility in financing and repayment, no limits on transaction size and medium- to long-term financing. For more information, visit Ex-Im Bank online at www.exim.gov.

State and Local Government

Many state, county and local governments and municipalities have loan and loan guarantee programs. In addition, they provide financial and tax incentives and grants. Contact the economic development or commerce departments of each agency in your area.

- **Community Development Corporations (CDC)**

  CDCs are comprised of banks and other financial institutions, municipalities, philanthropic organizations, neighborhood housing and community action agencies, private businesses and individuals that are linked to money, expertise and political power. These not-for-profit entities specialize in development and rehabilitation of real estate, and investments in business ventures and related activities specifically designed to address the housing, commercial redevelopment, employment and community facilities needs of low- and moderate-income persons and areas.

Local and national sources are channeled to CDCs in the form of project capital, operating subsidies and technical assistance grants. According to a national census of CDCs conducted by the National Congress for Community Economic Development (NACCED), there are an estimated 3600 such groups across the U.S. Since its emergence in the late 1960s, they've produced 247,000 private sector jobs and 550,000 units of affordable housing.

For more information or to obtain a copy of a study on community development corporations' programs, visit the NACCED online at www.nacced.org.

- **Community Reinvestment Act (CRA)**

Another source is through the Community Reinvestment Act (CRA) (12 USC 2901) which mandates financial institutions explore options available to expand their community development financing activities. In an effort to comply with CRA requirements, financial institutions have been authorized to engage in community development investments in a number of ways to include:

o Creating de novo community development corporations (CDCs) subsidiaries that invest in low- and moderate-income housing, commercial and industrial projects and community services facilities;

o Capitalizing multi-investor or consortium CDCs along with other financial institutions and public and private investors;

o Purchasing interests in limited partnerships formed to develop, rehabilitate, own and operate low- and moderate-income housing projects;

o Investing in local, state or national equity pools or master limited partnerships that provide capital for low- and moderate-income housing;

o Investing in CDCs, joint ventures or limited partnerships sponsored by community-based groups for community development purposes;

o Providing venture capital investments for start-up or expanding small and minority-owned businesses through the issuance of micro-loans in economically disadvantaged communities; and

o Organizing and operating entities that provide technical and advisory services for housing, community and economic development organizations and their projects.

For more information on the Community Reinvestment Act (CRA) program, visit the Federal Reserve online at http://www.federalreserve.gov/communitydev/.

All of the sources referenced above may be researched at your library, PTAC, business development center, incubator program, local SBA office, local telephone book or newspaper.

Equity Capital

- **Venture Capital**
  These are private firms that will invest directly in your company if they believe your business will be profitable and grow substantially. They expect high returns and usually want 20% to 40% minority positions and sometimes control. Even though investors take an equity position in a company and are usually actively involved, they seek to make money and exit the company within a five-year period.

  The National Venture Capital Association (NVCA) is a trade association that represents the U.S. venture capital industry. It's a member-based organization, which consists of venture capital firms that manage pools of risk equity capital designated for investment in high growth companies. For more information, contact NVCA online at www.nvca.org.

The National Association of Investment Companies (NAIC) is a trade association for diverse-owned investment management firms. NAIC is made up of 35 members, 31 of which re diverse-owned direct investment private equity firms who attract capital from government and corporate pension plans. For more information, visit the NAIC online at http://naicpe.com/.

Franchises

- **Franchising**
  Franchising is a method of distributing products and services. At least two levels of people are involved in a franchise system:

  1. the franchiser who lends his trademark or trade name and a business system; and

  2. the franchisee who pays a royalty and often an initial fee for the right to do business under the franchiser's name and system.

To get started in a franchise, identify companies offering franchises and contact them directly. Ascertain how much you can afford to invest and where you will secure the financing. But equally as important, you will need to closely examine what the franchise relationship entails. For example, you will need to know what type of training and support, location assistance, and sources of inventory and supplies they provide.

In addition, you need to obtain a copy of the Uniform Franchise Offering Circular (UFOC). It's the federal regulation that requires franchisers to prepare an extensive disclosure document. Within it are 23 categories of information about franchises to include required fees, basic investment, bankruptcy and litigation history, length of agreement, financial statements and earnings claims to mention a few.

To obtain a copy of the UFOC, contact the FTC online at www.ftc.gov/. For more information about international franchise opportunities, contact the International Franchise Association (IFA) at www.franchise.org of the American Association of Franchisees & Dealers (AAFD) at www.aafd.org.

Going Public

- **Initial Public Offering (IPO)**
  An IPO is the selling of stock to the public through the stock exchanges, but possibly selling to a "listed" company in exchange for stock. These public offerings usually involve issues of $5 million to $10 million or more. It is, however, possible to sell less, but it's probably unwise and definitely expensive because of legal fees, prospectus and underwriting costs.

Angel Networks

- **"Angels"**
  These are individuals who have money and want to invest in a company they believe may give them a good return on their investment. Some even play an active role in the companies they finance. Angel networks have been developed to match capital-seeking individuals with investors. It costs about $250 to sign up. Most angel networks can be found on college campuses, business incubator programs, state development agencies, or other not-for-profit organizations.

Other Sources of Financing

- **Leasing**
  The following are basic types of leasing. They include:

  - <u>Direct</u> – Where the leasing company arranges the original transaction from the beginning. This includes cars, trucks, computers, equipment, etc.

  - <u>Indirect</u> – In a three-way transaction, the supplier obtains the customer's signature on the lease and gives it to the leasing company who bills the user.

  - <u>Leveraged</u> – This is a partial equity investment position of 20% to 40% on the part of the user, with the remainder financed through leasing.

o <u>Sale-leaseback</u> – Used as a way to free up capital for operating purposes by selling real estate to a development company and leasing it back with a right to purchase at the end of 5 to 10 years.

- **Receivables Financing (Factoring)**
Accounts receivable financing allows a business to get cash from business receivables. This is possible even with a weak profile (e.g., prior bankruptcy, high debt to equity ratio, operating losses, etc.). The two types of receivables financing are:

  o Borrowing – A factor controls receivables and advances usually 80% of the total.

  o Invoice Purchase – A factor purchases accounts and pays them less their fee.

- **Suppliers**
The ability to negotiate with big suppliers is an often-overlooked source of capital. Even as a start-up, businesses may be able to develop a new market for a supplier's materials or semi-finished goods for much less than could be developed by the supplier.

- **Customers**
Small as well as large customers can help finance your business. This can be accomplished by accepting cash payments instead of credit, requiring deposits on orders, progress payments against work completed and equalized billings, especially for service businesses with long term customers who use periodic or cyclical peaks.

Meeting with Potential Lenders

Financial projections are intended to show your potential lender that the borrowed funds will significantly increase the profitability of your company and that you have the ability to repay. Marketing information will demonstrate your knowledge of your industry, detail how the products or services you provide can be sold, and to whom they will be sold.

Prior to meeting with a lender or investor, it's important to learn to speak the banker's language. Bankers are trained to look at the worse-case scenario.

Essential to the lending process are the "5 Cs" of borrowing. To determine whether the 5 Cs have been met, every lender will evaluate:

1. **CHARACTER**
   What type of person are you? What are your abilities in managing a business?

2. **CAPITAL**
   Have you made a reasonable investment in your business (e.g., cash, capital equipment, fixed assets, etc.)?

3. **CREDIT**
   Describe your personal and business credit experience. How much money will you need? What will the money be used for?

4. **COLLATERAL**
   What collateral, if necessary, will be used to secure the loan?

5. **CONDITIONS**
   What are the terms of the loan (e.g., repayment schedule, interest rate, etc.)?

In reviewing the loan documents and in the decision-making process, the lender will have particular interest in the following:

Business Performance

- Past earnings and future prospects indicating the ability to repay the loan and other fixed debt out of profits.

- Sufficient funds to have a reasonable amount at stake in the event of possible losses from the use of personal resources.

- Demonstrate that the money can be repaid and how it will be repaid.

General Business

- Are the books and records kept up to date?

- What is the condition of the accounts payable and notes payable?

- What are the salaries of owners, officers and managers of the company?

- Are all taxes current?

- What is the condition of the order backlog?

- How many employees are there?

- What type of insurance coverage is offered?

- Is there a succession plan detailing repayment in the event the business must be transferred or liquidated?

Accounts Receivable

- Have any accounts receivables been pledged?

- What is the accounts receivable turnover?

- Are any accounts receivable customers behind in their payments?

- Has a reserve been set up for bad debt?

- How much do the largest accounts owe, and what percentage of total accounts does this amount represent?

Inventories

- Is merchandise in good shape or will it have to be marked down?

- How much raw material is on hand?

- How much work is in progress?

- How much inventory is finished goods?

- Is there any obsolete inventory?

- Has an excessive amount of inventory been consigned to customers?

- Is inventory turnover comparable to other businesses in the industry?

- Is money tied up too long in inventory?

Fixed Assets

- What is the type, age and condition of the equipment?

- What are the depreciation policies?

- What are the details of mortgages or conditional sales contracts?

- What are the plans for future acquisitions?

- Are the any UCC filings on record with the Secretary of State?

Defining your reasons for borrowing money is as significant as the need to borrow itself. These reasons must be clear and your plans for repayment must be realistic. Borrowing money for multiple projects is usually not a problem. However, make sure each project is identified individually, particularly those that have the greatest economic return.

Crowdfunding

The concept of crowdfunding dates back as far as the 1700s when the Irish Loan Fund was established to give loans to low-income families. Beginning in 1997, crowdfunding emerged as a popular way for entrepreneurs and social organizations to fund projects or causes online. Now that commercial lending and government-backed business loans have become increasingly more difficult to obtain, especially for start-ups, crowdfunding has become a viable option for entrepreneurs to expose their ideas and secure funding.

The crowdfunding model has been used to fund projects from rock group tours to the development of independent films to software development and to fund the building a monumental base for the Statue of Liberty. The best thing about the crowdfunding model is that it uses the Internet to expose a company or individual(s) to millions of potential funders. Each funder can contribute a small amount to ultimately reach a financial goal and fund a project.

The following lists the three crucial components of crowdfunding:

1. The person, organization, or group with an idea or project;

2. Individuals or groups who are willing to support the idea or project; and

3. The platform that brings all parties together to launch the idea or project.

Depending on the type of funding, donors receive both tangible and/or intangible returns. Donation crowdfunding, debt crowdfunding and equity crowdfunding are the three main types of crowdfunding. They are defined as:

-   **Donation crowdfunding** – Generally cause related. Donors contribute because they believe in the cause (e.g., a person has a serious medical condition, saving wildlife, etc.) and have no expectation of receiving anything tangible in return.

-   **Debt crowdfunding** – Business related funding. Investors expect to receive their money back with interest. The return on investment is financial, and the investors contribute to an idea or project they believe in.

-   **Equity crowdfunding** – Also business-related funding. Investors have an equity position in the business or project.

Currently, there are hundreds of crowdfunding platforms in existence. Before deciding on which one will work best for your idea, project or cause, do your homework. Below is list of the most popular crowdfunding platforms:

-   **Kickstarter**
    https://www.kickstarter.com/

-   **Indiegogo**
    https://www.indiegogo.com/

-   **FundAnything**
    https://fundanything.com/en

- **Funder Hut**
  www.funderhut.com

- **Experiment**
  https://experiment.com/

When to Seek Financing

One of the biggest mistakes business owners make is waiting until they are near or at the point of desperation before applying for a loan or credit. A simple rule of thumb: **APPLY FOR A LOAN OR CREDIT BEFORE YOU NEED IT.** Three to four months lead time is good. This is the most pragmatic step any businessperson could take. Without question, it's better to have funds available and not need them, than to need them and be unable to obtain them.

At a minimum you will want to establish a line of credit (LOC). Situations inevitably arise which create a cash crunch for a company. In these instances, utilizing an LOC will alleviate cash flow problems. Even though an LOC usually has a higher interest rate, it costs nothing until the funds are used. Interest is then paid on those funds. LOCs are reviewed annually, and if a business has done well, a lower interest rate can be negotiated.

Obtaining Financing

At this point you should have clearly defined your borrowing needs based on financial and marketing data, assessed your current and future financial situation (including effectively projecting cash flow), and compiled supporting documents. This satisfy lenders that your business is strong enough to cover all operating obligations, cover the debt, and have enough cash available for contingencies. No prudent lender will loan more money than cash flows can support. You must have sufficient income to service current debt and well as cover new debt. The following are steps to take in securing financing:

1. **Obtain a copy of your credit report.**
   Your credit history is an important element in the lending process. You should know exactly what has been reported prior to contacting a lender. See page 304 or **CHAPTER 9, BUSINESS RESOURCES** under "**CREDIT & REPORTING**" on page 334.

2. **Target prospective lenders.**
   Consult with business acquaintances, family members and friends on lending sources. They may be able to provide you with sources you may not have already considered. However, don't be discouraged if their experiences with any of their referrals are less than favorable.

3. **Interview lending sources you've selected.**
   Call each lender you've selected (at least three to four). Schedule an appointment with a loan officer from each institution for the purpose of:

   a. obtaining information about the institution, loan programs available and lending criteria and policies;

   b. establishing a relationship with the lender and institution; and

   c. Giving a brief presentation about your company, project and financing needs, and to get feedback to assist in you structuring your written loan proposal.

4. **Prepare your loan proposal.**
   Once you've selected one or more lenders that you feel comfortable with, you will need to obtain any preprinted loan documentation they have. This includes loan applications, forms, and instructions listing all information they'll need before processing a loan. Follow instructions specifically and provide all documentation requested.

Preparing Your Loan Proposal

Loan proposals much like business plans come in various formats and styles. Regardless of the format, the necessary information is much the same. A complete proposal could easily contain up to 25 pages or more. The following are documents that are included in a loan proposal. Each lender will have specific information they require, but many of the documents below may be requested:

Business Information
- Loan proposal information
- Cover letter

- Loan application
- History and nature of business or business plan
- Succession Plan
- Financial statements
  - Balance Sheet
  - Income Statement
  - Operating Budget
  - Estimated Business Projections & Forecasts Statement
  - Sources & Uses of Cash
  - Cash Flow Analysis
  - Accounts Payable/Receivable Aging
- Schedule of Term Debt
- Trade References
- UCC Filings
- Business Federal Tax Returns
- Business Insurance
- Lease Agreements
- Partnership Agreement or Articles of Incorporation
- Franchise Agreement
- Affiliate Companies

Personal Information (for all owners, partners, officers)
- Personal Financial Statements (not more than 60 days)
- Personal Income Tax Returns (2 to 3 years)
- Personal Monthly Expense Report
- Résumés
- Statement of Facts

Miscellaneous Information
- Credit Authorization
- Tax Information Authorization Form 8821
- Request for Copy or Transcript of Tax Form 4506
- Letters of Reference
- Copy of Licenses
- Letters of Intent
- Executed Contract
- Purchase Orders
- Plans, Specifications

Collateral for Your Loan

Securing a loan or credit of any kind usually requires collateral. For short-term loans, current assets such as accounts receivable, inventory and marketable securities are most desirable. On the other hand, fixed assets such as buildings, equipment and machinery are preferred for long-term loans. While lenders seldom make decisions solely based on the strength of a borrower's collateral, they do, however, seek to secure the best collateral the borrower has to offer.

Article 9 of the UCC applies to security interests created by contract including pledge, assignment, chattel, mortgage, chattel trust, trust deed, factor's lien, equipment, conditional sale, trust receipt other lien or title retention contract and lease or consignment intended as security. It protects the creditor against the debtor's default. By filing a National Financing Statement form (UCC-1) and/or a security agreement with the Secretary of State, the creditor is legally allowed to recover the goods in the debtor's possession. Refer to **Exhibit 52 – UCC-1 Financing Statement** is located on page 307.

Negotiating the Loan

On a positive note, let's say you obtained approval for your loan. Congratulations!! The next step is negotiating its terms and conditions. Terms and conditions are contractual agreements made between you and the lender, provided that each party is legally empowered to enter into the agreement and everything in the contract is legal.

Regardless of how badly you need the money, hash out the lending terms before you sign on the dotted line. A good practice is to review loan documents in advance of the loan closing. Ask for a copy of the documents to take back to your office or home and examine them in a peaceful, comfortable atmosphere.

If you're an inexperienced borrower, as painful as it may be, read all loan documents carefully, word for word. Understanding the wording in the contract is very important, but more importantly, understanding the intent. If necessary, consult with your business associate or attorney.

Loan documents contain standard contract language that has been tested in court, with meaning that has been well established in the legal system. However, your lender should agree to minor changes that could improve the agreement in the opinion of both parties. At any rate, try to negotiate terms that you and your company can live with. A few questions you will want to ask your lender include:

1. When will the funds be available?

2. When are the principal and interest payable?

3. What will be the total cost of the loan?

4. Will there be any other fees charged?

5. Are there any prepayment penalties?

6. Are there any restrictions on the use of the funds?

7. Are there any provisions for extending or renewing the loan?

8. At what point will the loan be considered in default?

Loan Repayment

Simply stated, bankers and lenders are in business to make money. Extending loans to increase or ensure profitability of a business is but one way they make their money. So as a borrower, your job is to demonstrate to the lender that you're able to repay the loan on time and with interest.

Start-up, growth and expansion are the most common reasons businesses borrow money. So, obviously, the primary source of repayment is profits. However, a solid secondary source of repayment may be required in order to obtain a loan. Secondary sources would include insurance proceeds in the event the borrower dies or becomes disabled, or the collateral pledged to obtain the loan.

While many business owners underestimate the importance of a succession or contingency plan and consequently wait until it's too late to prepare one, bankers and lenders are extremely interested in them. Business continuation is given tremendous consideration in determining whether to approve a loan. Within your succession or contingency plan, make absolute certain that provisions for repayment are clearly spelled out.

Rejected Loan Proposals

Receiving word that your loan proposal has been rejected can be a humbling experience. With the amount of time, effort and energy that goes into its preparation, it's reasonable to think that all the information required and subsequently provided would clearly demonstrate the need for the funds and ability to repay. Some of the more common reasons for rejection of a loan proposal include:

1. not enough owner's equity in the business;

2. poor earnings;

3. insufficient collateral;

4. insufficient credit;

5. no financial track record; or

6. inadequate management experience.

In the event your loan proposal is rejected, it's imperative that you find out why. You don't want to continue applying for financing not understanding why you were denied previously. Ask your loan officer for a written statement in answer to the following questions:

1. What areas were deficient?

2. What would remedy any areas of deficiency?

3. Is there a possibility of reconsideration? If so, how could the current proposal be modified to prepare it for reconsideration?

4. What would be the timeframe for reapply or reconsideration?

5. What are suggestions for alternative funding sources?

If reconsideration is not an option, then the brighter side is that you have gained some experience with the lending process, and it'll be very beneficial in your next submission.

Credit and Creditworthiness

When personal and/or business credit is reason for rejecting a loan proposal, reasons for rejection may include:

1. **no credit** – never having established a credit history;

2. **credit too new to rate** – credit established for under two years prior;

3. **high credit usage** – credit cards charged to limits leaving low available credit;

4. **too many credit inquiries** – having applied for too many accounts in a two-year period; and

5. **derogatory credit** – negative credit, including judgements and charge-offs.

Credit Reporting Agencies

If the lender's reason for rejection is based on any of the above, then your first step is to find out the specifics. They may tell you, but it's best to obtain a copy of your credit report to review information that has been reported. If you request a copy within 30 days of being rejected, you will receive it free of charge. You can also receive on free credit report per year by contacting each of the major credit bureaus below. Contact them in writing or online, using the contact information below:

1. **Experian**
   www.experian.com
   475 Anton Boulevard, Costa Mesa, CA 92626
   955 American Lane, Schaumburg, IL 60173
   Phone: 888-397-3742

2. **Trans Union**
   www.transunion.com
   P.O. Box 2000, Chester, PA 19022
   Phone: 877-322-8228

3. **Equifax**
   www.equifax.com
   P.O. Box 740241, Atlanta, GA 30374
   Phone: 800-685-1111

4. **Dun & Bradstreet** (Business credit reporting)
   www.dnb.com
   103 JFK Parkway, Short Hills, NJ 07078
   Phone: 800-234-3867

Upon receipt of your credit report, review all information carefully for accuracy and completeness. Inaccurate and incomplete information can be investigated and corrected. Information that cannot be verified, has exceeded the time limitations or is incorrect will be deleted. The investigative process takes about 30 days. After the research is complete, a new credit report will be sent showing the results.

If rejection was based on lack of or insufficient credit, then it may be necessary for you to establish credit in one of the following ways:

1. **Endorser** – An individual contingently liable for the note they sign;

2. **Co-signer** – An individual who creates an obligation jointly with the borrower;

3. **Guarantor** – An individual who guarantees the payment of a note by signing a guarantee commitment; or

4. **Savings account assignment** – The bank gets an assignment of a personal savings account and the funds on deposit are kept as collateral.

If on the other hand derogatory credit is reported accurately, then there is little that can be done to correct this. In accordance with federal law, accurate, negative information, such as judgments, late payments or accounts turned over for collection can remain on your credit report for 7 years. Chapters 7, 11, 12 and 13 bankruptcies can remain on your credit report for up to 10 years. Credit bureaus are not required to remove this information before the reporting period has expired. Beginning on page 31, you will find an explanation of how credit is reported and how credit is scored.

Assistance with credit problems is available. There are organizations that promise debt consolidation, reorganization or counseling and "guarantee" to stop creditors' collection efforts. They charge substantial fees or a percentage of your debts. While there may be some reputable businesses that provide these types of services, there are many who don't deliver on their promises.

Consumer Credit Counseling Services (CCCS) is a not-for-profit organization with more than 2000 offices located in 44 states. CCCS counselors will arrange a repayment plan that is acceptable to you and your creditors. They charge little for services. You can locate the CCCS office nearest you online at www.credit.org or by calling 800-431-8157.

To find out about credit and federal laws involving credit including the Equal Credit Opportunity Act, the Fair Credit Reporting Act, the Truth in Lending Act, the Fair Credit Billing Act and the Fair Debt Collection Practices, or if you have a complaint that may involve a violation of consumer protection call, write or visit the FTC online at:

Federal Trade Commission
www.ftc.gov/
600 Pennsylvania Avenue, N.W.
Washington, D.C. 20580
Local: 202-326-2222 Toll free: 877-382-4357

UCC (Uniform Commercial Code) Filing

The Uniform Commercial Code (UCC) is a comprehensive set of laws governing commercial transactions (e.g., loans, leases, contracts and the sale of goods) between the U.S. and territories. A UCC-1 financing statement is the legal form that creditors file to give notice that it has or may have an interest in the personal property of a debtor.

The UCC filing serves as public notice for the creditor that they have a right to take procession of and sell certain assets for repayment of a specific debt with a certain priority. These notices are generally found in local newspapers. This process is called "perfecting the security interest" in the property. The UCC-1 financing statement is filed with the Secretary of State office in the state where the debtor is located, where the debtor resides or the state of incorporation or organization. **Exhibit 52 – UCC Financing Statement** is located on page 307.

Exhibit 52 – UCC Financing Statement

UCC FINANCING STATEMENT
FOLLOW INSTRUCTIONS

A. NAME & PHONE OF CONTACT AT FILER

B. E-MAIL CONTACT AT FILER

C. SEND ACKNOWLEDGMENT TO: (Name and Address)

| Print | Reset |

THE ABOVE SPACE IS FOR FILING OFFICE USE ONLY

1. DEBTOR'S NAME: Provide only one Debtor name (1a or 1b) (use exact, full name; do not omit, modify, or abbreviate any part of the Debtor's name); if any part of the Individual Debtor's name will not fit in line 1b, leave all of item 1 blank, check here ☐ and provide the Individual Debtor information in item 10 of the Financing Statement Addendum (Form UCC1Ad)

1a. ORGANIZATION'S NAME			
OR 1b. INDIVIDUAL'S SURNAME	FIRST PERSONAL NAME	ADDITIONAL NAME(S)/INITIAL(S)	SUFFIX
1c. MAILING ADDRESS	CITY	STATE POSTAL CODE	COUNTRY

2. DEBTOR'S NAME: Provide only one Debtor name (2a or 2b) (use exact, full name; do not omit, modify, or abbreviate any part of the Debtor's name); if any part of the Individual Debtor's name will not fit in line 2b, leave all of item 2 blank, check here ☐ and provide the Individual Debtor information in item 10 of the Financing Statement Addendum (Form UCC1Ad)

2a. ORGANIZATION'S NAME			
OR 2b. INDIVIDUAL'S SURNAME	FIRST PERSONAL NAME	ADDITIONAL NAME(S)/INITIAL(S)	SUFFIX
2c. MAILING ADDRESS	CITY	STATE POSTAL CODE	COUNTRY

3. SECURED PARTY'S NAME (or NAME of ASSIGNEE of ASSIGNOR SECURED PARTY): Provide only one Secured Party name (3a or 3b)

3a. ORGANIZATION'S NAME			
OR 3b. INDIVIDUAL'S SURNAME	FIRST PERSONAL NAME	ADDITIONAL NAME(S)/INITIAL(S)	SUFFIX
3c. MAILING ADDRESS	CITY	STATE POSTAL CODE	COUNTRY

4. COLLATERAL: This financing statement covers the following collateral:

5. Check only if applicable and check only one box: Collateral is ☐ held in a Trust (see UCC1Ad, Item 17 and Instructions) ☐ being administered by a Decedent's Personal Representative

6a. Check only if applicable and check only one box: ☐ Public-Finance Transaction ☐ Manufactured-Home Transaction ☐ A Debtor is a Transmitting Utility 6b. Check only if applicable and check only one box: ☐ Agricultural Lien ☐ Non-UCC Filing

7. ALTERNATIVE DESIGNATION (if applicable): ☐ Lessee/Lessor ☐ Consignee/Consignor ☐ Seller/Buyer ☐ Bailee/Bailor ☐ Licensee/Licensor

8. OPTIONAL FILER REFERENCE DATA:

FILING OFFICE COPY — UCC FINANCING STATEMENT (Form UCC1) (Rev. 01/02/15)   International Association of Commercial Administrators (IACA)

THE BUSINESS CENTER

Instructions for UCC Financing Statement (Form UCC1)

Please type or laser-print this form. Be sure it is completely legible. Read and follow all Instructions, especially Instruction 1; use of the correct name for the Debtor is crucial.
Fill in form very carefully; mistakes may have important legal consequences. If you have questions, consult your attorney. The filing office cannot give legal advice.
Send completed form and any attachments to the filing office, with the required fee.

ITEM INSTRUCTIONS

A and B. To assist filing offices that might wish to communicate with filer, filer may provide information in item A and item B.
C. Complete item C if filer desires an acknowledgment sent to them. If filing in a filing office that returns an acknowledgment copy furnished by filer, present simultaneously with this form the Acknowledgment Copy or a carbon or other copy of this form for use as an acknowledgment copy.

1. **Debtor's name.** Carefully review applicable statutory guidance about providing the debtor's name. Enter only one Debtor name in item 1 -- either an organization's name (1a) or an individual's name (1b). If any part of the Individual Debtor's name will not fit in line 1b, check the box in item 1, leave all of item 1 blank, check the box in item 9 of the Financing Statement Addendum (Form UCC1Ad) and enter the Individual Debtor name in item 10 of the Financing Statement Addendum (Form UCC1Ad). Enter Debtor's correct name. Do not abbreviate words that are not already abbreviated in the Debtor's name. If a portion of the Debtor's name consists of only an initial or an abbreviation rather than a full word, enter only the abbreviation or the initial. If the collateral is held in a trust and the Debtor name is the name of the trust, enter trust name in the Organization's Name box in item 1a.

1a. Organization Debtor Name. "Organization Name" means the name of an entity that is not a natural person. A sole proprietorship is not an organization, even if the individual proprietor does business under a trade name. If Debtor is a registered organization (e.g., corporation, limited partnership, limited liability company), it is advisable to examine Debtor's current filed public organic records to determine Debtor's correct name. Trade name is insufficient. If a corporate ending (e.g., corporation, limited partnership, limited liability company) is part of the Debtor's name, it must be included. Do not use words that are not part of the Debtor's name.

1b. Individual Debtor Name. "Individual Name" means the name of a natural person; this includes the name of an individual doing business as a sole proprietorship, whether or not operating under a trade name. The term includes the name of a decedent where collateral is being administered by a personal representative of the decedent. The term does not include the name of an entity, even if it contains, as part of the entity's name, the name of an individual. Prefixes (e.g., Mr., Mrs., Ms.) and titles (e.g., M.D.) are generally not part of an individual name. Indications of lineage (e.g., Jr., Sr., III) generally are not part of the individual's name, but may be entered in the Suffix box. Enter individual Debtor's surname (family name) in Individual's Surname box, first personal name in First Personal Name box, and all additional names in Additional Name(s)/Initial(s) box.

If a Debtor's name consists of only a single word, enter that word in Individual's Surname box and leave other boxes blank.

For both organization and individual Debtors. Do not use Debtor's trade name, DBA, AKA, FKA, division name, etc. in place of or combined with Debtor's correct name; filer may add such other names as additional Debtors if desired (but this is neither required nor recommended).

1c. Enter a mailing address for the Debtor named in item 1a or 1b.

2. **Additional Debtor's name.** If an additional Debtor is included, complete item 2, determined and formatted per Instruction 1. For additional Debtors, attach either Addendum (Form UCC1Ad) or Additional Party (Form UCC1AP) and follow Instruction 1 for determining and formatting additional names.

3. **Secured Party's name.** Enter name and mailing address for Secured Party or Assignee who will be the Secured Party of record. For additional Secured Parties, attach either Addendum (Form UCC1Ad) or Additional Party (Form UCC1AP). If there has been a full assignment of the initial Secured Party's right to be Secured Party of record before filing this form, either (1) enter Assignor Secured Party's name and mailing address in item 3 of this form and file an Amendment (Form UCC3) [see item 5 of that form]; or (2) enter Assignee's name and mailing address in item 3 of this form and, if desired, also attach Addendum (Form UCC1Ad) giving Assignor Secured Party's name and mailing address in item 11.

4. **Collateral.** Use item 4 to indicate the collateral covered by this financing statement. If space in item 4 is insufficient, continue the collateral description in item 12 of the Addendum (Form UCC1Ad) or attach additional page(s) and incorporate by reference in item 12 (e.g., See Exhibit A). Do not include social security numbers or other personally identifiable information.

Note: If this financing statement covers timber to be cut, covers as-extracted collateral, and/or is filed as a fixture filing, attach Addendum (Form UCC1Ad) and complete the required information in items 13, 14, 15, and 16.

5. If collateral is held in a trust or being administered by a decedent's personal representative, check the appropriate box in item 5. If more than one Debtor has an interest in the described collateral and the check box does not apply to the interest of all Debtors, the filer should consider filing a separate Financing Statement (Form UCC1) for each Debtor.

6a. If this financing statement relates to a Public-Finance Transaction, Manufactured-Home Transaction, or a Debtor is a Transmitting Utility, check the appropriate box in item 6a. If a Debtor is a Transmitting Utility and the initial financing statement is filed in connection with a Public-Finance Transaction or Manufactured-Home Transaction, check only that a Debtor is a Transmitting Utility.

6b. If this is an Agricultural Lien (as defined in applicable state's enactment of the Uniform Commercial Code) or if this is not a UCC security interest filing (e.g., a tax lien, judgment lien, etc.), check the appropriate box in item 6b and attach any other items required under other law.

7. **Alternative Designation.** If filer desires (at filer's option) to use the designations lessee and lessor, consignee and consignor, seller and buyer (such as in the case of the sale of a payment intangible, promissory note, account or chattel paper), bailee and bailor, or licensee and licensor instead of Debtor and Secured Party, check the appropriate box in item 7.

8. **Optional Filer Reference Data.** This item is optional and is for filer's use only. For filer's convenience of reference, filer may enter in item 8 any identifying information that filer may find useful. Do not include social security numbers or other personally identifiable information.

CHAPTER 7

BUSINESS
TECHNOLOGY

The Evolution of Technology

From the recent past we remember the typewriter, the mimeograph and the adding machine. With the use of this equipment, complex and even simple tasks took a lot of time and more than normal manpower to complete. Today, computers and peripherals, fax machines, copiers, telephone systems, digital devices and networking systems have revolutionized business processes. The current dependency on new technology makes us wonder how we ever survived without them.

With rapid technological advances comes greater sophistication in communications, security, information processing, data sharing, storage and retrieval. Access to resources, productive information flow, reduction in paperwork, and speedy execution of previously time-consuming tasks has created an efficient business environment. More significantly, with each technological advance, products are better, faster and cheaper.

Technology Impact on Business

Not having the proper technology in your business can inhibit your ability to grow, compete in the marketplace and experience any productivity gains. The investment in technology should be predicated on the specific type and needs of your business. Whatever technology you choose, it must be matched with overall company goals, improve processes and enable innovation.

Hardware, firmware, software and peripherals are the basic pieces of equipment used today in business, in education and at home. Each of these technological elements is defined as:

- <u>Hardware</u> – The circuitry and components which are a physical structure (e.g., monitor, motherboard, power supply, mouse);

- **Firmware** – Software instructions stored in the internal memory of the hardware;

- **Software** – Computer programs, applications and operating system stored either on a hard drive, CD, DVD or flash drive;

- **Peripherals** – Added components to include modems, printers, web cams, scanners, fax machines, speakers.

These basic technologies converged with 21st century technologies have revolutionized the way we work, are educated, play and do business. Today's most popular and widely-used technology trends include:

1. **WiFi** – A wireless networking technology that allows computers and other devices access internet services using adapters that create hotspots.

2. **Bluetooth** – Uses radio waves to connect to a phone, mobile device, radio, or computer in a short range.

3. **3D Printing** – Additive manufacturing process where three-dimensional objects are created from a digital file. Laying down of successive layers until an entire object is created.

4. **Robotics** – Used today to serve and assist people. At work, they can weld, cut and mold parts, deliver medical records in hospitals, disarm bombs, and can enter hazardous environments too dangerous for humans.

5. **E-commerce** – Electronic shopping platforms such as Big Commerce, Shopify which uses smartphones to make purchases

6. **Car-to-Car Communications** – Cars that talk to each to avoid crashes.

7. **Driverless Cars** – Cars powered with artificial intelligence utilizing input from video cameras inside the cars.

8. **Project Loon** – A reliable and cost-effective way to beam Internet service from the sky to places lacking service.

9. **Nano-architecture** – Tiny lattice material whose structures can be precisely tailored, are strong, flexible and extremely light.

10. **Google Glass** – Gives the ability to view social media feeds, navigate with GPS, text, and take photos.

11. **Oculus Rift** – 3D headsets that let you feel like you're actually inside a video game.

Above are some of the simpler, more recent innovations. Many believe that continued advancements in technology will soon create machines that will replace humans. The days of living like the '60s cartoon, the Jetsons, may not be as far off as we once thought. We already have computerized watches that act as cell phones, can access the Internet, perform calculations, serve as a monitoring device, and perform many of the functions like a computer.

Benefits of Technology

Technology provides a wide variety of benefits and should be integrated into every aspect of your business. It can bridge the gap between where you are and where you want to go. Making the right choice from the many solutions available can mean the difference between having an efficient, cost effective, streamlined operation, and business failure. In some cases, new technology can slow business, but usually only briefly. When properly implemented and executed, technology can:

1. build a company's overall performance;

2. automate manual functions;

3. allow companies to better communicate and exchange data more efficiently and expediently;

4. provide the agility needed to meet market changes;

5. make reporting more efficient and accurate;

6. improve work quality and productivity;

7. improve and decrease cycle times;

8. improve and increase the speed of business processes;

9. more efficiently coordinate work time while reducing production time;

10. improve responsiveness to customers and staff;

11. provide significant cost savings;

12. put small business on par with large business in the provision of good and services;

13. enable development of new and more innovative products or ways of providing services;

14. help businesses expand operations quickly, even globally;

15. upgrade skill sets of business owners and employees; and

16. promote continuous learning and innovating.

Technology Planning

Selecting the proper technology for your business takes serious planning. The latest and the greatest in solutions may sound nice, but isn't always best and may not provide the tools necessary to operate efficiently. Knowing how many computers you will need, the type of software, number of telephone lines, whether a combination fax/copier/printer will do versus standalone units and Internet speeds needed in your business is part of what technology planning encompasses.

Technology is intended to organize, streamline and modernize business processes. Employing the latest and the greatest technology in your business won't guarantee that your business functions optimally. In fact, the opposite can be true. You can spend a lot of money and get all the bells and whistles you can afford, but if all the accoutrements don't add value to your operation, don't meet your technology needs, or are not utilized properly or at all, you have wasted time and money.

So, when making your technology buying and implementation decisions, you should take into account:

1. the core functions of your business;

2. the company's goals over the long haul;

3. the technology needs of the company (requires a needs assessment);

4. technological expertise that already exists in the company;

5. technological expertise that will be needed;

6. how steep the learning curve will be for users;

7. technological architecture that will serve all units of the company;

8. how existing legacy systems will interoperate with new technology;

9. how operational performance will be measured based on the use of technology; and

10. how technological performance will be measured.

Types of Technologies

Based on your business needs, there are hardware, firmware and software solutions that will automate your business and make it function efficiently. Visit the websites of technology leaders or consult with technology experts to help you determine which solutions will work best for your company. Below is a list of the most widely-used products by businesses worldwide.

- Hardware
  - PC platform desktop, laptop or tablet
  - Apple platform, desktop, laptop or tablet
  - Desktop printer
  - Printer/fax/copier combination
  - 3-D printer

- Software
  - Microsoft Office (PC Windows and Mac OSX)
    - Word (word processing)
    - Excel (spreadsheets)
    - PowerPoint (presentation)
    - Access (database)
    - Publisher (publishing)

  - Communications
    - Microsoft Outlook (email, calendar, project management)

  - Graphics
    - Adobe PhotoShop
    - Adobe Illustrator
    - Adobe InDesign
    - Premiere Pro
    - CorelDraw
    - Printshop

  - Movies and Music
    - Windows Media Player
    - VideoStudio Pro
    - MovieMaker

  - Security and Antivirus
    - Norton
    - McAfee
    - Avg

- Web/Video Conferencing
  - Cisco WebEx Conferencing
  - Citrix GoToMeeting
  - Skype
  - Zoom Web Conferencing
  - Fuze
  - MeetingBurner

Implementing Technology in Your Business

Hardware and software used in business today varies widely. Once you've determined what will meet your technological needs, you must decide which of the many options available fits your budget.

When purchasing computer technology for your business, whether it is personal or mainframe, you will need to determine:

1. what platform(s) (e.g., Microsoft, Apple, IBM, Unix, SAP, etc.) will work best for your business;

2. will you be purchasing or leasing equipment;

3. what you want your computers to do (e.g., word processing, database management, financial accounting, use the Internet, graphic design, etc.);

4. what software programs will help you get the required and desired results (e.g., word processing, presentations, spreadsheets, database management, customer relationship management, graphic design, digital imaging, etc.);

5. what hardware requirements will be needed to support the software;

6. whether the technology is a viable replacement for manual processes;

7. what technical support (e.g., via phone, classes or training) is available after the purchase; and

8. what servicing is available to repair a computer if or when it becomes necessary.

Cloud Computing

Cloud computing is the use of a network of remote servers hosted on the Internet to store, process, collaborate, access and protect data. The Computer

Security Division Information Technology Laboratory of the National Institute of Standards and Technology (NIST) defines cloud computing as:

"...a model for enabling ubiquitous, convenient, on-demand network access to a shared pool of configurable computing resources (e.g., networks, servers, storage, applications, and services) that can be rapidly provisioned and released with minimal management effort or service provider interaction..."

As described by Wikipedia, cloud computing is a kind of Internet-based computing, where shared resources, data and information are provided to computers and other devices on-demand. Below is a graphic illustration of how cloud computing works:

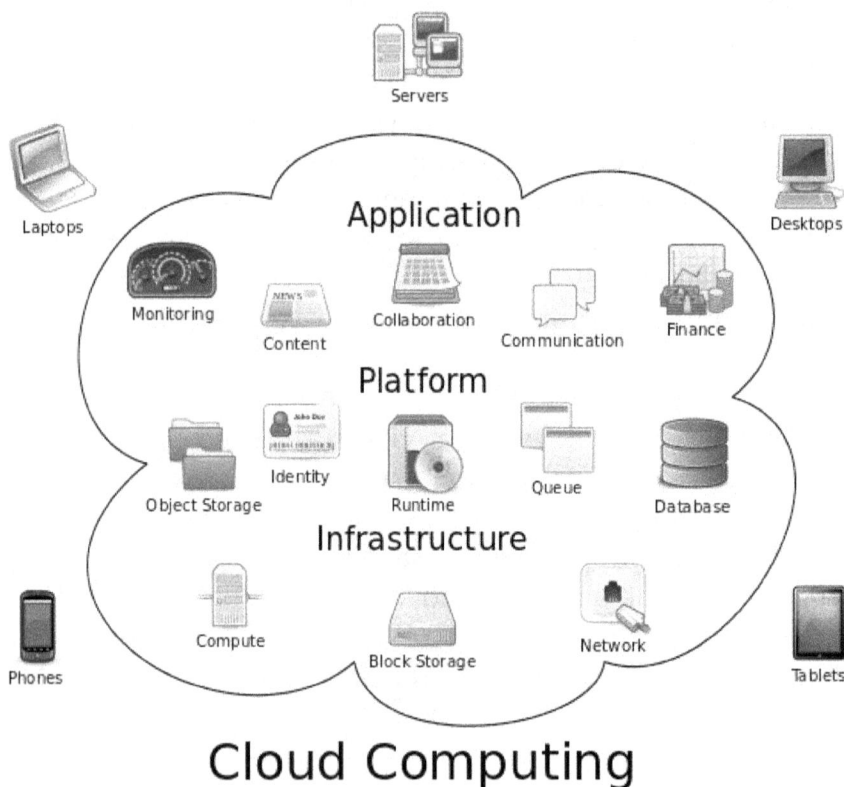

Cloud Computing

From Wikipedia https://en.wikipedia.org/wiki/Cloud_computing

Cloud computing has significantly transformed how we use, store and access data. Some of the many benefits to businesses small and large derived from the use of cloud computing includes:

316

1. Improved and measurable productivity within a corporate or organizational structure. Access to documentation and real-time collaboration is more easy and convenient.

2. Provides the agility needed for remote accessibility for a mobile workforce.

3. No capital expenditures in data centers or servers, and reduces maintenance and hardware upgrading costs.

4. Access is available through desktop and laptop computers, mobile devices, and tablets.

5. No capacity worries. Cloud space can be scaled up or down based on current needs.

6. Data is protected as it is developed.

As with every type of technology, there are some presumed disadvantages to cloud computing. Because an Internet connection is necessary to use the service, any disruptions to a connection or the cloud service will disrupt its use. There are a few cloud applications, however, that have offline capability, but more need an Internet connection. A second very important issue with cloud computing is security. Some companies are not comfortable with storing their sensitive or personal information on an Internet server.

A few of the top cloud computer systems that provide pay-as-you go options include:

- **Dell Cloud Computing**
  www.dell.com/cloud_computing

- **Equinix Cloud Solutions**
  www.equinix.com/cloud_exchange

- **Google Cloud Platform**
  https://cloud.google.com/

- **Microsoft Cloud Computing**
  https://resources.office.com

The future of cloud computing includes lower costs and more efficient allocation of IT (information technology) resources. Cloud hosting companies continue to resolve issues such as assurances of encryption technologies, privacy protection, improvements in web-based applications, and offline accessibility. This includes better security in the use of applications such as Skype, Facetime, Google Voice, social media, traditional desktop software, and others which are all web-based.

Technical Service & Support

Not every business owner is fortunate enough to have an IT person on staff. For the daring, but unfortunate many, you may want to ease the pain of technical difficulties over and above the services and support offered by your vendor by:

1. purchasing books or subscribe to magazines that claim to quickly and easily troubleshoot most any computer problem;

2. purchasing or obtaining anti-virus software such as Norton to mitigate or eliminate computer viruses or worms; and

3. joining a computer user's group to discuss and share computer hardware and software knowledge.

In **CHAPTER 9, BUSINESS RESOURCES** under the "**COMPUTER HARDWARE & SOFTWARE**" beginning on page 332 are a few of the major U.S. computer hardware and software dealers and manufacturers. Many of the solutions they provide have similar characteristics and functions but pricing will vary, sometimes significantly. So you'll need to visit their web sites or a store before settling on something that may not be beneficial to your operations.

SMALL, DISADVANTAGED, MINORITY, WOMEN, VETERAN-OWNED & SERVICE-DISABLED VETERAN BUSINESS ENTERPRISE DEVELOPMENT

History of Small Business

In 1932, the Reconstruction Finance Corporation (RFC), a federal lending program, was created by President Herbert Hoover to alleviate the financial crises of all businesses during the Great Depression. With the advent of World War II in 1942, Congress then created the Small War Plants Corporation (SWPC) to provide direct loans to private entrepreneurs, encourage large financial institutions to make credit available to small businesses, and to advocate small business interests to federal procurement agencies and large businesses.

After the war, the SWPC was dissolved and all lending and contract powers were handed over to the RFC though some of its responsibilities became that of the Office of Small Business (OSB) in the Department of Commerce. By 1952, a move was made to abolish the RFC. In an effort to continue the important functions of the earlier agencies, President Dwight Eisenhower proposed the creation of the Small Business Administration (SBA). And in July 1953, Congress created the SBA in the Small Business Act whose function was "to aid, counsel, assist and protect, insofar as is possible, the interests of small business concerns."

Over the many decades of its existence, the SBA has grown in terms of total assistance provided including financial and federal contract procurement assistance, management assistance and specialized outreach to women, minorities and armed forces veterans. In addition, it has loan programs to victims of natural disasters and specialized advice and assistance in international trade.

Small Business Size Standards

Chapter 13 of the Code of Federal Regulations (CFR) Part 121 (13 CFR 121) are the small business size standards established by the SBA. It is a numerical definition for all for-profit industries. Size standards represent the largest size that a business (including its subsidiaries and affiliates) may be to remain classified as a small business concern by NAICS codes in dollars or number of employees.

In determining what constitutes small business, the definition varies based on the industry. The purpose of using size standards is to make a determination as to the eligibility for SBA's financial assistance and other programs, as well as federal government procurement programs designed to help small businesses.

Below is a partial size standards table as an example:

NAICS Codes	NAICS INDUSTRY DESCRIPTION	SIZE STANDARDS IN MILLIONS OF DOLLARS	SIZE STANDARDS IN NUMBER OF EMPLOYEES
541712	Research and development in the physical, engineering and life sciences (except biotechnology)		1,000
Except	Aircraft engine and engine parts		1,500
Except	Other aircraft parts and auxiliary equipment		1,250
Except	Guided missiles and space vehicles, their propulsion units and propulsion parts		1,250
541720	Research and development in the social sciences and humanities	$20.5	
541810	Advertising agencies	$15.0	
541820	Public relations agencies	$15.0	
541830	Media buying agencies	$15.0	
541840	Media representatives	$15.0	
541850	Outdoor advertising	$15.0	
541860	Direct mail advertising	$15.0	
541870	Advertising material distribution services	$15.0	
541890	Other services related to advertising	$15.0	
541910	Marketing research and public opinion polling	$15.0	
541921	Photography studios, portrait	$7.5	
541922	Commercial photography	$7.5	
541930	Translation and interpretation services	$7.5	
541940	Veterinary services	$7.5	
541990	All other professional, scientific and technical services	$15.0	

To determine the size standard for your business, visit the SBA website at https://www.sba.gov/sites/default/files/files/Size_Standards_Table.pdf.

Minority, Disadvantaged Business Enterprise Development

Title VI of the Civil Rights Act of 1964 provides that:

"No person in the United States shall, on the grounds of race, color or national origin, be excluded from participation in, be denied the benefits of, or be otherwise subjected to discrimination in federally-assisted programs. And that all recipients of federal assistance must provide proper assurance of compliance with all the provisions of the Act."

Ultimately, the Executive Branch strengthened the federal government's role in fulfilling this initiative by issuing Executive Orders 11625 in October 1971 and 12138 in May 1979. Executive Order 11625 required federal agencies to develop comprehensive plans and programs to encourage minority business enterprise (MBE) participation in subcontracts on federal and federally-assisted activities and to establish regular performance monitoring and reporting systems.

A minority, disadvantaged small business concern was defined as owned and controlled 51% or more by one or more minority individuals of a presumptive minority group as follows:

- **Asian Pacific** – a person having origins in any of the original peoples of Japan, China, Taiwan, Korea, Vietnam, Laos, Cambodia, the Philippines, Samoa, Guam and the U.S. Trust Territories of the Pacific and the Northern Marians

- **African American** – a person having origins in any of the Black racial groups of Africa

- **Hispanic** – a person of Mexican, Puerto Rican, Cuban, Central or South America, or other Spanish or Portuguese culture or origin regardless of race

- **Native Americans** – a person having origins in any of the original people of North America, Eskimos, Aleuts or Native Hawaiians

Under Executive Order 11625, the Office of Minority Business Enterprise (OMBE) was changed to the Minority Business Development Agency (MBDA), which was established as a primary operating unit of the U.S. Department of Commerce. Their responsibility was to assist the Secretary in carrying out functions under the Order to include:

1. facilitating the coordination of the plans, programs and operations of the federal government which affect or may contribute to the establishment, preservation and strengthening of minority business enterprises;

2. promoting the mobilization of activities and resources of state and local governments, businesses and trade associations, universities, foundations, professional organizations, and volunteer and other groups towards the growth of minority business enterprises;

3. establishing operating centers for the development, collection, summarization and dissemination of information that will be helpful to persons and organizations throughout the nation in undertaking or promoting the establishment and successful operation of minority business enterprises;

4. providing financial assistance to public and private organizations so that they may render technical and management assistance to minority business enterprises;

5. establishing policies, standards, definitions, criteria and procedures appropriate and incident to the functions herein, and propose for the Secretary's consideration such additional measures as determined to be necessary for the implementation, interpretation and application; and

6. preparing a full report for the Secretary to submit to the President of the Department's activities during that year, and from time to time, submit to the Secretary recommendations for legislation or other actions deemed desirable to promote the purposes of the order.

Women Business Enterprise Development

Executive Order 12138 required each department and agency to take appropriate affirmative action through the issuance of regulations in support of women business enterprises (WBEs) that prohibited any actions or policies that discriminated against WBEs on the grounds of sex. As amended by Executive Order 12608 in September 1987, provides that a National Women's Business Enterprise Policy be created and prescribe arrangements for developing, coordinating and implementing a national program for women's business enterprises. Within the constraints of statutory authority and as otherwise permitted by law, responsibilities of the federal departments and agencies include:

1. taking appropriate action to facilitate, preserve and strengthen women's business enterprises and to ensure full participation by women in the free enterprise system;

2. taking affirmative action in support of women's business enterprises in appropriate programs and activities including, but not limited to, management, technical, financial, procurement assistance, as well as, business related education, training, counseling information and dissemination; and

3. requiring any department or agency empowered to extend federal financial assistance to any program or activity issue regulations requiring the recipient of such assistance take appropriate affirmative action in support of women's business enterprises and prohibit actions or policies that discriminate on the grounds of sex.

Veteran-Owned and Service-Disabled Veteran Business Enterprise Development

Public Law 106-50, The Veterans Entrepreneurship and Small Business Development Act of 1999, establishes the Office of Veterans Business Development (OVBD) to be administered by the Associate Administrator for Veterans Business Development (AAVBD). The AAVBD is responsible for the formulation, execution and promotion of policies and programs of the SBA that provide assistance to small businesses owned and controlled by veterans and service-disabled veterans.

The SBA is very supportive of the efforts to assist veterans and to increase their opportunities for small business success. A member of SCORE (Service Corp of Retired Executives) is appointed by SBA Administrator to act as a National Veterans Business Coordinator and to establish and maintain telephone and Internet access to provide veterans with information about entrepreneurship counseling and training to include technical assistance, financial assistance, procurement assistance.

Current State of Small Business Development

The Small Business Act (Public Law 85-536, as amended) states that, *"The essence of the American economic system of private enterprise is free competition."* But while the government wholly supports this philosophy for all Americans, there are still socially and economically disadvantaged individuals whose ability to compete in the free enterprise system remains impaired due to diminished capital, credit and contracting opportunities as compared to others in the same business area who are not socially or economically disadvantaged.

A study commissioned by Washington, D.C.-based Joint Center for Political and Economic Studies in partnership with the then Telecommunications Industry Group (TIG), of the National Minority Supplier Development Council (NMSDC) (now part of the Telecommunications Industry Association [TIA]) was conducted by the Asaba Group, Inc. of Boston, Massachusetts. The intent of the study was to determine how best to achieve sustainable minority-, women- and disabled veteran-owned businesses as suppliers in the telecommunications industry.

The study identified a number of issues that inhibit S/D/M/W/V/DVBE growth and sustainability, and made recommendations that would enable development to include:

1. corporate supplier development organizations playing a role in creating a more accurate picture of the procurement landscape for prospective S/D/M/W/V/DVBE suppliers;

2. advocacy organizations such as the National Supplier Development Council (NMSDC), Women's Business Enterprise National Council (WBENC), U.S. Hispanic Chamber of Commerce (USHCC), the U.S. Pan Asian American Chamber of Commerce (USPAAC), Women's Business Development Centers (WBDCs), and others, become more proactive in reinforcing the link between the corporations with active supplier diversity programs and their various constituencies;

3. developing a widely understood and internalized value proposition that will enable the creation of contractual requirements on the large tier-one suppliers; and

4. the TIA actively provide information about industry trends and emerging opportunities.

The study also recommended that supplier diversity managers create competitively viable suppliers, and evolve from current mindset to create a new paradigm that requires a:

1. shift from creating minority jobs to creating business capacity;

2. shift from creating access to bids to creating a strong competitive set of suppliers; and

3. shift from supplier diversity as corporate altruism to how can it enhance and enable competitive differentiations.

Section 8(a) Business Development Program

One of the many programs and services offered by the SBA is the Section 8(a) and 7(j) Minority Small Business and Capital Ownership Development Program. The purpose of this program is to assist eligible small disadvantaged business concerns compete in the American economy through business development.

A participant receives a program term of nine years from the date of SBA's approval letter certifying the concern's admission. Eligibility must be maintained during the tenure and the SBA must be informed of any changes that would adversely affect its eligibility. Upon completion of the nine years, a participant is deemed to have graduated. The term may be shortened only by termination, early graduation or voluntarily.

Business Certification

The integrity and credibility of any legislative or executive mandate depends on the establishment of systematic procedures that ensure only bona fide small businesses are independently owned and controlled in both substance and form by socially and economically disadvantaged individuals, women or armed forces veterans. To carry out these mandates, regulations were implemented so that qualifying firms must first certified, usually by a third party such as a local government agency or an independent entity contracted by a government agency.

Persons with disabilities are not presumed to be disadvantaged as other groups. If a disabled or handicapped individual applies for certification and is not a member of one of the presumptive groups, they would have to prove his or her social and economic disadvantage status based on their handicap. The disability must be shown to have been chronic, longstanding and substantial, not fleeting or insignificant, and to have negatively affected their entry into and/or advancement in the business world.

The procedure known as the "certification process" consists of three sequential steps to certify that the prospective firm is eligible to participate. The certifying agency must provide uniform eligibility standards to the prospective firms describing the process, rebuttals, recertification and due process. The steps are:

1. collecting the specified and necessary information from the firm;

2. applying the criteria for eligibility set forth in each certification program; and

3. certifying (or denying) that the prospective firm is eligible to participate in the program.

The first step requires that all prospective S/D/M/W/V/DV or disabled/handicapped firms complete an application. It is the responsibility of the applicant to provide the information deemed necessary by the certifying agency to ascertain eligibility. The information provided by the applicant is used as evidence in support of fulfilling all eligibility standards set forth by the certifying entity.

The next step is an on-site review as a part of the uniform certification process. It is an effective means to verify the applicant's home or office facilities and operations, and to validate the written application. In conjunction with the application and documents submitted, the on-site review will help determine whether a firm:

1. is in fact in existence, operational and in business for a profit;

2. possesses the resources or expertise to operate in this field of work;

3. owners and key persons listed in the application play a critical role in the company; and

4.   does not exist solely on paper and not organized in an attempt to take advantage of project goals.

Finally, a thorough, detailed and complete analysis of the application file with the supporting documents is conducted. The applicant is entitled to prompt action on its application and to be duly informed when any part of the application is deficient and/or incomplete. A formal decision can be made by management acting independently, or through a committee. Any firm denied certification would be afforded due process.

You can obtain minority, disadvantaged, woman and service disabled veteran certification from a variety of sources. In addition to the organizations listed below, contact your local city, county, quasi-government or state office and inquire about minority and women business certifications in your area. You may also obtain certification applications, as well as the statutes, process for certification and other information to assist you in becoming certified.

Minority Business Enterprise (MBE) Certification

National Minority Supplier Development Council (NMSDC)
www.nmsdc.org/
1040 Avenue of the Americas, 2nd Floor
New York, New York 10018
Phone: 212-994-2430

Section 8(a) Certification

Small Business Administration
www.sba.gov/sdb/indexsdbapply.html
Office of Small Disadvantaged Business Certification & Eligibility
409 – 3rd Street, S.W., MC 8800, SDB 8th Floor
Washington, D.C. 20416
Phone: 202-619-1850

Veteran-Owned, Service-Disabled Veteran Business Enterprise Certification

Department of General Services
www.pd.dgs.ca.gov/smbus/dvbecert.htm
Office of Small Business Certification & Resources
1531 I Street, Second Floor
Sacramento, CA 95814
Phone: 916-322-5060

American Society of Disabled Veterans
ASDV Clearinghouse
www.asdv.org/

Small & Disadvantaged Business Enterprise Certification

Department of Transportation
https://www.civilrights.dot.gov/disadvantaged-business-enterprise
Office of Civil Rights
400 – 7th Street, S.W.
Washington, D.C. 20590
Phone: 202-366-1605

Women Business Enterprise (WBE) Certification

Women's Business Enterprise National Council (WBENC)
www.wbenc.org/
1156 – 15th Street, N.W., Suite 1015
Washington, D.C. 20005
Phone: 202-862-4810

Woman-owned Small Business (WOSB) Federal Contracting Program and Economically Disadvantaged Women-Owned Business (EDWOSBs)

Small Business Administration
https://certify.sba.gov/
409 3rd Street, SW
Washington, DC 20416

Women's Business Development Center (WBDC)

http://www.wbdc.org/
8 S. Michigan Avenue, 4th Floor
Chicago, IL 60603
Phone: 312-853-3477

Woman/Minority Business Enterprise (MBE) Certification

The Supplier Clearinghouse
http://www.thesupplierclearinghouse.com/
10100 Pioneer Boulevard, Suite 103
Santa Fe Springs, CA 90670
Phone: 562-325-8685

CHAPTER 9

BUSINESS RESOURCES

Your Resource Center

(NOTE: At this release, all website addresses, email address, telephone numbers, company/organization names and descriptions were verified and active.)

ACCOUNTING

ADP
www.adp.com
Employee payroll solutions.

American Accounting Association (AAA)
www.aaahq.org
The largest community of accountants in academia. Shaping the future of accounting through teaching, research and a powerful network, ensuring a position as thought leaders in accounting.

American Institute of CPAs (AICPA)
www.aicpa.org/
Serves as the national representative of CPAs before governments, regulatory bodies and other organizations in protecting and promoting members' interests.

Financial Accounting Standards Board (FASB)
www.fasb.org/
Establishes and improves standards of financial accounting and reporting for guidance and education of the public including issuers, auditors and users of financial information.

Paychex
www.paychex.com
Small business payroll services.

Intuit QuickBooks
https://www.intuit.com/
Provider of accounting solutions designed to help people and businesses manage their finances, run their small businesses, pay employees, including taxes with TurboTax.

ADVERTISING

American Association of Advertising Agencies (AAAA)
www.aaaa.org/
A management-oriented association that offers its members the broadest possible services, expertise and information regarding the advertising agency business.

Advertising Self-Regulatory Council (ASRC)
www.asrcreviews.org/
Establishes the policies and procedures for advertising industry self-regulation, including the National Advertising Division (NAD), Children's Advertising Review Unit (CARU), National Advertising Review Board (NARB), Electronic Retailing Self-Regulation Program (ERSP) and Online Interest-Based Advertising Accountability Program (Accountability Program.) The self-regulatory system is administered by the Council of Better Business Bureaus.

AFFILIATE MARKETING

Amazon
https://affiliate-program.amazon.com/

Avangate
http://www.avangate.com/

CJ by Conversant
www.cj.com

Ebay Partner Network
https://www.ebaypartnernetwork.ebay.com/

Rakuten Linkshare
http://marketing.rakuten.com/affiliate-marketing

BANKING & FINANCE

American Express Small Business
https://www.americanexpress.com/us/small-business/

BB&T Small Business Banking
www.bbt.com/business

Bank of America Multicultural Supplier Diversity
www.bankofamerica.com/business

Business Consortium Fund (BCF)
www.bcfcapital.com/
A minority business development company created by the National Minority Supplier Development Council (NMSDC) to provide financing to NMSDC-certified MBEs across America through a network of participating banks and NMSDC affiliates.

Capital One for Business
www.capitalonecom/creditcards/businessrewards

Chase Business Banking
www.chase.com/forbusiness

Community Development Financial Institutions (CDFI) Fund
www.cdfifund.gov
Offers tailored resources and innovative programs that invest federal dollars alongside private sector capital, the CDFI Fund serves mission-driven financial institutions that take a

market-based approach to supporting economically disadvantaged communities.

Community Reinvestment Act (CRA)
www.federalreserve.gov/communitydev/
Financial institutions are authorized to engage in community development investments in any number of ways at their discretion.

Export-Import Bank of the United States (Ex-Im Bank)
www.exim.gov/
The official export credit agency whose mission is to assist in financing the export of U.S. good and services to international markets.

Overseas Private Investment Corporation (OPIC)
www.opic.gov/
Established as a development agency of the U.S. government to help U.S. businesses invest overseas, foster economic development in new and emerging markets.

Small Business Administration (SBA)
https://www.sba.gov/loanprograms
Aids, counsels, assists and protects the interests of small businesses. Ensures that small business concerns receive a fair portion of government purchases, contracts and subcontracts.

Wells Fargo Small Business
www.wellsfargo.com/biz/

BLOGGING

Blog Index
www.theblogindex.net/

Blog Index Web Directory
https://sites.google.com/site/blogsindex/web-directory

Blogger
www.blogger.com

Build Your Own Blog
http://www.buildyourownblog.net

Copyblogger
www.copyblogger.com
Gawker
http://gawker.com/

Mashable
www.mashable.com

Movable Type
www.movabletype.com

Tumblr (Foursquare)
www.tumblr.com

Typepad
www.typepad.com

WordPress
www.wordpress.com

BONDING

National Association of Surety Bond Producers (NASBP)
www.nasbp.org/
An international organization of surety bond producers and brokers, representing over 5000 personnel who specialize in surety bonding, performance and payment bonds for the construction industry and other types of surety bonds for the guaranteeing performance such as license and permit bonds.

Surety & Fidelity Association of America
www.surety.org/
Formerly known as the Surety Association of America, a trade association consisting of companies that collectively write the majority of surety and fidelity bonds in the United States.
These are the bonds that facilitate commerce, assist economic development, and protect consumers, taxpayers, and businesses.

Surety Information Office
www.sio.org/
Mission to increase the use of contract surety bonds in the private sector, and foster dissemination of positive information on the

important role of corporate suretyship in the public and private construction.

CERTIFICATION

American Society of Disabled Veterans (ASDV)
www.asdv.org/
Pioneer in inclusion of service disabled and prisoner of war veteran entrepreneurs (SDVE) on specially-assisted procurement programs of the federal and state governments and their private-sector contractors.

Disadvantaged Business Enterprise (DBE) Program 49 CFR Part 26
https://www.fhwa.dot.gov/civilrights/programs/dbess.cfm
Ensures that federally-assisted contracts for highway, transit and aviation projects are made available for small business concerns owned and controlled by socially and economically disadvantaged individuals.

National Minority Supplier Development Council (NMSDC)
www.nmsdc.org/
A membership organization that provides a direct link between corporate America and minority-owned businesses in an effort to increase procurement and business opportunities.

Small Business Administration (SBA)
Office of Small Disadvantaged Business Certification & Eligibility – 8(a) and SDB
https://www.sba.gov/content/about-8a-business-development-program
Provides a wide range of services to minority businesses to include support for government contracting, access to capital, management and technical assistance and export assistance.

Small Business/DVBE Outreach & Education
www.pd.dgs.ca.gov/smbus/sbcert.htm
Created to act as a liaison between DGS Procurement Division and certified small business suppliers. Objective is to promote the use of small business within state government.

Supplier Clearinghouse
http://www.thesupplierclearinghouse.com/
A full online application for new and renewing firms, a comprehensive directory search function, and relevant news and events for the MBE, WBE, DVBE, and LGBTBE communities and provides utility companies with a current database of all bona fide firms.

Women's Business Development Center (WBDC)
http://www.wbdc.org/
A non-profit focused on fueling the economy through entrepreneurship. As the oldest, largest and most comprehensive women's business assistance center in the United States, we have programs designed to help individuals in every phase of the business development and growth process.

Women-owned Small Business (WOSB) and Economically Disadvantaged Women-Owned Businesses (EDWOSBs)
https://certify.sba.gov/
A federal contracting set-aside program which authorizes contracting officers to restrict competition or award sole source federal contracts to eligible WOSBs and Economically Disadvantaged Women-Owned Small Businesses (EDWOSBs) in certain industries.

Women's Business Enterprise National Council (WBENC)
www.wbenc.org/
The nation's leading advocate of women-owned businesses as suppliers to America's corporations.

CHAMBERS OF COMMERCE

National Black Chamber of Commerce (NBCC)
http://www.nationalbcc.org/
Dedicated to economically empowering and sustaining African American communities through entrepreneurship and capitalistic activity within the U.S. and via interaction with the Black Diaspora.

U.S. Chamber of Commerce
www.uschamber.com/
Provides a voice of experience and influence in Washington, D.C. and around the globe with expert policy specialists, lobbyists and attorneys representing businesses, state and local chambers, business associations and American Chambers of Commerce abroad.

U.S. Hispanic Chamber of Commerce (USHCC)
www.ushcc.com/
Communicates the needs and potential of Hispanic enterprises to the public and private sectors by implementing and strengthening national programs that assist in economic development, increase business relationships and monitors legislation, policies and programs.

U.S. Pan Asian American Chamber of Commerce (USPAAC)
www.uspaacc.com/
A national not-for-profit business organization representing all Asian Americas and Asian American related groups in businesses, sciences, the arts, sports, education, public and community services.

CLOUD COMPUTING

Dell Cloud Computing
www.dell.com/cloud_computing

Equinix Cloud Solutions
www.equinix.com/cloud_exchange

Google Cloud Platform
https://cloud.google.com/

Microsoft Cloud Computing
https://resources.office.com

COMPUTER HARDWARE & SOFTWARE

Adobe Systems, Inc.
www.adobe.com/
Digital imaging, design and document technology platforms for consumers, creative professional and enterprises.

Apple
www.apple.com/business
Provides hardware and software business solutions for accounting, finance, general productivity, marketing, sales data, network management, mobile and wireless, one-line business.

Cisco Systems, Inc.
www.cisco.com/
Provides hardware and software networking, security, analytics, conferencing, switching, video broadband cable, access servers, wireless.

Computer Sciences Corporation (CSC)
www.csc.com/
Provides application services, big data and analytics, consulting, cloud solutions, cybersecurity mobility and social, next generation networks and service management solutions.

Dell Computer Corporation
www.dell.com/
Computer, printers, televisions, gaming and other consumer electronics for small, medium and large businesses and home.

Gateway, Inc.
www.gateway.com/
Sellers of personal computers, electronics, accessories, software, digital TV, on-line, retailers or direct sales force.

Hewlett-Packard Company
www.hp.com/
Desktop, workstations, notebooks, tablets, printing, handheld devices, monitors, projections, faxes, copiers, scanners, digital photography, supplies and accessories.

IBM Corporation
www.ibm.com/us/
Personal computing, servers, software, storage, microelectronics, printing systems.

Microsoft Corporation Small Business
www.microsoft.com/smallbusiness
Mobil and business solutions for small, medium and large business data analysis, business finance, mapping tools, office systems, games.

Oracle - Siebel
www.siebel.com/
Leader in customer relationship management software and a leader in providing of software applications for business intelligence and business integration.

Quark, Inc.
www.quark.com/
Leader in desktop publishing software with a suite of enterprise publishing software for custom publishing in a multi-channel environment. Industry leader in design, publishing, personalization and content management.

CONTRACTING

Dynamic Small Business Search (DSBS)
http://dsbs.sba.gov/dsbs/search/dsp_dsbs.cfm
A database of all small businesses that have registered in SAM (www.sam.gov). This listing is searched by both Federal agencies and prime contractors to locate small businesses that meet their requirements.

FedBizOpps
https://www.fbo.gov/
The official federal government procurement opportunities allowing contractors to retrieve services posted by government buyers.

Federal Acquisition Regulations (FAR/DFAR)
https://www.acquisition.gov/
A substantial and complex set of rules governing the federal government's purchasing process to ensure purchasing procedures are standard and consistent and conducted in a fair and impartial manner.

GSA eLibrary
http://www.gsaelibrary.gsa.gov/ElibMain/home.do
Source for the latest GSA contract award information. GSA offers unparalleled acquisition

solutions to meet today's acquisition challenges. GSA's key goal is to deliver excellent acquisition services that provide best value, in terms of cost, quality and service, for federal agencies and taxpayers.

System for Award Management (SAM) formerly CCR

https://www.sam.gov/

The official U.S government system that consolidated the capabilities of CCR/Federal Agency Registration, Online Representations and Certifications Applications.

USASpending.gov

https://www.usaspending.gov/

USAspending.gov is the publicly accessible, searchable website mandated by the Federal Funding Accountability and Transparency Act of 2006 to give the American public access to information on how their tax dollars are spent.

CREDIT & REPORTING

Consumer Credit.com

https://debthelp.consumercredit.com/

Provides budget counseling, educational programs, debt management assistance and housing counseling online, by telephone and in person.

Credit Karma

https://www.creditkarma.com/

Provides members free credit reports, scores and credit monitoring.

Dun & Bradstreet Corporation (D&B)

www.dnb.com/us/

Provider of global business information tools and solutions that customers rely on to make critical business decisions.

Equifax

www.equifax.com/

Provider of information technology enabling and securing global commerce across industries including financial services, retail, healthcare, telecommunications/utilities, brokerage, insurance and government agencies.

Experian

www.experian.com/

Provides U.S. consumers and businesses with the tools and services to help understand, manage and protect their personal credit profiles.

Federal Trade Commission (FTC)

www.ftc.gov/

Ensures that the nation's markets are vigorous, efficient and free of restrictions that harm customers and enforces federal consumer protection laws that prevent fraud, deception and unfair business practices.

Freecreditreport.com

https://www.freecreditreport.com/

Founded in 1995 to give consumers quick, easy, and inexpensive access to their credit histories. It is now the leading provider of online consumer credit reports, credit scores, credit monitoring, and other credit-related information.

FreeScoresAndMore.com

https://offer.freescoresandmore.com/

Provides credit scores from all three credit bureaus, crediting monitoring and alerts, and identify theft protection.

Standard & Poor's Credit Rating (S&P)

www2.standardandpoors.com/

Provider of credit ratings for globally-recognized financial market indices as the S&P 500, and provides a wide range of other products and services designed to help individuals and institutions make better-informed financial decisions.

Trans Union

www.transunion.com/

Global provider of technology-based business intelligence services with products including innovative credit decision and fraud prevention tools, advanced target marketing products, risk and profitability models and portfolio management that enables businesses manage financial risk and capitalize on market opportunities.

CROWDFUNDING

Experiment
https://experiment.com/

FundAnything
https://fundanything.com/en

Funder Hut
www.funderhut.com

GoFundMe
www.gofundme.com

Indiegogo
https://www.indiegogo.com/

Kickstarter
www.kickstarter.com

DOMAIN NAME REGISTRATION

Check Domains
www.checkdomain.com/

GoDaddy
www.godaddy.com/

InterNic
www.InterNIC.net/
Stands for "Internet Network Information Center." The InterNIC is an organization created by the National Science Foundation to provide Internet information and domain name registration services. InterNIC was started as a joint effort between Network Solutions and AT&T, it is now run by the Internet Corporation for Assigned Names and Numbers (ICANN).

iPage
www.ipage.com

Network Solutions
www.networksolutions.com

Register.com
www.Register.com/

Web.com
www.web.com/

Wix
www.wix.com

Yahoo
www.smallbusiness.yahoo.com/domains

EMAIL MARKETING

AWeber
www.weber.com

Benchmark Email
http://www.benchmarkemail.com/

Constant Contact
www.constantcontact.com

ExactTarget
www.exacttarget.com

GetResponse
http://www.getresponse.com

IContact
https://www.icontact.com

MailChimp
http://mailchimp.com/

Pinpointe
http://www.pinpointe.com/

EMPLOYEES

ADP
www.adp.com
Global provider of cloud-based Human Capital Management solutions such as payroll, talent, time, taxes and benefits administration.

Employee Benefits Research Institute (EBRI)
https://www.ebri.org/
Contributes to, encourages, and enhances the development of sound employee benefit programs and sound public policy through objective research and education.

Internal Revenue Service (IRS) Employee Benefits

https://www.irs.gov/Businesses/Small-Businesses-&-Self-Employed/Employee-Benefits

IRS guidelines to employee benefits to include fringe benefits, unemployment insurance, workers' compensation, and health plans.

Paychex

http://www.paychex.com

Recognized leader in payroll, human resources and benefits outsourcing.

ENTREPRENEURIAL EDUCATION

Financial Peace University – Ramsey Solutions

http://www.daveramsey.com/fpu/

A biblically-based money handling plan using video teaching, class discussions and interactive small group activities combined with practical steps that show individuals how to get rid of debt, manage money, spend, save and give wisely.

Kauffman Foundation, Ewing Marion

http://www.kauffman.org

Helps individuals attain economic independence by advancing educational achievement and entrepreneurial success, consistent with the aspirations of our founder, Ewing Marion Kauffman.

Lynda.com

http://www.lynda.com/

A leading online learning company that helps anyone learn business, software, technology and creative skills to achieve personal and professional goals. Through individual, corporate, academic and government subscriptions, members have access to the lynda.com video library of engaging, top-quality courses taught by recognized industry experts.

EQUITY INVESTORS

National Association of Investment Companies (NAIC)

http://naicpe.com/

The trade association for diverse owned investment management firms. The association is made up of 35 members, 31 of which are diverse-owned direct investment private equity firms who attract capital from government and corporate pension plans.

National Venture Capital Association (NVCA)

www.nvca.org/

A trade association that empowers its members and the entrepreneurs they fund by advocating for policies that encourage innovation and reward long-term investment. As the venture community's flagship trade association, the NVCA serves as the definitive resource for venture capital data and unites its over 300 member firms through a full range of professional services.

Private Equity International

https://www.privateequityinternational.com/

Provides a ranking of the world's top fund managers according to a very simple metric: how much capital they have raised for private equity investment in the last five years.

FEDERAL AGENCIES

Department of Agriculture (DOA)

www.usda.gov

Provides leadership on food, agriculture, natural resources, rural development, nutrition, and related issues based on public policy, the best available science, and effective management.

Department of Air Force

www.af.mil

Provides compelling air, space, and cyber capabilities for use by the combatant commanders. Excels as stewards of all Air Force resources in service to the American people, while providing precise and reliable Global Vigilance, Reach and Power for the nation.

Department of Army

www.army.mil

Conducts both operational and institutional missions. The operational Army consists of numbered armies, corps, divisions, brigades, and battalions that conduct full spectrum operations around the world. Institutional organizations provide the infrastructure necessary to raise, train, equip, deploy, and ensure the readiness of all Army forces.

Department of Commerce (DOC)

www.commerce.gov

Works with businesses, universities, communities, and the Nation's workers to promote job creation, economic growth, sustainable development, and improved standards of living for Americans.

Department of Defense (DOD)

www.defense.gov

Manages an inventory of installations and facilities to keep Americans safe. The Department's physical plant is huge by any standard, consisting of more than several hundred thousand individual buildings and structures located at more than 5,000 different locations or sites.

Department of Education

www.ed.gov

Establishes policies on federal financial aid for education, and distributing as well as monitoring those funds. Collects data on America's schools and disseminating research. Focuses national attention on key educational issues. Prohibits discrimination and ensuring equal access to education.

Department of Energy (DOE)

www.energy.gov

To ensure America's security and prosperity by addressing its energy, environmental and nuclear challenges through transformative science and technology solutions.

Department of Health and Human Services (HHS)

www.hhs.gov

Enhances and protects the health and well-being of all Americans by providing for effective health and human services and fostering advances in medicine, public health, and social services.

Department of Homeland Security (DHS)

www.dhs.gov

Secures the nation from the many threats through the dedication of more than 240,000 employees in jobs that range from aviation and border security to emergency response, from cybersecurity analyst to chemical facility inspector with a goal of keeping America safe.

Department of Housing and Urban Development (HUD)

www.hud.gov

Sponsors housing counseling agencies throughout the country that can provide advice on buying a home, renting, defaults, foreclosures, and credit issues.

Department of the Interior (DOI)

www.doi.gov

Responsible for the construction of the national capital's water system, the colonization of freed slaves in Haiti, exploration of western wilderness, oversight of the District of Columbia jail, regulation of territorial governments, management of hospitals and universities, management of public parks, and the basic responsibilities for Indians, public lands, patents, and pensions.

Department of Justice (DOJ)

www.justice.gov

Enforces the law and defend the interests of the United States according to the law; ensures public safety against threats foreign and domestic; provides federal leadership in preventing and controlling crime; to seek just punishment for those guilty of unlawful behavior; ensures fair and impartial administration of justice for all Americans.

Department of Labor (DOL)

www.dol.gov

To foster, promote, and develop the welfare of the wage earners, job seekers, and retirees of the United States; improve working conditions; advance opportunities for profitable employment; and assure work-related benefits and rights.

THE BUSINESS CENTER

Department of Navy

www.navy.mil

To maintain, train and equip combat-ready Naval forces capable of winning wars, deterring aggression and maintaining freedom of the seas.

United States Department of State

www.state.gov

The United States federal executive department responsible for the international relations of the U.S, equivalent to the foreign ministry of other countries.

Department of Transportation (DOT)

www.transportation.gov

Serves the United States by ensuring a fast, safe, efficient, accessible and convenient transportation system that meets vital national interests and enhances the quality of life of the American people, today and into the future.

Department of the Treasury

www.treasury.gov

Responsible for promoting economic prosperity and ensuring the financial security of the United States. Responsible for a wide range of activities such as advising the President on economic and financial issues, encouraging sustainable economic growth, and fostering improved governance in financial institutions.

Department of Veterans Affairs

www.va.gov

Serves America's Veterans and their families with dignity and compassion, and to be their principal advocate in ensuring that they receive medical care, benefits, social support, and lasting memorials promoting the health, welfare, and dignity of all Veterans in recognition of their service to this Nation

FORMS & DOCUMENTS

Application for Employer Identification Number (SS4)

www.irs.gov/pub/irs-pdf/fssf.pdf

Used to obtain an identification number (like a social security number) for a business that is a corporation, partnership or sole proprietorship with employees.

Employment Eligibility Verification (I-9)

https://www.uscis.gov/sites/default/files/files/form/i-9.pdf

Used for verifying the identity and employment authorization of individuals hired in the U.S.

Employee Withholding Allowance Certificate (W-4)

https://www.irs.gov/uac/About-Form-W4

Used by employers to withhold the correct federal income tax from an employee's pay.

Uniform Commercial Code Financing Statement (UCC-1)

Used by creditors as a notice that it has or may have a financial interest in the personal property of a debtor. Contact the Secretary of State's Office in your area. (See page 307)

Wage and Tax Statement (W-2)

https://www.irs.gov/pub/irs-pdf/fw2.pdf

An Internal Revenue Service form used to report wages paid to employees and the taxes withheld from those wages.

FOUNDATIONS & GRANTS

Encyclopedia of Associations

http://find.galegroup.com/gdl/help/GDLeDirEAHelp.html

The only comprehensive source of detailed information concerning nonprofit American membership organizations of national scope. A guide to more than 23,000 organizations in subjects such as Trade, Business, and Commercial; Legal, Governmental, Public Administration, and Military; Cultural; Educational; Veterans', Hereditary, and Patriotic; Athletic and Sports; Fan Clubs, and many more.

Foundation Center

http://foundationcenter.org/

Collects, organizes and communicates information on U.S. philanthropy and ensures public access to information.

Foundation Directory

https://fconline.foundationcenter.org/

A database of resources needed to search for foundations most likely to award grant and manage prospects through funding.

Grant Space

http://grantspace.org/

Provides easy-to-use, self-service tools and resources to help nonprofits worldwide become more viable grant applicants and build strong, sustainable organizations.

GuideStar

https://www.guidestar.org

The most complete source of information about U.S. charities and other nonprofit organizations there is. Search our database of more than 1.8 million IRS-recognized organizations to find a charity to support, benchmark your own nonprofit's performance, research the sector, and more.

FRANCHISING

American Association of Franchisees & Dealers (AAFD)

www.aafd.org/

A national not-for-profit trade association representing the rights and interests of franchisees and independent dealers throughout the U.S.

Consumer Guide to Buying a Franchise

www.ftc.gov/bcp/conline/pubs/invest/buyfran.pdf

The Federal Trade Commission, the nation's consumer protection agency, has prepared this Guide to help you decide if a franchise is right for you. It suggests ways to shop for a franchise opportunity and highlights key questions you need to ask before you invest. The Guide also explains how to use the disclosure document that franchisors must give you — under the FTC's Franchise Rule — so you can investigate and evaluate a franchise opportunity.

International Franchise Association (IFA)

www.franchise.org/

A membership organization of franchisers, franchisees and suppliers providing one-stop shopping experience for franchise information.

IMPORT/EXPORT

American Association of Exporters & Importers (AAEI)

www.aaei.org/

The only national trade association dedicated exclusively to representing the interests of both U.S. exporters and importers before U.S. government agencies, Congress, international organizations and foreign governments.

International Trade Administration (ITA)

http://www.trade.gov/

Works to improve the global business environment and helps U.S. organizations compete at home and abroad

PIERS — Directory of U.S. Importers and Directory of U.S. Exporters

https://www.piers.com/

The global import and export information service that provides powerful tools and data for measuring markets, analyzing competition and uncovering opportunities. Launched more than 35 years ago, PIERS was the first venture in digital global trade intelligence and quickly became the industry standard for accuracy, reliability and insight.

Trade Information Center (TIC) Export.gov

http://export.gov/

Export.gov brings together resources from across the U.S. Government to assist American businesses in planning their international sales strategies and succeed in today's global marketplace.

U.S. Importers Directory

http://www.usimportersdirectory.com/

An importer's directory that tracks the most reputable import distributors. This is a list of registered importers that lets you find which companies are in the business of importing what product.

United States Export Assistance Centers
https://www.sba.gov/managing-business/exporting/us-export-assistance-centers
Provide one-stop trade promotion, financing and export financing, as well as, export insurance programs.

HEALTHCARE PROVIDERS

Aetna Health Insurance
www.aetna.com/

BlueCross/BlueShield
www.bcbs.com/

Cigna
www.cigna.com/

Health Net
www.healthnet.com/

Humana
www.humana.com/

Tenet Healthcare
www.tenethealth.com/

UnitedHealthcare
www.unitedhealthcare.com/

INSURANCE

American Insurance Association
www.aiadc.org/
Leading property-casualty insurance trade organization.

American Risk & Insurance Association
www.aria.org/
Promotes education and research in risk and insurance.

Employee Benefit Research Institute
www.ebri.org/
Conducts research on employee benefits including pensions, IRAs, health insurance, social security and long term health care.

America's Health Insurance Plans
www.ahip.org/
Commercial health insurers, to include managed care and group insurance committee, disability insurance committee, Medicare administration committee and long term care task force.

Insurance Information Institute (III)
www.iii.org/
Publisher of helpful pamphlets and books that provide accurate and timely information on insurance subjects.

INTERNET SERVICE PROVIDERS

AT&T
www.att.com/

Comcast
www.comcast.net

Cox Communications
www.cox.com/

Time Warner Cable
www.timewarnercable.com/

Verizon
www.verizon.com/

LABOR RELATIONS

AFL-CIO
www.aflcio.org/
To bring social and economic justice to our nation giving working people a voice on the job, in government, in a changing global economy and their communities.

National Federation of Independent Unions
https://www.unionfacts.com/
Nationally-recognized voice of independent unionism in the U.S. through which individual, independent unions come together for a common purpose – protecting the rights of Americans, working families, both on and off the job.

LEGAL

American Bar Association
http://www.americanbar.org/
One of the world's largest voluntary professional organizations, with nearly 400,000 members and more than 3,500 entities. Committed to serving members, improving the legal profession, eliminating bias and enhancing diversity, and advancing the rule of law throughout the United States and around the world.

Avvo Legal
http://www.avvo.com/
An online legal services marketplace that provides immediate free information and advice from experienced attorneys on most common legal issues.

Lawyers.com
http://legal-malpractice.lawyers.com/
A free service from Martindale-Hubbell® designed specifically for individuals and small businesses, providing accurate and reliable profiles of 1 million lawyers and firms worldwide, a wealth of information to help users better understand the law, make more informed personal legal choices and identify high quality legal representation, and other services.

LegalShield
https://www.legalshield.com/
Delivers fee-based legal services through a network of independent provider law firms to over 1.4 million families across the U.S. and Canada.

LegalZoom
http://www.legalzoom.com
Provides fee-based legal advice to individuals through local, independent attorneys.

Nolo Law for All
www.nolo.com/
Publisher of plain-English books, software and forms to help people handle their own everyday legal matters.

National Consumer Law Center
http://www.nclc.org/
The nation's consumer law expert helping consumers, their advocates and public policy makers use powerful and complex consumer laws to assure justice for vulnerable, low income Americans.

Rocket Lawyer
https://www.rocketlawyer.com/
Simple and affordable access to legal services. Provides everyday law helps identify the little and big ways the law can make life better. Tips about timely legal topics, and learn how people manage their issues. Solo lawyers and small firms can also share information and discuss their challenges.

LEGISLATION

8(a) Business Development/Small Business Status Determination
www.sba.gov/9abd/

Affordable Care Act of 2016
https://www.healthcare.gov/
Comprehensive health insurance reforms that have improved access, affordability, and quality in health care for Americans that has helped people across the country.

Age Discrimination Act of 1975
http://www.dol.gov/oasam/regs/statutes/age_act.htm

Age Discrimination in Employment Act of 1967
http://www.eeoc.gov/laws/statutes/adea.cfm

Americans with Disabilities Act of 1990
http://www.dol.gov/general/topic/disability/ada

Airline Deregulation Act of 1978
https://www.gpo.gov/fdsys/pkg/STATUTE-92/pdf/STATUTE-92-Pg1705.pdf

Antitrust Civil Process Act
http://www.justice.gov/atr/file/761131/download

Automobile Information Disclosure Act of 1958
https://www.gpo.gov/fdsys/pkg/USCODE-2010-title15/html/USCODE-2010-title15-chap28.htm

Bankruptcy Abuse Prevention and Consumer Protection Act of 2005
https://www.gpo.gov/fdsys/pkg/BILLS-109s256enr/pdf/BILLS-109s256enr.pdf

Brady Law of 1993
https://www.atf.gov/rules-and-regulations/brady-law

Child Protection Act of 1966
https://www.uscis.gov/green-card/green-card-processes-and-procedures/child-status-protection-act/child-status-protection-act-cspa

Children's Television Act of 1990
https://transition.fcc.gov/Bureaus/Mass_Media/Factsheets/kidstv.txt

Civil Rights Act of 1964 – Amended 1991
http://www.eeoc.gov/eeoc/history/35th/1990s/civilrights.html

Clayton Antitrust Act of 1914 (Amended by Celler-Kefauver Anti-merger Act of 1950)
http://www.justice.gov/atr/file/761131/download

Community Reinvestment Act of 1977
http://www.federalreserve.gov/communitydev/cra_about.htm

Consumer Credit Protection Act of 1968
http://www.dol.gov/whd/regs/statutes/garn01.pdf

Consumer Goods Pricing Act of 1975
https://www.gpo.gov/fdsys/granule/STATUTE-89/STATUTE-89-Pg801

Consumer Product Safety Improvement Act of 20713
http://www.cpsc.gov/

Controlling the Assault of Non-solicited Pornography and Marketing Act of 2003 (CAN-SPAM)
https://www.ftc.gov/tips-advice/business-center/guidance/can-spam-act-compliance-guide-business

Disadvantaged Business Enterprise (DBE) Program 49 Code of Federal Regulations Part 26
https://www.fhwa.dot.gov/civilrights/programs/dbess.cfm

Equal Credit Opportunity Act of 1961
http://www.justice.gov/crt/equal-credit-opportunity-act-3

Equal Education Opportunities Act of 1974
http://www.justice.gov/crt/types-educational-opportunities-discrimination

Equal Pay Act of 1963
http://www.eeoc.gov/laws/statutes/epa.cfm

Export Administration Act of 2001
https://www.congress.gov/bill/107th-congress/senate-bill/149

Export-Import Bank Act of 1945
http://www.state.gov/t/isn/exportimport/

Fair Credit Billing Act of 1974
https://www.ftc.gov/sites/default/files/fcb.pdf

Fair Credit Reporting Act of 1970
http://www.consumer.ftc.gov/articles/pdf-0111-fair-credit-reporting-act.pdf

Fair Debt Collection Practices Act as Amended 1996
https://www.ftc.gov/enforcement/rules/rulemaking-regulatory-reform-proceedings/fair-debt-collection-practices-act-text

Fair Packaging and Labeling Act of 1966
https://www.ftc.gov/enforcement/rules/rulemaking-regulatory-reform-proceedings/fair-packaging-labeling-act

Fair Labor Standards Act (FSLA) of 1938 – As amended
http://www.dol.gov/whd/regs/statutes/fairlabo
rstandact.pdf

Family & Medical Leave Act (FMLA) of 1993
http://www.dol.gov/whd/regs/statutes/fmla.ht
m

Federal Acquisition Regulations (FAR)
https://www.acquisition.gov/?q=browsefar

Federal Acquisition Streamlining Act (FASA) of 1994
https://www.gpo.gov/fdsys/pkg/BILLS-
103s1587enr/pdf/BILLS-103s1587enr.pdf

Federal Cigarette Labeling and Advertising Act of 1967
https://www.ftc.gov/enforcement/statutes/fed
eral-cigarette-labeling-advertising-act-1966

Federal Food and Drug Act of 1906
http://www.fda.gov/RegulatoryInformation/Leg
islation/ucm148690.htm

Federal Reserve Act of 1913
http://www.federalreserve.gov/aboutthefed/fra
ct.htm

Federal Trade Commission Act of 1914 – Amendments of 2006
https://www.ftc.gov/sites/default/files/docume
nts/statutes/federal-trade-commission-
act/ftc_act_incorporatingus_safe_web_act.pdf

Federal Trade Commission Improvement Act of 1980
https://www.govtrack.us/congress/bills/96/hr6
589

Flammable Products Act of 1953
http://www.cpsc.gov/en/Regulations-Laws--
Standards/Statutes/Flammable-Fabrics-Act/

Foreign Affairs Reform and Restructuring Act of 1998
https://www.congress.gov/105/bills/hr1757/BIL
LS-105hr1757enr.pdf

Freedom of Information Act
www.foia.gov

Fur Products Labeling Act of 1951
https://www.ftc.gov/node/119458

Glass-Steagall Banking Act of 1933
http://www.justice.gov/sites/default/files/atr/le
gacy/2008/09/05/236665.pdf

Gun Control Act
https://www.gpo.gov/fdsys/pkg/USCODE-2011-
title18/pdf/USCODE-2011-title18-partI-
chap44.pdf

HUBZone Empowerment Contracting Program
http://gao.gov/products/OGC-98-62

Immigration Reform and Control Act of 1986
https://www.uscis.gov/

International Antitrust Enforcement Assistance Act of 1994
http://www.justice.gov/atr/file/761131/downlo
ad

Interstate and Foreign Travel or Transportation in Aid of Racketeering Enterprise
https://www.gpo.gov/fdsys/pkg/USCODE-2011-
title18/pdf/USCODE-2011-title18-partI-chap95-
sec1952.pdf

Magnuson-Moss Warranty Act of 1975
https://www.ftc.gov/enforcement/statutes/mag
nuson-moss-warranty-federal-trade-
commission-improvements-act

Miller-Tydings Resale Price Maintenance Act of 1937
https://www.ftc.gov/system/files/documents/p
ublic_statements/683391/19520602_macintyre
_statement._relative_to_proposed_legislation_
dealing_with_resale_price_maintenance.pdf

Minority Business Development Agency (MBDA) Development of - Executive Order 11458 of 1969
http://www.mbda.gov/main/mbda-
history/executive-order-11458

Motor Carrier Act and Staggers Rail Act of 1980
https://www.gpo.gov/fdsys/pkg/STATUTE-94/pdf/STATUTE-94-Pg1895.pdf

National Environmental Policy Act (NEPA) of 1969/1970
http://energy.gov/sites/prod/files/nepapub/nepa_documents/RedDont/Req-NEPA.pdf

National Firearms Act
https://www.gpo.gov/fdsys/pkg/USCODE-2011-title26/pdf/USCODE-2011-title26-subtitleE-chap53.pdf

National Labor Relations Act of 1935
https://www.nlrb.gov/resources/national-labor-relations-act

National Traffic and Motor Vehicle Safety Act of 1966
https://www.gpo.gov/fdsys/pkg/USCODE-2011-title49/pdf/USCODE-2011-title49-subtitleVI-partA-chap301.pdf

North American Free Trade Agreement of (NAFTA)
https://ustr.gov/trade-agreements/free-trade-agreements/north-american-free-trade-agreement-nafta

Nutrition Labeling and Education Act of 1990
http://www.fda.gov/ICECI/Inspections/InspectionGuides/ucm074948.htm

Occupational Safety & Health Act of 1970
https://www.osha.gov/pls/oshaweb/owasrch.search_form?p_doc_type=OSHACT

Privacy Act of 1974
http://www.justice.gov/opcl/privacy-act-1974

Public Health Cigarette Smoking Act of 1971
https://www.gpo.gov/fdsys/pkg/STATUTE-84/pdf/STATUTE-84-Pg87-2.pdf

Public Works Economic Development Act of 1965
http://legcounsel.house.gov/Comps/Public%20Works%20And%20Economic%20Development%20Act%20Of%201965.pdf

Robinson-Patman Act of 1936
https://www.ftc.gov/tips-advice/competition-guidance/guide-antitrust-laws/price-discrimination-robinson-patman

Securities Exchange Act of 1934
https://www.sec.gov/about/laws/sea34.pdf

Sherman Antitrust Act of 1890
http://www.justice.gov/atr/file/761131/download

Small Business Act
https://www.sba.gov/sites/default/files/files/Small%20Business%20Act.pdf

Small Business Investment Act of 1958
https://www.sba.gov/sites/default/files/policy_regulations/Small%20Business%20Investment%20Act%20of%201958_0.pdf

Small Business Research and Development Enhancement Act of 1992
http://thomas.loc.gov/cgi-bin/query/z?c102:S.2941.ENR:

Small Business Size Standards
https://www.sba.gov/sites/default/files/files/Size_Standards_Table.pdf

Telecommunications Act of 1996
https://transition.fcc.gov/Reports/tcom1996.pdf

Trademark Act (Lanham) of 1946
http://www.uspto.gov/sites/default/files/trademarks/law/Trademark_Statutes.pdf

Trafficking in Contraband Cigarettes and Smokeless Tobacco
https://www.gpo.gov/fdsys/pkg/USCODE-2011-title18/pdf/USCODE-2011-title18-partI-chap114.pdf

Trans-Pacific Partnership (TPP) Agreement
https://ustr.gov/tpp/

Truth in Lending Act of 1968
http://files.consumerfinance.gov/f/201306_cfpb
_laws-and-regulations_tila-combined-june-
2013.pdf

Uniform Commercial Code
https://www.law.cornell.edu/ucc

Uniform Franchising Offering Circular (UFOC)
www.nasaa.org/

Uniform Partnership Act of 1997
http://www.uniformlaws.org/shared/docs/part
nership/upa_final_97.pdf

**Uniform Trade Secrets Act with 1985
Amendments**
http://www.uniformlaws.org/shared/docs/trad
e%20secrets/utsa_final_85.pdf

**Veterans Education and Benefits Expansion Act
of 2001 - Public Law 107-103**
https://www.congress.gov/107/plaws/publ103/
PLAW-107publ103.pdf

**Veterans Entrepreneurship and Small Business
Development Act of 1999**
https://www.sba.gov/sites/default/files/files/pl
106-50.pdf

Wheeler-Lea Act of 1938
https://www.ftc.gov/system/files/documents/p
ublic_statements/676351/19380517_freer_whe
_wheeler-lea_act.pdf

**Whistleblower Protection Enhancement Act of
2012**
https://www.atf.gov/resource-
center/docs/foia/whistleblower-protection-
enhancement-act-2012/download

Wilson-Gorman Tariff Act of 1894
http://www.justice.gov/atr/file/761131/downlo
ad

**Women's Business Enterprise Executive Order
12138**
http://www.archives.gov/federal-
register/codification/executive-
order/12138.html

Wool Products Labeling Act of 1939
https://www.ftc.gov/node/119457

Workforce Investment Act of 1998
https://www.doleta.gov/programs/factsht/wial
aw.cfm

OFFICE LOCATIONS

1871 Chicago
http://www.1871.com/
Using the business incubator concept, 1817 is
where Chicago's brightest digital designers,
engineers and entrepreneurs are shaping new
technologies, disrupting old business models,
and resetting the boundaries of what's possible.

Alliance Business Center
www.abcn.com/
Leading provider of executive suites, virtual
offices and full serviced office space with over
500 locations in 32 countries.

HQ Global Workplaces
www.hq.com/
Nation's largest network of furnished, full-
supported office space providing outstanding
services to America's leading Fortune 100
companies and small business entrepreneurs.

**International Business Innovation Association
(INBIA)**
www.inbia.org/
Members are business assistance professionals
concerned with business start-ups,
entrepreneurship and effective small business
management.

MARKETING & PUBLIC RELATIONS

American Marketing Association (AMA)
www.ama.org/
One of the largest professional associations for
marketers with 38,000 members worldwide in
every area of marketing. An essential resource
providing relevant marketing information that
experienced marketers turn to every day.

Business Marketing Association

www.marketing.org/

Leading professional resource for business-to-business marketers and communicators. Develops and delivers benefits, services, information, skill enhancement and networking opportunities that help members grow, develop and succeed.

Duct Tape Marketing

http://www.ducttapemarketing.com/

Simple, effective, and affordable small business marketing and home of the *Duct Tape Marketing* Consultant Network.

HubSpot

http://www.hubspot.com/

An easy-to-use, integrated set of applications for businesses to use, attract, engage, and delight customers by delivering inbound experiences that are relevant, helpful and personalized.

Public Relations Society of America (PRSA)

www.prsa.org/

Primary objectives are to advance the standards of the public relations profession and provide members with professional development opportunities through continuing education programs, information exchange forums and research projects conducted on national and local levels.

URL Dr.

http://www.theurldr.com/

Years of experience in e-commerce and online marketing, plus over 36 years of experience in retail, management, and operations with clients of various sizes.

Social Media Examiner

http://www.socialmediaexaminer.com/

The world's largest social media marketing resource that helps millions of businesses discover how to best use social media to connect with customers, drive traffic, generate awareness and increase sales.

MENTOR-PROTÉGÉ PROGRAMS

Department of Defense (DOD)
Office of Small & Disadvantaged Business Utilization (OSDBU)

http://www.acq.osd.mil/osbp/sb/programs/mpp/

Department of Transportation
Mentor-Protégé Programs

https://www.transportation.gov/osdbu/procurement-assistance/mentor-protege-pilot-program

Department of the Treasury
Mentor-Protégé Programs

https://www.treasury.gov/resource-center/sb-programs/Pages/dcfo-osdbu-mentor-protege-index.aspx

Small Business Administration (SBA)
Section 8(a) Business Development

https://www.sba.gov/blogs/sbas-mentor-prot-g-program

NOT-FOR-PROFIT ASSISTANCE

Internal Revenue Service IRS

https://www.irs.gov/Charities-&-Non-Profits

Provide information on applying for tax exempt status and reporting for charitable organizations, churches and religious organizations, political organizations, private foundations, other non-profits and contributors.

Society for Nonprofits

https://www.snpo.org/resources/startup.php

A leading resource for nonprofit professionals and has been helping nonprofit leaders increase their knowledge and grow the capacity of their organizations for more than 30 years.

ONLINE MARKETPLACES

Amazon.com

www.amazon.com

eBAY

www.ebay.com

Etsy

https://www.etsy.com/

346

Fiverr
https://www.fiverr.com/

Offeritem
http://www.offeritem.com/

Rakuten.com (Buy.com)
www.buy.com

Sears.com
https://www.searscommerceservices.com/

Sell.com Marketplace
http://www.sell.com/

PROFESSIONAL ASSOCIATIONS

AARP
http://www.aarp.org/
A nonprofit, nonpartisan, social welfare organization with a membership of nearly 38 million that helps people turn their goals and dreams into real possibilities, strengthens communities and fights for the issues that matter most to families — such as health care, employment and income security, and protection from financial abuse.

American Association of Persons with Disabilities (AAPD)
www.aapd.com/
The largest national not-for-profit cross-disability member organization dedicated to ensuring economic self-sufficiency and political empowerment for the more than 56 million Americans with disabilities.

American Association of Product Developers
www.aapd-dc.org
Free membership organization for both consumer product developers and business product developers committed to developing high-quality products while being an active member of in their local, state, and regional community.

American Express OPEN Forum
https://www.americanexpress.com/us/small-business/openforum/explore/

Provides insights, inspiration and connections for small business owners to grow their businesses.

American Management Association
http://www.amanet.org/
A membership organization that offers a wide range of exclusive benefits, including preferred pricing on seminars and up-to-date management and business information to help professional development ongoing and promote management excellence for all employees.

American Society of Association Executives (ASAE)
https://www.asaecenter.org/
An organization for association management, representing both organizations and individual association professionals.

Asian Women in Business (AWIB)
www.awib.org/
A not-for-profit membership organization that assists Asian women to realize their entrepreneurial potential.

Association of Women in International Trade (AWIT)
www.wiit.org/
A non-partisan professional organization for individuals (particularly women) who share a strong interest in international trade. Recognized for its range of professional development support.

BizLaunch
http://www.bizlaunch.com/
A small business training company in North America who's worked with Fortune 500 companies to improve their brand presence with over 100,000 entrepreneurs by providing high quality webinars, seminars, marketing content and training.

Disabled Businesspersons Association Challenged America
www.disabledbusiness.com/
Charitable organization dedicated to assisting enterprising individuals with disabilities to maximize their potential in the business world.

Home Office Association of America (HOAA)

www.hoaa.com/

A for-profit organization providing advice and information to home office workers and business owners.

LaunchGrowJoy

http://www.launchgrowjoy.com/

Works with entrepreneurs to help them grow their online business through online courses, courses at Creative Live, events, conferences, blog posts and videos.

National Association for Community Economic Development (NACED)

http://www.nacced.org/?page=About

The trade association for community development corporations, community economic development industry as well as other community-based economic organizations, community action agencies, banks, foundations, corporations, individual practitioners, students and small business.

National Association for Home-based Businesses

www.usahomebusiness.com/

Affiliate of International association for Business Organizations; Small Business Networks.

National Association for the Self-employed (NASE)

www.nase.org/

Advocates and supports micro-businesses and the self-employed at the state and federal level.

National Association of Government Contractors (NAGC)

http://www.governmentcontractors.org/

One of the largest, most powerful voices for small contractors on Capitol Hill, and has developed from an advocacy organization into an association providing advocacy, education, business development and services to member companies.

National Association of Manufacturers

www.nam.org/

The nation's largest industrial trade association representing small and large manufacturers in every industrial sector.

National Association of Professional Women (NAPW)

https://www.napw.com/

An organization offering women the opportunity network with over 700,000 members at more than 200 local chapters. Provides an exclusive, highly advanced networking forum to successful women executives, professionals and entrepreneurs.

National Association of Women Business Owners (NAWBO)

www.nawbo.org/

National organization that advocates for women entrepreneurs with 75 chapters nationwide.

National Center for American Indian Enterprise Development

http://ncaied.org/

Promotes advocacy, education, and communication, business development, legislative alerts and members' native-owned businesses.

National Contract Management Association (NCMA)

www.ncmahq.org/

Membership-based professional society whose vision is to be the pre-eminent source of professional development for the practice of contract management.

National Women Business Owners Corporation (NWBOC)

www.nwboc.org/

Established to increase competition for corporate and government contracts through implementation of a pioneering economic development strategy for women business owners.

OWN IT

https://www.ownit.com/communities/ownit

A network of small business owners and the self-employed supporting each other in growing their businesses.

Service Corps of Retired Executives (SCORE)
https://www.google.com/
Local chapters nationwide that assists small businesses with free face-to-face and online workshops, mentoring and helpful templates and tools.

Social Media Examiner
http://www.socialmediaexaminer.com/
The world's largest social media marketing resource that helps millions of businesses discover how to best use social media to connect with customers, drive traffic, generate awareness and increase sales.

Telecommunications Industry Association (TIA)
http://www.tiaonline.org/about/
The Telecommunications Industry Association (TIA) is the leading trade association representing the global information and communications technology (ICT) industries through standards development, policy initiatives, business opportunities and networking, market intelligence, and worldwide environmental regulatory compliance.

United Inventors Association of America
http://www.uiausa.org/
A 501c3 non-profit educational foundation dedicated to providing educational resources and opportunities to the independent inventing community, while encouraging honest and ethical business practices among industry service providers.

United States Association for Small Business and Entrepreneurship (USASBE)
http://www.usasbe.org/
The largest independent, professional, academic organization in the world dedicated to advancing the discipline of entrepreneurship. With over 1000 members from universities and colleges, for-profit businesses, nonprofit organizations, and the public sector, USASBE is a diverse mix of professionals that share a common commitment to fostering entrepreneurial attitudes and behaviors.

World Intellectual Property Organization (WIP)
http://www.wipo.int/
A self-funded agency of the United Nations and a global forum of intellectual property (IP) services, policy, information and cooperation. The mission is to lead the development of a balanced and effective international IP system that enables innovation and creativity for the benefit of all.

PUBLICATIONS

Asian Enterprise Magazine
www.asianenterprise.com/
Largest Asian-American small business focused publication providing important inform to a growing number of Asian Pacific American entrepreneurs including WMBE policies and procedures, access to small business programs, public policy, legislative and fiscal impacts procurement and business opportunities.

Black Enterprise
www.blackenterprise.com/
Serves to seek out, analyze and disseminate information that is helpful to and provides a forum for the ideas, ambitions and expressions of African American people.

Business Week
www.businessweek.com/
A weekly magazine that features information on investing, small business, global business, technology and top business news.

DiversityInc. Media
www.diversityinc.com/
Provides education and clarity on the business benefits of diversity.

Enterprising Women
www.enterprisingwomen.com/
Published five times annually and recognizes top women-owned enterprises in the U.S.

Fast Company
www.fastcompany.com/
Chronicles how companies create and compete to highlight new business practices and to

showcase teams and individuals who are inventing the future and reinventing business.

Forbes
www.forbes.com/
America's leading business magazine on technology, money and inventing, market trends, portfolio strategy, entrepreneurs and Forbes life.

Fortune
www.fortune.com/
Known for breaking new ground with its long history of award-winning editorial and innovative design as the chronicler of the true drama of business.

Harvard Business Review
https://hbr.org/
To improve the practice of management and its impact on a changing world by collaborating to create products and services in the media that best service customers, individuals and organizations.

Inc. Magazine
www.inc.com/
Offers advice, tools and services to help business owners and CEOs start, run and grow their businesses successfully. Topics include business management, marketing, sales, finding capital, managing people and more.

Kiplinger Personal Finance
www.kiplinger.com/
Developed one of the nation's first successful newsletters and subsequently created the nation's first personal finance magazine dedicated to delivering sound, unbiased advice.

MBE Magazine
www.mbemag.com/
Serves as a nationwide forum for minority and women business owners, corporations and government agencies concerned with minority entrepreneurial development.

Minority Business News USA
http://mbnusa.biz/
Nation's awarding-winning resource for information on minority business

entrepreneurship and diversity to an audience of minority business owners, corporations, procurement managers, education professionals and government representatives.

Money
www.money.cnn.com/
Reports on jobs, the economy, national and international financial markets and stocks, business news, technology, mutual funds, etc.

Network Journal
www.tnj.com/
Published each month, except combined July/August and December/January. The magazine is dedicated to educating and empowering Black professionals and small business owners.

PC Magazine
www.pcmag.com/
Technology publication that delivers authoritative, labs-based comparative review of computing and Internet products to more than 6.6 million highly engaged technology buyers.

QUALITY CONTROL

American National Standards Institute (ANSI)
www.ansi.org/
A private not-for-profit organization that administers and coordinates the U.S. voluntary standardization and conformity assessment system. Enhances both the global competitiveness of U.S. businesses and the U.S. quality of life by promoting and facilitating voluntary consensus standards and conformity assessment systems, and safeguarding their integrity.

American Society for Quality
www.asq.org/
World's leading authority on quality which creates better workplaces and communities worldwide by advancing learning, quality improvement and knowledge exchange to improve business results.

International Organization for Standardization (ISO)

www.iso.org/

The monitoring organization that meets the requirements of business and quality, providing a reference framework, common technological language, and facilitating trade and transfer of the technology platform between suppliers and their customers.

QuEST Forum

www.questforum.org/

A consortium of telecommunications service providers, suppliers and liaisons joint to implement requirements to improve the quality of telecommunications products and services.

RESEARCH ORGANIZATIONS

Bureau of Labor Statistics (BLS)

http://www.bls.gov/

Bureau of the Census

www.census.gov/

Business Reference Services

https://www.loc.gov/rr/business/company/public.html

Provides information on privately-held companies

Corporate Directory of U.S. Public Companies Walker's Research, LLC

www.walkersresearch.com/

Essential financial and business data on more than 10,000 publicly traded and foreign companies filing American Depository Receipts (ADRs).

EDGAR (Electronic Data Gathering and Retrieval) – Securities Exchange Commission

https://www.sec.gov/edgar/searchedgar/webusers.htm

A database of disclosure documents that public companies are required to file with the SEC.

Encyclopedia of Business Information Sources

http://find.galegroup.com/gdl/help/GDLeDirEBISHelp.html

A bibliographic guide containing more than 34,000 citations covering over 1100 business, financial and industrial topics on a variety of business-related concerns including business functions, computer-related subjects, foreign trade and the information industry.

ESRI Business Information Solutions

www.esri.com/

Helps industry, government and not-for-profit organizations understand customers, analyze site locations, visualize and map marketing and demographic data, and identify untapped market potential.

The Gale Group, Inc.

www.gale.com/

Serves the world's information and education needs through vast and dynamic content pools used by students, and consumers in their libraries, schools and on the Internet.

GuideStar

http://www.guidestar.org/

Provides IRS data and other up-to-date information on not-for-profit organizations.

Hoover's Handbook of American Businesses

www.hoovers.com/

Delivers comprehensive company, industry and market intelligence that drives business growth with a database of 12 million companies with in-depth coverage of 40,000 of the world's top business enterprises.

Joint Center for Political & Economic Studies

www.jointcenter.org/

A not-for-profit research and public policy institution providing training and technical assistance to newly-elected black officials. Recognized as one of the nation's premier think tanks on a broad range of public policy issues of concern to African Americans and other communities of color.

LexisNexis

www.lexis-nexis.com/

Provides information to legal, corporate, government and academic markets and publishes legal, tax and regulatory information via on line, hardcopy and CD-ROM.

Standard & Poor's Industry Surveys
www.standardandpoors.com/
Survey of recent developments, industry basics and company data for each of the 52 industry covered. Ideal for management consultants, strategic planners, money managers, public and academic librarians, students and business faculty.

Wikipedia
www.wikipedia.org
A user-generated online encyclopedia.

RSS FEED AGGREGATORS

Feedly
https://feedly.com/

Feedbin
https://feedbin.com/

Newsblur
https://newsblur.com/

Feed Wrangler
https://feedwrangler.net/welcome.html

SAFETY

International Code Council (ICC)
http://www.iccsafe.org/
A member-focused association. It is dedicated to developing model codes and standards used in the design, build and compliance process to construct safe, sustainable, affordable and resilient structures.

International Safety Equipment Association (ISEA)
https://safetyequipment.org/
The leading association for personal protective equipment and technologies that enable people to work in hazardous environments, and an ANSI-accredited standards developing organization.

National Association of Safety Professionals (NASP)
http://www.naspweb.com/
Provides safety classroom and independent study courses for safety professionals in business and industry. Includes mock OSHA inspections, development of safety plans and programs as well as other safety consulting services across the U.S.

Underwriters Laboratories (UL)
http://ul.com/
Provides expertise across three strategic businesses to promote safe living and working environments around the world. Works closely with industries, authorities and customers to keep safety ahead of innovation in an evolving global landscape. In every market, every day, we're helping companies keep pace with regulatory demands while strengthening the position of their brand and business.

SCHEDULING ONLINE

Acuity Scheduling
https://acuityscheduling.com/

Calendly
https://calendly.com/

Doodle
http://doodle.com/

Vcita
http://www.vcita.com/

WhenToWork
http://whentowork.com/

SEARCH ENGINES

Aol
www.aol.com

Ask
www.ask.com/

Bing
http://www.bing.com/

Google
www.google.com/

Yahoo
www.yahoo.com

SOCIAL MEDIA

Facebook
www.facebook.com
Focused on interaction with friends, family and business.

Flickr
www.flickr.com
Photosharing site used to build awareness and drive traffic to product pages.

Foursquare
www.foursquare.com
Find the best restaurants, shopping and entertainment in any city in the world.

Google+
www.google.com
Product of Google with a heavy visual focus.

Hootsuite
www.hootsuite.com
A social media management tool that allows management of multiple social media platforms all on one dashboard.

Instagram
www.instagram.com
For sharing visual content using mobile devices.

iTunes
www.apple.com/
Podcasting interviews with industry experts or creating mini radio shows.

LinkedIn
www.linkedin.com
For building professional connections to aid in career development.

Meerkat
https://meerkatapp.co/

For live video streaming.

MyLife
https://www.mylife.com/
Allows control over background reports that everyone can see including employers.

Pinterest
www.pinterest.com
For building a virtual collection of photos and images.

Reddit
www.reddit.com
Source of the most popular news and whatever is trending.

Snapchat
www.snapchat.com
Easily talk with friends and view live stories from around the world.

Twitter
www.twitter.com
Microblogging platform used for everything from business to fun and games.

Vimeo
www.vimeo.com
A video-sharing site.

Yelp
www.yelp.com
Reviews places to eat, shop, drink, relax or play.

YouTube
www.youtube.com
For hosting and sharing video content.

SPEAKING ORGANIZATIONS

Clarity Media Group
http://www.claritymediagroup.com/
A team of seasoned journalists who have dedicated our careers to the art of communication. The extensive knowledge and keen insights we have amassed from our award-winning work as storytellers are at the heart of every coaching session.

THE BUSINESS CENTER

TED
http://www.ted.com
A nonprofit organization devoted to spreading ideas, usually in the form of short, powerful talks (18 minutes or less). TED began in 1984 as a conference where Technology, Entertainment and Design converged, and today covers almost all topics — from science to business to global issues — in more than 100 languages.

Toastmaster's International
https://www.toastmasters.org/
A world leader in communication and leadership development. Our membership is more than 332,000 memberships. Members improve their speaking and leadership skills by attending one of the 15,400 clubs in 135 countries that make up our global network of meeting locations.

STRATEGIC PLANNING

Association for Strategic Planning
http://www.strategyassociation.org/
A non-profit professional society whose mission is to help people and organizations succeed through improved strategic thinking, planning and action. The only not-for-profit professional association dedicated to advancing thought and practice in strategy development and deployment for business, non-profit and government organizations.

Hubert H. Humphrey Institute of Public Affairs
www.hhh.umn.edu/
Widely recognized for its role in examining public issues and shaping public policy at the local, state and national and international levels and for providing leadership and management expertise to public and not-for-profit organizations.

Strategic Planning Institute
http://pimsonline.com/index.htm
Manages and develops the profit impact of market strategy (PIMS) database that includes information on markets, competitor, quality, structure, environment and financial performance.

SUPPLIERS & MANUFACTURERS

ManufacturerSupplier.com
http://www.manufacturersupplier.com/
Lists thousands of manufacturer and supplier sites offering suppliers, manufacturers, distributors, exporters and importers, and many unique and exclusive industry sources.

Shopify
https://www.shopify.com/blog/13975985-how-to-find-a-manufacturer-or-supplier-for-your-product-idea
Provides the basics of sourcing a supplier for your next project, places to search, how to approach them and what to ask.

Thomas Register of American Manufacturers
www.thomasregisterdirectory.com/
Provides concise information on approximately 194,000 U.S. companies, primarily manufacturers, with over 50,000 product classifications.

TAXES

H&R Block Get Answers
https://www.hrblock.com/get-answers/

Liberty Tax Estimator
https://www.libertytax.com/calculators/tax-estimator/

IRS Taxes for Small Business/Self-Employed
www.irs.gov/businesses/

TurboTax
https://www.turbotax.com/l

TECHNICAL ASSISTANCE

Association of Procurement Technical Assistance Centers
http://www.aptac-us.org/
With over 300 local offices — form a nationwide network of procurement professionals working to help local businesses compete successfully in the government marketplace. PTACs are the bridge between buyer and supplier, bringing knowledge of both government contracting and

the capabilities of contractors to maximize fast, reliable service to our government with better quality and at lower costs.

Minority Business Opportunity Centers (MBOCs)

http://www.mbda.gov/businesscenters

Business Resource Centers that provide individualized management and technical assistance to minority entrepreneurship at every stage of business development. Coordinates federal, state and local business resources designed to identify business opportunities and leverage existing programs to increase market access for MBEs.

National Development Council

http://nationaldevelopmentcouncil.org/

National not-for-profit and economic develop organization in the U.S. Provides technical and financial assistance to minority business people. Includes the flow of capital for investment, jobs and community development in underserved urban and rural areas across the U.S.

Procurement & Technical Assistance Centers (PTACs)

https://www.sba.gov/offices/headquarters/ogc/resources/362381

Local resource available that provides assistance to business firms in making products and services available to federal, state and local governments.

Small Business Development Centers (SBDCs)

www.sba.gov/sbdc/

SBDCs, with efforts of the private sector, education community, federal, state and local governments, offer one-stop assistance to individuals and small business by providing a wide variety of information and guidance in control and easily accessible branch locations.

Women's Business Development Center (WBDC)

http://www.wbdc.org/

A non-profit focused on fueling the economy through entrepreneurship. As the oldest, largest and most comprehensive women's business assistance center in the United States, we have programs designed to help individuals in every

phase of the business development and growth process.

TECHNOLOGY

American Society for Testing and Materials (ASTM) International

http://www.astm.org/

An international standards organization that develops and publishes voluntary consensus technical standards for a wide range of materials, products, systems and services.

Computing Technology Industry Association

www.comptia.org/

Leading IT trade association with influence in all areas of the IT industry worldwide. Providing a unified voice, global advocacy and leadership and to advance industry growth through standards, competence, education and business solutions.

IEEE Computer Society

www.computer.org/

Dedicated to advancing the theory, practice and application of computer and information processing technology, and promotes an active exchange of information, ideas and technological innovation among its members.

Lynda.com

http://www.lynda.com/

A leading online learning company that helps anyone learn business, software, technology and creative skills to achieve personal and professional goals. Through individual, corporate, academic and government subscriptions, members have access to the lynda.com video library of engaging, top-quality courses taught by recognized industry experts.

TELECOMMUNICATIONS

Free Conference Call.com

www.freeconferencecall.com

Grasshopper Virtual Phone System

www.grasshopper.com

THE BUSINESS CENTER

TRADE SHOWS

ASD Market Week
http://www.asdonline.com/lv/about/show-overview.shtml

ASI (Advertising Specialty Institute)
http://www.asicentral.com/

Black Enterprise Entrepreneurs Summit
http://www.blackenterprise.com/events/entrepreneurs-summit/

CES (Consumer Technology Association
http://www.ces.tech/

Comic-Con International
http://www.licensingexpo.com/

IDA Expo
http://www.idaexpo.org/index.html

International Production & Processing Expo
www.myprocessexpo.com/chicago/expo

Licensing Expo
http://www.licensingexpo.com/

National Minority Supplier Development Council (NMSDC)
www.nmsdc.org

Quality Show (The)
http://www.qualityshow.com/index.php

Small Business Expo
https://www.thesmallbusinessexpo.com/about/

Sourcing at MAGIC
www.ubmfashion.com/shows/sourcing-magic

WEB CONFERENCING

Cisco WebEx Conferencing
www.webex.com

GoToMeeting
www.gotomeeting.com

Zoom Web Conferencing
www.zoom.ux/

Fuze
www.fuze.com/

Lifesize
www.lifesize.com/

MeetingBurner
www.meetingburner.com/

Skype
www.skype.com/

Zoom Video Conferencing
www.zoom.us/

WEBSITE BUILDERS

eHost.com
https://www.ehost.com/

GoDaddy
www.godaddy.com

iPage
www.ipage.com

SiteBuilder
https://www.sitebuilder.com/

Siteblog
https://www.siteblog.com/

Sitey
https://www.sitey.com/

Webs.com
www.webs.com

WebsiteBuilder.com
https://www.websitebuilder.com/

Weebly
http://www.weebly.com/

Wix
www.wix.com

PART V

EPILOGUE

EPILOGUE

SELECTED READING

Suggested Publications

BUSINESS DEVELOPMENT

Business Development for Dummies, Anna Kennedy (2015)

Business Development: A Practical Guide for the Small Professional Services Firm, Sherran S. Spurlock (2013)

Business Development for Professionals: How to Eat an Elephant, One Bite at a Time, William C. Johnson (2011)

Innovation and Entrepreneurship, Peter F. Drucker, (1983)

BUSINESS COMMUNICATIONS

Business Communication: Polishing Your Professional Presence, Barbara G. Shwom and Lisa Gueldenzoph Snyder (2013)

Business Communication: Building Critical Skills, Kitty Locker and Stephen Kaczmarek (2013)

Business Style Handbook, The, Helen Cunningham, Brenda Greene (McGraw-Hill 2002)

Elements of Style, The, William Strunk, Jr. and E.B. White (Longman 2000)

BUSINESS MODELS

The Business Model Canvas: Let Your Business Thrive with This Simple Model, Magali Marbaise and Carly Probert (2017)

The Business Model: How to Develop New Products, Create Market Value and Make the Competition Irrelevant, Alexander Chernev (2017)

Platform Scale: How an Emerging Business Model Helps Startups Build Large Empires with Minimum Investment, Sangeet Paul Choudary (2015)

BUSINESS PSYCHOLOGY

Act Like a Success, Think Like a Success: Discovering Your Gift and the Way to Lie's Riches, Steve Harvey (2014)

The Power of Habit: Why We Do What We Do in Life and Business, Charles Duhigg (2014)

EPILOGUE

E-Myth Revisited: Why Most Small Businesses Don't Work and What to do About It, Michael E. Gerber (Harper Collins 2001)

Who Moved My Cheese, Spencer Johnson, M.D. (G.P. Putnam's Sons 1998)

7 Habits of Highly Effective People, Steven R. Covey (Simon & Schuster 1989)

CONTRACTING & CONSULTING

So You're Going Contracting: Unleash Your Inner Entrepreneur, Paul Reynolds (2015)

Nonprofit Consulting Essentials: What Nonprofits and Consultants Need to Know, Penelope Cagney (2010)

Demystifying Outsourcing: The Trainer's Guide to Working With Vendors and Consultants, Debbie Friedman (2006)

Consulting to Family Businesses: Contracting, Assessment, and Implementation, Jane Hillburt-Davis (2002)

CREDIT

Credit Repair: Make a Plan, Improve Your Credit, Avoid Scams, Robin Leonard, JD and Amy Loftsgordon (2015)

Hidden Credit Repair Secrets: Step-by-Step 6 Letter Dispute Plan Included, Mark Clayborne (2010)

Everything Get Out of Debt Book, The, Cheryl Kimball and Faye Kathryn Doria, CFP (Adams Media Corporation 2002)

Life After Debt, Bob Hammond (Career Press 2001)

ENTREPRENEURSHIP

Boss Life: Surviving My Own Small Business, Paul Downs (2016)

Killing It: An Entrepreneur's Guide to Keeping Your Head Without Losing Your Heart, Sheryl O'Loughlin and Steven Blank (2016)

The Little Big Small Business Book, Micah Fraim (2015)

The Entrepreneur Mind: 100 Essential Beliefs, Characteristics, and Habits of Elite Entrepreneurs, Kevin D. Johnson (2013)

FINANCE, ACCOUNTING & TAXES

Financial Statements: A Step-by-Step Guide to Understanding and Creating Financial Reports, Thomas R. Ittelson (2009)

The Essentials of Finance and Accounting for Nonfinancial Managers, Edward Fields (2011)

Business Math Essentials, Robert J. Hughes (Irwin Mirror Press 1993)

J.K. Lasser's Small Business Taxes, Barbara Weltman (John Wiley & Sons 2005)

FRANCHISING & LICENSING

The Franchise MBA: Mastering the 4 Essential Steps to Owning a Franchise, Nick Neonakis and Sagar Rambhia (2013)

Franchising & Licensing: Two Powerful Ways to Grow Your Business in Any Economy, Andrew J. Sherman (2011)

How to Buy a Franchise, James A. Meaney (Sphinx Publishing 2004)

Franchising 101: The Complete Guide to Evaluating, Buying and Growing Your Franchise Business, The Association of Small Business Development Centers and Ann Dugan (1998)

GRANTS & PROPOSALS

Grant Writing for Dummies, Bev Browning (2014)

The Only Grant Writing Book You'll Ever Need, Ellen Karsh and Arlen Sue Fox (2014)

Winning Grants Step by Step: The Complete Workbook for Planning, Developing and Writing Successful Proposals, Tori O'Neal-McElrath (2013)

The Everything Grant Writing Book, Nancy Burke Smith, Judy Tremore (Adams Media Corporation 2003)

HUMAN RESOURCES

The Employer's Legal Handbook: Manage Your Employees & Workplace Effectively, Fred S. Steingold (2015)

Winning Grants Step by Step: The Complete Workbook for Planning, Developing and Writing Successful Proposals, Tori O'Neal-McElrath (2013)

Hire Your First Employee: The Entrepreneur's Guide to Finding, Choosing, and Leading Great People, Rhonda Abrams (2011)

The Essential HR Handbook: A Quick and Handy Resource for Any Manager or HR Professional, Sharon Armstrong and Barbara Mitchell (2008)

IMPORT/EXPORT

Export/Import Procedures and Documentation, Donna L. Blade (2015)

EPILOGUE

Start Your Own Import/Export Business: Your Step-By-Step Guide to Success, Krista Turner (2014)

Export-Import Theory, Practices, and Procedures, Belay Seyoum (2013)

Import/Export: How to Take Your Business Across Borders, Carl Nelson (2009)

LEADERSHIP

The Ordinary Leader: 10 Key Insights for Building and Leading a Thriving Organization, Randy Grieser (2017)

LEADERSHIP: 10 Steps to Being a Successful Leader, Dale Whitman (2015)

How to Build Team Habits: Improve Your Customer Experience, Increase Efficiency, and Enjoy Better Business Results, Kyle Havill (2016)

21 Irrefutable Laws of Leadership: Follow Them and People Will Follow You, John C. Maxwell (2007)

Principle-Centered Leadership, Stephen R. Covey (1992)

LEGAL

How to Start And Run Your Own Corporation: S-Corporations For Small Business Owners, Peter I. Hupalo (2014)

Legal Writing in Plain English: A Text with Exercises, Bryan A. Garner (2013)

The Copyright Handbook, Stephen Tishman, JD (2011)

The Legal Analyst: A Toolkit for Thinking About the Law, Ward Fransworth (2007)

Hiring Independent Contractors: The Employer's Legal Guide, Stephen Fishman and Amy Delpo (2003)

MANAGEMENT & ORGANIZATION DEVELOPMENT

The 27 Challenges Managers Face: Step-by-Step Solutions to (Nearly) All of Your Management Programs, Bruce Tulgan (2014)

How to Improve Your Leadership and Management Skills – Effective Strategies for Business Managers, Meir Liraz (2013)

The First-Time Manager, Loren B. Belker and Jim McCormick (2012)

Practicing Organization Development: A Guide for Leading Change, William J. Rothwell and Jacqueline M. Stavros (2009)

MARKETING & PROMOTIONS

The New Rules of Marketing and PR: How to Use Social Media, Online Video, Mobile Applications, Blogs, News Releases, and Viral Marketing to Reach Buyers Directly, David Meerman Scott (2015)

The Marketing Blueprint: Lessons to Market & Sell Anything, Jules Marcoux (2015)

Guerilla Marketing: Easy and Inexpensive Strategies for Making Big Profits from Your Small Business, Jay Conrad Levinson and Jeannie Levinson (2007)

The 22 Immutable Laws of Marketing: Violate Them at Your Own Risk!, Al Ries and Jack Trout (1994)

PERSONAL FINANCE

The Index Card: Why Personal Finance Doesn't Have to Be Complicated, Helaine Olen and Harold Pollack (2016)

The Total Money Makeover: A Proven Plan for Financial Fitness, Dave Ramsey (2013)

The Millionaire Next Door: The Surprising Secrets of America's Wealthy Thomas J. Stanley and William D. Danko (2010)

Think and Grow Rich: The Landmark Bestseller – Now Revised and Updated for the 21st Century, Napoleon Hill and Arthur R. Pell (2005)

REFERENCE

The World Almanac and Book of Facts 2016, Sarah Janssen (2015)

Patent, Copyright & Trademark: An Intellectual Property Desk Reference, Richard Stim (2014)

Dictionary of Computer and Internet Terms, Douglas Downing, Ph.D., Michael Covington, Ph.D., Melody Mauldin Covington (2012)

The Everyday Internet All-in-One Desk Reference for Dummies, Peter Weverka (2005)

RESEARCH

The Oxford Guide to Library Research, Thomas Mann (2015)

Research Strategies: Finding Your Way Through the Information Fog, William Badke (2014)

How to Find Out Anything, Don MacLeod (2012)

Research Methodology: A Step-by-Step Guide for Beginners, Ranjit Kumar (2010)

EPILOGUE

SOCIAL MEDIA

Social Media Marketing Workbook: How to Use Social Media for Business, Jason McDonald, Ph.D. (2015)

A Social Strategy: How We Profit From Social Media, Mikolaj Jan Piskorski (2014)

500 Social Media Marketing Tips: Essential Advice, Hints and Strategy for Business: Facebook, Twitter, Pinterest, Google+, YouTube, Instagram, LinkedIn, and More!, Andrew Macarthy (2013)

Socialnomics: How Social Media Transforms the Way We Live and Do Business, Erik Qualman (2012)

The Social Media Bible: Tactics, Tools & Strategies for Business Success, Lon Safko (2010)

TECHNOLOGY

Smarter Than You Think: How Technology Is Changing Our Minds for the Better, Clive Thompson (2014)

How Computers Work: The Evolution of Technology, Ron White and Timothy Edward Downs (2014)

Technology In Action, Complete, Alan Evans and Kendall Martin (2013)

PCs All-In-One for Dummies, Mark L. Chambers (2013)

GLOSSARY OF TERMS

Business Terms

3D Printing – *Additive manufacturing process where three-dimensional objects are created from a digital file. Laying down of successive layers until an entire object is created.*

8(a) Program – *Business development program of the SBA that provides various forms of management and technical assistance to foster growth of socially- and economically-disadvantaged individuals.*

Acceptance – *A communicated acknowledgement whereby there is a meeting of the minds and an offer presented is accepted.*

Accounting - *A system of recording, summarizing, analyzing and verifying business and financial transactions and reporting the results.*

Accounting equation – *What a company owns is equal to what the company owes plus the owner's equity.*

Accounting notes – *Notes included with financial statements to provide detailed explanation of what the numbers mean.*

Accounts payable – *The balance due to a creditor on a current account.*

Accounts receivable – *A balance due from a debtor on a current account.*

Accounts receivable aging – *The length of time an account receivable has been outstanding divided by the number of number of days.*

Accounts receivable turnover - *The number of times it takes to turn accounts receivables into cash.*

Accrual based accounting – *The reporting of all revenues in the period earned, all expenses in the period consumed, all assets in the period purchased and all liabilities in the period incurred.*

Acid test ratio – *See quick ratio.*

Acquisition – *The number of visits that come from other social media platforms.*

Acronym – *An abbreviation formed from the initial letters of other words and pronounced as a word (e.g., ISP [Internet Service Provider]).*

Adjudicate – *To make an official decision about who is right in a dispute.*

Advertising - *The act of calling something to the attention of the public through paid announcements.*

Advisory Board – *A body of individuals acting in an advisory capacity to a business or organization.*

Affiliate marketing - *A way website owners earn commissions by promoting online businesses' products on their sites to build partnerships between merchants (online sellers of goods and services) and publishers (website owners).*

Affiliation – *A close connection as a member or branch to an organization or association.*

Alpha testing – *The first level of testing by potential users, customers or an independent testing team before a product is complete so that minor changes can be made.*

Alternative production – *A secondary method of production instituted when the primary method is not used.*

Amplification rate – *The number of reshares or retweets on average for each post.*

Analytical – *Relating to using analysis or logical reasoning.*

Angel networks – *A consortium of individuals who have money and want to invest in companies they believe may give them a good return on their investment.*

Annual industry sales - *Total dollar amount in sales at year end for an industry.*

Articles of Incorporation – *A corporate charter.*

Assemblage of assets – *The value of assets in place, but not used to conduct business operations used in business valuation.*

Assessment – *The determination of the importance, size or value of something.*

Asset approach – *A valuation approach that focuses on a company's net asset value or the fair market value to its total assets minus its total liabilities.*

Assets – *Total resources of a company to include cash, accounts receivable, inventories, plant and equipment and property under capital leases.*

Assumed name – *See Fictitious Business Name.*

Assumptions – *Facts or statements (e.g., proposition, axiom, postulate or notion) that are taken for granted.*

Attrition – *Action or process of gradual reduction of strength or effectiveness of someone or something through sustained attack or pressure.*

Audit – *A formal or official examination and verification of financial reports and accounting records.*

Authority – *The control, power or right of an individual to give orders, make decisions and/or enforce obedience.*

Average collection period – *The average number of days it takes a company to collect receivables.*

Average fixed cost – *Fixed cost divided by the number of units produced.*

Average total cost – *Total cost divided by number of units produced.*

Average variable cost – *Total variable cost divided by the number of units produced.*

Bad debt – *The operating expense incurred because of a failure to collect on receivables.*

Balance sheet – *The financial statement which reports the company's financial position at a certain period.*

Bankrupt – *The state in which a person or organization becomes insolvent.*

Barriers to entry/exit – *Situations such as finances, expertise or relationships that inhibit a company's ability to enter or exit a particular market.*

Barter – *To trade by exchanging one commodity or service for another.*

Beta testing – *Second level of testing, usually a external pilot test before a product becomes commercially available.*

Bid – *An announcement stating a specific undertaking that an organization or agency requests of suppliers or prospective suppliers.*

Bid Bond – *Provides financial assurance that the bid has been submitted in good faith and the contractor intends to enter into the contract at the price bid and provide the required performance and payment bonds.*

Blog - *Defined by Wikipedia as: ". . . a discussion of informational site published on the world wide web consisting of discrete entries ("posts") typically displayed in reverse chronological order."*

Blog indexes - *For bloggers to promote their blogs or identify blogs with content relevant to their business or interests.*

Blogging applications – *Tools that allow creation of blogs.*

Blogosphere – *A collection of blogs and their interconnections.*

Board of Directors – *A body of individuals elected by stockholders who meet periodically to determine the corporate policies and to select officers to manage the corporation.*

Bona fide – *Genuine, made in good faith without fraud or deceit.*

Bonding – *A surety that guarantees the contractor will complete the contract in accordance with the plans and specifications and all labor and materials will be paid.*

Bookkeeping – *The act of recording all transactions in a business.*

Bottom line – *A colloquial expression referring to the profit (or loss) of a company as reflected in the profit and loss statement.*

Bounce rate – *The number of visitors to your page, but leave without viewing other pages on your site.*

Brand(ing) - *A marketing strategy involving the creation of a differentiated name and image to establish presence in consumers' minds.*

Breach of contract - *The act of breaking the terms set out in a contract.*

Breakeven analysis – *A study to determine when there is neither a profit nor a loss.*

Breakeven point – *The point at which revenues from sales are exactly equal to the cost of goods sold plus expenses.*

Bricks and mortar - *An office or store where business is conducted face to face that is owned or rented.*

Broadband technology – *The amount of data that can be carried by a digital communications medium expressed in hertz.*

Budget – *An estimate of income and expenditures for a specific period of time.*

Business continuation – *A plan that provides for continuation of a business in the event of death, illness, disability or withdrawal of any of its owners or key employees.*

Business imperatives – *Issues that are critical to business success such as specific knowledge, technical expertise, proper resources, etc.*

Business incubator – *An organization that assists start-ups with management and technical assistance, and office space.*

Business Interruption Insurance – *Covers loss of income resulting from a fire or other catastrophe that disrupts the operation of the business.*

Business model - *A conceptual, textual and/or graphical representation roadmap of a firm's business design, how it captures value in the form of revenue, profit and discretionary funds of a customer, and how it drives its brand in the marketplace.*

Business plan – *A document prepared to serve as a roadmap for the operation and ultimate success of a business.*

Business Umbrella Insurance – *Adds another level of protection when liability coverage is not sufficient and ensures your business is protected when serious situations arise.*

Business valuation - *Process and procedures used to estimate the economic value of an owner's interest in a business and the price for which a business can be sold.*

Buy-out – *To purchase the shares or interest of any individual within an organization.*

Buy-sell agreement – *A legal agreement between shareholders setting out the conditions under which each may sell their shares.*

By-laws – *Rules adopted by an organization chiefly for the governance of its members and the regulation of its affairs.*

Call to action – *Instruction to readers that encourage them to take immediate action (e.g., click, call, write, subscribe, etc.).*

Campaign – *Work performed in an organized and active way to reach a particular goal either politically or social.*

Capacity – *The legal ability of an entity or individual to perform an act such as creating a binding contract.*

Capacity constraints – *Where limits of an organization's resources have been met creating a bottleneck in production.*

Capital – *Cash contributed by the owners or secured in the form of debt or equity financing in a business enterprise.*

Capital equipment – *Accumulated tangible goods used for the production of other goods that depreciates over many years.*

Capital expenditures – *Expenditures for long-term additions.*

Capital intensive – *A business or industrial process requiring the investment of large sums of money.*

Capitalization - *Total investment of the owner(s) in a business enterprise.*

Carry-back agreement – *An agreement by where a seller agrees to retain a portion of a sale for a specified amount of time.*

Cash based accounting – *The reporting of all revenues and expenses in the period during which cash is received or paid.*

Cash flow – *The timing of the flow of cash in and out of a company.*

Cash ratio – *Percentage of cash to liabilities.*

Census – *A periodic count of population, usually prepared by a governmental agency.*

Certification – *A document validating that an individual or firm has met the requirements of a program or field.*

Certified Public Accountant (CPA) – *Public accountants licensed by the state(s) in which they practice accountancy.*

Chain of command – *A hierarchy of authority dictating who's in charge and from where permission should be asked and granted.*

Channels of distribution – *A series of firms involved in the process of moving a product from production to end user.*

City charter – *A legal document establishing a municipality as a city or town.*

Classification - *Systematic arrangement in groups or categories according to established criteria.*

Clean (unclean) hands - *A rule in the law that a petitioner (defendant) for a court order must be free from unfair or unethical conduct with regard to their own matters in the case.*

Closely-held corporation – *A legal structure with few shareholders whose shares aren't available to the general public.*

Cloud computing - *The use of a network of remote servers hosted on the Internet to store, process, collaborate, access and protect data.*

Collateral – *Property pledged by a borrower to protect the interests of a lender.*

Collect on Delivery (COD) – *Payment made upon delivery of a product/service.*

Collection period – *The average number of days it takes a company to collect on receivables.*

Commercial Auto Insurance – *Usually the same coverage for personal auto insurance (e.g., liability, collision, comprehensive, personal injury) only it carries the name of the company.*

Commercial space – *Office or plant located in an area specifically for the purpose of commerce.*

Commingling funds – *To mix or combine funds making it difficult to determine which funds belongs to or comes from one account, client, etc. or another.*

Common stock – *The basic ownership class of corporate capital stock.*

Community development corporations – *Not-for-profit entities that specialize in the development and rehabilitation of real estate, investments in business ventures and related activities.*

Community foundations – *Publicly-sponsored organizations that make grants for social, educational, religious or other charitable purposes in a specific community or region.*

Company culture – *The beliefs and behaviors of a company or organization that determine how management and employees interact and handle outside business transactions.*

Company-sponsored foundations – *Legally and independent grantmaking organization with close ties to the corporation providing the funds.*

Compensation – *Payments made equivalent to services rendered or payments made to unemployed or injured workers.*

Competency – *Related skills, abilities, commitments or knowledge that enable a person to act effectively.*

Competition – *The effort of two or more parties acting independently to secure the business of a third party by offering the most favorable terms.*

Competitive advantage – *Attributes of a company that increases their chances of success over their competition.*

Competitive strategy – *A long-term action plan designed to give a company a competitive advantage.*

Compliance – *A state of being in accordance with established guidelines, regulations or specifications.*

Concept – *A thought or notion conceived in the mind.*

Confidentiality agreement – *A formal agreement between entities to safeguard process, procedures, intelligence, trade secrets, etc.*

Conglomerate – *A merger with companies that have nothing in common or with companies that want product or market extensions.*

Consequential damage – *Damage made by a product.*

Consideration – *A benefit of value that must be bargained for between parties and the essential reason for parties to enter into a contract.*

Consumer – *A person who purchases goods and services for personal use.*

Contingency plan – *A plan placed in effect in the event of a possible, but uncertain occurrence.*

Contract – *A legally enforceable promise using clear, specific language stating the understanding of all parties, oral, written or implied.*

Conversion – *The desired results from a post. This includes sales, signing up for a newsletter or coupon, completing a form, etc.*

Copyright – *The exclusive legal rights to reproduce, publish and sell the matter and form of literary, musical or artistic work.*

Core competencies – *Primary areas of a company where the greatest knowledge and expertise exists.*

Corporation – *A body formed and authorized by law to act as a single entity although constituted by one or more persons and legally endowed with various rights and duties including the capacity of succession.*

Cost of capital – *The opportunity cost of making a specific investment.*

Cost of goods sold – *Total original purchase price of merchandise sold during a fiscal period.*

Covenant of non-compete – *An agreement by where ex- employees or partners agree to withhold from direct competition for a specified amount of time.*

Co-venturer – *Participants in a joint venture.*

Credentials – *A qualification, achievement, personal quality or aspect of a person's background, such as a document or certificate as in a degree proving a person's identify or qualifications.*

Credit profile – *A document containing a person's credit history.*

Credit rating - *An estimate or evaluation of an individual's or business' standing or level of responsibility.*

Creditworthiness – *A valuation performed by lenders considering the repayment history and credit score which determines the possibility a borrower may default on his debt obligation.*

Critical path – *The longest sequence of activities in a project plan which must be completed on time for the project to complete on due date.*

Crowdfunding - *Model that uses the Internet to expose a company or individual(s) to millions of potential funders. Each funder can contribute a small amount to ultimately reach a financial goal and fund a project.*

Current assets – *Cash or other assets that can be turned into cash within a year.*

Current liabilities - *Debts that are due and payable in six months or less.*

Current ratio – *The ratio of current assets to current liabilities.*

Curriculum Vitae (CV) – *A short account of one's career and qualifications prepared typically by an applicant for a position.*

Customer acquisition cost - *Expenditures in any medium that determine whether the cost for acquiring the customers they attracted were worth the expense.*

Customer satisfaction – *A measurement of how products or services meets or exceed customer expectation.*

Customization – *A modification of something to suit a particular individual or task.*

Cyber squatters – *Those who purchase domain names with no intention of ever using them; only reselling them at a premium.*

Damages – *The amount of money a plaintiff (the person brining a case) is awarded in a lawsuit.*

Data – *A collection of facts and statistics for reference of analysis*

Database – *The organization of collected information so that it can be easily accessed, managed and updated.*

Debt crowdfunding – *Business related funding where investors expect to receive their money back with interest. The return on investment is financial, and the investors contribute to an idea or project they believe in.*

Debt financing – *Borrowed money from an outside source to be repaid at a specific point.*

Debt ratio – *Proportion of total assets provided by the firm's creditors.*

Debt-to-equity ratio – *The amount of debt being used to finance assets relative to the shareholders' equity.*

Demographic – *Statistical data relating to the population and particular groups within it.*

Deploy – *Methodical procedure of introducing an activity, process, program or system to all applicable areas of an organization.*

Depreciation – *The periodic cost expiration of all plant assets except land.*

Direct labor – *Wages of workers charged directly to a specific project.*

Directors and Officers Liability Insurance – *Offers reimbursement for losses or advancement of defense costs in the event an insured suffers a loss as a result of a legal action brought for alleged wrongful acts while in the capacity as a director or officer.*

Disability Insurance – *Replaces income that is lost during a short-term (e.g., pregnancy, accident, etc.) or permanent (e.g., long-term illness or condition) disability.*

Disabled Veteran-owned Business Enterprise (DVBE) – *A small business concern owned 51% or more by one or more disabled veterans.*

Disadvantaged Business Enterprise (DBE) – *A small business concern owned 51% or more by one or more minorities or women.*

Disbursement - *Funds that are paid out.*

Disclosure – *An act or instance of making something known or public.*

Disposition – *The act of transferring or relinquishing of property to another's care or possession. In litigation, it is a court's final determination of a case of issue.*

Distribution channels – *A network of individuals, businesses or organizations involved in getting a product or service from the provider to the user.*

Distributor – *One who markets a commodity.*

Domain name – *A name that identifies a web site.*

Domain name registration – *The process of registering a domain name identifying IP (internet protocol) addresses.*

Donation crowdfunding – *Where donors contribute because they believe in the cause (e.g., a person has a serious medical condition, saving wildlife, etc.) and have no expectation of receiving anything tangible in return.*

Due diligence – *The act of investigating a business or person prior to signing a contract.*

DUNS (Data Universal Numbering System) number - *The standard for keeping track of the world's businesses.*

E-commerce (electronic commerce) – *The exchange of business information using electronic technologies.*

Economic development – *The act of providing financial assistance to meet the needs of distressed communities throughout the U.S. that assists in creating wealth, minimizing poverty by attracting private capital investment and higher-skill, higher-wage jobs.*

Economically disadvantaged – *Socially-disadvantaged individuals whose ability to compete in the free enterprise systems has been impaired by diminished capital or credit opportunities.*

Economies of scale – *A proportionate cost savings gained by an increase in production.*

Economy – *The structure of economic life in a country, area or period.*

Educating the customer – *Methods used for providing information about a product or service to consumers.*

Electronic Data Interchange (EDI) – *The standardized computer-to-computer exchange of routine business documents (e.g., purchase orders, invoices, quotations, bids, etc.).*

Electronic Funds Transfer (EFT) - *The electronic transference of funds from one institution to another.*

Electronic mail (e-mail) – *The electronic transmission of information in a non-standardized format.*

Elevator pitch - *An approximately 60-second overview of your business, products or services used in face-to-face business networking.*

Email address – *Identifies an email box to which emails are delivered.*

Email etiquette – *Known as "Netiquette" (net etiquette) is the following of basic rules of preparing, sending and responding to email.*

Email marketing – *Direct marketing a message to a group of people via email.*

Emerging market – *Any market that is progressing towards becoming more advances via rapid growth and industrialization.*

Employment Practices Liability Insurance (EPLI) – *Covers businesses against claims by workers that their legal rights as employees have been violated.*

Engagement – *The rate of how much your followers/audience are engaged in responding to posts. This includes "likes", "shares", and comments on any post.*

Entrepreneur – *One who organizes, manages and assumes the risks of a business of enterprise.*

Environmental – *Relating to the natural world and the impact of human activity on its condition.*

Equity crowdfunding – *Also business-related funding. Investors have an equity position in the business or project.*

Equity financing – *Money provided by investors for an ownership interest in a company.*

Errors & Omissions Insurance – *Coverage for professional liability limited to acts of negligence.*

Estimated projections – *Use of historical information obtained by mechanical means to project the future.*

Ethical – *Relating to moral principles or the branch of knowledge dealing with these, and being in accordance with the rules and standards for proper conduct or practices.*

Execution excellence - *When people, processes and products/services are in total alignment to meet overall company goals and achieve business success.*

Executive Branch – *The branch of U.S. government responsible for implementing, supporting and enforcing laws made the Legislative Branch and interpreted by the Judicial Branch.*

Exit rate – *The rate at which people leave your site at a given page.*

Expert(ise) – *One who acquired special skills or knowledge in a particular field.*

Exposure – *State or condition of being unprotected and open to damage, danger, risk or suffering a loss in a transaction.*

External – *Coming or derived from an outside source.*

Factoring – *Also called receivables financing which allows businesses to get cash from business receivables.*

Fair market value – *A selling price for an item to which a buyer and seller can agree.*

Feasibility – *The state or degree of being easily or conveniently done, effected or accomplished.*

Federal Bond (non-contract) – *Required by the federal government (e.g., Medicare and Medicaid providers, customs, immigration, excise and alcoholic beverages).*

Federal Employer Identification Number (FEIN) - *A nine-digit number (e.g., 12-3456789) assigned to sole proprietors, corporations, partnerships, estates, trusts and other entities for tax filing purposes.*

Federal Supply Classification Code (FSC) – *Codes used to group products into logical families for management purposes.*

FICO score – Acronym for the credit scoring system used by most lenders, most often today that was invented by the Fair Isaac Corporation.

Fictitious business name (also known as "assumed name" or "DBA" [doing business as]) - *A business name used instead of the business owner's that is conventionally or hypothetically assumed or accepted.*

FIFO (first in, first out) – *Units acquired first are sold first.*

Financial plan – *A written statement of a financial strategy that includes financial statements and budgets.*

Financial status - *An individual's existing financial position.*

Fitness for duty - *An employee's physical and mental capability of safely and competently performing the essential functions of their position.*

Fixed assets – *Tangible assets used in the business of a permanent or fixed nature.*

Fixed costs – *Costs that remain constant regardless of amount of business conducted.*

Flowchart – *A diagram of the sequence of movements or actions of people or things showing step-by-step progression through a complicated procedure or system.*

Footprint (or service territory) – *The amount of space a particular unit of hardware, software or products occupy or the amount of territory products and services sales covers.*

Forecasts – *The calculation or prediction of some future event, usually as a result of rational study and analysis of available pertinent data.*

Foundation – *An organization or institution established for the purpose of providing money (in the form of a grant) to other organizations, institutions or individuals to promote a variety of humanitarian causes.*

Franchise – *The right or license granted to an individual or group to market a company's goods or services.*

Free on Board (FOB) – *Terms of an agreement between buyer and seller requiring the buy to absorb the transportation costs.*

Fringe benefits - *Benefits provided by an employer to an employee, contractor or partner (some tax-exempt) when certain conditions are met.*

Funding vehicle – *Any financial instrument that provides for immediate cash, usually insurance policies.*

Furniture and fixtures – *Sometimes known as FF&E (furniture, fixtures and equipment), are considered depreciable property unless affixed to real property.*

General and Administration (G&A) – *Expenses incurred in the general operation of a business.*

General Ledger (GL) – *A book containing a group of accounts to which debits and credits are posted from books of original entry.*

General Partnership – *A legal relationship that exists between two or more persons contractually associated as joint principals in a business.*

Generally Accepted Accounting Principles (GAAP) – *Generally accepted guidelines for the preparation of financial statements.*

Gentrification – *The process of renovating and improving an area or district for the purpose of conforming to middle-class taste.*

Geographic – *Belonging to or characteristics of the natural features, population, industries, etc. of a region or regions.*

Global – *Relating to the entire world; worldwide.*

Goal – *The end toward which effort is directed.*

Going concern – *An assumption that an entity will remain in business for the foreseeable future and will not be forced to halt operations and liquidate assets.*

Goodwill – *The value of customer lists, trade reputation and brand that is assumed to go with a company and its name.*

Google Glass – *Gives the ability to view social media feeds, navigate with GPS, text, and take photos.*

Gross Domestic Product (GDP) – *The monetary value of all the finished goods and services produced within a country's borders in a specific period of time, usually one year.*

Gross margin – *Percentage of each sales dollars remaining after the firm has paid for its goods.*

Gross national product (GNP) – *Measures the market value of all final goods and services produced by a country's citizens or residents, excluding activities in America owned by foreigners, but not American economic activity in other countries.*

Gross profit margin – *The excess of net revenue from sales over the cost of merchandise sold.*

Gross receipts – *Earnings before taxes or expenses.*

Guarantee – *An assurance of the quality of or the length of use to be expected from a product offered or sale, often with a promise of reimbursement.*

Health and Dental Insurance – *Covers the cost of the covered individuals' medical and surgical expenses for overall health and dentistry.*

Homebased business – *A business enterprise located and operating in a home.*

Horizontal merger – *Firms operating in the same space merging or consolidating their companies.*

Identify Theft Insurance – *Protects individuals whose personal information has been unlawfully used to impersonate them, steal from bank accounts, establish phony insurance policies, open credit card accounts or obtain bank loans.*

Impossibility of performance – *Whereby a party may be released from a contract on the grounds that uncontrollable circumstances have rendered their performance impossible.*

Impressions – *The number of visitors who saw your post.*

Inbound links – *The number of sites linking back to your website or page.*

Income approach – *A valuation approach commonly used by appraisers computed by taking the net operating income of rent collected and dividing it by the capitalization rate.*

Income statement – *Also known as the profit and loss statement, measures results of financial information for a specific period of time, usually one month.*

Indemnity – *Security or protection against a loss or other financial burden.*

Independent foundations – *Established to aid social, educational, religious or other charitable activities.*

Indirect costs – *Costs not identifiable with a specific product, function or activity.*

Indirect labor – *Labor not identifiable with a specific product, function or activity.*

Industrialization – *The development of industries in a country or region on a wide scale.*

Industry – *A distinct group or productive or profit-making enterprises.*

Industry best practices – *Techniques or methodologies proven through experience and research to be reliable and lead to a desired result.*

Industry sector – *A distinctive part of an industry as a whole.*

Industry standard (industry practices) – *A set of criteria generally accepted within an industry relating to the standard or best practice in functioning and carrying out of operations in their respective fields of production.*

Information economy - *An economy in which knowledge is the primary raw material and source of value.*

Information Management Systems (IMS) – *The manner in which data is collected, input, classified, calculated, analyzed, summarized, stored and retrieved.*

Infringement – *An encroachment or trespass on a right or privilege.*

Initial Public Offering (IPO) – *Selling stock to the public through the stock exchanges.*

Initiative – *An organization's way of setting a priority for actions that will direct its vision for improving the organization.*

Innovation – *The introduction of a new idea, method or device.*

Insurance – *Coverage by contract whereby one party agrees to guarantee another against a specific loss.*

Intellectual property – *Inventions, literary and artistic works, symbols, names and images used in commerce.*

Internal – *Belonging to or situated on the inside.*

International Organization for Standardization (ISO) - *Quality certification for the manufacture of a product, information technology and information technology management.*

Internet – *A digital communications network connection of thousands of smaller networks from all countries in the world.*

Internet Service Providers (ISPs) - *Organizations that provide the connection that enables you to surf the web and exchange electronic mail (e-mail).*

Inventory – *The quantity of goods or materials on hand.*

Inventory turnover – *The number of times the average level of inventory is sold.*

Investment – *The outlay of money usually for income or profit.*

Investor – *A person or organization that puts money into a financial scheme, business, property, etc. with the expectation of receiving a return on that investment.*

Invitation for Bid (IFB) – *A formal method by which prospective bidders are invited to bid on providing a product/service.*

Job diversification – *To give employees training that will expand skill levels.*

Joint venture – *A legal structure where companies combine resources and expertise to construct a major project.*

Journalizing – *The process of recording transactions into a journal before debits and credits are transferred to the accounts.*

Judicial and Probate Bond – *Also referred to as fiduciary bonds, secures the performance on fiduciaries' duties and compliance with court order, (e.g., administrators, executors, guardians, trustees of wills, liquidators, receivers).*

Judicial Branch – *The branch of the U.S. government that interprets the laws out of the Legislative Branch and administers justice.*

Judicial Proceedings Court Bond – *Injunction, appeal, indemnity to sheriff, mechanics lien, attachment, replevin and admiralty.*

Jurisdiction – *The authority of a sovereign power to govern or legislate within specific limits or territories.*

Key person – *Individuals within an organization that could include owners, executives and subject matter experts.*

Key Person Insurance – *Provides a death benefit to the company when the key employee dies. Policy is owned by the company that pays the premiums and that company is the beneficiary.*

Key results areas (KRA) – *Areas where an organization must achieve success for it to grow and prosper.*

Kidnap and Ransom Insurance – *Covers some of the expenses of dealing with kidnappers and their demands to include hostage negotiation fees, lost wages and ransom amount.*

Leads – *Visitors with the need or interest in your product/service.*

Lease agreements – *A contract by which one conveys real estate, equipment or facilities for a specified term and a specified fee.*

Leaseback – *To sell real estate or capital equipment and lease it back with an option to purchase at the end of a specified time.*

Legal structure – *Refers to the form of business ownership (e.g., sole proprietorship, partnership, corporation) established by law.*

Legislative Branch – *The part of the U.S. government that writes, debates and passes laws.*

Liabilities – *Debts of a business enterprise.*

Liability Insurance – *Covers legal responsibility for the harm it may cause to others (i.e., things that employees fails to do in the business that may cause bodily injury or property damage due to defective products, faulty installations and errors in services).*

License – *Permission and authority granted by a state agency giving individuals the right to legally practice a profession.*

License and Permit Bond – *Required by state law or local regulations in order to obtain a license or permit to engage in a particular business (e.g., contractors, motor vehicle dealers, securities dealers, employment agencies, health spas, warehouses, liquor and sales tax).*

Licensing - *Leasing of a single or combination of legally-protected trademarks, patents, designs, slogans, characters, etc. owned by another entity.*

LIFO (last in, first out) – *Units acquired last sold first.*

Limited Liability Company (LLC) – *A legal structure which allows a business to operate like a traditional partnership and have the protection from personal liability provided by the corporate structure.*

Limited Liability Partnership (LLP) – *A legal formation with one or more general partners and one or more limited partners.*

Line of Credit (LOC) – *An approved credit amount established for a customer by which interest is paid only on the amount used.*

Liquidated damages – *Damages whose amount the parties designate during the formation of a contract for the injured party to collect as compensation upon a specific breach.*

Liquidation – *The act of converting assets into cash.*

Liquidity – *Consisting of or capable of ready conversion into cash.*

Litigants – *Persons involved in a law suit.*

Litigation – *Carrying on a legal contest by the judicial process.*

Loan guarantee – *An agreement by a third party to undertake a debt in the event of a default.*

Long arm of the law – *The far-reaching power of authorities such as the court system to exercise authority over other jurisdictions.*

Long-term assets - *Instruments with a true value that's known after several years or even decades. See fixed assets.*

Long-term debt – *Debts not due for a long period of time, usually one year or more.*

Machinery – *Tools containing one or more parts using energy, usually chemical, thermal or electrical means, to perform an intended task (e.g., printer, cutter, folder, forklift, tractor, lathe, drill, backhoe, crane, etc.).*

Maintenance Bond – *Normally guarantees against defective workmanship or materials for a specified period.*

Management Information Systems (MIS) – *A manual or electronic system designed to ensure efficient use of information generated in the day-to-day operations of a business.*

Marginal cost – *Cost of producing each additional unit; indicates the minimum extra revenue that should be generated by each additional unit.*

Market approach – *A business valuation method used to calculate the value of property or as part of the valuation process or to determine the value of a business ownership interest, security or intangible asset.*

Market extension merger – *When two companies dealing in the same products, but separate markets to gain access to larger markets and client bases.*

Market penetration – *Increase of sales of a firm's present products in its present markets.*

Market position – *The ranking by dollar sales volume of competitors in a particular market.*

Market potential – *The entire size of a market for a product or service at a specific time.*

Market research – *The systematic gathering and interpretation of information using statistical and analytical methods and techniques to gain insight or support decision making.*

Marketing – *The act or process of selling or purchasing in a market.*

Marketing plan – *A written statement of a marketing strategy and the time-related details for carrying out the strategy.*

Marketplace – *The world of trade or economic activity.*

Mark-up amount or percent – *An amount or percentage added to the cost to determine the selling price.*

EPILOGUE

Mark-up chain – *The sequence of mark-ups used by firms at different levels in the channel of distribution.*

Merger – *See conglomerate, horizontal merger, vertical merger, market extension merger, product extension merger.*

Method – *A systematic or established way, technique or process for accomplishing or approaching something.*

Metrics - *A measuring system that quantifies an art, process, science, trend.*

Mezzanine debt – *Also called subordinated debt, is debt that is subordinate to senior debt giving it a second claim on a company's assets much like a second mortgage.*

Microloans – *Loans of $25,000 and below granted usually from community development corporations.*

Minority-owned Business Enterprise (MBE) – *A small business concern owned and controlled 51% or more by one or more minority individuals of a presumptive minority group (e.g., Asian, African American, Hispanic, Native American).*

Miscellaneous Bond – *Lost securities, lease, guaranteed payment of utility bills, guarantee employer contributions for union fringe benefits and workers compensation for self-insurers.*

Mission - *What the business wants to do for its owners, customers, and employees.*

Mission statement - *A brief statement describing why an organization exists, its products/services, customers served, and its goals and philosophies.*

Mitigate damages – *To cause to become less harsh or hostile by minimizing the effects and losses resulting from the injury.*

Monitoring – *To watch, keep track of, observe, especially for a specific purpose.*

Municipalities – *Primarily urban political units having corporate status and usually powers of self-government.*

Mutuality – *The consent by both parties to a contract to pay, yield or give up something in return for the benefits received.*

NAICS codes (North American Industrial Classification System) – *Formerly the SIC code is a unique, all-new system for classifying business establishments.*

386

Nano-architecture – *Tiny lattice material whose structures can be precisely tailored, are strong, flexible and extremely light.*

Net fixed assets – *Book value of fixed assets.*

Net income – *The final figure in the income statement when revenue exceeds expenses.*

Net loss – *The final figure in the income statement when expenses exceed revenues.*

Net worth – *Capital belonging to the owners as opposed to lenders or others.*

Niche - *A market where products or services are sold to only a particular kind or group of people.*

Non-recurring/recurring - *Not to occur OR to occur again after an interval.*

Notes to financial statements - *Accounting notes that are prepared to explain, in detail, what the numbers actually mean.*

Not-for-profit (non-profit) – *A corporation not conducted or maintained for the purpose of making a profit.*

Objective – *A strategic position to be attained or purpose to be achieved.*

Obsolescence – *The process of becoming obsolete or the condition of being nearly obsolete.*

Oculus rift – *3D headsets that let you feel like you're actually inside a video game.*

Offer – *To do an act or to give something on condition that the party to whom the proposal is made do some specified act make a return promise.*

Online presence – *Having visibility of a company, organization, event, etc. using social media or a website.*

Operability – *Capable of operating suitably.*

Operating budget – *A financial statement that provides an estimate of sales and expenses for a specific period of time.*

Operating expenses – *Costs such as overhead, general and administrative, salaries directly related to operating a business.*

Operating foundations – *Organizations that use its resources to conduct research or provide a direct service.*

Operating income – *Gross income minus the day-to-day operating costs.*

Operational efficiency - *Capability of an enterprise to deliver cost effective products/services to its customers and ensuring value, high quality and support.*

Operational risk - *The risk of loss that can result from inadequate or failed internal processes, people, systems or external events.*

Opportunity cost - *The loss of a potential gain when a particular alternative is chosen.*

Ordinances – *An authoritative law, decree or direction from a governmental entity.*

Outsourcing – *The act of utilizing the services of an outside entity to perform specific functions.*

Overhead – *Business expenses not chargeable to a particular part of the work or product.*

Overhead rate – *Percentage or hourly rate of overhead costs are allocated to each product or service.*

Owner's equity – *The rights of the owners in a business enterprise.*

Partnership – *A legal form of business where two or more persons are contractually associated as joint principals in a business.*

Patent – *The exclusive right of an inventor to make, use or sell his invention for a specified number of years.*

Payment Bond – *Guarantees the contractor will pay certain subcontractors, laborers and material suppliers associated with the project.*

Performance Bond – *Protects the owner from financial loss should the contractor fail to perform the contract in accordance with its terms and conditions.*

Performance metrics – *Of or relating to the art, process or science of measuring the execution of an action.*

Peripherals – *Any auxiliary device such as a mouse, keyboard, speaker, camera, external drive, etc. that connects to a computer.*

Personal credit history – *A record showing a borrower's responsible repayment of debt.*

Personal liability – *A financial obligation for which an individual is responsible for which may be satisfied with his/her own personal assets, usually cash or from the sale of assets.*

Personal net worth – *The difference between what you own (assets) minus what you owe (liabilities).*

Personal property - *Personal items valued at whatever one believes it is worth in its present condition.*

Posting – *Transferring data from the journals to the ledger.*

Prepaid expenses – *Purchased commodities or services that have not been consumed at the end of an accounting period.*

Prerequisite – *Something that is required as a prior condition for something else to happen or exist.*

Press release – *Sometimes called a news release and used as a publicity mechanism containing fewer than 300 words and distributed to print and electronic media.*

Pricing model – *A method for deciding how a product or service will be priced.*

Pricing policies – *Policies established to determine how products and services will be priced and what allowances and discounts will be given.*

Prior agreement – *An agreement put in place previously; prior to a current agreement.*

Private sector – *Non-governmental entities such as small businesses and U.S. publicly-traded corporations.*

Pro forma statements – *Information before the fact.*

Procedure – *An established or official way of doing something.*

Process – *A series of actions or steps taken in order to achieve an expected end.*

Process improvement – *In an organization or business where a series of actions are taken by a process owner to identify, analyze and improve the existing processes to meet new goals and objectives.*

Product – *An article of substance that is manufactured or refined for sale.*

Product extension merger – *Where merging firms use common or related production processes and/or marketing and distribution channels, but not as competitors.*

Professional Liability Insurance – *Protects professionals deemed to have extensive technical knowledge or training in their particular area of expertise.*

Professional licenses – *Issued through the secretary of state's office in each state legislatively charged to administer and enforce specific laws relating to the licensing and regulation of certain occupations and professions.*

Professional services – *Contracted outside services including legal, accounting and other consulting.*

Profit and Loss statement (P&L) – *Also known as the income statement used to report revenue and expenses.*

Profitability – *The ability of a firm to earn income.*

Profits – *Net result of income minus expenses and taxes.*

Promissory note – *An agreement between the buyer and seller identifying specific amounts to be paid over a specific period of time.*

Proof of concept/principle - *Demonstration that a concept or theory is feasible and has the potential for real-world application.*

Proof of mechanism – *Refers to early clinical development as it pertains to an evaluation of the effect of a new treatment on disease biomarkers.*

Propaganda – *Information of a biased or misleading nature used to promote or publicize a particular political cause or point of view.*

Property Insurance – *Provides coverage for the building and its contents.*

Proposal – *A formal offer by a supplier to provide a service as required in an RFP.*

Prototype – *An original model of which something is patterned.*

Psychographics – *Classification of people according to their psychological criteria such as attitudes, aspirations, interests.*

Public Official Bond – *Guarantees the performance of duty by a public official (e.g., treasurers, tax collectors, sheriffs, judges, court clerks, notaries).*

Public relations – *The business of inducing the public to have an understanding for and goodwill toward a person, firm or institution.*

Public sector – *Governmental entities.*

Quality certifications - *Formal recognition that individuals have demonstrated their proficiency and expert knowledge of a specific subject.*

Quality control – *An aggregate of activities designed to ensure adequate quality in manufactured products.*

Quality organizations – *Entities that exist for its members to share relevant knowledge and develop international standards for their industry.*

Quality standards – *A set of rules that govern the activities designed to ensure adequate quality in manufactured products.*

Quasi-government – *An organization having a partly government character by possession of rights to make rules and regulations having the force of law.*

Quick ratio – *Also known as the acid test ratio, cash or assets minus inventory that can be converted into cash within one year minus inventory.*

Raw materials – *Material whether, crude or processed, that can be converted by manufacture, processing or combination into a new and useful product.*

Reach – *The growth rate of an audience, including new followers.*

Real estate – *Property in the form of buildings and land.*

Receivables financing – *See factoring.*

Regulations (regulatory) - *Rules or order having the force of law issued by an executive authority of government.*

Reliability testing – *Experiments, tests or measuring procedures used to ensure that repeated trial yield the same result.*

Request for Proposal (RFP) – *A formal request of prospective consultants propose to provide a consultant service.*

Request for Qualifications (RFQ) – *A formal request in which expertise and education are requested from prospective supplier to provide a product/service to an agency or firm.*

Rescission of a contract – *The unwinding or unmaking of a transaction bringing the parties involved back to the position they were in before entering into a contract.*

Research and Development (R&D) - *The creation of new technology or information aimed to improve the effectiveness of products or make the production of products more efficient.*

Resource – *A stock or supply of money, materials, staff or other assets that can be utilized by an organization in order to function efficiently.*

Response rate – *The speed at which comments and replies are made on social media, and how quickly marketing and sales leads are followed up on.*

Resume - *Introduction of one's experience and skills relative to the position they are seeking.*

Retained earnings – *Net income retained in a corporation.*

Retention – *The continued possession, use or control of something.*

Return on capital – *Net profits computed on the basis of capital in the company instead of sales.*

Return on equity – *Return earned on the owner's investment.*

Return on investment (ROI) - *The measure in a percentage of net profit over the investment needed to generate that profit.*

Revenue – *The total income produced for goods sold or services rendered.*

Revenue multiple – *A valuation method that measures the value of a stock compared to a company's enterprise to its revenue.*

Reverse auctions – *Utilizing the Internet, multiple vendors compete in an open and interactive environment to provide goods at the lowest selling price.*

Risk – *The degree of probability that a loss or damage could occur.*

Robotics – *Mechanical units used today to serve and assist people that can weld, cut and mold parts, deliver medical records in hospitals, disarm bombs, and can enter hazardous environments too dangerous for humans.*

Royalties - *Monies paid to one party from another for the right to use an asset.*

RSS (really simple syndication) – *The way to automatically share website content and keep track of new content on favorite websites.*

Search engine – *The mechanical means of searching for information via the Internet.*

Search Engine Optimization (SEO) - *The methodology of the strategies, techniques and tactics used to rank content based on the number of visitors to a website in the search results page of a search engine improving the site's visibility.*

Secured debt – *A loan that is collateralized.*

Securities – *Publicly-traded assets to include bonds, stocks, mutual funds, warrants and options.*

Selling price – *Cost of goods sold plus mark-up.*

Service – *A helpful act for someone that does not produce a tangible commodity.*

Shareholder's equity – *A firm's reinvested earnings over time.*

Shareholders – *Sometimes called stockholders, individuals with ownership interest in a corporation.*

Small business – *A small business concern whose annual average gross receipts or number of employees over a three-year period do not exceed a size standard set for its industry.*

Small Disadvantaged Business (SDB) – *A small business concern owned 51% or more by one or more minorities and/or women.*

Social media - *Computer-mediated tools that allow people to create, share, or change information, career interests, ideas and pictures/videos in virtual communities and networks.*

Social media marketing – *Marketing utilizing one or more social media platforms.*

Social media platforms – *Applications used in social media such as Facebook, Twitter, Instagram, Pinterest, etc.*

Socially disadvantaged – *Individuals who have been subjected to racial or ethnic prejudice or cultural bias because of their identity as a member of a minority group without regard to their individual qualities.*

Sole Proprietorship – *A business concern owned by one individual or a husband and wife.*

Source documents – *A transaction record, usually in the form of a sales slip, invoice, time card or check.*

Spam - *Officially known as Unsolicited Commercial Email [UCE], is the junk mail sent to numerous email address without permission, and is illegal.*

Spreadsheet – *An electronic document in which data is arranged in the rows and columns of a grid and can be manipulated and used in calculations.*

Stakeholders – *Individuals with an interest or concern in something, especially a business.*

Start-up costs – *Initial costs of starting a business.*

State-of-the-art – *Highest level or cutting edge in the development of a device, procedure, process, technique or science at a given time.*

Stockkeeping units (SKUs) – *Identification code for a product or service line.*

Strategic plan – *The managerial process of developing and maintaining a match between the resources of an organization and its market opportunities.*

Strengths, Weaknesses, Opportunities and Threats (SWOTS) - *Analyzing the current situation of a business for the purpose of long range and strategic planning.*

Subchapter S corporation – *A corporation that generally avoids corporate taxation and has all profits and losses passed through to corporate shareholders in proportion to their respective stock ownership.*

Subcontractor – *An individual or company contracting to perform part or all of another's contract.*

Subdivision Bond – *Guarantees to a city, county or state that the principal will finance and construct certain improvements such as streets, sidewalks, curbs, gutters, sewer and drainage.*

Subordinated debt – *See mezzanine debt.*

Succession plan – *A plan that specifically states the order in which or the conditions under which one person after another succeeds to a property, dignity, title or throne.*

Supplier development – *Providing suppliers with training and mentoring for the purpose of growing and expanding their current situation.*

Supply shortage – *A deficit of available supplies.*

Sustainability – *The ability to keep up or prolong.*

System – *A set of organized principles, procedures or methods according to which something is done.*

System for Award Management (SAM) - *Formally known as Central Contractor Registration [CCR]), is the official U.S. government system that consolidated the capabilities of CCR/Federal Agency Registration, ORCA and EPLS.*

Systematic – *An approach to a process that is methodical in procedure or plan.*

Tactical objective – *Specific objective used to achieve a specific goal.*

Task – *An assigned piece of work often to be finished within a certain time.*

Taxes - *A charge imposed by authority upon persons or property for public purposes.*

Technical assistance – *Providing consultation, advice or training.*

Technical proposal – *A formal document usually requested by an agency or organization that details processes or procedures to be performed in response to an RFP.*

Technology – *A technical method through the use of equipment for achieving a practical purpose.*

Telecommunications – *Communications by electronic means over distance by cable, telegraph, telephone or broadcasting.*

Tenant improvements – *Customized alterations to a building that an owner makes to rental space as part of a lease agreement.*

Theory – *A supposition or a system of ideas intended to explain something, especially one based on general principles independent of the thing to be explained.*

Time on site – *The length of time visitors stay on your site before exiting.*

Timeline – *A graphic or linear representation of important events in the order in which they should or have occurred.*

Total asset turnover – *A firm's ability to use its assets to generate sales dollars.*

Total liabilities and equity – *Total liabilities of the company plus worth of the company.*

Trade association – *Networking organizations specific to an industry that help establish contacts and keep abreast of developments in that industry.*

Trade publication – *Literature prepared and distributed to members of trade associations.*

Trade secrets – *A formula, process, compilation of information or device used in a business that is not published or divulged and that thereby gives an advantage over competitors.*

Trademark – *Words, symbols or marks legally registered for use by a single company.*

Trans Pacific Partnership (TPP) – *The trade agreement between the United States, Japan, and 10 other Pacific nations.*

Transaction – *A financial event, act, process or instance of transacting, especially a business deal, that affects assets, liabilities and owner's equity.*

Transfer of ownership – *Conveyance of title, rights or interest from one person to another.*

Trends – *The general movement during the course of time of a statistically detectable change.*

Trial balance – *A listing of titles of the accounts and their balances in order of which the accounts appear in the ledger.*

Troubleshooting - *Solving serious problems for a company by tracing and correcting faults.*

Turnaround time – *The time it takes for an action to reach its potential.*

Turnkey – *An operation or project that is constructed and ready to be sold and used by any buyer as a completed product.*

Turnover in working capital – *Complete replacement of working capital using available funds.*

Uncontrollable factors – *Factors that cause an inability to control.*

Uniform Commercial Code (UCC) – *A uniform set of rules to govern commercial transactions in an effort to bring uniformity to interstate trade and commerce.*

Uniform Resource Locator (URL) – *A standard way of specifying the location of a particular resource.*

Unique selling proposition (USP) – *Factors in advertising and promotion presented by the seller reason(s) one product/service is different from and better than that of the competition.*

Unsecured debt – *Credit granted without requiring collateral.*

Valuation – *See business valuation.*

Value add – *Having features added to a basic line or model for which a buyer is prepared to pay an additional cost.*

Value Added Network (VAN) – *Provides communications between standard data formats, detects and corrects errors and provides messages encryption and decryption for security.*

Value proposition - *A business statement summarizing the reasons why a company's products or services offer more value, worth, utility or importance than other companies.*

Value statement – *A statement that describes the intrinsic quality or importance of something.*

Variable costs – *Costs that change depending on production.*

Venture capital – *Money received from an outside source in exchange for ownership interest and a substantial return on investment.*

Verification – *The process of establishing the truth, accuracy or validity of something.*

Vertical merger – *When two companies operating at separate stages for a specific finished product merge operations.*

Vetting – *Making a careful and critical examination of something or someone, through investigation to ensure loyalty or trustworthiness.*

Vision - *Unusual wisdom in foreseeing what is going to happen.*

Vision statement – *A statement that describes a business, its commitment, customer and philosophy for the future.*

Visits and unique visits – *Visits are the number of times each person visits your website. Unique visits are counted only once.*

Warranty – *Promises a seller makes to a buyer about their products regarding the integrity and the maker's responsibility for the repair or replacement of defective parts.*

Web address or URL (Uniform Resource Locator) - *The standard way developed to specify the location of particular resource in your website.*

Web browser – *A program that enables one to search randomly through information provided by a specific type of server.*

Web conferencing – *Real-time communications in which multiple computer users are connected to the Internet all viewing the same computer screen at the same time.*

Web site – *A specific location of a business' information on the world wide web.*

Weighted average – *Used when inventory is stirred or mixed together and it's physically impossible to determine what has been sold.*

Wikipedia - *A multi-lingual, web-based, free-content encyclopedia project supported by the Wikimedia Foundation based in San Francisco, California.*

Woman-owned Business Enterprise (WBE) – *A small business concern owned 51% or more by one or more women.*

Workers Compensation Insurance – *Provides payments to injured workers for time lost from work and for medical and rehabilitation services without regard to who was at fault in the accident, or death benefits to surviving spouses and dependents.*

Working capital – *The excess of total current assets over total current liabilities at a particular point in time.*

World Wide Web (WWW) – *A loosely organized set of computer sites that publish information that anyone can read via the Internet using hypertext transfer protocol (http).*

Zoning laws – *Ordinances put in place by municipalities to ensure that sections of a city, borough or township are used for specific purposes.*

APPENDIX

List of Exhibits

Exhibit No.	**Document Name**	**Page**
1	Assessment of Personal Strengths & Weaknesses	26
2	Setting Personal Financial Goals and Addressing Concerns	28
3	Current Personal Financial Status	30
4	Monthly Budget	35
5	Assessment of Start-up Costs	38
6	Google Advanced Search	44
7	Legal Forms of Business	47
8	SS4 – Application for Employer Identification Number	58
9	Federal, State and Local Government Agencies	91
10	Business Start-up Checklist	112
11	Cover Page	128
12	Cover Letter of Introduction	131
13	Table of Contents	133
14	Authorizations Page	135
15	Executive Summary	138
16	The Operating Plan	143
17	Fixed Asset Inventory List	146
18	Key Operating Metrics	147
19	The Marketing Plan	156
20	Product & Service Pricing Models	159
21	Breakeven Analysis	160
22	Press Release	161
23	Customer Acquisition Model	162
24	Fact Sheet	163
25	Market Position & Annual Industry Sales	164
26	Key Marketing Metrics	165

Exhibit No.	Document Name	Page
27	Service Contract	166
28	Limited Warranty	167
29	Money Back or Replacement Guarantee	168
30	The Management Plan	171
31	Organizational Chart	174
32	Staffing Plan Chart	176
33	Resume/Curriculum Vitae	178
34	Key Management Metrics	179
35	Balance Sheet	185
36	Income Statement	186
37	Cash Flow Analysis	187
38	Operating Budget	188
39	Estimated Projections & Forecasts Statement	189
40	Key Financial Metrics (Terms, Ratios & Formulas)	190
41	Strategic Plan	201
42	Goals & Objectives	203
43	Key Results Areas (KRAs)	210
44	Strengths, Weaknesses, Opportunities & Threats (SWOTs)	211
45	Strategic Implementation Plan	212
46	Status Report	213
47	Key Strategic (Long Range) Plan Metrics	214
48	Succession Plan	218
49	Key Succession Plan Metrics	222
50	Appendix	224
51	Glossary of Terms	225

INDEX

Index

A

Accessing Your Market, *229*

Accounting, *III, VI, 71, 92, 99, 173, 181, 182, 190, 204, 329, 360, 365, 379, 387*

   Accrual Based, *365*

   Receivable, *190, 295*

   Receivable Turnover, *365*

Acquisition, *V, 93, 151, 162, 233, 234, 278, 333, 342, 365, 399*

Advertising, *329, 366*

Advisory Board, *169, 171, 366*

Affiliate Marketing, 329, *366*

Americans with Disabilities Act (ADA), *76*

Assets, 366

   Current Assets, *29*

   Long-term, *29*

   Personal Property, *29*

   Real Estate, *29*

   Securities, *29*

Associations and Foundations, *238*

Assumed Name, *367*

B

Banking & Finance, *330*

Barriers to Entry, *11, 367*

Barriers to Exit, *8, 11, 15, 367*

Bids & Proposals

   Preparing, *251*

Blog, 330, 368

Board of Directors, 169, 171, 173

Bona Fide, *368*

Bonding, *81, 368*

   Bid Bond, *82, 331, 367*

   Federal Bond, *83, 378*

   Judicial and Probate Bond, *83, 382*

   Judicial Proceedings Court Bond, *83, 383*

   Maintenance Bond, *82, 385*

   Miscellaneous Bond, *83, 386*

   Paymenet Bond, *82, 388*

   Performance Bond, *82, 388*

   Public Official Bond, *83, 390*

   Subdivision Bond, *82, 394*

Bounce Rate, *368*

Branding, *63, 368*

Breakeven Analysis, 150, 160, 368, 399

Breakeven Point, *368*

Budget, *34, 35, 133, 175, 183, 188, 198, 202, 207, 300, 368, 399, 400*

Business, *39*

   Bank Account, *56*

   Continuation, *369*

   Execution Excellence, *105*

   Expansion & Improvement, *142, 145*

   Fictitious Business Name, *55*

   Incubator, *369*

   Location, *141, 143, 164, 205*

   Model, *40, 146, 151, 162, 166, 167, 168, 225, 369, 373, 399*

   Naming, *53*

   Organizing the Development, *39*

   Valuation, *369*

Business Development

   Section 8(a), *325*

   Centers, *19, 290*

   Enterprise Certification, *26, 325, 327, 328, 331, 370*

Business Enterprise
  Minority, Disadvantaged, *321*
  Veteran-Owned and Service-Disabled
    Veteran, *323*
  Women, *322*
Business Interruption Insurance, *80*
Business model, *40, 140*
Business Plan Development
  Authorizations Page, *134, 135, 254, 399*
  Cover Letter of Introduction, *129, 130, 131,*
    237, 253, 399
  Cover Page, *126, 127, 128, 197, 253, 399*
  Executive Summary, *121, 122, 124, 133, 136,*
    138, 197, 254, 399
  Financial Plan, *180*
  Finished Document, *124*
  Importance, *117*
  Management Plan, *121, 123, 133, 137, 139,*
    169, 171, 400
  Marketing Plan, *121, 123, 133, 137, 139, 148,*
    154, 156, 399
  Operating Plan, *121, 123, 133, 137, 138, 140,*
    141, 143, 399
  Sample Plan, *125*
  Strategic Plan, *193*
  Succession Plan, *215*
  Table of Contents, *122, 124, 132, 133, 134,*
    197, 253, 399
  Update, *125*
  What Is, *115*
  Writing, *I, IV, V, IV, XV, XVIII, 111, 116, 118,*
    206, 253, 361, 362, 407
Business Umbrella Insurance, *80*
Business Valuation, *107*
  Asset Approach, *108, 366*
  Income Approach, *109, 381*
  Market Approach, *108, 385*
  Multiplier Method, 109

C

Capacity Constraints, *110, 370*
Capital Intensive, 7

Capitalization, *3, 370*
Cash Flow, *370*
Certification, *331*
Chambers of Commerce, *332*
Channels of Distribution, *370*
Clean (Unclean) Hands, *10, 371*
Close and Closely-held Corporations, *48*
Cloud Computing, *315, 332, 371*
Collateral, *371*
Collect on Delivery (COD), *371*
Collection Period, 371
Commercial Auto Insurance, *81*
Commercial Space, *371*
Community Development Corporations, *371*
Computer Hardware and Software, *332*
Contracts, *III, 85, 153, 155, 158, 204. 333*
  Acceptance, *VIII, 86, 255, 365*
  Agreement, *49, 50, 51, 77, 81, 82, 85, 86, 87,*
    88, 156, 166, 171, 202, 216, 219, 220, 250,
    256, 283, 291, 301, 302, 343, 369, 370,
    372, 373, 379, 384, 389, 390, 395, 396
  Breach of Contract, *86, 368*
  Competency and Capacity, *86*
  Completion, *44, 87*
  Consideration, *86, 372*
  Execution, *III, IV, 85, 105, 377*
  Federal Contracting Opportunities, *234*
  Mutuality, *86, 386*
  Not-for-Profit Organizations, *238*
  Offer, *VIII, 86, 255, 387*
  Performance, *20, 82, 83, 86, 120, 153, 157,*
    158, 171, 172, 179, 193, 194, 195, 198,
    206, 208, 214, 221, 243, 249, 251, 254,
    256, 259, 311, 313, 321, 331, 338, 354,
    367, 380, 382, 390
  Private Sector, *237*
  Prior Agreement, *86, 389*
  Rescission, *87, 391*
  Rules and Regulations, *233*
  State, Local and Quasi-Government, *236*
  Terminated, *86, 250*
  Valid, *III, 85, 86, 152, 200*
  Verbal (or Oral), *85*

Written, *86*

Copyrights, *83, 223, 224*

Corporation, *46, 47, 48, 51, 52, 57, 79, 112, 138, 173, 217, 231, 239, 246, 247, 248, 250, 251, 252, 253, 368, 371, 383, 387, 392, 393, 394*

County Government *100*

    Recorder, *54*

Credit, *334*

    Creditworthiness, *304*

    History, *31*

    Rating, *73, 373*

    Reporting Agencies, *304*

Crowdfunding, *XV, 296, 297, 334, 374, 375, 377*

    Debt, *191, 220, 282, 283, 284, 297, 300, 306, 342, 360, 374*

    Equity, *IX, 190, 191, 192, 282, 290, 297, 336, 377*

Curriculum Vitae, *169, 177, 178, 254, 400*

Customer

    Acquisition Model, *151*

    Building Relationships, *245*

    Educating, *102*

    Relationship Management, *VIII, 246*

    Service, *101, 155, 157*

D

Demographics, *374*

Directors and Officers Liability Insurance, *80*

Disability Insurance, *80*

Domain Name, *60, 112, 375*

    Registration, *335*

Dun & Bradstreet, *54, 72, 73, 79, 112, 231, 305, 334, 375*

E

Economy, *XVII, 209, 211, 361, 376*

Elevator Pitch, *102, 376*

Email, *61, 168*

    Creating Effective, *259*

    Marketing, *268, 335*

    Unwanted and Unsolicited, *258*

Employees, *335*

    Contract Employee, *76*

    Fitness for Duty, *75, 378*

    Fringe Benefits, *76, 379*

    Hiring, *74*

    Staffing, *VI, 14, 56, 104, 125, 128, 131, 133, 136, 141, 143, 146, 147, 161, 162, 163, 164, 165, 170, 175, 176, 197, 209, 210, 211, 212, 213, 214, 222, 400*

Employment Practices Liability Insurance, *81*

Entrepreneurship, *15*

    Personal Strengths & Weaknesses, *20, 26*

    Readiness, *17*

    Skills and Abilities, *22*

    Traits, *15*

Equal Pay Act (EPA), *76*

Equifax, *32, 304, 334*

Equity Investors, *336*

Errors and Ommissions Insurance, *80*

Experian, *32, 304, 334*

Exporting

    Export Ready, *240*

    Risks, *241*

F

Fact Sheet, *150, 163, 399*

Fair Labor Standards Act (FLSA), *76*

Family and Medical Leave Act (FMLA), *76*

Federal Agencies, *336*

Federal Employer Identification Number (FEIN), *57*

FICO® score, *33*

Finances

    Goals, *27*

    Personal, *27*

    Personal net worth, *29*

    Status, *27*

Financial Planning, *VI, 180, 181*

Financial statements

    Assumptions, *183, 209, 367*

Balance Sheet, *133, 183, 185, 222, 300, 400*
Cash Flow Analysis, *133, 183, 187, 300, 400*
Estimated Projections & Forecasts Statement,
 133, 183, 189, 400
Income Statement, *133, 183, 186, 300, 400*
Notes to, *184, 387*
Operating Budget, *183*
Financing
 "5 Cs" of Borrowing, 294
 Angel Networks, *292*
 Crowd Funding, *296*
 Equity Capital, *290*
 Franchises, *291*
 Going Public, *292*
 Government, *284*
 Obtaining, *298*
 Other Sources, *IX, 292*
 Source of Capital, *282*
 Types of, *282*
 Understanding Needs, *281*
 When to Seek, *X, 298*
Fixed Asset Inventory List, *142, 146, 399*
Foundations & Grants, *338*
Franchising, *4, 19, 40, 46, 50, 51, 115, 122, 138,*
 153, 291, 339
Franchise, *19, 50, 51, 100,* 223, 224, 291, 300,
 338, 339, 360, 361, 379
Funding Vehicle, *379*

G

General Partnership, *46, 48, 49, 56*
General Services Administration Schedules (GSA
 Schedules), *235*
Goals & Objectives, *197, 199, 209, 400*
Government
 County, *100*
 Local, *III, VIII, 19, 70, 89, 90, 91, 101, 236,*
 288, 289, 306, 348, 354, 399
 State, *III, VIII, XI, 67, 70, 74, 76, 89, 90, 91, 96,*
 99, 100, 135, 236, 288, 337, 377, 394, 399,
 407

U.S. Federal, *III, 89, 91*
Gross Domestic Product (GDP), *380*
Gross National Product (GNP), *380*

H

Health and Dental Insurance, *80*
Healthcare Providers, *339*
Hiring, *8, 9, 24, 54, 74, 75, 76, 118, 170, 171,*
 175, 177, 180, 210, 217, 222
 Compensation & Benefits, *169, 171*
 State "At Will", *76*

I

Identify Theft Insurance, *81*
Import/Export, *339*
Industry, *II, V, 24, 42, 91, 99, 122, 152, 154, 156,*
 164, 203, 234, 242, 324, 333, 351, 355, 381,
 399
Information Economy, *43, 381*
Information Management Systems (IMS), *142,*
 144
Innovation, *4, 93, 345, 359, 381*
Insurance, *79, 80, 81, 98, 203, 218, 223, 224,*
 284, 300, 339, 340, 369, 371, 375, 376, 377,
 380, 382, 383, 389, 390, 398
Intellectual Property, *8, 9, 84, 85, 109, 139, 141,*
 142, 144, 243, 349, 364
International Markets, *239*
International Organization for Standardization
 (ISO), *382*
International Trade Administration (ITA), *243*
Internet Service Providers (ISPs), *62,* 340, *382*
Inventories, *295*

J

Joint Venture, *46, 51, 138, 249, 373*
Jurisdiction, *383*

K

Key Person Insurance, *80, 383*
Key Results Areas (KRAs), *199, 206, 210,* 383, *400*
Kidnap and Ransom Insurance, *81*

L

Labor Relations, *340*
Legal and Regulatory Issues, *I, 8*
Legal Issues, *XXII, 8, 218, 340*
    Business Licenses or Registrations, *70*
    City and County Ordinances, *69*
    Clean (Dirty) Hands Doctrine, *10*
Legal Structure, *46, 112, 203, 222, 383*
    Close or Closely-Held Corporation, *48*
    Corporation, *47*
    Franchise, *50*
    General Partnership, *49*
    Joint Venture, *51*
    Limited Liability Company (LLC), *51*
    Limited Liability Partnership (LLP), *49*
    Not-for-Profit (NFP), *52*
    Professional or Personal Services Partnership, *50*
    Sole Proprietorship, *47*
    Subchapter S Corporation, *48*
Legislation, *341*
Liabilities
    Current Liabilities, *29*
    Real Estate, *29*
Liability Insurance, *79*
License, *70, 74, 82, 383, 384*
Licensing Agreements, *87, 152*
    Royalties, *87, 392*
Limited Warranty, *153, 167, 400*
Loan
    Collateral, *301*
    Negotiating the, *301*
    Proposal, *299*
    Rejected, *303*
    Repayment, *302*
Location
    Bricks and Mortar, *67*
    Commercial Space, *39, 67, 68, 69, 141, 211, 270*
    Homebased, *67*
    Office, 345
    Selecting, *66*
Logo (Business/Company), *54, 65, 126*

M

Management Information Systems (MIS), *142, 144*
Market Position & Annual Industry Sales, *152, 164, 399*
Marketing
    7 Ps, *148*
    Advertising & Promotion, *155, 157, 162*
    Competition, *155, 157, 204, 372*
    Objective, *137, 138, 155, 196, 213, 267, 331, 387*
    Public Relations, *34*
    Sales Objectives, *V, 155, 156, 160, 162, 164, 165, 173, 186, 191, 192, 203, 212, 214, 260, 268, 399*
Mentor-Protégé Programs, *249, 346*
Mergers, *215, 218*
    Conglomerate, *372*
    Horizontal, *220, 380*
    Product Extension, *389*
    Market Extension, *385*
    Vertical, *220*
Metrics, *III, V, VI, VII, IX, XVI, 71, 103, 104, 142, 145, 147, 153, 154, 155, 158, 165, 170, 172, 179, 180, 184, 190, 198, 202, 214, 217, 222, 278, 386, 399, 400*
    What Gets Measured and How, *104*
Mezzanine Debt, *386*
Mission Statement, *I, 13, 14, 39, 136, 138, 197, 203, 206, 331, 386*
Money Back or Replacement Guarantee, *153, 168, 400*

N

Niche, *5, 387*

North American Industrial Classification System (NAICS), *41, 112*

Not-for-Profit, *XX, 45, 46, 47, 52, 238, 245, 286, 289, 292, 306, 332, 338, 346, 347, 350, 351, 353, 354*

O

Occupational Safety & Health Act (OSHA), *76*

Online Marketplaces, *346*

Operational Efficiency, *106*

Operational Risk Management, *12, 387*

Ordinances, *III, 70, 388, 398*

Organizational Chart, *133, 169, 173, 174, 400*

P

Patent & Trademark Office (USPTO), *54, 60*

Patents, *83, 223, 224*

Personal Financial Status, *II, 29, 30, 31, 399*

Press Release, *150, 161, 399*

Problem Solving, *VI, 200*

Procurement and Technical Assistance Center, *19*

Product & Service Pricing Models, *149, 159, 399*

Products, *I, 4*
    Manufacturing & Production, *141, 143*
    Packaging & Distribution, *145*

Professional Associations, *346*

Professional Liability Insurance, *80*

Professional or Personal Services Partnership, *50*

Professional Services, *76, 169, 171, 359*

Project Plan, *197*

Proof of Concept, *I, 6*

Proof of Mechanism, *7*

Property Insurance, *80*

Publications, *349*

Q

Qualifying as a Supplier, *231*

Quality Certifications
    ASQ (American Society for Quality), *73*
    ISO (International Organization for Standardization), *73*
    NAHQ (National Association for Healthcare Quality), *73*
    TL 9000 QuEST Forum, *73*

Quality Control, *350*

R

Registering
    Government Contracting Opportunities, *235*
    Registration, *60, 70, 78, 79, 85, 100, 112, 335, 375*

Regulatory Issues, *10*

Research, *XVII, 7, 20, 42, 43, 45, 91, 92, 93, 96, 110, 112, 173, 203, 213, 223, 224, 230, 249, 257, 335, 340, 344, 350, 363, 391*

Research and Development (R&D), *6, 7, 391*

Research Organizations, *350*

Résumé, *133, 169, 177, 178*

Return on Investment (ROI), *392*

Reverse Auctions, *244*

RSS Feed Aggregators, *351*

S

Safety, *351*

Scheduling Online, *352*

Search Engine Optimization (SEO), *352, 392*

Secretary of State, *48, 50, 52, 54, 74, 296, 301, 306, 338*

Service Contract, *153, 166, 400*

Small Business, *319*
    Size Standards, *320*

Small Business Administration, *19, 83, 98, 122, 250, 285, 319, 327, 328, 330, 331, 346, 407*

Small Business Development, *XI, 323, 324, 344, 354, 361*

Small, Disadvantaged, Minority, Woman, Veteran-Owned & Service- Disabled Veteran Business Enterprise Certification, *78*

Social Media, *63, 210, 257, 262, 263, 265, 266, 267, 278, 279, 346, 348, 352, 362, 363, 364*
    Planning, *265*
    Platforms, *263*

Sole Proprietorship, *46, 47, 48, 56, 138, 173, 216, 383*

Speaking Organizations, *353*

Staffing Plan Chart, *170, 175, 176, 400*

Start-up Costs, *II, 36, 37, 38, 399*
    Non-recurring, *36*
    Recurring, *36*

Strategic Alliances, *248*

Strategic Planning, *353*

Strengths, Weaknesses, Opportunities or Threats (SWOTs), *201*

Subchapter S Corporation, *48*

Supplier
    Development Initiatives, *247*
    Diversity, *247*
    Suppliers & Manufacturers, *354*

System for Award Management (SAM)
    Registration, *78*

T

Taxes, *III, 72, 204, 354, 360, 395*
    Filing income, *72*

Technical Assistance, *236, 241, 354*

Technology, *66, 91, 93, 96, 173, 210, 212, 213, 231, 309, 311, 312, 315, 350, 353, 355, 364, 395*
    Benefits of, *311*
    Impact on Business, *X, 309*
    Implementing, *315*
    Planning, *312*

Technical Service & Support, *X, 318*
    Types of, *313*

Telecommunications, *355*

Trade Information Center (TIC), *243*

Trade secrets, *83, 344*

Trade shows, *157, 356*

Trademarks, *83, 223, 224*

Trans Union, *32, 304, 334*

Transfer of the Business, *216*

U

U.S. Department of Transportation, *83, 250, 407*

UCC Filing (Uniform Commercial Code), *306, 396*

Understanding Your Competitive Advantage, *232*

Uniform Resource Locator (URL), *396*

V

Value Proposition, *13, 397*

Vision, *3, 136, 138, 197, 206, 397*

W

Warranties & Guarantees, *158*

Web Conferencing, *355*

Website
    Affiliate Marketing, *276*
    Blog, *271*
    Builders, *355*
    Developing, *65*
    Marketing, *269*
    RSS Feed, *274*
    Search Engine Optimization (SEO), *275*
    Website Address, *127, 167*

Workers Compensation Insurance, *80*

X Y Z

Zoning, *68, 398*

EPILOGUE

ABOUT THE AUTHOR

KIMBERLY LOUISE JOHNSON

After working over 25 years in corporate America, I, like millions of other Americans decided to take the entrepreneurial leap. Drawing on many years of professional experience, having earned a bachelor's degree in business administration and studying human behavior at the graduate level, I put all my skills, knowledge and abilities to work as an author, speaker and business development consultant.

My journey began with attending any and every low-cost or no-cost seminar or workshop throughout Southern California. While I didn't find the information being disseminated difficult to comprehend, I did, however, find it vague and not very helpful. And more often than not, walked away not knowing any more than what I knew when I walked in.

It seemed that for every question asked, the only response given by the speaker was, *"well if you'd like to schedule an appointment with my office, we can. . ."* Needless to say, not only did I feel cheated in having spent the time attending these sessions, I also felt as though I was simply a part of an audience for basically unknown consultants to peddle their wares.

This was the impetus to the first edition of the 1997 first edition of *"The Start of Something BIG: Your Ultimate Guide to Writing a Dynamic Business Plan."* It was created to give the business novice clear and easy-to-understand direction in the business start-up and planning process. Also, provide the experienced entrepreneur with the necessary tools to grow, expand and sustain their existing businesses.

As a result of publishing and the national distribution of *"The Start of Something BIG: . . ."* I had the pleasure of being featured in an 8-part series on business planning in *Black Enterprise* magazine. In addition, I've had the opportunity to share the stage in conferences, workshops and seminars with Fortune 100 companies such as ExxonMobil, Walt Disney Company, Texaco, Bank of America, and federal government agencies to include U.S. Department of Commerce, U.S. Department of Transportation and the U.S. Small Business Administration just to name a few.

In 2010, I earned a Master of Arts Degree in Strategic Communications. Prior to that accomplishment was my successful completion and certification in the Working Ahead: The National Workforce and Career Development Instructor Training Program, a joint initiative of the U.S. Department of Labor, the Prudential Foundation, the Fund for New Jersey and Rutgers, the State University of New Jersey Edward J. Bloustein School of Planning and Public Policy.

Today, I reside in Bolingbrook, Illinois with my sons Marcus, Daniel and James. As a Bolingbrook Host for the internationally-known organization, The Founding Moms and a member of Women Entrepreneurs Secrets of Success (WESOS), my goal is to continue to promote entrepreneurship by providing the most helpful, innovative and contemporary instruction available.